Guide to
MUSICALS

Rexton S. Bunnett

ly & John Muir

Publishers

To Michael

HarperCollins*Publishers*
Westerhill Road, Bishopbriggs, Glasgow G64 2QT

First published in hardback 1997
This updated and expanded edition in paperback 2001

© HarperCollins*Publishers* 1997, 2001

ISBN 0 00 712268-3

Reprint 10 9 8 7 6 5 4 3 2 1 0

A catalogue record for this book is available from the British Library

Printed and bound in Great Britain by
Omnia Books Limited, Glasgow G64

Contents

About the Authors

REXTON S. BUNNETT is the honorary musical theatre consultant at the Theatre Museum in Covent Garden. He has written extensively on the musical theatre, revue and, as a discographer, he has had published *London Musical Shows on Record*. He is is the joint curator of the Overtures Collection. His four-part BBC Radio 2 series on composer Harold Arlen was recently broadcast and he also wrote Ned Sherrin's *Review of Revue* series.

MICHAEL PATRICK KENNEDY was *The (Glasgow) Herald* musical reviewer for a number of years. He principally worked in the record industry at EMI's World Records and Conifer Records, where he developed and expanded the range of releases of vintage recordings. Sadly, Michael died in 1998.

JOHN MUIR is joint curator of the Overtures Collection, probably the most comprehensive collection in the UK of recordings of musical shows, posters, programmes, libretti and sheet music, which will be bequeathed to the London Theatre Museum.

Acknowledgments

The authors would like to thank the following people, whose practical help and encouragement have contributed to the creation of this book: Rexton Bunnett, Austin Bennett, Bradley Bennett, Thomas Connor, Martin Moritz, Richard Norton, Warren Seamans, our patient and indefatigable editor Ian Brooke and the staff of HarperCollins Publishers.

Various reference sources have been consulted for the checking of facts. These include: the American and British national press, the Theatre Museum, the US Library of Congress, *Theatre World*, *Theatre Week*, and works of erudition and scholarship by the following authors: Ken Bloom, Gerald Boardman, Kurt Gänzl, David Ewen and Stanley Green.

How to Use this Book

Collins Musicals is an invaluable guide to the fascinating world of the stage musical, featuring numerous examples of this hugely popular art form.

The main body of the book contains an alphabetical listing of 195 well-known, and some less well-known, stage musicals. The entries appear on a double-page spread, giving details of composers and lyricists, characters, casts and plot, music and songs, and recommended recordings. Each stage musical also has a Did You Know? section featuring useful background information and some appropriate media comment.

A biographies section includes details on the life and works of over 70 composers and lyricists. A cross-reference system enables the reader to find further information on other personalities within the biographies section, as well as indicating the musicals which are covered in greater detail in the main body of the book.

A comprehensive index will enable the reader to track down favourite songs to their musical 'home'.

An introduction on the development of the stage musical, a listing of the different forms of musical and a glossary of terms round out this indispensable reference source.

Most recommended recordings are available on CD throughout the world in specialist shops and on the Internet. Unfortunately, record companies sometimes delete recordings from their catalogues quickly, thus making the CDs harder to find.

Introduction

Musicals are the most popular form of theatrical entertainment. In any one week around half the stages in London's West End will be offering musical plays. That means between eighteen and twenty-three out of forty-three (or more) active stages. London is not unique. New York has a similar bias. It's not merely by chance, either.

Music has been used to enhance drama for centuries, in Greek and Roman times, and in the theatres of India and China. And in Shakespeare's time plays usually included a song or two, but they could not be classed as musicals by any stretch of the imagination.

The development of the musical – an entertainment which weaves song, story and often dance into a single homogeneous whole – is comparatively recent. Whereas ballet and opera were originally court entertainments financed by powerful patrons, kings and princes throughout Europe, musical comedy has always had to pay its own way, and to find its audiences not exclusively from among the rich and the nobility, but principally from the middle and lower classes, who paid for their seats and on whose patronage the success or failure of the shows depended. This is not to say that the early forerunners of musical comedy did not borrow from the grander forms of music. The tunes in John Gay's 1728 success *The Beggar's Opera* were cheerfully filched not merely from popular ditties and folk songs, but from classics by Handel and Purcell, among others.

The Victorian era, for all its seeming prudishness, entertained some of the most savage lampooning of its public figures in cartoon and other forms on the printed page. This was reflected in the musical theatre of the time. The comic operas of William Schwenck Gilbert and his composer Arthur Seymour Sullivan, direct forerunners of the modern musical comedy, were brimful of topical allusions satirising – to give just two examples – the aesthetic movement of Oscar Wilde and Aubrey Beardsley in *Patience* and the craze for everything Japanese in *The Mikado*. Their brilliant series of works remains as topical today as yesterday, each crammed with adroit portraits of human fallibility in an entertaining and melodic form.

The mid- to late 19th century, indeed, brought a great expansion of entertainment, centred principally on London, but also with the building of chains of theatres in the main towns and cities. Improved roads, better forms of transport and the resulting prosperity meant that there was greater opportunity for leisure pursuits, and these included going to the theatre. Christmas was a traditional time for theatregoing, and that meant pantomime.

For many years pantomime held sway in Great Britain and, to a lesser extent, in the United States of America. A zesty bran pie of delights offering song, dance, a fairy tale story, topical jokes and audience participation with games and prizes, the traditional British Christmas pantomime was an eagerly-awaited treat for the whole family. With a dame normally played by an elderly male comic, and a principal boy played by a shapely girl in tights, there was fun for all the family. And the habit of going to the pantomime may well have created the desire among its loyal public to visit other musical shows at other times of the year, especially as there were many touring companies who took shows on the road throughout Britain and America. Indeed, a New York run often proved less important and profitable than the years of touring for many important shows.

Other popular entertainments were also evolving. The ballad operas which set new verses to famous tunes gave way to burlesques which were parodies of well-known stories and plays. But we shall probably never see a production of *Flora*, which delighted audiences in Charleston in 1735 and which can lay claim to being the precursor of musical comedy in America.

The extravaganza, which offered elements of song, dance and comedy plus elaborate special effects, was an extension of the pantomime. The outstanding example of this was *The Black Crook*, mounted at Niblo's Gardens, New York, for 474 performances from 12 September 1866. Musical theatre folklore tells us that this was an invention born of necessity when a French ballet company found itself homeless, and a less-than-successful melodrama needed help. Originally it ran for five and a half hours with a plot reminiscent of the German opera *Der Freischutz* with its magic bullets and devilish supernatural interventions. There was a female chorus, scantily clad, to perform ballets and other dances, spectacular scenic effects and lots of songs and elaborate production numbers. It was followed a few years later by a successful burlesque of Longfellow's *Evangeline* with original music, and the musical pastiche *Adonis* (1884).

In Britain there was a flood of adaptations of French musical plays, which were often witty and topical, with music by French 'light' composers such as Offenbach, Lecocq and Planquette. There were heavier romances from Austria and Germany which dealt with kings and queens and princelings, and mythological characters who often dallied with comely servant girls, usually in disguise. (Early works by serious opera composers like Verdi, Donizetti and Bellini also had their parallels in comic operas of the period.)

Yet native early musicals were firmly anchored among the middle and working classes. The last quarter of the 18th century brought *The Quaker* (1775), *No Song, No Supper* (1790) and *The Waterman* (1794), which remained in common currency for a century or more.

By the middle of the next century, English and Irish composers like Balfe, Wallace and Benedict were producing still-remembered, if no longer performed, romantic favourites – *Maritana*, *The Bohemian Girl* and *Lily of Killarney* – with completely original scores. This was a great step forward. Composers were able to obtain limited copyright protection on their own melodies and start to make a decent living from them. Even so, the French-sounding but English by nature Planché's parodies on existing tunes and stories were still popular in the early and middle years of the 19th century. His successors moved to more direct parody and comment; *Windsor Castle* by Burnand, with an original score, was highly successful.

These developments attracted such writers as the previously noted W.S. Gilbert, who teamed up with Arthur Sullivan for a series of glittering comic operas whose sharp wit and social comment have remained as acute today as when first seen. And they were not alone. *Billee Taylor* by Edward Solomon got better reviews at the time than its contemporary *The Pirates of Penzance*. It would be nice to see why. Jakobowski's *Erminie* was another hit of the time – wildly popular in London and the provinces before proving equally successful in America. Will we ever see a revival of Alfred Cellier's *Dorothy*? It holds the record for the longest run of a 19th-century musical play in Britain and certainly counts as an early musical comedy.

As all but the Gilbert and Sullivan shows lost their appeal, the modern form of musical comedy was fast developing, offering good tunes, romantic stories, glamorous choruses, elaborate dance numbers, gorgeous settings and costumes, and often played in modern (i.e. contemporary) dress. Its flexibilty and immediate eye and ear appeal took the musical comedy ahead of the comic opera and ballad opera models from which it sprang. A broader, less high-brow appeal produced a wider audience that flocked to the new theatres.

George Edwards mounted show after show at the Gaiety Theatre in London. Ivan Caryll and Lionel Monckton were the house composers. At Daly's Theatre the shows, while generally adhering to the tuneful, lavishly staged formula so successful at the Gaiety, were operetta in form. This was an early golden age for the embryonic musical comedy that crossed the Atlantic with great success, and London was exporting its vibrant new entertainments to the United States and every corner of the English-speaking world. Leslie Stuart was mainly responsible for *Florodora*'s score, an outstanding hit of the period that dealt with perfume making in the South Seas.

An import, Franz Lehár's *The Merry Widow,* was very influential, and not merely in fashion – the Widow's hat was especially admired and imitated. An operetta on the continent, the show had extra elements of coarse comedy for London and settled in happily as a musical comedy. Although the old-fashioned, more staid comic opera could still score successes, as Edward German's *Tom Jones* and *Merrie England* proved, the arrival of *The Maid of the Mountains* (1917) and *Chu Chin Chow* (1916) marked the end of the old and the beginning of the new. The general public now demanded spectacle, exoticism, melody and – stars! Gertie Millar, José Collins, Evelyn Laye and Cicely Courtneidge were the new names that would fill the auditoriums.

The centre for the musical's development was firmly in Europe. Jerome Kern learnt his trade in London where he wrote songs before returning to the United States to write additional numbers for English imports. Almost another hundred years would pass before the main traffic would be from England to America again. This is not to say that the European influences would not still be felt in the interim. Many an American lyricist acknowledges to this day a great debt to Gilbert's wit and lyric style.

An American failure, *The Belle of New York*, travelled across the Atlantic with Edna May and Dan Daly, its original stars, in tow and became a huge hit in London in 1898. This was much more significant than it may have seemed at the time. While London remained alert to its own shows, and enjoyed a regular stream of imports from the continent, as the 20th century wore on the work of the prime American composers was welcomed in Britain. Indeed, George Gershwin's first important score, *Primrose,* was written for London and was successful – it even received extensive coverage on disc. Its style was daintily cute and showed little of the rhythmic and melodic verve that would mark its composer's later output.

America was developing its own style of musical comedy provided by expatriate Europeans such as Victor Herbert, Sigmund Romberg and Rudolf Friml. The first exodus from Europe had been caused by the unsettled conditions in Europe, including anti-Semitic pogroms in Eastern Europe that expelled many talented musicians to Britain and especially to America. This meant in America at least a Hungaro/ Germanic cast to the melodies and also to the plots of early musical comedies. Unlike British scores of the period, the influx of such composers to America meant that their plots were originally set, as were their parallel European equivalents, in exotic far-off places, with *The Desert Song* in the African desert, *The Vagabond King* in Paris during the Middle Ages, and *The Student Prince* in Heidelberg. There was little attempt to re-create local melodic styles. As in European shows of the time, these shows demanded well-trained singers of near-operatic standard. At this stage realistic acting and other niceties were not required.

Younger, native-born Americans such as George Gershwin, Richard Rodgers and Jerome Kern were learning their craft by producing songs for insertion in musicals and revues by others. Irish-born, German-trained Victor Herbert scored with *The Fortune Teller* (1898) and *Babes in Toyland* (1903). He was to turn out hit shows almost every other year for some considerable time, each full of endearing, opulent melody, but none of which developed the style of the musical comedy. Flagwaving, irrepressible George M. Cohan had his first success with *Little Johnny Jones* (1904), and proceeded with aggressively patriotic shows that made you feel that every day was the Fourth of July!

A British import, *The Girl from Utah,* arrived in America in 1914, embellished with seven songs by Jerome Kern (the sixth show he had contributed to, and the most substantial to date). The same year, Irving Berlin composed the score for *Watch Your Step* (the first of twenty-one). A year later *The Blue Paradise* introduced the sentimental romantic style of Sigmund Romberg that would see him through fifty-seven shows.

The first successful Princess Theater show – *Very Good, Eddie* – was mounted in 1915 with a full score by Jerome Kern. This was an intimate show designed for a small theatre, and for some the sequence of Princess Theater shows represents the dawn of modern musical comedy. Kern, the supreme melodist, was beginning a string of musical hits that would stretch into the 1940s and include some of the finest musical comedy scores for both stage and screen ever written.

Wartime, much longer in Europe (1914–18) than for the United States (1917–18), meant the British audiences had significantly different requirements from their theatres. Britain wanted happy, upbeat entertainment, and that's what they got. Shows with a Germanic background or origin were swiftly removed. Lavish revues and musical comedies, including the *Passing Shows* and the *Bing Boys* series, offered patriotism and sentiment. *The Maid of the Mountains* and *Chu Chin Chow* each offered exotic escapism, and were two extremely profitable shows by composers who were never to equal these achievements again (Frederic Norton and Harold Fraser-Simpson).

When World War I came to an end, the English musical continued its largely separate way from its American counterpart and offered, for the most part, star vehicles created around leading players of the day, leavened with the odd American import. The Astaires, singers and dancers (brother and sister) Fred and Adele, came with three shows, of which two were classics – *Lady, Be Good!* and *Funny Face.* These were the work of the Gershwins, and composer George Gershwin brought a fresh and original musical style, jazzy, syncopated and confident in its melodic originality, that showed how the American musical comedy was pulling well ahead of its now old-fashioned-seeming British equivalent.

Not everything was totally new, however. Friml's *Rose Marie* was a good old-fashioned wallow in the Rockies. Romberg's prince-and-serving girl show *The Student Prince* was a determinedly old-fashioned romance – the only kind Romberg knew how to write – and it was a massive hit. The remainder of the 1920s found Friml in France with *The Vagabond King*, Berlin in cahoots with the Marx Brothers for *The Cocoanuts*, Kern at the circus for *Sunny*, the Gershwins with bootleggers in *Oh, Kay!* and Youmans all at sea with *Hit the Deck.* All had their individual styles. Irving Berlin was the most chameleon-like. He could and did write every kind of song and in every conceivable style. Kern was the supreme melodist, with tunes that unfolded both beautifully and with a complete inevitability. The Gershwin melodies throbbed with an inner rhythmic impetus and Youmans' tunes had a simple step-by-step catchiness with the kind of infuriatingly simple melody you just couldn't forget – remember 'Tea for two'?

The vigour of American folk music, blues and jazz began to influence American classical and popular music from 1924 onwards, for that was the year of Gershwin's *Rhapsody in Blue*, a classical composition that broke down the barriers of popular and classical music. The theatregoing public looked for excitement and zip in their shows and they got it.

For sheer cleverness there were Rodgers and Hart. They explored early American history with *Dearest Enemy* and made a trip back to King Arthur's Camelot with *A Connecticut Yankee*. Their songs were witty, memorable and tuneful. Rodgers would have two separate careers. Firstly, a frustrating but rewarding time as the partner of urbane Larry Hart, whose sophisticated, often despairing lyrics hymned the joys and sadnesses of metropolitan life. Towards the end of their time together came the real masterpieces – *Pal Joey, On Your Toes* and *Babes in Arms*. Secondly, he found a new partner, and even greater success, with Oscar Hammerstein II.

Jerome Kern and Oscar Hammerstein II came up with the best musical of 1927 – some say of any year – in their massive, masterful adaptation of Edna Furber's *Show Boat*. In every way this impressive and eventful musical pageant, loosely based round the River Mississippi, proved what musical comedy was capable of. Its wide panorama of events spanned forty years and offered a depth of characterisation hitherto unseen on the Broadway stage coupled with a score of matchless purity, excitement and beauty that showed the influences of not merely operetta, but also of the blues and current dance forms, including the Charleston.

In 1929 in Britain we were offered Noël Coward's affecting, enduring *Bitter Sweet* and Vivian Ellis' captivating sex-reversal version of *Cinderella – Mr Cinders*. The former show visited Broadway – the latter didn't. While Coward's plays were witty contemporary comedies of manners, his musical comedies were costume melodramas and didn't have the staying power of some others.

Among the most popular shows in Britain in the 1930s were the musicals of Ivor Novello, including *Glamorous Night* and *The Dancing Years*. They were romantic, old-fashioned spectacular extravaganzas that harked back to European models of earlier decades, and each was illuminated by the star presence of their matinée-idol nonsinging hero, their composer and creator Ivor Novello himself. None of them received American productions. Vivian Ellis was another successful creator of British musical comedy. From *Jill Darling* to *Bless the Bride* and *Big Ben*, his shows, though unexportable, filled London's theatres. Indeed, *Bless the Bride*'s record-breaking run still stands high in the list of British all-time successes.

The 1930s and '40s, though, were a golden period for the American musical comedy. The Gershwins opened their decade with the bright and bouncy *Girl Crazy* and followed up with three political satires – *Strike Up the Band, Of Thee I Sing* and *Let 'Em Eat Cake*. The great depression which followed the stock market crash of 1929 left many families ruined, but there was still enough prosperity to fuel the successful production of shows with long runs.

The arrival of sound on film from 1927 onwards brought a great number of filmed musicals that expanded the potential audience for live theatre. The great heritage of folk and blues and the development of jazz forms was reflected in musical comedy. The Gershwin masterpiece *Porgy and Bess*, which dealt with the lives of poor negroes in the South, drew on all of these for its feeling and power. The witty Cole Porter produced an authentic-sounding spiritual for his smash hit *Anything Goes*. When the celebrated German composer Kurt Weill escaped to New York he produced a musical comedy entitled *Down in the Valley* that sounded as if it was entirely composed of folk songs. He also created a powerful anti-war tract in *Johnny Johnson*. Musicals of social realism seldom reached as far as Broadway, but surfaced in the work of such composers as Harold Rome with his union-based revue *Pins and Needles*, written for garment workers, and Marc Blitzstein's *No for an Answer*, with a strong left-wing bias, which were mounted off-Broadway.

Cole Porter produced a stream of bright and bouncy hit musicals that were pleasant enough vehicles for great Broadway stars, but it was with his post-war shows, especially *Kiss Me Kate*, that Porter found true greatness. The show offered a backstage story of quarrelling stars in a Shakespeare play and a clutch of fine songs. Audiences loved the combination of wit and melody.

Rodgers and Hart achieved their best shows right at the end of the 1930s. *On Your Toes* enchanted audiences with its brave mix of tap and ballet dancing as the basis for a show. The novelty of *Pal Joey* was that it offered an unsympathetic conman as hero; the result was a bright, sassy and forward-looking show. The musical comedy was now offering grown-up, adult stories.

During and after World War II, Rodgers, with his new partner Oscar Hammerstein II, took over the main thrust of musical comedy with shows from *Oklahoma!* to *The Sound of Music*. These built on solid characterisation, strong books and fine music and lyrics. Not only were these to find great success at home, but they proved in almost all cases to find favour internationally. Unlike their predecessors, they did not rely on larger-than-life star performances from star performers, but the stories were driven forward by the songs which were totally integrated. The satisfying result often included elaborate dancing, and had a believability that was comparatively uncommon up to that time. *Oklahoma!* offered a simple story of life on the prairies; *Carousel* a doomed marriage between a New England fairground barker and his sweetheart; *South Pacific* was with the US marines in the fight against the Japanese; and an English governess taught the children of the Siamese court in *The King and I*. All these shows involved their fascinated audiences in the problems and predicaments of real people in real situations. And in wartime and afterwards, musical comedies offered two hours or more of escape into another world. For tourists in New York as in London, the escapism offered was worth its extra cost.

After the Second World War, not only did the Rodgers and Hammerstein shows make the running abroad, but so also did Irving Berlin's excellent *Annie Get Your Gun*, a vigorous tale of a travelling wild west show which enjoyed a longer run in London than on Broadway. The sheer zip and elan, and the professionalism of staging and performance, was exhilarating. The combination of Vienna's Frederick Loewe and America's Alan Jay Lerner would also find two of their shows, *Paint Your Wagon* and *Brigadoon*, run for longer in Britain than on Broadway. Later on, the talented team produced their greatest success, one of the last great operettas, based on George Bernard Shaw's *Pygmalion* – *My Fair Lady*. It combined glamour, well-realised characters, a strong story and gorgeous songs.

A new generation of composer/lyricists was appearing, who took note of the greater mood of social realism and incorporated it in their shows. Leonard Bernstein, after a couple of fairly conventional shows which gloried in the greatness of New York, turned to novice lyricist Stephen Sondheim and playwright Arthur Laurents for his startling new twist on the story of Romeo and Juliet. The harshly realistic *West Side Story*, also set in New York, took both Broadway and London by storm with its depiction of street gangs and their fights to the death. The effective work of Jerome Robbins marked the growing importance of dance in shows. In fact, from this show on, the increasing importance of the dance led many choreographers to become successful directors. As well as Robbins, examples are Bob Fosse, Michael Bennett and Gower Champion.

The brilliant Cy Coleman was responsible, with crack veteran lyricist Dorothy Fields, and Neil Simon's brilliant book, for *Sweet Charity*, a diamond-hard celebration of a down-at-heel ballroom hostess unsuccessfully searching for love. Matching this team in putting an unfeeling spotlight on mankind's foibles and dishonesties, John Kander and Fred Ebb came up with – and continue to produce – a stream of successes that can leave audiences shifting uneasily in their seats, but which are emotionally satisfying nevertheless. *Cabaret* opened up the sleazy world of Berlin nightlife in the late 1930s. *Chicago* revealed the dishonesty and hypocritical dealings of the judicial and political system of pre-war America, sparing no one's feelings in the process. The same visceral punch resulted from *Fiddler on the Roof*, a warmly emotional record of the upheaval of a Jewish village in Tsarist Russia. It was the work of Jerry Bock and Sheldon Harnick.

Side by side with these new-style musicals Broadway still found room for good old-fashioned star vehicles; Jule Styne's *Funny Girl* for Barbra Streisand and *Bells are Ringing* for Judy Holliday are good examples. One of the newcomers, Jerry Herman, was also solidly in the old-fashioned mould and came up with *Hello Dolly!* for Carol Channing and *Mame* for Angela Lansbury.

Jule Styne was also responsible for the best of all the backstage musicals. It brought together Laurents and Jerome Robbins with their *West Side Story* collaborator Stephen Sondheim. The show, starring Ethel Merman, was *Gypsy*, a celebration of a striptease artiste and her monstrous stage mother. The story was top notch, the songs were marvellously memorable and the casting well-nigh perfect.

There were a number of attempts to combine current rock and popular idioms with musical comedy in *Godspell*, *Hair* and *Grease* – the latter was originally intended as a satire, an element that has disappeared with blown-up revivals playing on the film's success.

13

Stephen Sondheim moved over to create the music as well as the lyrics for future shows and came up with a series of dazzling masterpieces that were also creative breakthroughs. They tackled difficult subjects and brought them off successfully. In *Follies* he examined the possible breakdown of two marriages against the background of a showgirl reunion. In *Sweeney Todd* it was mass murder, cannibalism and madness. *Sunday in the Park with George* examined with subtlety and depth the selfishness of creativity. *Merrily We Roll Along* dealt with the demands of friendship as opposed to ambition. *Passion* centres on the overpowering demands of love. Sondheim has consistently burst through the imagined boundaries of the musical to produce works which are constantly challenging, and always rewarding. As his shows do not pander to passing fashion, they have not always been as successful as they deserve. It is perhaps significant that revivals of his shows have often proved more prof-itable than the original runs, at least in Britain.

Back in Britain the left-wing Unity Theatre and the Theatre Royal Stratford East nurtured Lionel Bart, who eventually produced the classic adaptation from Charles Dickens – *Oliver!* – which successfully combined strains of folk song and music hall into a pleasing and dramatic whole. David Heneker's *Half a Sixpence* was a successful version of H.G. Wells' *Kipps* that also drew on the rich heritage of folk and music-hall styles. Both these shows, plus Sandy Wilson's *The Boy Friend*, a pleasing pastiche of the 1920s, proved successful at home and abroad in the 1960s.

These composers also wrote many other shows which were native successes only; in Lionel Bart's case *Blitz* and *Maggie May*, his most strongly folk-influ-enced show of all, consolidated his reputation. Heneker came up with a string of other musicals, the highly successful *Charlie Girl* among them. Julian Slade's *Salad Days* turned out not to be exportable and other fine shows like *Trelawny* were not even optioned. Ron Grainer's *Robert and Elizabeth*, the finest British operetta-musical of the post-war years, ran into legal trouble at the time in the United States, and the clock moved on.

But the pendulum has moved back, even if only temporarily, across the Atlantic to Britain, from where the longest-running shows are currently origi-nating. This appears to be due to two factors arriving at once: the composing and producing talents of Andrew Lloyd Webber and the entrepreneurial skill of Cameron Mackintosh. These together run the most important and influential production houses at the end of the century. There's also Bill Kenwright, vying for third place with his imaginative production programme. As far as America is concerned there may be an additional reason. As prices of American theatre seats rose sharply, audiences became more demanding. They wanted to go to smash hits only. As a result producers could no longer afford to nurse shows that were less than totally successful. Many therefore closed within days of opening if the reviews were unfavourable, and one publication in particular, the *New York Times*, appeared to have the power to influence the fate of a show more than any other. A show already proved to be a hit in Britain appears to have a greater chance of success in the United States. (British producers also seem more ready to nurse a show than their American counterparts. *The Phantom of the Opera, Evita* and *Blood Brothers* all survived less than satisfactory reviews on Broadway to run profitably.)

Apart from Marvin Hamlisch's long-running, exceptional, one-of-a-kind *A Chorus Line,* the most successful shows of recent years on Broadway have been created in Britain. They are the ones that run for years. However, the pendulum may well swing back as more American home-grown hits shine forth.

Andrew Lloyd Webber shows combine a classical flavour with the composer's love of popular music, and have found great success throughout the world. At the time of writing, the West End is playing host to *Cats, Starlight Express, Phantom of the Opera* and, his latest, *The Beautiful Game.* The classic *Evita* was recently and successfully filmed with Madonna playing the title role. This is a tally of success that is unmatched by any other composer. *Cats* is the longest-running London and Broadway show of all time, and was chosen as the first of Lloyd Webber's productions to be filmed for video issue even while its 'now and forever' run continues in London. Videos of *Joseph and the Technicolor Dreamcoat* and *Jesus Christ Superstar* have also been issued.

Lloyd Webber's first collaborator, lyricist Tim Rice, has found success working in the United States, first in Hollywood and then on Broadway. His *The Lion King,* written with pop superstar Elton John, started life as a Disney animated film and developed into a magical theatre piece. A totally original Disney musical called *Aida,* using the same story as Verdi's opera, has followed this from the same collaboration. *The Lion King* goes some way to making up for the disappointment when the musical Rice had written with two members of the Swedish pop group ABBA, called *Chess,* which ran for two years in Britain, swiftly folded on Broadway. *Blondel,* his musical about Richard I at the Crusades, with Stephen Oliver has not travelled abroad either.

An Anglo-French collaboration, nursed by producer Cameron Mackintosh, resulted in the Jean-Michel Schonberg–Alain Boublil show *Les Miserables,* a long-runner everywhere but France, followed by a modern-day version of the plot of Puccini's *Madama Butterfly – Miss Saigon.* These are established all-time international successes. Their third collaboration, *Martin Guerre,* after substantial revision, managed a West End run and, with further changes, it toured. Another production opened in the United States without success. Mackintosh was co-producer of early Lloyd Webber shows and through his charitable foundation actively supports new writers and writing, as well as offering funding to help produce shows in subsidised theatres, the most recent being the critically-acclaimed revivals of *Carousel, Oklahoma!* and *My Fair Lady* at the Royal National Theatre. He is now represented on the commercial London stage with a new musical comedy called, and based upon the film of the same name, *The Witches of Eastwick.*

What can we look forward to in the future? Intriguingly, the two longest-running shows of all time are plotless. They are disguised revues in that they each consist of a series of character sketches, revealing various personality traits: *A Chorus Line* focuses on the selection of members of a Broadway chorus and *Cats* is a cycle of poems about various felines and what they get up to. Do they point out a new direction? Andrew Lloyd Webber has indicated that he believes the days of the spectacular show are drawing to a close and his latest production, with book and lyrics by comedian/writer Ben Elton, is a powerful social statement called *The Beautiful Game* which depends more upon directorial, choreographic and writing skills than spectacular diversions. On Broadway, the spectacular *The Lion King* has a new competitor as the hottest ticket in town with the musical version of the comedy motion picture *The Producers*. Yet at the same time, three of the other Broadway hits are revivals of shows from the Broadway golden period: *Annie Get Your Gun*, *Kiss Me, Kate* and *The Music Man*. The success of *Rent*, a contemporary version of Puccini's *La Boheme* and the rock-scored *Aida* show there is a place for musicals closer attuned to the rock and pop music of the time. In London *Mamma Mia!* uses the almost nostalgic soft rock songs of ABBA to produce a mega hit. Stars are still important and, indeed, some shows totally depend upon their names above the show's title; but, there is a trend which makes the show the star, which, of course, is a producer's dream.

Whatever the mix of musical shows that play in London or New York may be, the future of the musical comedy will depend on three main factors: the development and nurturing of new talent, the courage of producers to find the money to mount new work, and the willingness of audiences to attend the shows. If musical comedy is to continue to occupy over half of the available stages, it must continue to offer entertainment, stimulation and satisfaction. Long may it continue to do so.

Forms of Musical

The modern musical comedy, from its various roots, has evolved into a number of different forms, some of which overlap. The main forms are:

THE OPERETTA MUSICAL

The oldest form, and one in which Friml, Romberg and sometimes Kern operated. A prime requisite is well-trained semi-operatic voices. The music will be well crafted, and though the plots and even the sentiments may sometimes seem silly, the musical result is likely to be glorious. In general, convincing acting is not necessarily a prime requisite – although it would be nice. The plots are likely to involve princes, kings, queens, strange foreign kingdoms, and simple folk who go to the big city and are hurt by city sophisticates before retiring hurt to where they came from. But the main thrust involves unhappy, or unfulfilled romances between kings and commoners. Examples are *The Student Prince in Heidelberg*, *The Vagabond King* and *Bitter Sweet*.

THE STORY MUSICAL

In general this is a form that is not cast with stars but with able performers capable of both acting and singing with conviction and sincerity. The focus is on story and character. The hero and/or heroine come through some trial or test, becoming better and stronger people, or at least gaining in a self-knowledge that will enable them to advance more successfully in their lives. Rodgers and Hammerstein were masters of this kind of show, even if they were sometimes star vehicles as well. *Oklahoma!* and *Carousel* did not contain major stars, yet they proved to be the first in a long line of successful story musicals that began with *Show Boat*, and later *Oklahoma!*, which brought new standards in acting, singing and decor, and extended the boundaries of song and dance. The 1940s, '50s and '60s exploded with such fare: Adler and Ross' *The Pajama Game* and *Damn Yankees*, Frank Loesser's *Guys and Dolls* and Bock and Harnick's *Fiddler on the Roof* show just how good such shows can be. More recently *Les Miserables*, *Miss Saigon* and *Aspects of Love* have continued this fine tradition.

THE POP/ROCK MUSICAL

Usually the form that dates most easily, since the musical style reflects contemporary pop fashions, or revives and comments on past musical trends. Most conventional Broadway composers have veered away from this form. As a result, the majority of shows in this genre were written by composers new to Broadway or to London. Unhappily, they usually only enjoyed one hit. Where are the follow-up hits by Galt McDermot (*Hair*), Jim Jacobs and Warren Casey (*Grease* was originally a satire, but this strain has been lost in the film and revivals). Stephen Schwartz has managed it with *Pippin* following *Godspell* and in Broadway-style songs for Disney films, but he's been the exception. Hal David and Burt Bacharach brought their pop hit writing skills to Broadway with *Promises, Promises*, and Barry Manilow offered *Copacabana* to London. While both shows enjoyed satisfactory runs, they appear to be one-offs. The black rock musical is a subdivision of the pop/rock musical – modern and realistic, street smart with music that reflects the contemporary black music scene. The stories reflect current situations and oppressions. Examples are Gary Geld's *Purlie*, Charlie Smalls' *The Wiz* and Henry Krieger's *Dreamgirls* and *The Tap Dance Kid*. Previous generations have been offered shows by, usually, non-Afro-American writers which explored earlier concerns. Examples are Kurt Weill's *Lost in the Stars*, Harold Arlen's *House of Flowers* and *Jamaica*, and Jule Styne's *Hallelujah Baby*.

THE DISGUISED ROCK CONCERT (SOMETIMES BIOGRAPHICAL)
A format devised largely by the British. In these a series of pop and rock hits are confected into a suitable format to fit a storyline. The evening invariably ends with an uninterrupted series of numbers performed by the cast. Some of these musicals are semi-biographical: *Buddy, Good Rocking Tonight, Are You Lonesome Tonight?, Ferry Cross the Mersey* and *Return to the Forbidden Planet*, which is a rock and roll version of Shakespeare's *The Tempest*.

THE STAR VEHICLE
Normally the mainstay of Broadway in the vintage years, these are shows built round stars who rightly or wrongly are the main box office draw. The stars also have the lion's share of the best numbers too. Star vehicles are Rosalind Russell in *Wonderful Town*, Carol Channing in *Hello Dolly!*, Ethel Merman in *Gypsy* and *Annie Get Your Gun*, Angela Lansbury in *Mame*, Julie Andrews in *Victor/Victoria*, Barbra Streisand in *Funny Girl* and a succession of stars in *Sunset Boulevard*. Jule Styne and Jerry Herman have usually, if not always, written for stars and their shows have the strengths and weaknesses inherent in this format. The danger comes when stars' contracts are up. Can their replacements maintain the audiences?

THE NON-LINEAR MUSICAL
There is no real storyline. Other elements are considered much more important. Shows like Sondheim's *Company* and *Pacific Overtures*, Hamlisch's *A Chorus Line*, and Lloyd Webber's *Cats* offer events and characters but do not aim for a coherent storyline. They rely on the strength of the music and lyrics, often combined with strong characterisation, to create an interesting and satisfying evening.

THE ALMOST-AN-OPERA MUSICAL
Although Sondheim may not thank anyone for saying so, *Sweeney Todd* falls into this category, where it is joined by Loesser's magnum opus *The Most Happy Fella*. The grace and style of Sondheim's *A Little Night Music* makes this another candidate. These shows have a lot of music in them, which is both taxing and rewarding for the performers. Revivals are often undertaken by opera companies.

REVUE
Originally a form of mixed entertainment, the revue consists of a series of unrelated songs and sketches. A very popular form on both sides of the Atlantic with *The Band Wagon* (all songs by Schwartz and Dietz), *The Music Box* revues

(Berlin), *As Thousands Cheer* (Berlin) and *At Home Abroad* (Schwartz and Dietz) representing America. Also into this category fall the *Ziegfeld Follies* and *The George White Scandals*. English revues developed independently in two forms, the spectacular and the intimate. The former was typified by the Crazy Gang shows and, in earlier times, the Charles B. Cochran star-packed extravaganzas. The intimate style is characterised by small casts playing in smaller theatres; they were the province of impresarios such as André Charlot and created stars like Gertrude Lawrence, Jack Buchanan and Beatrice Lillie. During the Second World War revues such as the *Sweet and Low* series were a major part of the London theatre scene. The death of revue in Britain came with the advent of satire (*Beyond the Fringe*) and television with its own variety programmes and, with programmes like *That Was The Week That Was*, instant topicality.

THE MUSICAL SURVEY
A very popular, and often economically efficient, form of musical entertainment. Shows in this category consist of a collection of songs by one, two or more collaborators that can be mounted more easily with a small group of singers and orchestral backing than would have been the case with the shows the songs came from (if indeed they came from any show). *Side by Side by Sondheim* and *Marry Me a Little* (Sondheim), *Closer than Ever* and *Starting Here, Starting Now* (Maltby and Shire), *Spread a Little Happiness* (Ellis), *Ain't Misbehavin'* (Waller), *The World Goes Round* (Kander and Ebb), *Cowardy Custard* (Coward) and *Cole* (Porter), and just recently *Smokey Joe's Cafe* (Lieber and Stoller) and *Sophisticated Ladies* (Duke Ellington), are just a few of these.

> **Note**
>
> In order to limit the number of shows covered in this guide, we concentrate upon the book shows created for the theatre and exclude revues and musical surveys.

Annie

LYRICS ✶ Martin Charnin
MUSIC ✶ Charles Strouse
BOOK ✶ Thomas Meehan, based on the cartoon strip *Little Orphan Annie*

First Performance

New York, Goodspeed Opera House, 10 August 1976
Transferred to Alvin Theater, 21 April 1977 (2377 performances)
London, Victoria Palace, 2 May 1978 (1485 performances)

Principal Characters

Annie ✶ An orphan
Miss Hannigan ✶ In charge of the orphanage
Oliver Warbucks ✶ A millionaire, friend of the Mighty
Grace Farrell ✶ His charming and astute secretary
Rooster and Lily ✶ Alias Ralph and Shirley Mudge, a couple of villains

Original New York Cast

Andrea McArdle, Dorothy Loudon, Reid Shelton,
Sandy Faison, Robert Fitch, Barbara Erwin

Original London Cast

Andrea McArdle/Ann-Marie Gwatkin, Sheila Hancock, Stratford Johns,
Judith Paris, Kenneth Nelson, Clovissa Newcombe

Plot

It's 1933 and the very depths of the Depression. Annie is 11 years old, living in the Municipal Orphanage on New York's Lower East Side. Miss Hannigan is in charge and could give some useful pointers to the Wicked Witch of the West. Annie decides to escape and seek her parents. This proves unsuccessful, but Grace Farrell, secretary to Oliver Warbucks, the well-known millionaire, is looking for an orphan to invite home for Christmas. Despite initial disappointment that Annie isn't a boy, Oliver Warbucks takes to her and organizes a nationwide search for her real parents. Miss Hannigan interferes, and coaches her brother, Rooster, so that he and his girlfriend 'Lily' can claim Annie, and the reward. Meanwhile, Annie is in Washington, cheering up the president, F.D.R. (Roosevelt). Back in New York Annie is claimed by Rooster and his girlfriend, but Grace smells a rat – she's seen Rooster in Miss Hannigan's office. The fraudulent couple are exposed, and it is discovered that Annie's parents died some time ago. Warbucks plans to adopt Annie, and her fellow orphans are invited to Warbucks' home to share in a wonderful Christmas Day of celebrations, as America looks forward to future prosperity and a New Deal.

Music and Songs

A joyous, easy-to-hum score, packed with good tunes and witty lyrics. Broadway magic at its most effervescent, with echoes of the great songwriters of the past – Gershwin, Porter and de Sylva, Brown and Henderson to name but five. The hit number, 'Tomorrow' (Annie), is a tribute to the get-up-and-go spirit that yanked America out of the Depression. Not to be overlooked: 'NYC' (the company), a valentine to New York, and 'You're never fully dressed without a smile' (Bert Healy, Boylan Sisters), a cute pastiche of a 30s radio song.

Did You Know?

✴ *Annie* is one of the very few successful musical shows to be based on an American cartoon strip.

✴ Although the original Broadway *Annie* played the London opening, Anne Marie Gwatkin eventually took over, and appeared on the London cast album.

✴ After one attempt at a sequel – *Annie II: Miss Hannigan's Revenge* – a third musical actually reached New York under the title of *Annie Warbucks* in 1993. The same creative talents were involved, but the show did not repeat the success of the original. Incidentally, at the end of this third show, Grace and Warbucks marry and adopt the orphans.

The Critics

Annie received high critical praise:
'It's pure magic' – *Daily Express*
'The charm of Annie is irresistible' – *Daily Mirror*
'A blockbusting smash hit' – *Daily Mail*

Recommended Recording

Broadway cast (CD) OBC Sony SK 60723
The original recording is a fine Broadway cast album and contains many pleasing performances. Andrea McArdle is the finest Annie, a little girl with a lot of heart and a will to live life for the best. For those who like their Broadway shows to be brash, tuneful and totally entertaining.

Film

Columbia Pictures, 1982. Starring Aileen Quinn, Carol Burnett, Albert Finney, Ann Reinking, Tim Curry and Bernadette Peters. Directed by John Huston.

Annie Get Your Gun

LYRICS ✶ Irving Berlin
MUSIC ✶ Irving Berlin
BOOK ✶ Herbert and Dorothy Fields

First Performance

New York, Imperial Theater, 16 May 1946 (1147 performances)
London, Coliseum, 7 June 1947 (1304 performances)

Principal Characters

Annie Oakley ✶ A sharpshooter
Frank Butler ✶ Another marksman
Charlie Davenport ✶ Advance publicist for Buffalo Bill
Winnie Tate ✶ Charlie's niece
Tommy Keeler ✶ Her beau
Buffalo Bill Cody

Original New York Cast

Ethel Merman, Ray Middleton, Marty May, Betty Ann Nyman,
Kenny Bowers, William O'Neil

Original London Cast

Dolores Gray, Bill Johnson, Hal Bryan, Wendy Toye,
Irving Davies, Ellis Irving

Plot

The Buffalo Bill Wild West Show is tented near Cincinnati. The main attraction is sharpshooter Frank Butler. Enter Annie Oakley and her four siblings. Annie can't read or count but what she can do is challenge Frank in a shooting contest. Before this, she meets him and is smitten. He, on the other hand, prefers feminine women – all peaches and cream. That isn't Annie! But she wins the shooting match and is invited to join the show. She accepts and her star billing makes Frank jealous. He leaves to join the rival Pawnee Bill show.

Frank Butler is a hit with the rival show and moves easily into smart society. Annie turns up, festooned with medals at a grand ball at the Brevoort Hotel. Everyone thinks both troupes are rich, but they're not. The solution is a merger of Buffalo Bill's and Pawnee Bill's shows. But, this will only happen if both Annie and Frank remain as attractions – and all depends on the result of a grand shooting contest. Her friends interfere with Annie's rifle sights to ensure she loses. Unfortunately, Frank lends Annie his rifle. It is only when Sitting Bull, her friend, gives Annie some advice that she decides to lose the contest to win her man. Now the new Wild West Show will feature Mr and Mrs Frank Butler!

Music and Songs

A wonderful example of what the Broadway conventional musical score is. Every song is a hit and draws on the rich legacy of American popular music. 'There's no business like show business' (Frank, Annie and company) is the ultimate showbiz anthem. 'The girl that I marry' (Frank) and 'My defenses are down' (Frank) are standouts, as is the great 'me too' duet 'Anything you can do' (Annie and Frank). 'They say it's wonderful' (Annie) and 'I got the sun in the morning' (Annie) display the soft and optimistic side of the heroine with passion and tenderness, while 'Doin' what comes natur'lly' (Annie) and 'You can't get a man with a gun' (Annie) show her brash side.

Did You Know?

✲ The show was produced by the songwriting team of Richard Rodgers and Oscar Hammerstein II, whose first choice as composer was Jerome Kern. Unfortunately Kern died suddenly and Berlin was asked to take over. Dorothy Fields, who originally was to have written the lyrics, agreed to remain on the show and worked with her brother Herbert on the book.

✲ In London the conductor was the distinguished bandleader Lew Stone, and Dolores Gray scored a massive personal triumph as Annie.

✲ Judy Garland started filming the title role but ill health stopped her completing it, and Betty Hutton was brought in to replace her.

✲ The recent Broadway revival was made politically correct in the characterisation of Annie and the portrayal of the Indians.

The Critics

'No use trying to pick a hit tune for all the tunes are hits' – *New York Post*
'The Irving Berlin songs form a fascinating web of wit and melody' – *New York Herald Tribune*
'*Annie Get Your Gun* is far and away the best musical in town' – *New York Journal American*

Recommended Recording

Original cast (CD) MCA MCAD 10047
While there are excellent full recordings of the score (**EMI CDC 7 542062** with Kim Criswell and **TER CDTER1229** with Judy Kaye), Ethel Merman wins with an excitement and thrill less evident elsewhere.

Film

MGM, 1950. Starring Betty Hutton and Howard Keel. Directed by George Sidney.

Anyone Can Whistle

LYRICS ✶ Stephen Sondheim
MUSIC ✶ Stephen Sondheim
BOOK ✶ Arthur Laurents

First Performance

New York, Majestic Theater, 4 April 1964 (9 performances)
Cheltenham, UK, Everyman Theatre, 21 August 1986 (22 performances)

Principal Characters

Cora Hoover Hooper ✶ It's her town
Nurse Fay Apple ✶ From the lunatic asylum, the Cookie Jar
Dr Hapgood ✶ A visitor
Police Chief Magruder ✶ Police chief
Comptroller Shub
Treasurer Cooley

Original New York Cast

Angela Lansbury, Lee Remick, Harry Guardino, James Crawley,
Gabriel Dell, Arnold Soboloff

Original UK Cast

Pip Hinton, Marilyn Cutts, Michael Jayes, Jonathan Stephens,
Bill Bradley, John Griffiths

Plot

A small town in America is bankrupt and needs a miracle to save it. Cora, the unpopular mayoress, is the richest person in town and even she can't do anything to improve the situation. A trip to the rock on the outskirts of the town provides the answer. A youngster is thirsty, licks the rock, and water gushes forth – it's a miracle! Enter Nurse Apple with forty-nine patients from the successful Dr Detmold's hospital, the Sanitarium for the Socially Pressured. Can they be cured? Probably not, for the miracle is a fake, engineered by corrupt town officials. The patients mingle with pilgrims – becoming indistinguishable from them. Nurse Apple refuses to identify them; she believes the patients have as much right to be cured as anybody. The nurse longs for a hero to rescue her and right on cue J. Bowden Hapgood arrives, a doctor who is to become the assistant of Dr Detmold. He'll sort out the mad from the sane – won't he? He divides the people into two groups and announces that everybody is mad.

Nurse Apple reappears in heavy disguise as a French investigator come to check out the rock. She's taken the records of the patients to prevent identification. Hapgood sees through her disguise and tries to seduce her, but fails. He urges her to destroy the patients' records. When she refuses, he starts to do so himself, and admits that he's no doctor but a former professor of statistical philosophy – and the fiftieth patient!

The nurse tears up the records. Meanwhile, Cora and company decide to reveal the hoax and blame it, and everything else, on Hapgood. Nurse Apple, no longer in disguise, is charged with identifying and returning the patients to the hospital. She chooses forty-nine citizens at random. Dr Detmold demands the records from Nurse Apple, but she cannot supply them. Sadly she collects the forty-nine she's forced to identify (but not Hapgood) and leads them past the now dry 'miracle' rock. She encounters Hapgood, they embrace and for the first time in her life she's able to whistle. Suddenly water bursts from the rock – a real miracle at last!

Music and Songs

Anyone Can Whistle is an eclectic, ravishingly beautiful, astonishing score whose music recalls Jerome Moross' Big Country film score, classical music by Harris and Copland, plus Arlen's Over the Rainbow and smart Kay Thompson-type revue numbers. 'Anyone can whistle' (Nurse Apple), 'Me and my town' (Cora), 'With so little to be sure of' (Hapgood), and 'There won't be trumpets' (Nurse Apple) are typical of the show's richness of style and content.

Did You Know?

✷ Anyone Can Whistle's fame and influence is remarkable in view of its run of only nine performances. It's equally praiseworthy that an original cast album was actually made – and is a classic.

✷ Playwright Tom Stoppard, a friend of the composer, named one of his plays Hapgood.

✷ If all the people who now claim to have seen the show had actually done so, it would have run for months – not just over a week.

The Critics

'An exasperating musical comedy' – New York Herald Tribune
'They have taken an idea with possibilities and pounded it into pulp' – New York Times
'A merry abundance of theatrical ingenuity' – New York World Telegram & Sun

Recommended Recording

Original Broadway cast (CD) Columbia CK 2480
The show that introduced Angela Lansbury to the Broadway stage. It is an inventive score recorded beautifully by the king of Broadway record producers, Goddard Lieberson. A concert version with Angela Lansbury narrating lacks consistency, but a promised new recording with Julia McKenzie may well be rewarding. Notwithstanding, Angela Lansbury is outstanding and Lee Remick charming and it is doubtful that anyone could better these performances.

Anything Goes

LYRICS ✳ Cole Porter
MUSIC ✳ Cole Porter
BOOK ✳ Guy Bolton and P.G. Wodehouse
(revised by Howard Lindsay and Russel Crouse)

First Performance

New York, Alvin Theater, 21 November 1934 (420 performances)
London, Palace Theatre, 14 June 1935 (261 performances)

Principal Characters

Reno Sweeney ✳ Former evangelist and currently nightclub singer
Billy Crocker ✳ An old friend
Moonface Martin ✳ Public Enemy No.13, disguised as Rev. Moon
Hope Harcourt ✳ A beautiful heiress

Original New York Cast

Ethel Merman, William Gaxton, Victor Moore, Bettina Hall

Original London Cast

Jeanne Aubert, Jack Whiting, Sydney Howard, Adele Dixon

Plot

A shipload of passengers are sailing on the SS *American* from New York to London. (The original production began in a cocktail bar on shore, but subsequent productions have started on the ship itself.) We meet Hope Harcourt and her fiancé, the rich but dumb Sir Evelyn; a bishop and two Chinese converts; the entertainers Reno Sweeney and her Angels; and Billy Crocker (who doesn't have a ticket, but is offered one by Moonface Martin, a gangster disguised as a priest). Billy is attracted by Hope and tells Reno, a friend of long standing. Billy has to hide from his boss (also on board) and further complications arise. Billy's ticket was originally intended for a notorious killer and Billy is mistaken for him. Billy tries to evade capture by dressing up in various disguises. Meanwhile, Moonface gambles with the two Chinese converts and loses everything. Billy is 'exposed' as the killer and becomes the celebrity of the hour. Moonface is imprisoned, and is joined by Billy when he is revealed as an ordinary stockbroker and not the criminal he has been impersonating.

The ship docks at Southampton; Billy and Moonface escape, having won a game of strip poker against the Chinese. They visit Sir Evelyn at his home, accompanied by Reno who accuses Evelyn of having fathered a Chinese child. He can no longer marry Hope! Billy's employer buys Hope's company instead. Billy pairs off with Hope, Reno with Sir Evelyn. It also turns out that Moonface is no longer a wanted man. Happiness reigns.

Music and Songs

A wonderful vintage Cole Porter score, full of wit and merriment, ranging from old time revivalist numbers, such as 'Blow, Gabriel blow' (Reno), to zesty show-stoppers – 'You're the top' (Billy and Reno), 'I get a kick out of you' (Reno), 'Anything goes' (Reno and sailors) – and tender, intense love songs, including 'All through the night' (Billy and Hope).

Did You Know?

✳ The original show's plot involved a shipwreck. This had to be changed when the SS *Morro Castle* caught fire during a cruise from Havana – one of the major maritime disasters of the 1930s.

✳ Ethel Merman recreated her role as Reno Sweeney both on film and television.

✳ *Anything Goes* is one of the few 1930s shows to be revived successfully.

✳ P.G. Wodehouse wrote new lyrics for 'You're the top' and the title number for the London production.

The Critics

'Dashing score and impish lyrics' – *New York Times*
'A jubilant and expert affair' – *New York Evening Post*

Recommended Recording

Complete recording (CD) EMI CDC 749848 2
An inspired John McGlinn recording using the original orchestrations where they survive. It is the most comprehensive, authentic and the best recording of the score with a ballsy Kim Criswell taking on the Merman role.

Films

Paramount, 1936. Starring Bing Crosby and Ethel Merman. Directed by Lewis Milestone. The film used only four songs from the show alongside original numbers.
Paramount, 1956. Starring Bing Crosby, Zizi Jeanmaire, Mitzi Gaynor and Donald O'Connor. Directed by Robert Lewis. This bore even less resemblance to the stage version.

Applause

LYRICS * Lee Adams
MUSIC * Charles Strouse
BOOK * Betty Comden and Adolph Green,
based on the film *All about Eve* (screenplay by Joseph Mankiewicz),
adapted from the short story *The Wisdom of Eve* by Mary Orr

First Performance

New York, Palace Theater, 30 March 1970 (896 performances)
London, Her Majesty's Theatre, 16 November 1972 (382 performances)

Principal Characters

Margo Channing * A star actress
Bill Samson * Her director and fiancé
Eve Harrington * An ambitious girl
Howard Benedict * A powerful producer
Karen Richards * Wife of . . .
Buzz Richards * A playwright
Duane Fox * A flamboyant dresser
Bonnie * The lead female dancer
(in London, Sheila was the name of the lead female dancer)

Original New York Cast

Lauren Bacall, Len Cariou, Penny Fuller, Robert Mandan, Ann Williams,
Brandon Maggart, Lee Roy Reams, Bonnie Franklin

Original London Cast

Lauren Bacall, Eric Flynn, Angela Richards, Basil Hoskins, Sarah Marshall,
Rod McLennan, Ken Walsh, Sheila O'Neill

Plot

At the Tony ceremony on Broadway, successful, mature actress, Margo Channing, hands the Best Actress award to young Eve Harrington, and thinks back to when the manipulating, scheming Eve entered the lives of Margo and her circle, wreaking emotional havoc in her ruthless climb to the top. Was it only a year and a half ago? From just a fan, Eve rapidly becomes Margo's Girl Friday, then her understudy, making a play for the show's producer, Howard, as well. Margo is the first to see Eve for what she really is. Friends refuse to believe Margo, putting her fears down to paranoia. To teach her a lesson, Karen, wife of Buzz, the playwright, ensures that Margo misses a performance, and Eve scores a hit.

Eve lets the fame go to her head, snubbing former backstage friends, and dismissing Margo by suggesting in a newspaper article that she is one of the 'aging stars'. After an unsuccessful attempt to ensnare Bill, Margo's fiancé and director, Eve settles on playwright Buzz, until her plans are thwarted by the more powerful producer, Howard, who can give her what she wants – the lead in a new play. Meanwhile, Margo realizes that what she really wants out of life is Bill.

Music and Songs

Artfully tailored to enable its Hollywood star to make an impact on Broadway, the score of *Applause* combines a set of showstoppers such as 'Applause' (Bonnie and chorus) and 'Welcome to the theater' (Margo), with zesty character songs like 'But alive' (Margo) and, in wistful contrast, 'Hurry back' (Margo).

Did You Know?

✳ The original story was based on a real-life situation.

✳ One of the performers who took over the lead as Margo on tour in America was the actress who created the role of Eve in the original film – Anne Baxter.

✳ Ron Field won Tony awards for both his direction and choreography. It was also voted best musical of the season with Lauren Bacall winning the best actress award.

✳ Lauren Bacall recreated her role as Margo Channing in a television production of the show.

The Critics

'Whatever it is Miss Lauren Bacall possesses she throws it around most beautifully, most exquisitely and most excitingly' – *The New York Times* '*Applause* takes the familiar story of the understudy who substitutes for the absent star and wins a great personal success, and turns it upside down. The musical comedy based on the film *All About Eve*, which opened last night at the Palace Theater, is a sardonic view of backstage life, and, although I thought it eased off considerably after a brilliant start, it is so filled with entertainment values that it is surely destined to be a gigantic hit' – *New York Post*

Recommended Recording

Original Broadway cast (CD) Decca 012 159 404-2
The only recording of this clever star vehicle show – Miss Bacall may not have the voice but she certainly has the power and ability to put a song over. The score has worn well and is a far wittier show than perhaps one first thought.

Film

The original version was the non-musical *All About Eve*, starring Bette Davis. The show was recorded in London for American television with a mixture of the New York and London casts.

The Arcadians

LYRICS ✴ Arthur Wimperis
MUSIC ✴ Lionel Monckton and Howard Talbot
BOOK ✴ Mark Ambient, Alexander M. Thompson and Robert Courtneidge

First Performance

London, Shaftesbury Theatre, 29 April 1909 (809 performances)
New York, Liberty Theater, 17 January 1910 (136 performances)

Principal Characters

Peter Doody ✴ A morose, ill-starred jockey
Eileen Cavanagh ✴ The niece of . . .
Simplicitas ✴ Alias James Smith, an aviator and restaurateur
Jack Meadows ✴ A not-too-well-off racehorse owner
Sombra ✴ An inhabitant of Arcady
Mrs Smith ✴ James' wife and Eileen's aunt
Chrysea ✴ An Arcadian

Original London Cast

Alfred Lester, Phyllis Dare, Dan Rolyat, Harry Welchman,
Florence Smithson, Ada Blanche, May Kinder

Original New York Cast

Percival Knight, Julia Sanderson, Frank Moulan, Alan Mudie,
Ethel Cadman, Connie Ediss, Audrey Maple

Plot

Arcady, an ideal land lying some way above the North Pole, is the home of the lovely Sombra. She has dreamt of a great serpent arriving from a place called England – a place where they tell lies. Old Father Time decides to provide the serpent – or in this case an aeroplane – piloted by James Smith. He lands in what he believes to be the Garden of Eden. He meets Sombra, lies to her and is dropped in the Well of Truth, from which he emerges as a good-looking young Arcadian shepherd called Simplicitas, with a warning that he will lose his handsome looks if he lies again. Sombra seizes the opportunity to take him back to wicked London and present him as a convert to the good and simple life.

The scene changes to Askwood racetrack. Jack Meadows has an untamed horse entered in the main race. The only jockey who'll agree to the ride is the morose Peter Doody, a born loser. Meanwhile, Jack spies Eileen, James Smith's lovely niece, and falls in love. But her aunt has found her a more suitable (i.e. wealthy) match elsewhere, racehorse owner Sir George. Thunder and lightning herald the arrival of the Arcadians. Simplicitas (James) falls from a tree and flirts with his own wife. She sees the business opportunities, assumes the arrival of the Arcadians is a publicity stunt, and decides to open the Arcadian Restaurant using

James's skills. Jack's horse has attacked Doody but Sombra saves the day by being able to converse with animals and, she guarantees a win.

The restaurant is a success, Jack and Eileen are getting on well even if there is a misunderstanding regarding the pretty Sombra, and James is having the time of his life – although not telling lies is difficult. But Sombra decides to go home, James tells a lie on purpose and returns to his old self and there is a happy ending. Unfortunately, Sombra and Chrysea's mission has failed – but then that is London for you.

Music and Songs

One of the greatest triumphs of the Edwardian era. With lyrics and music of the standard of Gilbert and Sullivan, *The Arcadians* offers witty, adroit numbers that illuminate character, and melody of boundless charm in a style that bridges the gap between Sullivan and Jerome Kern. 'The pipes of Pan' (Sombra) is the best-known number from the radiant score, but there's much more, including 'The girl with the brogue' (Eileen), 'Charming weather' (Eileen and Jack) and 'My Motter' (Peter).

Did You Know?

✶ After its original success, the show toured the UK for over 30 years and became staple fare for amateur operatic societies.

✶ The show was presented and directed by Robert Courtneidge. Cicely Courtneidge, his daughter, made her London debut in the play in its second year and, during the run, succeeded Phyllis Dare as Eileen, Jack's beloved. Miss Courtneidge also played the role in London in the 1915 revival.

The Critics

The critics were pleased:
'A more exquisite or amusing entertainment has not been seen since the days when genuine comic opera was the vogue' – *Play Pictorial*

Recommended Recording

Studio cast and original cast recording (CD) EMI 0 777 89057 2
An issue utilising two studio cast recordings from the EMI vaults to give as complete a recording of the show as possible. The bonus is tracks from the original cast sounding as pristine as the day they were first heard.

Film

Gaumont, 1927 (silent). Starring Doris Bransgrove, Ben Blue, Jeanne de Casalis and Gibb McLauchlin.

Aspects of Love

LYRICS ✶ Charles Hart and Don Black
MUSIC ✶ Andrew Lloyd Webber
BOOK ✶ Charles Hart and Don Black,
adapted from the novel of the same title by David Garnett

First Performance

London, Prince of Wales Theatre, 17 April 1989 (1325 performances)
New York, Broadhurst Theater, 8 April 1990 (377 performances)

Principal Characters

Alex Dillingham ✶ A young soldier
Rose Vibart ✶ His mistress
Uncle George ✶ His uncle
Giulietta ✶ A sculptress

Original London Cast

Michael Ball, Ann Crumb, Kevin Colson, Kathleen Rowe McAllen

Original New York Cast

Michael Ball, Ann Crumb, Kevin Colson, Kathleen Rowe McAllen

Plot

The young soldier, Alex Dillingham, entranced by the young actress, Rose Vibart,
meets her after a performance of *The Master Builder* in a theatre in Montpellier,
and impulsively invites her to spend some time with him at his wealthy uncle's
mansion in Pau. Uncle George is away and the actress agrees. Meanwhile, the
gardener informs Alex's uncle about the visit, and George Dillingham decides to
investigate things for himself. He leaves behind in Paris his young mistress, an
Italian sculptress, Giulietta, and travels to Pau. He meets and charms Rose who
shocks him by wearing a dress belonging to his late wife. When he returns to
Paris, Alex and Rose enjoy an idyllic holiday before she leaves in answer to a
telegram from her stage manager. Two years pass.

Visiting his uncle's Paris flat, Alex finds that Rose has now moved in with
George. There's a struggle, Rose is winged by Alex's gunshot and George leaves,
to rejoin Giulietta. Rose now turns up at Giulietta's studio and the two are
attracted to each other. Nevertheless Rose asks George to marry her. He does so.

Twelve years later, Rose is performing in Paris when the 30-year-old Alex
reappears. She takes him down to Pau where George lives with their daughter
Jenny. Young Jenny now falls in love with Alex. Alex is initially unwilling to
acknowledge his reciprocal affection, but George is aware of the situation and
takes to spying on the couple when they are together. In so doing he suffers a fatal
heart attack. Rose asks Alex to stay on after the funeral. But this is an impossible
situation for him, caught as he is between Rose and Jenny – the two women he

loves and who love him. There is another option – the simple primal love of Giulietta. As for Rose, she will ensure she is anything but lonely.

Music and Songs

A wonderfully mature and complex score – a great achievement using very difficult subject matter and yet retaining sympathy for characters who are both amoral and not necessarily likeable. Michael Ball took 'Love changes everything' (Alex) into the charts. The rich score also includes the popular 'Anything but lonely' (Rose), 'The first man you remember' (George and Jenny) and 'Seeing is believing' (Alex and Rose). At the time the score and the show were considerably undervalued.

Did You Know?

✳ Roger Moore was originally cast as Uncle George, but relinquished the part in rehearsals.

✳ A revised, more intimate, version of the show, based on an Australian production, toured Britain and paid a subsequent visit to the West End.

The Critics

The critics were, by and large, respectful – unlike their American counterparts:
'A remarkably daring piece of work . . . a rare example of theatrical intimacy succeeding in large-scale circumstances' – *The Observer*
'Lloyd Webber's best so far' – *The Daily Telegraph*
'It generates as much heated passion as a trip to the bank' – *New York Times*

Recommended Recording

Original London cast (CD) Polydor 841 1262
Like a good wine, the score of *Aspects of Love* improves with age and, in retrospect, can be considered one of Lloyd Webber's best scores. The original cast recording is a remarkable experience and an essential recording for lovers of the musical.

Babes in Arms

LYRICS ✴ Lorenz Hart
MUSIC ✴ Richard Rodgers
BOOK ✴ Rodgers and Hart

First Performance

New York, Shubert Theater, 14 April 1937 (289 performances)
There has been no London West End performance, although the show was
successfully mounted at the Regent's Park Open-Air Theatre in the 1990s

Principal Characters

**Valentine LaMar, Billie Smith, Peter Jackson, Baby Rose,
Ivor and Irving DeQuincy, Gus Fielding, Dolores Reynolds,
Sam Reynolds, Marshall Blackstone**
✴ All the characters are Babes in Arms

Original New York Cast

Ray Heatherton, Mitzi Green, Duke McHale, Wynn Murray, Harold Nicholas,
Fayard Nicholas, Rolly Pickert, Grace McDonald, Ray McDonald, Alfred Drake

Plot

We're in Seaport, Long Island, where actors live. The adults are off on tour for five
months, leaving their kids behind. Twenty-year-old Val LaMar meets an
attractive hitchhiker, Billie Smith. He wants an extended acquaintance, but the
local sheriff arrives to escort Val to a work farm. Val will have none of it, and calls
a meeting with other kids in Seaport to explore other opportunities. After lively
discussion, the kids decide to mount their own show. The sheriff gives them two
weeks to stage a revue and raise enough money to make themselves self-
sufficient.

With backer, Lee Calhoun, and a top star, Baby Rose, the kids are off and
running. But Lee doesn't want the black kids, Ivor and Irving DeQuincy, to
participate. Two weeks later the show is mounted at Seaport's Red Barn. Calhoun
causes trouble when Ivor DeQuincey performs, and closes the show.The kids are
shipped off to a work camp. Billie, ever an optimist, believes good luck will come
right out of the sky. A famous pilot, René Flambeau, is flying overhead; his plane
is running out of fuel. He makes a forced landing on LaMar's field. He is quickly
trussed up by the kids, and Val takes his place before reporters, using the
opportunity to promote the field (owned by his family) as an ideal site for an
airport. Soon major companies are bidding against each other for the land.
Flambeau is rescued by Calhoun, who makes further trouble, but the pilot takes
pity on the kids and all ends happily.

Note: A revised plot, the work of George Oppenheimer, was prepared for
postwar performances.

Music and Songs

A wonderful, happy score stuffed with songs that show the wit and melody of Rodgers and Hart at their peak. There are many fine standards, including 'Where or when?' (Val and Billie), 'I wish I were in love again' (Gus and Dolores), 'My funny Valentine' (Billie), 'Johnny One Note' (Billie), 'Way out West' (Billie and ensemble) and 'The lady is a tramp' (Billie).

Did You Know?

✶ Although most of the score was ditched by MGM for the Mickey Rooney and Judy Garland film, many of the songs popped up in other films, including *Pal Joey* and *Words and Music*.

✶ The Valentine of the song 'My funny Valentine' refers to the show's hero, and has nothing to do with 14 February!

✶ The list of reasons given as to why 'The lady is a tramp' prove her to be quite the reverse – an aficionado of culture, in fact!

The Critics

The critics loved the show and the cast:
'As nice a group of youngsters as ever dove into an ice cream freezer at a birthday party' – *New York Times*
'A field day for a Hollywood talent scout' – *Variety*

Recommended Recording

Original 1999 New York cast (CD) DRG 94769
A beautifully reconstructed version that was performed in concert as part of the annual New York Encore series. This is the only recording that can boast of almost the complete original score – a score packed with hits and treated so well on this disc. It has more the feel of young hopefuls than the more maturely cast studio cast (**CD – New World NW 386-2**). Unfortunately, the song 'All dark people' is omitted from both recordings – presumably in the interests of political correctness.

Film

MGM, 1939. Starring Judy Garland, Mickey Rooney and Charles Winniger. Directed by Busby Berkeley. Naturally the plot was altered.

Babes in Toyland

LYRICS ✳ Glen MacDonough
MUSIC ✳ Victor Herbert
BOOK ✳ Glen MacDonough

First Performance

New York, Majestic Theater, 13 October 1903 (192 performances)

Principal Characters

Wicked Uncle Barnaby
Alan ✳ His nephew
Jane ✳ His niece
Contrary Mary
Tom Tom
Little Bo Peep

Original New York Cast

George W. Denham, William Norris, Mabel Barrison,
Amy Ricard, Bessie Wynn, Nella Webb

Plot

The plot is happily old fashioned. It offers a villainous Uncle Barnaby, a scheming miser who is planning to do away with his niece (Jane) and nephew (Alan) so that he can claim their inheritance. Through his activities the youngsters are shipwrecked on an island, where they meet their favourite Mother Goose and fairy-tale characters. Uncle Barnaby forecloses on Mother Hubbard's house and is thrown into a pond. He then plans for his niece and nephew to be abandoned in the Forest of No Return. Luckily they're rescued by gypsies. They now land in Toyland which is ruled by Toymaker, a tyrant who is killed by his own toys when one of his spells brings them alive. Alan is about to be unjustly hanged for the deed but the truth emerges just in time. Undaunted, Barnaby now tries to poison both of them but mistakenly takes the poison himself. The children are now rich and free and all is well as the curtain falls on the traditionally happy ending.

Music and Songs

Charming, old-fashioned songs, bridging the gap between operetta and early musical comedy. 'I can't do the sum' (chorus) and 'Go to sleep, slumber deep' (Alan) are typical. 'The march of the toys' is still thrilling. 'I can't do the sum' has an ingenious accompaniment of chalk on slates.

Did You Know?

✱ Dublin-born Victor Herbert was not enamoured of Britain. He was trained in Germany and lived in America all his professional life. This helps to explain why his shows were, apart from the very earliest, never mounted in London's West End.

✱ Although by different authors, the show was planned as an attempt to emulate the success of *The Wizard of Oz*, a stage version mounted in 1901 that long preceded the film and had different music.

✱ *Babes in Toyland* was the first Herbert show planned for an extended rather than a limited run.

✱ The composer wrote a sequel, *Wonderland*, which did not achieve the same success.

The Critics

'A perfect dream of delight to the children and will recall the happy days of childhood to those who are facing the realities of life' – *New York Dramatic Mirror*
'Music a hundred times better than is customary in shows of this sort' – *The New York Sun*

Recommended Recording

Historical reconstruction (CD) AEI 6591-10044
Taken mainly from a radio broadcast this CD gives a good overview of the score and story line. There are some bonus tracks that include Victor Herbert conducting his orchestra and Bessie Wynn singing 'Toyland' which she introduced in the original production.

Films

MGM, 1934. Starring Laurel and Hardy, and Charlotte Henry. Directed by Gus Meins and Charles Rogers.
Walt Disney, 1961. Starring Ray Bolger, Ed Wynn and Tommy Sands. Directed by Jack Donohue.

Barnum

LYRICS ✶ Michael Stewart
MUSIC ✶ Cy Coleman
BOOK ✶ Mark Bramble

First Performance

New York, St James' Theater, 30 April 1980 (854 performances)
London, London Palladium, 11 June 1981 (655 performances)

Principal Characters

P.T. Barnum ✶ A great showman
Charity (Chairy) Barnum ✶ His wife
Jenny Lind ✶ An international soprano
Tom Thumb ✶ An extremely small gentleman
Joice Heth ✶ Claimed to be George Washington's nurse

Original New York Cast

Jim Dale, Glenn Close, Marianne Tatum,
Leonard John Crofoot, Terri White

Original London Cast

Michael Crawford, Deborah Grant, Sarah Payne,
Christopher Beck, Jennie McGustie

Plot

P.T. Barnum believes there's a sucker born every minute – and this biographical show proves him right. He buys fairground attraction, Joice Heth, claimed to be the oldest woman alive, dubs her George Washington's nurse and is off in the world of showbusiness. With the money he makes he builds a museum of curiosities. Barnum acquires the midget, Tom Thumb, and tours him round the world. Then there's the Swedish nightingale, Jenny Lind, who captivates all who encounter her. Barnum presents her first American concert and falls in love with her. Eventually he realizes she's not for him and returns to his faithful wife, Chairy. At his wife's insistence, Barnum tries to become an ordinary businessman and attempts, unsuccessfully, to enter politics. Chairy becomes seriously ill and, after her death, Barnum feels the old showbusiness excitement coursing through his veins once more. He meets James Bailey and together they found the greatest show on earth – Barnum and Bailey's Circus.

Music and Songs

Cy Coleman writes the greatest Broadway marches and 'Come follow the band' is one of his most stirring. The score has the zest and excitement of the circus, plus some excellent patter songs mainly for Barnum ('Out there', 'The Prince of Humbug' and 'There is a sucker born ev'ry minute'), and an affecting ballad, 'The colors of my life' (Barnum).

Did You Know?

✴ In order to portray the most quintessentially American of conmen and showmen, an Englishman, Jim Dale, was chosen to lead the Broadway original cast, perhaps because of the impact he'd made in a British import, a version of Molière's *Scapin*. He scored a huge success – as did Michael Crawford in London – in two separate seasons.

✴ It is estimated that over two and a half million people attended the London production.

✴ Glenn Close was discovered for a part in a Hollywood movie while playing her role of Charity Barnum on Broadway.

The Critics

'Barnum's a beaut' – *News of the World*
'A triumph of energy over art, Barnum will be around for a long time' – *New Standard*
'An evening of raucously enjoyable technicolor popular theatre' – *The Guardian*
'Beat the drum – it's brilliant' – *Daily Mail*

Recommended Recording

Original Broadway cast (CD) Columbia CK 36576
Both Jim Dale (Broadway) and Michael Crawford (London) give outstanding performances and both are captured superbly on disc. However, the original Broadway cast has the edge and, of course, the added attraction of Glenn Close before becoming a film star. There is a feel of the circus on this CD.

Film

The London production starring Michael Crawford was recorded and issued on video.

The Beautiful Game

LYRICS ✳ Ben Elton
MUSIC ✳ Andrew Lloyd Webber
BOOK ✳ Ben Elton

First Performance

London, Cambridge Theatre, 26 September 2000 (still running)

Principal Characters

John ✳ A football-crazy youth
Mary ✳ John's girlfriend
Thomas ✳ A member of the IRA
Father O'Donnell ✳ The football coach
Del ✳ A Protestant football player
Christine ✳ His Catholic girlfriend

Original London Cast

David Shannon, Josie Walker, Michael Shaeffer, Frank Grimes, Ben Goddard, Hannah Waddingham

Plot

It is Belfast, 1969 and the Troubles are starting. There is a local football team run by the Catholic priest, Father O'Donnell. One of its members is Del, the only Protestant on the team, and he is warned off playing by Thomas. John, another of the team, has taken a shine to Mary and after some innocent banter it is obvious she is falling in love with him. Del is going out with Christine, Mary's friend who is a Catholic. As the conflict worsens their relationship grows stronger, but in the end it drives them away to find a new home in the United States.

The team is doing well and after their victory in the cup they celebrate with a grand party. At the party, Ginger, the overweight goalie, finds that Bernadette has taken a fancy to him – it is first love. On the way home early next morning, he is set upon by a gang of Protestants and is left for dead. He dies soon after at the age of eighteen. But life goes on and John and Mary wed. On their wedding night there is a telephone call from Thomas – he needs help in escaping from the police. John goes to him and drives him away.

There is a chance that John will be picked for an English professional football club but the police get to him first; he has been named as a collaborator and is sent to prison. There his hatred grows and he becomes an IRA member; he also becomes a father, but his relationship with Mary has taken a turn for the worse. Thomas kneecaps another lad, saying it was he who told the police about John, but John knows differently. It was Thomas who exchanged John's name for his freedom, and on his release John kills Thomas. As John sees Mary for the last time he gives her a package for their son – it is his prized football. His son will take on his father's ambition to be a football player in a professional side.

Music and Songs

Ben Elton has come up with a mighty piece of theatre built on a subject that is full of prejudices. Amazingly, this is his first musical and the first lyrics he has written. Andrew Lloyd Webber has responded to this intelligent, adult base with a fine score, perhaps one of his best. The title number (company) sets the show's overall theme, while 'God's own country' (Mary and a protestant girl) shows brilliantly both sides of the political coin. The show's anthem is 'If this is what we're fighting for' (Mary). There is also the charming honeymoon night song 'The first time' (Mary and John) and the powerful 'Our kind of love' (Christine).

Did You Know?

✶ Ben Elton was first approached by Andrew Lloyd Webber to help on an update of *Starlight Express* – instead he offered to come up with a new show after Lloyd Webber mentioned a true story about a Belfast football team.

✶ Meryl Tankard, the choreographer, watched football matches to get the movements she wanted, and the outcome is one of the most inventive dance sequences on the London stage.

The Critics

'Webber not only extends his musical range but comes up with two or three lively numbers, each packed with his trademark yearning' – *The Times*
'Elton's book boasts generous lashings of a gritty populist wit' – *Variety*
'Lloyd Webber trademark soaring melodies' – *Variety*

Recommended Recording

Original London cast (CD) Telstar TCD 3160
A new Andrew Lloyd Webber recording is always something to look forward to and this is no exception. The cast is extraordinary, with Josie Walker and David Shannon as Mary and John, intimate and loving. Hannah Waddingham as Christine is also a standout. It would be hard to think of a better recording of this wonderful new entry into the world of musicals.

The Beauty and the Beast

LYRICS ✶ Howard Ashman and Tim Rice
MUSIC ✶ Alan Menken
BOOK ✶ Linda Woolverton

First Performance

New York, Palace Theatre, 18 April 1994 (still running)
London, Dominion Theatre, 13 May 1997 (1064)

Principal Characters

Belle ✶ Maurice's beautiful daughter
Maurice ✶ An inventor
Beast ✶ The prince in his punishment outer form
Gaston ✶ The local handsome hunter
Lumiere ✶ A candle holder
Mrs Potts ✶ A tea-pot
Chip ✶ Her chipped-cup son
Cogsworth ✶ A clock
Lefou ✶ Gaston's sidekick

Original New York Cast

Susan Egan, Tom Bosley, Terrence Mann, Burke Moses, Gary Beach, Beth Fowler, Brian Press, Heath Lamberts, Kenny Raskin

Original London Cast

Julie-Alanah Brighton, Barry James, Alasdair Harvey, Burke Moses, Derek Griffiths, Mary Millar, Ben Butterfield, Norman Rossington, Richard Gauntlett

Plot

A beggar lady offers a single rose to a handsome prince who turns her away. His lack of compassion shows he has no love in his heart and, when the beggar lady is transformed, she puts a curse on him and turns him into a beast. Some twenty years on he has made himself his own prisoner, surrounded by his faithful servants who have been changed into household objects. The rose has little time left before it dies and that is all the time he has to rid himself of the curse. The only way he can do this is to fall in love and have someone fall in love with him.

Belle is an oddity in her little village for she loves books and shows no interest in the local heartthrob, Gaston. Maurice, her father, is an inventor and he has just designed an automatic log cutter that he plans to show at the local fair. He sets forth with it but gets lost in the dark and finds himself at the castle where Cogsworth, Lumiere and Mrs Potts make him welcome, but the Beast makes him a prisoner. Maurice's horse returns home alone, and takes Belle back with him to the castle where she pleads with the Beast to let her take her father's place. He agrees and, instead of the tower cell, she is given a room and allowed to go anywhere she likes – except the west wing.

The Beast is trying hard to be a gentleman but his temper still gets the better of him, especially when he discovers Belle in the west wing. She escapes but is set upon by wolves, which the Beast fights off. He is hurt in the fight and Belle nurses him. He is now in love with her and she is beginning to see through his ugliness. But she misses her father and, through the Beast's magic mirror, she sees that he has lost his way and she goes to his rescue. When she gets him back home she discovers that Gaston wants her father committed to an asylum in an attempt to get Belle's hand. In the magic mirror he sees the Beast, and he and the villagers attack the castle where they are beaten off, except for Gaston who is after the Beast. The Beast puts up little fight believing he has lost Belle – but when he sees her he fights back and Gaston falls to his death. The Beast is dying and Belle now knows she loves him. Amid fireworks the Beast takes back the form of the Prince and recovers fully, his servants become human again, and all live happily ever after

Music and Songs

Tim Rice came to Broadway to help put the score on stage and so there are many differences between the film soundtrack and the Broadway show. Remaining from the film are all the favourites such as the title song (Mrs Potts), 'Be our guest' (Lumiere, Mrs Potts and Cogsworth) and the amusing 'Gaston' (Gaston, Lefou and the customers of the tavern). Among the delightful new songs are 'If I can't love her' (Beast) and 'Home' (Belle).

Did You Know?

✳ The lyricist, Howard Ashman, died in 1991 at the age of 41 before the show reached the stage.

✳ While not receiving any major awards it did win the Tony for the best costume designs.

✳ This was the first Disney venture into the theatre and its success has opened a whole new world for the Disney Empire.

The Critics

'Enough of the ten million pounds budget has been spent on spectacular effects to ensure that if your brain-cells begin to ooze away or your eardrums to gum up, your eyes will remain ravished' – *The Times*

Recommended Recording

Original Broadway cast (CD) Walt Disney Productions 60861-7
A charm score that has become loved through the original film but augmented with some excellent new numbers by Time Rice and the film's composer Alan Menken. There are many recordings including the London cast version but Susan Egan and Terrance Mann are hard acts to follow.

Bells are Ringing

LYRICS ✳ Betty Comden and Adolph Green
MUSIC ✳ Jule Styne
BOOK ✳ Betty Comden and Adolph Green

First Performance

New York, Shubert Theater, 29 November 1956 (924 performances)
London, Coliseum, 14 November 1957 (292 performances)

Principal Characters

Ella Peterson ✳ A telephonist
Jeff Moss ✳ A playwright
Sue Summers ✳ Proprietress of Susanswerphone
Sandor ✳ Her musical friend
Inspector Barnes
Blake Barton ✳ A subscriber to Susanswerphone
Larry Hastings ✳ Another subscriber
Carl ✳ A dancer

Original New York Cast

Judy Holliday, Sydney Chaplin, Jean Stapleton, Eddie Lawrence,
Dort Clark, Frank Aletter, George S. Irving, Peter Gennaro

Original London Cast

Janet Blair, George Gaynes, Jean St. Clair, Eddie Molloy,
Donald Stewart, Franklin Fox, Robert Henderson, Harry Naughton

Plot

Ella Peterson is a switchboard operator at Susanswerphone, a telephone
answering service. She falls in love over the phone with subscriber Jeff Moss, a
playwright. They have never met and Jeff thinks she's just 'Mom', a lady of
mature years. When Ella decides to help his career along and encourage him over
a writer's block, she adopts the name Melisande Scott and goes to his flat. The
mutual attraction is instant, and he takes her out on the town to a smart party,
then to Central Park and to some nightclubs, in one of which, thanks to Ella's
efforts, a dentist subscriber has succeeded in having some of his own songs
performed.

Meanwhile, there's trouble back at Susanswerphone. Proprietress Sue's friend,
Sandor, asks if he can run a record company from there. Unbeknown to Sue, this
is a cover for a gambling operation. When customers ring to order records (in fact
to place bets) Ella helpfully interferes and causes chaos. Jeff, alone in a nightclub,
meets up with other subscribers, all of whom realize that they owe their lucky
breaks to Susanswerphone. Jeff visits their offices, unmasks 'Mom' as Melisande
and all ends happily.

Music and Songs

A classic, mature Jule Styne score that includes some of Broadway's best point numbers: 'It's a perfect relationship' (Ella and Jeff) and 'Is it a crime?' (Ella) as well as the wonderful 11 o'clock number for the star, 'I'm going back' (Ella), and major hit songs 'The party's over' (Ella), 'Long before I knew you' (Ella) and 'Just in time' (Jeff and Ella).

Did You Know?

✶ The 1928 Broadway show *The Five O'Clock Girl* also featured a telephone operator who fell in love with a young man, sight unseen.

✶ The premise of the plot is now virtually outdated. The answering machine has taken over from the answering service for most potential customers.

✶ The show was Judy Holliday's first Broadway musical starring role and her only musical hit – *Hot Spot* was a failure some years later.

The Critics

The critics enjoyed Miss Holliday's performance:
'She sings, dances, clowns – and also carries on her shoulders one of the most antiquated plots of the season' – Brooks Atkinson

Recommended Recording

Original Broadway cast (CD) Columbia CK 2006
There is little choice other than the film version with a reduced and changed score. Even so, it would be hard to imagine a better recording for this captures the vibrancy of the original as well as the magical performance of the unique Judy Holliday. Her early death robbed the theatre of one of its greatest individualistic performers.

Film

MGM, 1960. Starring Judy Holliday and Dean Martin. Directed by Vincente Minnelli.

Bitter Sweet

LYRICS ✷ Noël Coward
MUSIC ✷ Noël Coward
BOOK ✷ Noël Coward

First Performance

London, Her Majesty's Theatre, 12 July 1929 (697 performances)
New York, Ziegfeld Theater, 5 November 1929 (157 performances)

Principal Characters

Sarah Millick/Sari ✷ Our heroine
Carl Linden ✷ Her singing tutor
Manon ✷ A singer
Vincent Howard ✷ A pianist
Hugh Devon ✷ Sarah's fiancé
Marquis of Shayne

Original London Cast

Peggy Wood, George Metaxa, Ivy St. Helier,
Robert Newton, Norah Howard, Alan Napier

Original New York Cast

Evelyn Laye, Gerald Nodin, Mireille,
Tracey Holmes, Sylvia Leslie, John Evelyn

Plot

It's 1929. The Marchioness of Shayne is giving a dance party at her home in Grosvenor Square. Dolly and her friend, Henry, quarrel and are observed by the Marchioness who asks Dolly, who is attracted to the band's pianist, Vincent, what she intends to do about both men. Her indecision prompts her hostess to tell her own story. In 1875 Sarah Millick is just sixteen, and engaged to Hugh Devon. Shortly before her wedding, she elopes with her singing teacher, Carl Linden, moving with him to Vienna.

Five years on, Sarah, now known as Sari, is engaged as a dancer/hostess in Schlick's Café. Carl is the conductor of the orchestra and his friend Manon is the featured singer. Sari refuses to have supper (and probably more) with an influential customer, much to Herr Schlick's annoyance. After an entertainment in which Manon sings 'If love were all', Captain August Lutte claims her as his dance partner, but his increasingly amorous advances annoy Carl, who is challenged to a duel. Carl is fatally wounded, dying in Sari's arms.

Fifteen years pass. Lord Shayne is giving a party to welcome the famous singer, Madam Sari Linden. Delightedly, the guests recognize their old friend, Sarah. With exquisite tact she bridges an embarrassing meeting with her former fiancé and his wife. Lord Shayne asks her, not for the first time, to marry him. This time she will think it over. She sings a couple of songs, the lights dim and we're back in 1929. Dolly is moved to declare her love for Vincent, who moves over to the piano and plays 'I'll see you again' as a foxtrot. Sarah laughs and, in fond farewell to Carl and the vanished era, sings the last lines of the song: 'Though my world has gone awry, I shall love you till I die – Goodbye!'

Music and Songs

While the sumptuous, hugely romantic score contains a fair amount of typically Coward wit in 'Green carnation' (Four lords) and 'Ladies of the town' (chorus), it also includes many of the composer/lyricist's most heartfelt romantic creations, including 'I'll see you again' (Carl and Sarah), 'If love were all' (Manon), 'The call of life' (Sarah) and 'Zigeuner' (Sari).

Did You Know?

✶ Noël Coward's most successful romantic operetta was originally intended for Gertrude Lawrence, but her vocal limitations forced the author to look elsewhere. Evelyn Laye, because of her antagonism towards Charles Cochran because she blamed him for the loss of her husband to Jessie Matthews, refused the part, which went to the American actress Peggy Wood. (Miss Laye later made up with Cochran, headed the New York company, and then replaced Miss Wood for two months in London.)

✶ Coward, who got the idea for the Viennese setting while listening to a recording of *Die Fledermaus*, was motivated to write *Bitter Sweet* because he felt the time was ripe for a romantic renaissance in the theatre.

The Critics

'The stupendous opus which is this operetta – a thundering job' – *The Sunday Times*

Recommended Recording

London Revival cast (CD) TER 21160
This complete recording of the show includes material dropped from the revival. It captures the romance of the story and the lushness of the music. It is also beautifully sung.

Films

British and Dominion, 1933. Starring Anna Neagle and Ferdinand Graavey with Ivy St Helier reproducing her role as Manon. Directed by Herbert Wilcox.
MGM, 1941. Starring Jeanette MacDonald and Nelson Eddy. Directed by W.S. Van Dyke.

Bless the Bride

LYRICS ✳ A.P. Herbert
MUSIC ✳ Vivian Ellis
BOOK ✳ A.P. Herbert

First Performance

London, Adelphi Theatre, 26 April 1947 (886 performances)

Principal Characters

Lucy Veracity Willow ✳ An English rose
Pierre Fontaine ✳ A dashing French actor
Thomas Trout ✳ An Englishman
Suzanne Vallois ✳ Pierre's friend in France

Original London Cast

Lizbeth Webb, Georges Guétary, Brian Reece, Betty Paul

Plot

It's July 1870. The Willow family are playing croquet on their lawn. Lucy is to marry Thomas Trout the following day. But she believes him to be a liar, and as her middle name is Veracity, this is a marriage that cannot take place. Thomas introduces the family to his French friends, Pierre and Suzanne. Pierre and Lucy are immediately attracted to each other. They kiss. The next day Pierre turns up at the wedding disguised as the doctor. Pierre and Lucy decide to elope to France before the ceremony. When her family discover what has happened, they follow the couple to France with the aim of bringing Lucy to Thomas in England.

Meanwhile, Lucy and Pierre are on the beach at Eauville under the disapproving eye of Suzanne, who wants Pierre for herself. Lucy's family turn up in heavy disguise. Eventually they persuade Lucy to return with them after the (Franco-Prussian) war has begun and Pierre has gone off to fight.

A year later at Lucy's twenty-first birthday party, Thomas Trout arrives with an engagement ring and some flowers – but Lucy can't forget Pierre, even though she believes he has been killed in battle. Suzanne now turns up with a special present. It's Pierre; rumours of his death had been much exaggerated. Thomas joins the happy couple together and gives Pierre the engagement ring for him to use. All ends happily with a celebratory polka.

Music and Songs

The finest of the Ellis and Herbert collaborations produced catchy animated songs, as well as passionate love songs and lively dances that recall the music of Edward German and Roger Quilter. Highlights include 'Ma belle Marguerite' (Pierre), 'This is my lovely day' (Pierre and Lucy), 'I was never kissed before' (Lucy) and the comedy number 'Ducky' (Nanny).

Did You Know?

∗ The musical, Cochran's last but one, was the famous producer's longest-running production.

∗ The run was curtailed while still successful, to make way for another show by Vivian Ellis.

∗ Like *Bitter Sweet*, the plot involves a young girl who elopes to the Continent just before marriage – but in this case, all ends happily.

∗ A recent revival in a small London Fringe Theatre changed the role of Suzanne to a male.

The Critics

'*Bless the Bride* proves that Englishmen can still write songs as well as any people in the world' – *The Sunday Times*

Recommended Recording

Original cast (CD) AEI-CD 015
Astonishingly, this radio broadcast of the show survived almost complete and is only now being made available. It features the original cast and, of the important songs, only 'Silent heart' and 'The family' are missing. As few songs were recorded at the time, this is an important and worthwhile document of one of the greatest postwar musical successes of the London stage. The cast are exemplary. The sentiments expressed on the broadcast will do little for Anglo-French relations, however.

Blitz!

LYRICS ✳ Lionel Bart
MUSIC ✳ Lionel Bart
BOOK ✳ Lionel Bart

First Performance

London, Adelphi Theatre, 8 May 1962 (568 performances)

Principal Characters

Mrs Blitztein, Carol Blitztein, Harry Blitztein, Siddy Blitztein, Rachel Blitztein,
Cissy Blitztein, Alfred Locke, Georgie Locke, Frances Locke, Ernie Near
✳ All are inhabitants of the East End

Original London Cast

Amelia Bayntun, Grazina Frame, Tom Kempinski, Kaplan Kaye, Rose Hill,
Julie Cohen, Bob Grant, Graham James, Deborah Cranston, Edward Caddick,
– and the voice of Vera Lynn

Plot

In Petticoat Lane, in the East End of London, Mrs Blitztein has a pickled herring
stall next to Alfred Locke's fruit stall. Mrs B hates Alfred almost as much as she
loathes Hitler. Their respective children, Carol and Georgie, act as go-betweens
and almost inevitably fall in love. As if that isn't enough, Mrs Blitztein's eldest
son, Harry, returns on leave with a gentile girlfriend. His mother and former
girlfriend, Elsie, gang up to put a stop to such nonsense – but there is worse to
come. Carol is blinded in an air raid and Harry deserts from the army.

Georgie returns, embittered, from the war front. Mrs B accepts the inevitable
and brings Carol and Georgie together. There's a Jewish wedding for the happy
pair to which Georgie's father, Alfred, and his sidekick, Ernie, bring their own
food – fish and chips. The party guests leave the café but Mrs Blitztein is still there
when an unexploded German bomb finally detonates. Alfred returns and pulls her
from the wreckage. But there's no reason to end their (mutually enjoyable) feud.
'You took long enough to get here didn't you?' she cries. Things are back to
normal.

Music and Songs

Lionel Bart has written a tuneful score with the authentic sound of the wartime
forties. There is also more than a splash of music hall vitality, and of traditional
Jewish and folk melodies. Shirley Bassey enjoyed success with 'Far away' (Carol).
Other songs include 'The day after tomorrow' (heard on the radio, sung by Vera
Lynn), 'Mums and dads' (the kids) and 'Who's this geezer Hitler?' (Mrs Blitztein
and company).

Did You Know?

✳ Grazina Frame dubbed the singing voice for Carole Gray, Cliff Richard's co-star in *The Young Ones*, the successful musical flm.

✳ Cast member Tom Kempinski subsequently became a distinguished playwright (*Duet for One*).

✳ The National Youth Theatre successfully revived the show in the early 1990s.

✳ Noel Coward is reported to have said the show was twice as long and twice as noisy as the real thing.

✳ There were plans to take the show to the United States but they were dropped for fear that the subject matter would mean little to audiences.

The Critics

The critics described the show as 'immense', 'stunning' and 'riveting'. Sean Kenny's sets were 'amazing' and 'spectacular' – and the production matched them.
'Allegedly the most expensive British musical to date. As in *Oliver!* Mr Bart has included a chorus of children, and they collected the loudest cheers of the first-night audience. The show as a whole depends much more on its crowd scenes than on separate performances. As a piece of ensemble it has plenty of spirit and pace but not much finesse' – *The Times*
'A stage set of quite staggering magnificence ... lifelike replicas of the bombing' – *The Times*

Recommended Recording

Original London cast (CD) EMI CDP 7 97470 2
Originally issued on LP with an additional EP with four extra numbers included.
These four tracks have been restored to their original positions in the show.
While there is no alternative it would be hard to contemplate a better recording of this atmospheric score.

Blood Brothers

LYRICS ✶ Willy Russell
MUSIC ✶ Willy Russell
BOOK ✶ Willy Russell

First Performance

Originated at Liverpool Playhouse, 8 January 1983
London, Lyric Theatre, 11 April 1983
Remounted at Albery Theatre, 28 July 1988
Phoenix Theatre, 21 November 1991 (still playing)
New York, Music Box Theater, 25 April 1993 (839 performances)

Principal Characters

Narrator
Mrs Johnstone ✶ Mother of the twins
Mrs Lyons and Mr Lyons ✶ The 'adoptive' parents
Mickey ✶ Mrs Johnstone's twin son
Eddie ✶ Mickey's twin brother
Sammy ✶ The twins' elder brother
Linda ✶ Loved by both Mickey and Eddie

Original London Cast

Andrew Schofield, Barbara Dickson, Wendy Murray, Alan Leith, George Costigan,
Andrew C. Wadsworth, Peter Christian, Amanda York/Kate Fitzgerald

Original New York Cast

Warwick Evans, Stephanie Lawrence, Barbara Walsh, Ivar Brogger, Con O'Neill,
Mark Michael Hutchinson, James Clow, Kate Fitzgerald

Plot

A modern version of *The Corsican Brothers* story also used in *Jean de Florette*, *Manon des Sources* and Verdi's opera *Il Trovatore*.

Mrs Johnstone, an impoverished Liverpool housewife, deserted by her husband, is expecting twins. Although warned against the idea by the show's narrator, she separates them and one, Eddie, is brought up as a rich kid by Mr and Mrs Lyons, for whom Mrs Johnstone works. Mrs Lyons fakes a pregnancy to pass Eddie off as her own child. The other, Mickey, remains with his natural mother, and is brought up in poverty. As they grow up, the twins become friends, but no one tells them of their close family relationship. Indeed, their mothers forbid them to play together, as Mrs Lyons heads for a mental breakdown under fear of the secret being discovered. Nevertheless, the twins go through the ceremony of becoming Blood Brothers.

Growing up, they both fall for the same girl, Linda. Mickey wins out and marries Linda. She falls pregnant. Then Mickey loses his job and, desperate to earn some money for Christmas, acts as a lookout in an armed robbery for his elder brother Sammy. There's a killing and Mickey is sent down for seven years. Back on the outside, Mickey sees Linda and Eddie together and jumps to the wrong conclusion, urged on by the unbalanced Mrs Lyons. Mickey goes after Eddie with a gun which accidentally goes off, killing Eddie, after his mother has revealed that the two are brothers. The police then gun down Mickey and Mrs Johnstone is left to mourn her two children. The day that the boys found out they were brothers was also the day they died.

Music and Songs

A good folk-flavoured score with at least two outstanding songs – the haunting 'Tell me it's not true' (Mrs Johnstone), and 'I'm not saying a word' (Eddie), plus 'Marilyn Monroe' (Mrs Johnstone) and 'Living on the never never' (Mrs Johnstone).

Did You Know?

✱ *Blood Brothers* is a show that refused to die. After a respectable first run in London, the producer Bill Kenwright remounted the musical a few years later, and this version has already run for more than ten years – over 3000 performances.

✱ After the mixed notices in New York the same producer insisted on keeping the show running, against the advice of American colleagues who are used to closing a show swiftly when notices are bad. He was proved right and the show ran for years.

✱ Willy Russell is one of the very rare book-lyricist-composers – perhaps the first since Sandy Wilson and Noël Coward. To date *Blood Brothers* is his only completely original musical.

The Critics

'A powerful folk-influenced score' – *The Herald*
'There are so many good things to shout and sing about in this brave and angry new musical that Willy Russell, who has spread his talents thickly over book, songs and lyrics, must not be offended when I say that the music is not, perhaps, what first springs to the lips' – *Daily Mail*

Recommended Recording

Original London cast (CD) Legacy LLMCD 3007
The original Mrs Johnstone, Barbara Dickson, has the edge on all the talented ladies who have followed her in this role. This is an emotional performance that makes the score shine. The lady who played the role longer than any other was the late Stephanie Lawrence who also recorded the show and, perhaps, the most famous is Petula Clark who played the part in New York. Their recordings are fine as well.

Bloomer Girl

LYRICS ✶ E.Y. Harburg
MUSIC ✶ Harold Arlen
BOOK ✶ Sig Herzig and Fred Saidy,
based on an unproduced play by Lilith and Dan James

First Performance

New York, Shubert Theater, 5 October 1944 (654 performances)

Principal Characters

Evelina Applegate ✶ The youngest daughter of . . .
Horatio Applegate ✶ The maker of hoop skirts
Jeff Calhoun ✶ A young man from a good Southern family
Pompey ✶ A slave
Dolly ✶ Also known as Amelia Bloomer, an early fighter for women's rights
Serena Applegate ✶ Evelina's mother
Julia and Daisy ✶ Young girls of Cicero Falls

Original New York Cast

Celeste Holm, Matt Briggs, David Brooks, Dooley Wilson, Margaret Douglass,
Mabel Taliaferro, Toni Hart, Joan McCracken

Plot

The setting is the small Southern town of Cicero Falls at the time of the American Civil War. Evelina is the only unmarried daughter of the principal manufacturer of hoop skirts for crinolines. Her father, Horatio, has picked out a nice suitor from a good Southern family, Jeff Calhoun. In spite of that, Evelina falls for him. But there is a problem: Jeff owns slaves. Evelina, influenced by her aunt Dolly, is an abolitionist and, for good measure, a believer in women's and civil rights. Jeff naturally soon has a change of heart and arranges to help his own slave, Pompey, escape to freedom in the North, through a secret underground railway. Evelina, meanwhile, is to model a new super skirt for her father. But at the garden party she lifts her skirt to show that she is clad in bloomers, in support of her aunt and her causes. Jeff's brother, an unreconstructed slave owner, causes trouble and Evelina, Dolly and the slaves are all thrown into gaol.

On release they mount a performance of *Uncle Tom's Cabin*. News then comes of the firing on Fort Sumpter. The American Civil War has begun. Evelina and Jeff's romance must wait. He goes to enlist in the Confederate Army. Meanwhile, her brothers-in-law have enlisted in the Zouave regiment of the Union Army and they wear trousers that look like bloomers! The Applegate factory, under the joint direction of Horatio Applegate and Dolly Bloomer, is turned over to the manufacture of bloomers. Jeff has a change of allegiance after hearing Lincoln speak and returns to Evelina as the curtain falls.

Music and Songs

This is perhaps Arlen's richest and most varied score. It ranges from blues and folk melody to passionate love songs and does not shirk, helped by Harburg's lyrics, from exploring the sombre side of life. 'Right as the rain' (Evelina and Jeff), 'The eagle and me' (Pompey) and 'Tomorra, tomorra' (Daisy) indicate the depth and range of the score.

Did You Know?

✶ This was Celeste Holm's first show after her success as Ado Annie in *Oklahoma!*

✶ The choreography for the show was by Agnes de Mille who created the ballets for *Oklahoma!* the previous year.

✶ *Bloomer Girl* was the first show to be produced for television and recreated the Agnes de Mille ballets. It starred Barbara Cook.

The Critics

'Not to scurry about for exotic phrases, *Bloomer Girl* is an unusually good musical' – Louis Kronenberger
'A show of magical delight . . . it blends songs, dancing, drama and spectacle in an enchanting and prodigal entertainment' – *New York Herald Tribune*
'The town's newest musical show is what the town has been awaiting for some time' – *The Times*

Recommended Recording

Original Broadway cast (CD) Decca Broadway 440 013 561-2
Originally issued as a 78 rpm album it became one of the first LPs. And it can still be heard here in all its mono glory. The charming opening of 'When the boys come home' sung by the five daughters sets the scene and it continues to be a joy right up to the closing reprise of the same song. The latest reissue includes three bonus tracks, including Bing Crosby singing 'Evelina' and 'The eagle and me'.

The Boy Friend

LYRICS ✶ Sandy Wilson
MUSIC ✶ Sandy Wilson
BOOK ✶ Sandy Wilson

First Performance

London, Wyndham's Theatre, 14 January 1954 (2084 performances)
New York, Royale Theatre, 30 September 1954 (485 performances)

Principal Characters

Polly Browne ✶ Daughter of . . .
Percival Browne ✶ The famous millionaire
Tony ✶ The Brockhurst heir in disguise
Madame Dubonnet ✶ Proprietress of a finishing school in Nice
Bobby Van Husen ✶ A young American
Lord and Lady Brockhurst
Hortense ✶ A vivacious maid
Nancy, Maisie and Dulcie ✶ Perfect young ladies

Original London Cast

Anne Rogers, Hugh Paddick, Anthony Hayes, Joan Sterndale-Bennett,
Larry Drew, John Rutland, Beryl Cooke, Violetta, Juliet Hunt,
Denise Hirst, Maria Charles

Original New York Cast

Julie Andrews, Eric Berry, John Hewer, Ruth Altman,
Bob Scheerer, Geoffrey Hibbert, Moyna MacGill, Paulette Girard,
Millicent Martin, Ann Wakefield, Dilys Lay (later Laye)

Plot

The show is set on the French Riviera in the 1920s in the Villa Caprice (Madame Dubonnet's finishing school), where the perfect young ladies are contemplating with excitement the upcoming carnival ball. All have partners, except Polly Browne. Enter Tony, a delivery boy – or so it seems. They strike up an instant rapport; he suggests that she go as Pierrette and he'll be her partner. Lord and Lady Brockhurst arrive and catch sight of their son, Tony. They cry 'Stop that man' and Polly, overhearing, takes him for a thief or conman, only after her money. She won't be going to the ball after all . . .

Polly's father arrives, unexpectedly, at the villa and recognizes Madame Dubonnet as his old flame, Kiki. Polly is persuaded to go to the ball, where her friends have all vowed to give their beaux an answer to their proposal of marriage at midnight. Tony turns up at the ball, dressed as Pierrot, and kisses Polly. His parents recognize him and reveal his identity as the Honourable Tony Brockhurst, and Percival Browne reveals himself as Polly's father, and a millionaire to boot.

Percival will now marry Madame Dubonnet, all the young ladies accept their marriage proposals and, best of all, Polly and Tony are united. After all, it's carnival time!

Music and Songs

A wonderfully varied score – perhaps the best evening of pastiche in the history of musical comedy – recalling popular show songs from the 1920s by Kern, Gershwin, Rodgers and Hart and Cole Porter. It includes 'I could be happy with you' (Polly and Tony), 'A room in Bloomsbury' (Polly and Tony), 'Fancy forgetting' (Madame Dubonnet) and 'It's never too late to fall in love' (Dulcie and Lord Brockhurst).

Did You Know?

✶ Sandy Wilson's affectionate spoof of flapper-era musical comedy began life at the Players Club, London on 14 April 1953 as part of the club's 'Late Joys' programme and had a three-week run. Because of its success it was expanded to a three-act production, which reopened at the club on 13 October and ran for six weeks. Though considered a questionable project for the West End, the musical was eventually transferred to Wyndham's Theatre, where its 2084 performance-run disproved this.

✶ There was a sequel to *The Boy Friend* called *Divorce Me, Darling* that ran for 91 performances at London's Globe Theatre in 1965 and was revived at Chichester in 1997.

✶ Moyna MacGill, who played Lady Brockhurst in the original Broadway production, was Angela Lansbury's mother.

The Critics

'It is hard to say which is the funnier: the material or the performance' – *New York Times*
'*The Boy Friend* is a happy, amiable and funny show' – *New York Daily News*

Recommended Recording

1984 London revival cast CDTER 1095
The original London cast recording has not been re-issued on CD and nor has the excellent (and best) version of the 1967 revival been transferred. So, the choice goes to the none-too-successful 1984 revival recording which has a fine feeling for the score and bags of charm. The cast includes Tony winner Anna Quayle, Rosemary Ashe and Simon Green. For those wanting to hear Julie Andrews becoming a Broadway star, then the campy original Broadway recording is for you (**RCA Victor GD 60056**).

Film

MGM, 1971. Starring Twiggy and Christopher Gable. Directed by Ken Russell.

The Boys from Syracuse

LYRICS ✶ Lorenz Hart
MUSIC ✶ Richard Rodgers
BOOK ✶ George Abbott

First Performance

New York, Alvin Theater, 23 November 1938 (235 performances)
London, Drury Lane Theatre, 7 November 1963 (100 performances)

Principal Characters

Antipholus of Syracuse
Antipholus of Ephesus
Dromio of Syracuse
Dromio of Ephesus
Luce
Adriana
Luciana

Original New York Cast

Eddie Albert, Ronald Graham, Jimmy Savo, Teddy Hart, Wynn Murray,
Muriel Angelus, Marcy Westcott

Original London Cast

Bob Monkhouse, Denis Quilley, Ronnie Corbett, Sonny Farrar, Maggie Fitzgibbon,
Lynn Kennington, Paula Hendrix

Plot

The Comedy of Errors by William Shakespeare provides the story. Antipholus and
his servant, Dromio, have come to Ephesus in Ancient Greece from their home in
Syracuse to find their long-lost twins, unaware of the crucial fact that each pair of
twins is identical and that each pair also has the same name. This leads to many
farcical misunderstandings as each is in turn mistaken for the other. Even the
servants can't distinguish one master from the other – and the confusion is
mutual. The Ephesus Dromio is having a stormy relationship with his wife, Luce.
His master is faring no better with his wife, Adriana. When the Syracuse
Antipholus turns up and pays court to Adriana's sister, Luciana, the trouble
accelerates. He and his servant are entertained by their seeming wives. When the
Ephesus couple return, they are chased away.

   Total misunderstanding is soon the order of the day, principally involving a
gold chain ordered by one Antipholus and delivered to the other. Syracuse's
Antipholus can't understand why Luciana rejects him and Adriana claims him as
her husband – and his Dromio is in similar trouble. Eventually, both sets of twins
finally meet, the mystery is solved and all ends happily.

Music and Songs

Delightful, mature Rodgers and Hart score with the pair at the peak of their powers. The rich and rewarding score includes 'Falling in love with love' (Adriana), 'Sing for your supper' (Luce, Adriana and Luciana) and 'This can't be love' (Antipholus and Luciana).

Did You Know?

✶ Only one authentic line from the original play made its way into the musical – 'The venom clamours of a jealous woman poison more deadly than a mad dog's tooth' – and was duly acknowledged as such when a Dromio popped his head round from the wings and announced, 'Shakespeare!'

✶ You can't keep a good plot down. It also did service for the 1980s musical *Oh Brother* that unhappily did not emulate the success of its predecessor.

✶ The original plot was taken from *Menachaechmi* by the Roman playwright, Plautus.

The Critics

The critics were kind:
'I believe it will be regarded as the greatest musical comedy of its time' – *New York World Telegram*
'If you have been wondering all these years just what was wrong with *The Comedy of Errors*, it is now possible to tell you. It has been waiting for a score by Rodgers and Hart and direction by George Abbott' – *New York Herald Tribune*

Recommended Recording

Concert Version (CD) DRG 21471-4767
The most complete recording of this score as performed for the New York City Center Encores series. This uses the original orchestrations and has a young, lively cast. The successful 1963 off-Broadway revival also made it onto disc (**Broadway Angel ZDM 7 64695 2**) and is a good second choice.

Film

RKO, 1940. Starring Allan Jones, Joe Penner and Martha Raye. Directed by A. Edward Sutherland.

Brigadoon

LYRICS ✶ Alan Jay Lerner
MUSIC ✶ Frederick Loewe
BOOK ✶ Alan Jay Lerner

First Performance

New York, Ziegfeld Theater, 13 March 1947 (581 performances)
London, His Majesty's Theatre, 14 April 1949 (685 performances)

Principal Characters

These are the New York production names. In London the surnames were
changed, as shown in brackets.

Tommy Albright ✶ An American tourist
Fiona MacLaren ✶ His sweetheart (MacKeith)
Meg Brockie ✶ The comic foil
Charlie Dalrymple ✶ The bridegroom (Cameron)
Jeff Douglas ✶ Tommy's American friend
Harry Beaton ✶ A Brigadoon hothead (Ritchie)

Original New York Cast

David Brooks, Marion Bell, Pamela Britton, Lee Sullivan,
George Keane, James Mitchell

Original London Cast

Philip Hanna, Patricia Hughes, Noele Gordon, Bill O'Connor,
Hiram Sherman, James Jamieson

Plot

The time is the present. Two American tourists, Tommy and Jeff, have lost their
way in the Highlands of Scotland. Through the trees they glimpse a village and
enter it. This is Brigadoon. There's something strange about it, though. The
clothes and manners of the villagers seem to come from the 18th century. Time
has passed it by, perhaps? Gradually they discover the truth, thanks to the village
dominie (schoolmaster). In order to protect the people from harm, Brigadoon's
minister had made a pact with God that it should disappear, emerging for 24 hours
in each century. As his own sacrifice, the minister would be left behind. Jeff and
Tommy are confused and appalled. Tommy has already fallen in love with Fiona.

Meanwhile, two villagers are about to get wed – Charlie and Jean. Harry, the
village wild child, who still loves Jean, threatens to leave and by so doing
condemn Brigadoon to total oblivion. He must be stopped! He is, and dies in an
accident. Midnight approaches and Tommy and Jeff prepare to depart. Tommy
could stay, but his love is not strong enough. He bids a sad farewell to Fiona and
the village sinks back into the mist.

Back in New York, Tommy finds he's thinking more and more of Brigadoon and of Fiona. Eventually the lure is too strong. He returns to Scotland and, in the depths of the Highlands he watches in amazement as the village materialises before his eyes. The dominie, Mr Lundie (Mr Murdoch), appears and reveals that love can conquer anything – including time.

Music and Songs

Does the score sound more Irish than Scottish? Either way it sounds appropriately Celtic. The collaboration sounds hugely authentic, with stirring music from the past, tender lyric ballads and ribald comedy numbers that find the team at the top of their versatile creative powers. High points include 'Come to me, bend to me' (Charlie), 'Almost like being in love' (Tommy and Fiona), 'There but for you go I' (Tommy and Fiona), 'My mother's wedding day' (Meg), 'Waitin' for my dearie' (Fiona) and 'From this day on' (Fiona).

Did You Know?

∗ The comic lead in London, Noele Gordon, subsequently enjoyed huge success on television as the proprietress of the Crossroads motel – she was also a Meg!

∗ In America, the creative talents rated their producer Jean Dalrymple so highly that each night the bride, a Jean, married a Dalrymple.

The Critics

The New York Drama Critics Circle loved *Brigadoon*, citing it Best Musical of the Season: 'Because it is an altogether original and inventive blending of words, music and dance; because its taste, discretion and thoughtful beauty mark a high note in any season; and because it finds the lyric theatre at its best.'
'A bonny thing for Broadway, a scintillating song and dance fantasy that has given the theatregoers reason to toss tam o' shanters in the air' – *New York Herald Tribune*

Recommended Recording

Complete studio recording (CD) Broadway Angel 0777 7 54481 2 2
A wonderful John McGlinn reconstruction with the original orchestrations and the complete score recorded for the first time. The cast includes three terrific Broadway performers in Brent Barrett, Judy Kaye and Rebecca Luker.

Film

MGM, 1954. Starring Gene Kelly, Cyd Charisse and Van Johnson. Directed by Vincente Minnelli.

Bye Bye Birdie

LYRICS ✶ Lee Adams
MUSIC ✶ Charles Strouse
BOOK ✶ Michael Stewart

First Performance

New York, Martin Beck Theater, 14 April 1960 (607 performances)
London, Her Majesty's Theatre, 15 June 1961 (268 performances)

Principal Characters

Albert Peterson ✶ Manager and songwriter for . . .
Conrad Birdie ✶ A rock 'n' roll singer
Rose Grant ✶ Albert's girlfriend
Mae Peterson ✶ Albert's mother
Mr MacAfee ✶ Father of . . .
Kim MacAfee ✶ A teenager
Hugo ✶ Her boyfriend

Original New York Cast

Dick Van Dyke, Dick Gautier, Chita Rivera, Kay Medford, Paul Lynde,
Susan Watson, Michael J. Pollard

Original London Cast

Peter Marshall, Marty Wilde, Chita Rivera, Angela Baddeley, Robert Nichols,
Sylvia Tysick, Clive Endersby

Plot

Bye Bye Birdie was the first successful musical to deal with the phenomenon of
rock 'n' roll. It was inspired by the drafting of Elvis Presley into the US army. The
show's rock star, named Conrad Birdie, is similarly about to join up. Before he
does so, he's to perform a new song written for the purpose by his harassed
manager Albert Peterson, and kiss a specially-selected teenager on an Ed Sullivan
television coast-to-coast broadcast. She's Kim MacAfee, from Sweet Apple, Ohio,
so Albert, together with girlfriend Rose, and Birdie go there. Birdie stays with the
MacAfee family, much to the disgust of Hugo, Kim's understandably jealous
boyfriend. A further complication arises: the arrival of Albert's mother, who
theatens to kill herself if Albert marries Rose.

Tired of close supervision, Birdie slips out to have a good time with Kim and
her friends. Meanwhile, Rose and Hugo share their problems in a local bar, before
Rose storms out and disrupts a meeting of the Shriner's Club with a dazzling
dance routine. Kim and her friends, meanwhile, find Birdie really boring, and
Hugo realizes there's nothing to worry about. Albert proposes marriage to Rose
and promises a quiet existence in Pumpkin Falls, Iowa. This sounds good to her.
Conrad Birdie joins the army and Sweet Apple returns to its normal identity as a
small town in which nothing much ever happens.

Music and Songs

A lively score that masquerades under rock 'n' roll colours, but most of the tunes are conventional Broadway show songs – the first to reach Broadway from Charles Strouse and Lee Adams. In a dynamic and enjoyable set, 'Put on a happy face' (Albert), 'A lot of livin' to do' (Conrad) and 'Kids' (the parents) stand out.

Did You Know?

∗ This was Gower Champion's first success as a director. His previous career had been as half of the dancing team of Marge and Gower Champion, whose grace and elegance featured in many '50s film musicals.

∗ A sequel in 1991, *Bring Back Birdie*, survived four performances.

∗ Sammy Davis made a personal hit with 'A lot of livin' to do'.

∗ The new television soundtrack recording (1996) included further original songs.

∗ Marty Wilde, who played Birdie in London, was a genuine pop star whose daughter, Kim, has followed successfully in her father's footsteps.

The Critics

Critical reaction included John Chapman's assertion in the *New York Daily News* that the show was 'the funniest, most captivating and most expert musical comedy one could hope to see in several seasons of showgoing'.

Recommended Recording

Original Broadway cast (CD) Columbia CK 2025
Dick Van Dyke in his best role as Albert and Chita Rivera blossoming as a true Broadway star. He went on to make the film and she recreated her role in London. A case where there are excellent alternatives such as the film, the London cast and a revival television version, but with the original cast version there is a brightness and newness that somehow is lost in them.

Film

Columbia, 1963. Starring Ann-Margret, Bobby Rydell, Jesse Pearson, Janet Leigh and Dick Van Dyke. Directed by George Sidney. A fine stage-to-screen adaptation – some new songs too.

By Jupiter

LYRICS ✶ Lorenz Hart
MUSIC ✶ Richard Rodgers
BOOK ✶ Rodgers and Hart,
based on the play *The Warrior's Husband* by Julian Thompson

First Performance

New York, Shubert Theater, 2 June 1942 (427 performances)

Principal Characters

Sapiens ✶ The king, and husband of . . .
Hippolyta ✶ An Amazon queen
Antiope ✶ The queen's sister
Theseus ✶ A warrior
Pomposia ✶ A female warrior
Heroica ✶ Another female warrior
Homer ✶ Another warrior's husband
Hercules ✶ Another warrior

Original New York Cast

Ray Bolger, Constance Moore, Benay Venuta, Ronald Graham, Bertha Belmore, Margaret Bannerman, Berni Gould, Ralph Dumke

Plot

On the island of Pomus in Asia Minor in far-distant times, the roles of the sexes are reversed. Queen Hippolyta leads a fearsome Amazon warrior band. The men cook and look after the homes their wives leave behind when off making war. This situation is all due to the girdle of the goddess Diana, worn by the queen. But if she loses it, she loses her power, and dominance as well. Theseus and Hercules, with some Greek troops, arrive on the island to try and obtain the girdle. Instead of open warfare, the men decide to rely on their sex appeal. They are successful, obtain the girdle and, as a result, the women revert to their traditional roles. Hippolyta's husband, Sapiens, changes from being the weakest, most servile and cowardly husband of all, to assuming his role as a great and mighty king. Meanwhile, Theseus has fallen in love with Hippolyta's sister, Antiope, and she with him – so all ends neatly.

Music and Songs

A delightful and currently neglected score. The reason why it does not contain the list of hits that one tends to expect from a Rodgers and Hart score, is that it is their most integrated. So there are the war cries in 'For Jupiter and Greece' (Greek men) and 'Ride, Amazon, Ride' (Amazon warriors), the sex reversal songs such as 'The boy I left behind me' (Amazons) and charmers like 'Wait till you see her'

(Theseus), 'Everything I've got' (Hippolyta and Sapiens) and 'Nobody's heart' (Antiope).

Did You Know?

✶ This was Rodgers and Hart's last original musical together. Satisfyingly, it also gave them their longest run – which could have been longer, had not Ray Bolger departed to entertain troops in war zones.

✶ Bertha Belmore, the battleaxe and stalwart of British stage and screen in the thirties, was ideally cast as Pomposia in this Broadway show.

✶ The original title of the show was *All's Fair* (presumably in love and war).

✶ The original non-musical play made Katherine Hepburn a star. It was called *The Warrior's Husband*, filmed in 1933 and its principal stars were Elissa Landi and Ernest Truex. The latter was ideally cast as a downtrodden husband.

The Critics

'A lush and lavish musical comedy, extravagant, adult and betimes amusing' – *Variety*

Recommended Recording

1967 revival cast (LP) RCA LSO-1137
To date this spirited and highly entertaining cast album has not been released on CD. With the Richard Rodgers centenary in 2002 one can only hope that this splendid recording will get issued as part of the celebrations.

Cabaret

LYRICS ✳ Fred Ebb
MUSIC ✳ John Kander
BOOK ✳ Joe Masteroff, based on Christopher Isherwood's *Berlin Stories*
and John van Druten's play *I am a Camera*

First Performance

New York, Broadhurst Theater, 20 November 1966 (1165 performances)
London, Palace Theatre, 28 February 1968 (336 performances)

Principal Characters

Sally Bowles ✳ An English girl
Cliff Bradshaw ✳ An American writer
Herr Schulz ✳ An elderly German greengrocer
Fräulein Schneider ✳ A landlady
Fräulein Kost ✳ A tenant
Master of Ceremonies ✳ A performer in a Berlin nightclub
Ernst Ludwig ✳ A sinister entrepreneur

Original New York Cast

Jill Haworth, Bert Convy, Jack Gilford, Lotte Lenya, Peg Murray,
Joel Grey, Edward Winter

Original London Cast

Judi Dench, Kevin Colson, Peter Sallis, Lila Kedrova, Pamela Strong,
Barry Dennen, Richard Owens

Plot

American traveller, Cliff Bradshaw, arrives in Berlin in the 1930s and lodges with Fräulein Schneider. Another tenant is Sally Bowles, from Chelsea in England, who sings in the local Kit-Kat Club. Cliff supplements his income by giving English lessons. One of his pupils is Ernst Ludwig, who is later revealed as a Nazi go-between. Germany is bankrupt and taking its pleasures in nightclubs like the Kit-Kat, where the Master of Ceremonies sings songs with a bitter political flavour. Back at his lodgings, Cliff observes the burgeoning romance between his landlady and an elderly beau, Herr Schulz – until she is warned off the liaison by Nazi elements who also invade the nightclub and beat up Cliff when he remonstrates with them.

Sally reveals she's pregnant and Cliff plans to marry her and take her away. But Sally can't face this or any long-term emotional commitment. She has an abortion and remains behind, singing in the club, while Cliff sadly leaves Berlin after promising to dedicate his book, when he writes it, to Sally Bowles – *Goodbye to Berlin*.

Music and Songs

Wonderfully evocative of the Brecht/Weill songs of decadent 1930s Germany, Kander and Ebb's brilliant, sometimes erotic, sometimes deeply frightening score summons up the period with pinpoint accuracy. 'Cabaret' (Sally) was a hit. 'Willkommen' (Master of Ceremonies), 'So what?' (Fräulein Schneider), 'Tomorrow belongs to me' (Nazi rally members) and 'Why should I wake up?' (Cliff) typify this many-layered, memorable score.

Did You Know?

✶ The original title of the show was *Welcome to Berlin*. British composer Sandy Wilson had previously worked on an adaptation of the stories called *Goodbye to Berlin*.

✶ A radically new production in 1993 at the intimate Donmar Theatre in London, subsequently filmed for television, offered a believable Sally (Jane Horrocks) who had the courage to sing in deliberately second-rate fashion – as indicated in the original Isherwood story. Alan Cumming's Master of Ceremonies was the most sinister yet.

✶ Lotte Lenya was the wife of Kurt Weill who was the inspiration behind much of the music.

The Critics

'A marionette's-eye view of a time and place in our lives that was brassy, wanton, carefree, and doomed to crumble' – *New York Times*
'It has bright music, magnificent production numbers, touches of comedy and tragedy' – *Variety*

Recommended Recording

Original London cast (CD) Sony West End SMK 53494
Although this version does not have the remarkable Joel Grey it surpasses with every other performance on the recording. Judy Dench, in the first of three major musical roles, is a fine Sally who brings out the vulnerability of the character, and does not shy away from showing the limited talent the character really has as a singer.

Film

Allied Artist Films, 1972. Starring Liza Minnelli, Michael York and Joel Grey. Directed by Bob Fosse. This featured an altered story with some additional songs – the raunchy 'Mein Herr' and 'Maybe this time'.

Cabin in the Sky

LYRICS ✶ John LaTouche
MUSIC ✶ Vernon Duke
BOOK ✶ Lynn Root

First Performance

New York, Martin Beck Theater, 25 October 1940 (156 performances)

Principal Characters

Petunia Jackson ✶ A committed Christian
Joe Jackson ✶ Her weak husband
Lawd's general ✶ A heavenly messenger
Lucifer Junior ✶ A young devil
Georgia Brown ✶ A real temptation
Brother Green ✶ A pastor

Original New York Cast

Ethel Waters, Dooley Wilson, Todd Duncan, Rex Ingram,
Katherine Dunham, J. Rosamond Johnson

Plot

Petunia Jackson is a wife of simple but unquenchable faith, who lives with her weak-willed husband in a modest home in the American South. Joe is obviously intended for Hell unless Petunia can do something about it. Joe's lying on his deathbed, injured in a crap game. It seems he's dead but heavenly emissaries arrive and Joe's soul pleads for a second chance. Because of Petunia, Joe is given a six-month trial to whitewash his soul. The devil is furious and resolves to provide many temptations, beginning with a winning sweepstake ticket. How will Joe cope with being rich? But Joe can't read and ignores the telegram announcing his win.

It's time to bring on Georgia Brown, who reads the telegram and tells Joe of his good fortune. As they share a hug, Petunia arrives, and throws Joe out of the house. But she can fight back, too. When Joe turns up in John Henry's café with Georgia, Petunia makes an entrance, dressed up to the nines. She tells her husband she's no longer interested in him, only in her share of the sweepstake win. Domino Jackson asks her to dance and wants to take liberties. Joe punches Domino on the jaw. The latter pulls a gun and Petunia receives the bullet intended for Joe. But a second bullet reaches its target and Joe dies. There's a violent storm and after Petunia's pleading on Joe's behalf, the ghosts of Petunia and Joe are led up to Heaven – to the Cabin in the Sky.

Music and Songs

The poetic imagery of John LaTouche is perfectly aligned with Vernon Duke's smoky, blues-, gospel- and folksong-influenced score that never descends to vaudeville or cakewalk caricature. 'Cabin in the sky' (Petunia and Little Joe), 'Taking a chance on love' (Petunia), and 'Honey in the honeycomb' (Georgia) remain Broadway standards and cabaret mainstays.

Did You Know?

✶ This was Vernon Duke's major Broadway show.

✶ *Cabin in the Sky* was choreographer George Balanchine's first show as director.

✶ Ira Gershwin, the first choice as lyricist, was unable to comply. However, he did write additional lyrics for extra songs added to the film.

The Critics

George Jean Nathan considered *Cabin in the Sky* the best musical of the year. *The New York Times* praised 'its cornucopia of songs and the earthy vitality of Ethel Waters'.

Recommended Recording

New York revival cast (CD) Angel ZDM 0777 7 64892 2 3
The most comprehensive version that also has additional material by Vernon Duke written for this production, which stars Rosetta Le Noire in what was originally the Ethel Waters role. The few original tracks that Miss Waters recorded are available on a combination CD with tracks from other shows (AEI CD 017).

Film

MGM, 1944. Starring Ethel Waters, Eddie Anderson and Lena Horne. Directed by Vincente Minnelli.

La Cage aux Folles

LYRICS ✱ Jerry Herman
MUSIC ✱ Jerry Herman
BOOK ✱ Harvey Fierstein, based on the play by Jean Poiret

First Performance

New York, Palace Theatre, 21 August 1983 (1761 performances)
London, London Palladium, 7 May 1986 (301 performances)

Principal Characters

Georges ✱ Our host
Albin ✱ Star of 'La Cage'
Jean-Michel ✱ Georges' son
Anne Dindon ✱ His fiancée
Edouard Dindon ✱ Her father
Madame Dindon ✱ Her mother

Original New York Cast

Gene Barry, George Hearn, John Weiner, Leslie Stevens,
Jay Garner, Merle Louise

Original London Cast

Denis Quilley, George Hearn, Jonathon Morris, Wendy Roe,
Brian Glover, Julia Sutton

Plot

We are in St Tropez and at the nightclub called La Cage aux Folles. The club's star is Za Za, a middle-aged drag queen and lover of the club's owner, Georges. Za Za's real name is Albin and he is highly temperamental. In a short relationship, some twenty-five years before, Georges had fathered Jean-Michel and the gay couple brought him up. Jean-Michel has now met Anne and they want to marry – the problem is that Anne's father is an anti-gay politician and he, and his wife, are coming to meet Jean-Michel's parents. Jean-Michel wants Albin out of sight and Georges agrees, only he finds it impossible to tell him. Albin finds out when he catches father and son removing his belongings from their flat and, emotionally upset, he performs a moving 'I am what I am' and leaves the club.

In the morning Georges tries to patch up the situation and suggests that Albin could come to the dinner as Uncle Al, only the lesson he has to make him appear 'butch' does not work. Georges is now very annoyed with his son, who is acting selfishly and without feeling for Albin who has brought him up. The flat has been stripped of every camp item and when the Dindons arrive they are duly impressed; as they are with Jean-Michel's 'mother', Albin, helping to save the day. They all go off to a local restaurant, Chez Jacqueline, where Albin is invited to sing – only he forgets what he is doing and on the final note he tears off his wig allowing the Dindons to see him for what he really is. Back at the flat, Jean-Michel acknowledges that what he did was wrong. Also, the press have been tipped off that Deputy Dindon is on the premises and the only way to get him out is in drag. And so, a happy ending. Jean-Michel and Anne go off to get married, the Dindons are just thankful for not being sucked into a political storm and, most importantly, Georges and Albin can continue their life together.

Music and Songs

An engagingly tuneful score with an authentic French flavour and Jerry Herman at his most accessible and endearing. Highlights include 'I am what I am' (Albin), 'Song on the sand' (Albin and Georges) and 'The best of times' (Jacqueline and company).

Did You Know?

✴ Unusually, the French play, film and American musical all used the same title.

✴ The show proved itself to be the most popular Broadway musical of its era on European stages – though not in England nor in Australia.

✴ The show won Tonys for best musical, book, director, costumes and star (George Hearn).

The Critics

'Terrific! Yes it is. And fun-filled' – *New York Post*
'The best Broadway musical in years. Slick, stunning and fun!' – *WNEW tv*

Recommended Recording

Original Broadway cast (CD) RCA Red Seal BD84824
This shows off Jerry Herman's magnificently tuneful score with the ultimate performances – it just cannot be bettered.

Films

There is no film of the musical, although a Hollywood version of the story entitled *The Birdcage* and starring Nathan Lane was released in 1996. There is an excellent French film of the original play.

Call Me Madam

LYRICS ✴ Irving Berlin
MUSIC ✴ Irving Berlin
BOOK ✴ Howard Lindsey and Russel Crouse

First Performance

New York, Imperial Theater, 12 October 1950 (644 performances)
London, Coliseum, 15 March 1952 (485 performances)

Principal Characters

Sally Adams ✴ The new Ambassador to Lichtenburg
Cosmo Constantine ✴ Prime Minister of Lichtenburg
Kenneth Gibson ✴ Sally's aide
Congressman Wilkins
Pemberton Maxwell ✴ A member of the embassy
Sebastian Sebastian ✴ A minister in Lichtenburg
Princess Maria of Lichtenburg

Original New York Cast

Ethel Merman, Paul Lukas, Russell Nype, Pat Harrington, Allan Hewitt,
Henry Lascoe, Galina Talva

Original London Cast

Billie Worth, Anton Walbrook, Jeff Warren, Sidney Keith, Donald Burr,
Stanley van Beers, Shani Wallis

Plot

'The play is laid in two mythical countries. One is called Lichtenburg, the other the United States of America.' Washington socialite party-giver Sally Adams is appointed American ambassador to the postage stamp-sized principality of Lichtenburg in central Europe. Once there, her vivacity and charm overcome the lapses in protocol that she inadvertently commits. She finds herself attracted to the country's prime minister, Cosmo Constantine. Her aide, Kenneth Gibson, is similarly taken with the young Princess Maria.

Sally tries to obtain a loan of $100 million for the principality, expecting Cosmo to be pleased. He isn't, believing his country needs to stand on its own feet with no handouts. Furthermore, Sally's meddling in Kenneth's romance has her recalled to Washington. Luckily the show ends happily with Sally reunited with Cosmo and Kenneth with Princess Maria.

A nice touch was the appearance, at the curtain call only, of a Harry Truman lookalike, as the president had, seemingly, been on the other end of Sally's telephone calls to the States.

Music and Songs

The last great score by 'Mr American Music', *Call Me Madam* shows the old wizard at his wittiest, and calling on that boundless outpouring of catchy melody that makes Berlin the 20th-century popular equivalent to Schubert. There's his best antiphonal duet, 'You're just in love' (Sally and Kenneth), wonderful upbeat ditties such as 'It's a lovely day today' (Maria and Kenneth), and some barnstorming character-establishing numbers for 'The hostess with the mostes' on the ball' (Sally), plus a tender love duet – 'The best thing for you' (Sally and Constantine).

Did You Know?

✴ The song 'They like Ike' was used as a campaign song by the future president, and may have helped sweep Eisenhower to victory.

✴ The show was Irving Berlin's last major hit.

✴ Both Ethel Merman and Irving Berlin won Tony awards, Merman for her performance and Berlin for his score.

The Critics

The critics had a fine time:
'It is genuine comedy because the character grows and develops in the course of the play and because Ethel Merman puts into it good will as well as swaggering self-confidence' – Brooks Atkinson
'The Irving Berlin songs and a superb production make *Call Me Madam* the gala that it promised to be' – *New York Herald Tribune*

Recommended Recording

Ethel Merman (CD) MCAD-10521
Call Me Madam without Merman is just not *Call Me Madam*! The show was written for her unique voice and it shows. For contractual reasons she was not released from her record company to make the original cast recording and so she recorded her role assisted by Dick Haymes for Decca. The rest of the cast went into RCA's studio and recorded it with Dinah Shore trying valiantly (but losing) to match the Merman verve.

Film

20th Century Fox, 1953. Starring Ethel Merman, George Sanders, Donald O'Connor and Vera-Ellen. Directed by Walter Lang.

Camelot

LYRICS ✶ Alan Jay Lerner
MUSIC ✶ Frederick Loewe
BOOK ✶ Alan Jay Lerner,
based on T.H. White's novel *The Once and Future King*

First Performance

New York, Majestic Theater, 3 December 1960 (873 performances)
London, Drury Lane Theatre, 19 August 1964 (518 performances)

Principal Characters

King Arthur ✶ King of England
Queen Guenevere ✶ His wife
Merlyn ✶ A magician
Morgan LeFay ✶ A temptress
Sir Lancelot ✶ A knight
Mordred ✶ Arthur's illegitimate son
Sir Lionel and Sir Dinadan ✶ Two of Arthur's knights
King Pellinore ✶ A friend of King Arthur

Original New York Cast

Richard Burton, Julie Andrews, David Hurst, M'el Dowd, Robert Goulet,
Roddy McDowall, Bruce Yarnell, John Cullum, Robert Coote

Original London Cast

Laurence Harvey, Elizabeth Larner, Miles Malleson, Moyra Fraser, Barry Kent,
Nicky Henson, Raymond Edwards, Victor Flattery, Cardew Robinson

Plot

Camelot is set in ancient England. Guenevere, arriving at Camelot to marry the king, gets lost in the woods where she meets King Arthur for the first time. They fall in love before she realizes his identity. They marry and the deeply idealistic Arthur founds the Round Table to establish new standards of conduct, friendship and loyalty. Among the knights who come to join the brotherhood is Sir Lancelot. The queen challenges him to joust with three knights, and Lancelot emerges unscathed from the contest. As he finds that he has also fallen in love with the queen, he leaves, but two years later he returns to be inducted into the Round Table. Arthur's illegitimate son, Mordred, has designs on the throne. He catches Guenevere and Lancelot together in a compromising situation and uses their guilt to his own advantage. Mordred has Lancelot locked up and plans a death at the stake for Guenevere. Lancelot escapes from prison and flees to France with Guenevere.

Arthur's world has been shattered but his love for both Guenevere and Lancelot remains. War is declared on France and Arthur discovers and forgives the runaways. Arthur is now pitted against Mordred and his forces. Arthur's spirits are raised by hearing a young boy recounting his dream of Camelot and, as a final act on the field of battle, he knights him and sends him back to England to continue the tradition and live up to the ideals that he himself had established – at the Round Table in Camelot.

Music and Songs

A tuneful score by Lerner and Loewe, showing yet again their ability to recreate the idioms of another time in another land. The score sounds more English even than *My Fair Lady*, with a vein of wistful folk melody and the full panoply of English music at its most ceremonial. The fine score includes the hit song 'If ever I would leave you' (Lancelot). Others are 'Camelot' (King Arthur), 'I wonder what the king is doing tonight?' (Arthur and Guenevere) and 'How to handle a woman' (Arthur).

Did You Know?

✶ Surprisingly, because of the success of *My Fair Lady*, there was no great rush for tickets and it was only the sight of Richard Burton dancing with Julie Andrews on television's Ed Sullivan show that created a hit.

✶ When John F Kennedy was assassinated in 1963 it was mentioned by his wife that his favourite song was the title song from the show and he used to play it often before retiring to bed. That night when the song was sung in the theatre the audience and cast burst into tears and the show had to stop for a few minutes.

The Critics

The critics were respectful:
'A very handsome musical play with many lovely and imaginative things in it' – Richard Watts Jnr

Recommended Recording

Original Broadway cast (CD) Sony SK 60542
Julie Andrews, as expected, gives a fine performance in another of her great 'English' roles. However, the surprise is Richard Burton who is superb as the king. Robert Goulet is the definitive Sir Lancelot.

Film

Warner, 1967. Starring Vanessa Redgrave and Richard Harris. Directed by Joshua Logan. In many ways the film represented a deeper emotional experience than the original stage show.

Can-Can

LYRICS ✶ Cole Porter
MUSIC ✶ Cole Porter
BOOK ✶ Abe Burrows

First Performance

New York, Shubert Theater, 7 May 1953 (892 performances)
London, Coliseum, 14 October 1954 (394 performances)

Principal Characters

La Môme Pistache ✶ Owner of the Bal du Paradis
Aristide Forestier ✶ A judge
Boris Adzinidzinadze ✶ A Bulgarian sculptor
Claudine ✶ A soubrette
Hilaire Jussac ✶ An art critic
Théophile and Etienne ✶ Parisians

Original New York Cast

Lilo, Peter Cookson, Hans Conried, Gwen Verdon, Eric Rhodes,
Phil Leeds, Richard Purdy

Original London Cast

Irene Hilda, Edmund Hockridge, Alfred Marks, Gillian Lynne, George Gee,
Warren Mitchell, Alan Gilbert

Plot

La Môme Pistache owns a café in Paris' Montmartre district in the latter years of the 19th century. One of the prime features of the entertainment it offers is a scandalous dance, the can-can. Our heroine is frequently in trouble with the law as a result.

As the show opens, the can-can girls are being released yet again from the court, as no policeman will testify against them. In frustration, Judge Aristide decides to go to the café himself to gather evidence. Meanwhile, Claudine, a laundress cum can-can girl, is fending off a pass from Hilaire, an art critic – she's already involved with a sculptor. Aristide arrives at the café and he and the proprietress fall for each other. He does not reveal his identity and La Môme employs all her tricks to evade the prosecution of her girls. She bribes the police and names names. The judge's identity is revealed by the girls and in the middle of the can-can, there's the flash of a camera. The judge has his evidence. Meanwhile, Hilaire plans to hold an elaborate ball at the café. Claudine agrees to dine with him, to ensure a favourable review for her sculptor, Boris.

But with the café girls and the proprietress locked up, thanks to Aristide, can the ball go ahead? Yes, of course – they are released pending prosecution, and Aristide, in an attack of conscience, urges Pistache to escape. He kisses her, and click, another compromising camera shot – this time of the judge. Next day the papers print his photograph and Hilaire's panning of Boris' work. Boris challenges Hilaire to a duel and promptly faints. Hilaire is shamed into writing a rave review of Boris' work. Aristide is expelled from the bar and ostracised by his legal colleagues. Pistache arranges for Aristide and herself to be arrested, to give him a chance to clear his name in court. Together they prove, with the aid of the girls, that there's nothing wrong with a little harmless can-can.

Music and Songs

The fifth of Porter's musicals with French settings brought out a cornucopia of lively songs, many tinged with garlic or the French musette. The Continental influence extended to the titles – 'Allez-vous-en' (Pistache), and 'C'est magnifique' (Pistache) – as well as the melodies – 'It's all right with me' (Aristide) and 'I love Paris' (Pistache).

Did You Know?

✳ A first featured appearance on Broadway as Claudine by Gwen Verdon stole the notices from Lilo. From then on, Gwen was a star in her own right – her next show was *Damn Yankees*.

✳ Gwen Verdon received her first Tony award for *Can-Can* and the choreographer, Michael Kidd, also won a Tony.

✳ The role of Claudine in London was a major stepping stone for Gillian Lynne, later the choreographer of *Cats* and *Phantom of the Opera*.

The Critics

Walter Winchell claimed on radio that the show was 'a surefire click'. Others felt the show had 'a score by Cole Porter that falls pleasantly on the ears' and praised 'some good Cole Porter tunes'.
'Lilo went into the show a star and Gwen Verdon came out of it a star' – *New York World Telegram & Sun*
'Cole Porter's score is by no means his most distinguished' – *New York Herald Tribune*

Recommended Recording

Original Broadway cast (CD) Broadway Angel ZDM 7 64664 2 2
More complete than the much-changed film version and a good record of a fine Porter score.

Film

20th Century Fox, 1960. Starring Frank Sinatra, Maurice Chevalier and Shirley MacLaine. Directed by Walter Lang. The story was altered, and more Cole Porter songs added.

Candide

LYRICS ✳ Richard Wilber
MUSIC ✳ Leonard Bernstein
BOOK ✳ Lillian Hellman
Based on Voltaire's satire

First Performance

New York, Martin Back Theatre, 1 December 1956 (73 performances)
London, Saville Theatre, 30 April 1959 (60 performances)

Principal Characters

Dr Pangloss * The teacher
Candide * The boy
Cunegonde * The girl
Old Lady * The maid
Governor of Buenos Aires * The same
Marquis and Sultan * Parisian house owners

Original New York Cast

Max Adrian, Robert Rounseville, Barbara Cook, Irra Petina, William Olvis, Boris Aplon, Joseph Bernard

Original London Cast

Laurence Naismith, Denis Quilley, Mary Costa, Edith Coates, Ron Moody, Victor Spinetti, James Cairncross

Plot

Candide and Cunegonde are to be married and, as the philosopher Dr Pangloss says, it is the best of all possible worlds. Unfortunately, however, the marriage does not take place because Westphalia and Hesse go to war, and Cunegonde is believed dead. Candide and Dr Pangloss set out for Lisbon where the Inquisition is under way and they are sentenced to death. An earthquake saves Candide but the doctor dies. Alone, Candide makes for Paris where Cunegonde is found, very much alive and in the house of the Marquis and the Sultan admiring her jewellery. Candide has a duel and kills both the Marquis and Sultan and he and Cunegonde, together with her maid, the Old Lady, flee. They meet up with a band of pilgrims on their way to the New World and sail for Buenos Aires. When they arrive all but Cunegonde and the Old Lady are made slaves. Cunegonde is pursued by the Governor, while Candide, enthused by the tales of riches in Eldorado, escapes, vowing to return for Cunegonde.

Candide makes his fortune and returns only to find the Governor has tired of Cunegonde and has put her and the Old Lady on a boat. He tells Candide that they have sailed to Europe and sells him a ship which, when Candide sets forth on it, sinks. Candide is rescued and is astonished by the unexpected appearance of a raft, bearing Dr Pangloss.

In Venice, Cunegonde has taken up the post of a scrubwoman and the Old Lady a woman of fashion. Candide and the doctor arrive, and Candide manages to lose what remains of his fortune. They make their way back to the now-ruined Westphalia where Candide eventually throws out Dr Pangloss's optimistic ideal and decides to live a more sensible life.

Music and Songs

Bernstein's majestic score has long been a favourite of show collectors. The overture is one of the most brilliant for a Broadway show. Cunegonde's 'Glitter and be gay' helped make Barbara Cook a star. And there are the delightful 'Best of all possible worlds' (Candide, Cunegonde and Dr Pangloss), 'I am easily assimilated' (Old Lady) and 'What's the use' (Old Lady).

Did You Know?

* While neither of the original New York or London productions was successful, the show had a cult following and this has led to many revivals, each a little different from the previous one, with Hugh Wheeler and Stephen Sondheim (among others) aiding with the alterations.

* The 1973 Broadway revival was staged in the round with the audience on benches. It was a hit and ran for 740 performances.

The Critics

'Lillian Hellman's libretto ... bears her own strong impress, which is foreign to Voltaire's. When Voltaire is ironic and bland, she is explicit and vigorous. When he makes lightning, rapier thrusts, she provides body blows. When he is diabolical, playwright Hellman is humanitarian' – *Time*

Recommended Recording

Original London 1999 Revival cast (CD) First Night Cast CD 75
An almost impossible choice to make, there are so many excellent recordings of this score. This is the most recent and the production was, perhaps, one of the most satisfying of a show that originally found little success. The strong acting in this Royal National Theatre version was evident on stage and on disc it shows a fine singing ensemble. Simon Russell Beale is a wonderful Voltaire / Pangloss and both Alex Kelly and Daniel Evans as Cunegonde and Candide are delightful. The show has been blessed with many fine singers playing Cunegonde. Two outstanding ones also correspond with the other recommended recordings: Barbara Cook in the original Broadway cast (**Sony Broadway SK 48017 mono**) and Marilyn Hill Smith in the Scottish Opera production (**TER CDTER 1156**).

Carmen Jones

LYRICS ✶ Oscar Hammerstein II
MUSIC ✶ Georges Bizet
BOOK ✶ Oscar Hammerstein II, based on Henri Meilhac and Ludovic Halévy's
opera libretto, adapted from Prosper Mérimée's novel *Carmen*

First Performance

New York, Broadway Theater, 2 December 1943 (502 performances)
London, Old Vic Theatre, 15 April 1991, for a season

Principal Characters

Carmen Jones ✶ A parachute factory worker
Joe ✶ A soldier
Husky Miller ✶ A fighter
Cindy Lou ✶ Joe's sweetheart
Frankie ✶ Carmen's friend
Remo the Drummer

Original New York Cast

Muriel Smith/Muriel Rahn, Luther Saxon/Napoleon Reid, Glenn Bryant,
Carlotta Franzell/Elton J. Warren, June Hawkins, Cozy Cole

Original London Cast

Wilhelmenia Fernandez/Sharon Benson, Damon Evans/Michael Austin,
Gregg Baker, Karen Parks, Carolyn Sebron, Robin Jones

Plot

Carmen Jones is a worker in a Southern parachute factory. It's wartime and
Carmen always appears to be at the heart of any fight that's going on. Corporal
Joe is detailed to arrest and guard her after a particularly serious brawl, but Joe is
bewitched by her, and she's much taken with him. Joe lets her escape and is put
under arrest. Meanwhile, Carmen has attracted another beau, Husky Miller, a
prize-fighter, who wants her to go to Chicago with him. She refuses because of
Joe but when he is released he kills another soldier in a drunken jealous state and
has to disappear. Carmen follows Husky to Chicago where he's in training for an
important fight. She discards Joe without a second thought when he arrives in
Chicago, but shaking him off is not as easy.

Carmen arrives outside the stadium where Husky Miller is to fight; there she is
accosted by a haggard fugitive from justice. It's Joe, and he's desperate. All that
matters is his love for Carmen – can't they start again? Carmen demurs. Joe was
yesterday; Husky Miller is what matters to her today. Maddened with frustration,
Joe stabs her fatally as the crowd inside the stadium acclaims Husky Miller the
winner of the fight. Joe waits outside for the police to arrest him.

Music and Songs

The music is that of Bizet's lively, infectiously melodic opera set in Spain, with very little alteration made to accommodate its new status as a musical. Hammerstein's lyrics are an amazing achievement. Highlights are 'Dat's love' (Carmen), 'You talk just like my maw' (Joe), 'Beat out dat rhythm on a drum' (Frankie), 'Stan' up and fight' (Husky), 'Dis flower' (Joe) and 'My Joe' (Cindy Lou).

Did You Know?

✶ On the first day of rehearsal only one of the 115 cast members had been on stage before.

✶ Due to French copyright laws, without the permission of Bizet's descendants *Carmen Jones* cannot yet be performed in France.

✶ Other operas adapted for Broadway musicals include Rossini's *The Barber of Seville* (*Once Over Lightly*, 1942) and Verdi's *Aida* (*My Darlin' Aida*, 1952). A number of opera plots have also been reused; current examples are *Madama Butterfly* (*Miss Saigon*, 1992) and *La Bohème* (*Rent*, 1996).

The Critics

The critics enjoyed the show:
'Wonderful, just wonderful. Hammerstein has not written a parody in any sense but simply a parallel' – *New York Times*
'A memorable milestone in the upward and onward course of the great American show' – Robert Garland
'It is superb. It is enchantingly beautiful; it is musically and visually stirring. Hammerstein, the best lyric writer in the business, has done a poet's job with the libretto. His incandescent imagination sets your own afire' – *New York Daily News*

Recommended Recording

Original London cast (CD) EMI Classics CDC 7 54351 2
The successful London revival recording that shares Carmen's songs between the alternate leads, Wilhelmenia Fernandez and Sharon Benson. This recording is a great improvement on both the original Broadway cast and the film soundtrack.

Film

20th Century Fox, 1954. Starring Dorothy Dandridge, Harry Belafonte, Diahann Carroll and Pearl Bailey. Directed by Otto Preminger.

Carnival

LYRICS ✳ Bob Merrill
MUSIC ✳ Bob Merrill
BOOK ✳ Michael Stewart, based on the film *Lili* by Helen Deutsch,
adapted from the story *The Love of Seven Dolls* by Paul Gallico

First Performance

New York, Imperial Theater, 13 April 1961 (719 performances)
London, Lyric Theatre, 8 February 1963 (34 performances)

Principal Characters

Lili ✳ A young orphan
Marco ✳ A magician
Paul Berthalet ✳ A puppeteer
Rosalie ✳ Marco's assistant
Jacquot ✳ A youngster of the circus
Schlegel ✳ The circus owner

Original New York Cast

Anna Maria Alberghetti, James Mitchell, Jerry Orbach, Kaye Ballard,
Pierre Olaf, Henry Lascoe

Original London Cast

Sally Logan, James Mitchell, Michael Maurel, Shirley Sands,
Bob Harris, Peter Bayliss

Plot

Carnival is set on the outskirts of a small town in southern Europe. Although it occasionally imagines itself to be the Grand Imperial Circus of Paris, this circus is in reality shabby and down at heel, with few attractions. A young orphan, Lili, from the town of Mira, comes to visit, looking for a friend of her father. For her, the circus is a source of wonder and magic. She's particularly enchanted by the magician, Marco the Magnificent, although probably not as much as he is by himself. He has an assistant, Rosalie, who is the subject of his most elaborate illusions.

When Lili encounters the puppets of Paul Berthalet she treats them as friends and they respond in kind. Paul himself is a bitter, unpleasant cripple who can only express his love and emotion through his puppets. He falls in love with Lili, but what chance does he have? Lili is given a job with the circus in which she talks to the puppets, all of whom curiously seem to exhibit character traits also possessed by members of the carnival. In due course, helped by the puppets, Lili realises where her true feelings lie; she's in love – not with Marco, but with the puppeteer Paul, and by the end of the show the two are together.

Music and Songs

A tuneful, conventional Broadway score with an appropriate circus feeling and a wistful other-worldly quality by Bob Merrill. Songs include 'Love makes the world go round' (Lili), 'Mira' (Lili), 'Always, always you' (Marco and Rosalie) and 'A sword and a rose and a cape'(Marco).

Did You Know?

✷ The show failed to find the same success in Britain as it had enjoyed on Broadway.

✷ Despite his activities as composer/lyricist, which continued, Bob Merrill acted as lyricist only on shows like *Funny Girl*, to Jule Styne's music. No Bob Merrill show has been a success in London and even *Funny Girl* ran only while Barbra Streisand was the star.

✷ The only Tony Award the show won was for its young star, Anna Maria Alberghetti, who shared best actress in a musical award with Diahann Carroll in Richard Rodger's *No Strings*.

The Critics

The American critics liked the show:
'It bursts with the vitality of Broadway know-how' – *New York Times*
'The Best Musical of the Season' – *New York World Telegram & Sun*
'The happiest musical of the season' – *Newsweek*

Recommended Recording

Original Broadway Cast (CD) Polydor 837 195-2
While there was a London cast recording it lacks the charm of the original and the outstanding performances of Jerry Orbach and Kaye Ballard. The CD has bonus tracks which include the composer singing five of his songs and Richard Chamberlain singing 'Love makes the world go round'.

Film

MGM, 1952 (called *Lili*, and on which the musical was based). Starring Leslie Caron and Mel Ferrer. Directed by Charles Walters. The film had a few songs, none of which were by Merrill. None were used in the stage show.

Carousel

LYRICS ✶ Oscar Hammerstein II
MUSIC ✶ Richard Rodgers
BOOK ✶ Oscar Hammerstein II, based on Ferenc Molnar's play *Liliom*

First Performance

New York, Majestic Theater, 19 April 1945 (890 performances)
London, Drury Lane Theatre, 7 June 1950 (566 performances)

Principal Characters

Billy Bigelow ✶ A fairground barker
Julie Jordan ✶ A mill girl
Carrie Pipperidge ✶ Her friend
Enoch Snow ✶ A fishing boat owner
Nettie Fowler ✶ Julie's aunt
Jigger Craigin ✶ A bad lot
Starkeeper ✶ A heavenly visitor
Louise Bigelow ✶ Billy and Julie's child
Mrs Mullin ✶ Owner of the carousel
June ✶ A girl

Original New York Cast

John Raitt, Jan Clayton, Jean Darling, Eric Mattson, Christine Johnson, Mervyn Vye, Russell Collins, Bambi Linn, Jean Casto, Iva Withers

Original London Cast

Stephen Douglass, Iva Withers, Margot Moser, Eric Mattson, Marion Ross, Morgan Davies, William Sherwood, Bambi Linn, Marjorie Mars, Mavis Ray

Plot

Set in New England, *Carousel* presents a tough fairground barker, Billy, who falls for simple mill girl, Julie, who pays regular visits to the fairground carousel (or merry-go-round if you're British) where he works. The owner of the attraction, Mrs Mullin, is jealous and sacks Billy (although she tries to re-employ him immediately). Billy and Julie are truly in love, and marry. He is unemployed. As a result the couple live with, and off, Julie's aunt, Nettie. Julie is pregnant and Billy is overjoyed, though worried about how he'll provide for his child.

Julie's friend, Carrie, marries a local fish merchant, Mr Snow, who offers Billy a job. Billy, with his criminal friend, Jigger, has other ideas. There's a clambake on a nearby island. Billy and Jigger will take part but slip back to rob Mr Bascomb, the mill owner, of his payroll.

Billy is killed in the bungled attempt at robbery. He's not good enough to go to heaven but the Starkeeper allows him a day on earth to help his (now teenage) daughter. As a visible presence, Billy goes back but when Louise won't accept the gift of a star he's brought her, he slaps her. She rushes inside her home and Julie comes out. Billy, now invisible, is given permission to attend Louise's graduation, where he manages to give hope and optimism to both his wife and daughter. He is now allowed to ascend to heaven.

Music and Songs

The score and the lyrics show just how great a musical can be. *Carousel* has one of the greatest scores ever composed for a musical, bursting with abundant life and full of memorable melodies and acute lyrics. 'Soliloquy' (Billy) is a wonderful piece of extended plotting and characterization. 'If I loved you' (Billy and Julie) is a fine ballad of growing affection, and the anthem 'You'll never walk alone' (Julie and Nettie) is one of the most beloved of all show tunes. In addition there is the rousing 'June is bustin' out all over' (Nettie, Carrie, Chorus), 'A real nice clambake' (Chorus) and, not to be forgotten, 'Carousel waltz' (Orchestra).

Did You Know?

✶ The song 'This was a real nice clambake' was originally written for *Oklahoma!* as 'This was a real nice hayride'.

✶ Gerry Marsden, Liverpool pop star, took the song 'You'll never walk alone' twice into the British charts.

✶ *Carousel* featured more wonderful dances by Agnes de Mille, following her success with *Oklahoma!*

✶ *Carousel* was the favourite score of its composer, Richard Rodgers.

The Critics

'This is the most glorious of the Rodgers and Hammerstein works' – Brooks Atkinson
'One of the finest musical plays I have ever seen. I shall remember it always' – John Chapman

Recommended Recording

Original Broadway cast (CD) Broadway Gold MCA Classics 0881-10799
This mono original has that freshness and indefinable magic of a great original cast album. If stereo is wanted then a studio cast version on MCA (**DMCG 6028**) with Barbara Cook, Samuel Ramey and Sarah Brightman is the one to go for.

Film

20th Century Fox, 1956. Starring Shirley Jones and Gordon MacRae. Directed by Henry King.

Cats

LYRICS ✳ T.S. Eliot
MUSIC ✳ Andrew Lloyd Webber
BOOK ✳ Based on T.S. Eliot's *Old Possum's Book of Practical Cats*

First Performance

London, New London Theatre, 11 May 1981 (still running)
New York, Winter Garden Theater, 7 October 1982 (7393 performances)

Principal Characters

Grizabella ✳ A cat of faded beauty
Rum Tum Tugger ✳ An athletic cat
Asparagus ✳ The theatre cat
Growltiger ✳ A sinister cat
Mister Mistoffolees ✳ A magician cat
Deuteronomy ✳ A wise old cat
Skimbleshanks ✳ A railway cat
Rumpleteazer ✳ A cat burglar
Mungojerrie ✳ A cat burglar
Munkustrap ✳ A story-teller
Jennyanydots ✳ A mature cat

Original London Cast

Elaine Paige, Paul Nicholas, Stephen Tate, Wayne Sleep, Brian Blessed,
Kenny Wells, Susan Jane Tanner, Bonnie Langford, John Thornton,
Jeff Shankley, Myra Sands

Original New York Cast

Betty Buckley, Terrence V. Mann, Stephen Hanan, Timothy Scott, Ken Page,
Reed Jones, Bonnie Simmons, Christine Langner, Rene Clemente,
Harry Groener, Anna McNeely

Plot

Cats doesn't really have a plot as such. Based on T.S. Eliot's children's book, *Old Possum's Book of Practical Cats*, the show introduces us to a succession of different cats. A brilliant explosion of song and dance, it's set on a giant rubbish dump. The cats include the humorous, generously proportioned Gumbie Cat, the athletic Rum Tum Tugger, the elegant Bustopher Jones and cat burglars Mungojerrie and Rumpleteazer. All good theatres have a cat – so here's Asparagus to tell the tale of the frightening Growltiger and his cat friend Griddlebone. Skimbleshanks is the railway cat. There's a magician cat too – Mister Mistoffolees – and the mysterious cat is Macavity. Lastly, there's the veteran presence of Grizabella, who is finally lifted up to the cat heaven – the Heaviside Layer – after singing 'Memory'.

Music and Songs

Lloyd Webber shows his versatility and thorough musical training in this suite of songs that vividly characterizes the various feline characters depicted. The music is inevitably highly melodic and shows influences of a pop music tradition that had yet to make a mark on Broadway. The lovely 'Memory' (Grizabella) is perhaps atypical of the score in its soft romantic warmth (no wonder there are 600-plus recordings). The remainder are character/action songs, bursting with vitality and rhythmic bounce, such as 'Mr Mistoffolees' (Mistoffolees).

Did You Know?

✴ *Cats* is the longest-running musical in the history of the West End theatre.

✴ In July 1997 the show overtook *A Chorus Line* as the longest-running musical in the history of Broadway.

✴ Judi Dench was to play Grizabella (and one other cat as well), but had to bow out due to a leg injury. When Elaine Paige took over she needed a big number and that became 'Memory'.

✴ This is one of the very few cases where the lyricist, in this case the important and influential author of *The Cocktail Party* and *Four Quartets*, T.S. Eliot, had died decades before the show was conceived and created.

✴ One song, 'Memory', has a lyric by the show's director, Trevor Nunn. It has made him a millionaire.

The Critics

'It is powerfully melodic theatre music' – *The Times*
'Cats isn't perfect. Don't miss it' – *The Observer*
'In the end one comes back to Lloyd Webber's remarkable ability to find tunes that fit each specific feeling' – *The Guardian*

Recommended Recording

Original London cast (CD) Polydor 817 810-2
The original and still the most exciting. It is virtually complete on two CDs and features definitive performances from many of the cast who have gone on to further success since this show.

Film

A video and DVD starring Elaine Paige and Sir John Mills has been issued.

Charlie Girl

LYRICS ✶ David Heneker and John Taylor
MUSIC ✶ David Heneker and John Taylor
BOOK ✶ Hugh and Margaret Williams with Ray Cooney,
based on a story by Ross Taylor

First Performance

London, Adelphi Theatre, 15 December 1965 (2202 performances)

Principal Characters

Joe Studholme ✶ A servant at the home of . . .
Lady Hadwell ✶ The impoverished owner of a stately home
Kay Connor ✶ A rich American ex-chorus girl
Charlie ✶ Lady Hadwell's tomboy daughter
Nicholas Wainwright ✶ Representative of a football pools company
Jack Connor ✶ Kay's handsome son

Original London Cast

Joe Brown, Anna Neagle, Hy Hazell, Christine Holmes,
Derek Nimmo, Stuart Damon

Plot

Charlie Girl is an updated version of the 'Cinderella' story with Buttons (Joe) winning Cinders (Charlie).

The story, set in the stately home of Hadwell Hall, now a tourist attraction, concerns tomboy Lady Charlotte Hadwell (Charlie), who is more interested in cars than boys at the beginning of the show. Mind you, she's quite taken by Jack, the son of her mother's old friend, Kay, who's staying at the hall. Before too long the mothers are plotting to marry him off to one of Lady Hadwell's three daughters (none of whom is ugly, by the way).

Meanwhile, Joe is the unwilling winner of the football pools. The pools company's persistent representative, Nicholas Wainwright, tries to make him take the money. Nicholas in turn is soon in love with one of Charlie's sisters. There's a celebration ball but when Charlie is kissed there by Jack, there's no romantic magic. That leaves Joe who, after foiling a burglary, turns out to be the man for her. He accepts the pools money and everyone lives happily ever after. Even Jack, who is soon snapped up by the remaining Hadwell daughter.

Music and Songs

A very pleasant, typically enjoyable score from David Heneker and his colleagues who followed up the success of *Half a Sixpence*'s 'Flash! Bang! Wallop!' with another knees-up show-stopper, 'Fish and chips' (Joe), in a varied evening that offered nicely satirical insights such as 'What's the magic?' (Jack), as well as the poignant 'My favourite occupation' (Joe) and a juicy duet for two mothers – 'Let's do a deal' (Lady Hadwell and Kay).

Did You Know?

✷ This was Anna Neagle's first musical in 12 years. Her engaging co-star, Joe Brown, was a pop singer and the combination worked well.

✷ Whereas the oh-so-British Lady Hadwell was played in the revival by American dancer Cyd Charisse, the part of Kay has always been played by English actresses – first by Hy Hazell, with Dora Bryan in the revival.

✷ The marriage of theatre and film people into the aristocracy is quite common – Maureen Swanson became Countess of Dudley. A predecessor in the same family was the great Edwardian star Gertie Millar. Also, Jamie Lee Curtis, the American film actress, is now Lady Haden-Guest.

✷ *Phil the Fluter*, the follow-up by the same collaborating team which used the same formula of aging star (Evelyn Laye), fading pop star (Mark Wynter) and comedian (Stanley Baxter) failed.

The Critics

The show survived a critical lambasting – 'Brash, charmless, vulgar, obvious and wilfully lacking in wit' opined *The Daily Telegraph* – to become a long-runner, perhaps partly due to extremely astute casting.

Recommended Recording

Original London cast (CD) Sony West End SMK 66174
A pleasant more than a great score but it has some wonderful performances from pop star Joe Brown and Broadway professional Stuart Damon, as well as a bit of nostalgia from Anna Neagle and Hy Hazel.

Chess

LYRICS ✴ Tim Rice
MUSIC ✴ Benny Andersson and Bjorn Ulvaeus
BOOK ✴ Tim Rice, reworked for Broadway by Richard Nelson

First Performance

London, Prince Edward Theatre, 14 May 1986 (1209 performances)
New York, Imperial Theater, 28 April 1988 (68 performances)

Principal Characters

Frederick Trumper ✴ USA world chess champion
Florence Vassy ✴ His second
Anatoly Sergeievsky ✴ The USSR challenger
Alexander Molokov ✴ His second
Walter de Courcy ✴ A broadcasting executive
The Arbiter
Svetlana Sergeievsky ✴ Anatoly's wife

Original London Cast

Murray Head, Elaine Paige, Tommy Körberg, John Turner, Kevin Colson,
Tom Jobe, Siobhan McCarthy

Original New York Cast

Philip Casnoff, Judy Kuhn, David Carroll, Harry Goz, Dennis Parlato,
Paul Harman, Marcia Mitzman

Plot

The World Chess Championship is taking place in Merano. The combatants are Frederick Trumper from America and Anatoly Sergeievsky from Russia. Trumper is flamboyant, aggressive and unpleasant. His entourage includes his manager and his Hungarian-American girlfriend, Florence Vassy. Sergeievsky has far more people in his team, headed by the dishonest, scheming Molokov, his manager, who intends to ensure that his client wins by fair means or foul. The judge or arbiter is meant to be impartial – but is he? There are so many commercial considerations and merchandising spin-offs to consider.

Florence and Anatoly become friends, to the distress of Frederick, who loses his confidence and thus the match. Florence has had enough. She walks out and joins the now defecting Russian. In his new role as champion he defends his title in Bangkok. The Soviets undermine Anatoly by bringing his wife, Svetlana, out to rejoin her husband. Frederick is shocked by what's happening and helps Anatoly to win. Anatoly now decides to help Florence by going back behind the Iron Curtain, to see if Florence's father is still alive and do what he can to reunite father and daughter, at whatever cost to himself.

Note: This is the original London story. It was somewhat altered for Broadway, with Anatoly lured back to Russia in exchange for a CIA agent, and Florence discovering that her father is already dead.

Music and Songs

The music was provided by the male members of a world-famous, middle-of-the-road pop group, ABBA. As a result, the music has a contemporary music feeling absent from Broadway shows of the time. And it had its crop of hits, including the wistful, rueful 'I know him so well' (Florence and Svetlana), the equally touching 'Heaven help my heart' (Florence), 'One night in Bangkok' (Frederick and chorus) and a wonderful national anthem – 'My land' (Anatoly).

Did You Know?

✳ Illness prevented Michael Bennett from directing this show, so Trevor Nunn took over, using scenic elements already established by Bennett.

✳ When Trevor Nunn restaged the show for New York all aspects of the original Michael Bennett concept were dropped. It failed to reach the success it had in London.

✳ Sir Tim Rice has revisited the book and score since the Broadway failure.

The Critics

'Tim Rice's lyrics come as further proof that he is the most wittily stylish rhymer since Noël Coward' – Sheridan Morley

Recommended Recording

Original concept recording (CD) RCA PD70500(2)
Features some members of the original London cast, including Elaine Paige, Murray Head and Tommy Körberg. Barbara Dickson joins Miss Paige for the hit version of 'I know him so well'. One of the best scores of the 1980s given a perfect showcase.

Chicago

LYRICS ✻ Fred Ebb
MUSIC ✻ John Kander
BOOK ✻ Fred Ebb and Bob Fosse, based on the play by Maurine Dallas Watkins

First Performance

New York, 46th Street Theater, 3 June 1975 (898 performances)
London, Cambridge Theatre, 10 April 1979 (603 performances)

Principal Characters

Roxie Hart ✻ A young woman
Amos ✻ Her husband
Velma Kelly ✻ A fellow prisoner
Billy Flynn ✻ A charismatic lawyer
Mary Sunshine ✻ A journalist
Wardress Mama Morton

Original New York Cast

Gwen Verdon, Barney Martin, Chita Rivera, Jerry Orbach,
M. O'Haughey, Mary McCarty

Original London Cast

Antonia Ellis, Don Fellows, Jenny Logan, Ben Cross,
G. Lyons, Hope Jackman

Plot

We're in big, bold, brassy Chicago in the late 1920s. Our heroine, Roxie Hart, has just killed her erstwhile lover, Fred Casely. At her trial Roxie's husband, Amos, is no help at all, revealing that Fred was more than just an acquaintance and not the burglar that Roxie's defence counsel claims. So Roxie ends up in prison with a mixture of criminals and innocent victims, all looked after and wisely counselled by wardress Mama Morton. How will Roxie escape the consequences of her crime? Venal lawyer, Billy Flynn, has the answer. He is able to manipulate local reporter, Mary Sunshine, as well as the rest of the press. Mary has one big surprise of her own (but unless you've guessed her secret already, you'll have to see the show to find out what that is). Billy is successful in his activities. Roxie and her new friend Velma (another inmate) become celebrities, only to be pushed aside by a newer murder that captures the public's attention. So Roxie announces that she's pregnant. She's a girl who thinks on her feet.

Velma is furious that Roxie is always upstaging her while Amos believes the tale of the baby and even claims paternity – not that that matters, as he still isn't noticed. Billy plans to pull out all the punches in his showbusiness-style defence and uses Velma's ideas to aid Roxie. He succeeds in getting her acquitted but her moment of fame is shortlived when a new, more sensational, crime is committed.

There is only one way forward and that is for Roxie and Velma to join up in a sister act – they deserve each other.

Music and Songs

A tuneful, mature, ruthlessly and cynically brilliant Kander and Ebb score, with the old-time vaudeville touch which eschewed sentiment and a love story for that old 'Razzle dazzle' (Billy). Other fine numbers include 'All that jazz' (Velma), 'My own best friend' (Roxy), 'Mr Cellophane' (Amos), 'Nowadays' (Roxie and Velma) and the witty 'Class' (the company).

Did You Know?

✶ This was the longest run in Britain of any Kander and Ebb show to date. Gwen Verdon's last Broadway show enabled her to play a part she'd longed to play ever since seeing the film as a child.

✶ A recent Broadway semi-staged revival has proved to be a greater hit than the original, both in New York and London.

✶ When Gwen Verdon had to take time off for an operation, Liza Minnelli stepped in.

✶ The actor playing the role of Mary Sunshine only uses the initial of their given name.

The Critics

The critics had mixed opinions, of which this is typical:
'It's really an overstaged show, the height of theatrical decadence; everything we're meant to react to is in the staging. It's strange to think of (director) Fosse as the last German Expressionist – strange that his own decadence as an artist should take such a visually corny and alien form' – Arlene Croce

Recommended Recording

Original Broadway cast (CD) Arista 7822-18952
Top-notch performances by Gwen Verdon and Chita Rivera ably assisted by another great Broadway star Jerry Orbach. This has Broadway oozing out of every note and proves that lust and murder are just part of the all-American success story.

Film

TCF, 1942. Starring Ginger Rogers and Adolphe Menjou. Directed by William Wellman. Non-musical version called *Roxie Hart*.

The Chocolate Soldier

LYRICS ✶ Stanislaus Stange
MUSIC ✶ Oscar Straus
BOOK ✶ Stanislaus Stange, based on *Der tapfere Soldat* by Rudolph Bernauer and
Leopold Jacobson, and adapted from George Bernard Shaw's
play *Arms and the Man*

First Performance

New York, Lyric Theatre, 13 September 1909 (296 performances)
London, Lyric Theatre, 10 September 1910 (500 performances)

Principal Characters

Lieutenant Bumerli ✶ A serving officer
Colonel Kasimir Popoff
Nadina Popoff ✶ His daughter
Mascha ✶ A kinswoman
Major Alexius Spiridoff ✶ A pompous hero

Original New York Cast

J.E. Gardner, William Pruette, Ida Brooks Hunt,
Flavia Arcaro, George Tallman

Original London Cast

C.H. Workman, John Dunsmure, Constance Drever,
Amy Augarde, John Cunningham

Plot

It's the 1880s and there's war between the Serbs and the Bulgarians. Colonel
Popoff has a house in Bulgaria. Colonel Popoff's wife, their daughter Nadina and
kinswoman Mascha long for the return of their menfolk. Nadina is engaged to the
dashing Major Alexius Spiridoff. Under gunfire, a man called Bumerli arrives. He
turns out to be a Swiss mercenary, escaped from the Bulgarians and who has run
out of his favourite chocolate drops. Nadina refuses to feed and shelter the enemy
but soon comes to like him. He reveals the truth behind Alexius' so-called heroic
charge (the horse ran away with him). Bumerli is asleep in Nadina's room when
soldiers, accompanied by Mascha, arrive looking for him. Neither gives the hiding
place away. Both girls place photographs of themselves in the pockets of the coat
they give Bumerli to escape in.

Six months later the war is over. Nadina lets Alexius know that she doesn't
believe in all his heroic exploits. Meanwhile, the colonel tells the story of a Swiss
soldier helped to escape by some women – all of whom had fallen in love with
him! Right on cue, Bumerli turns up, ostensibly to return the coat he'd escaped in,
but in reality to see Nadina again. Captain Massakroff also turns up for the
wedding of Nadina and Alexius and recognizes Bumerli as the soldier he was

chasing. The photographs are produced and cause trouble. Bumerli is challenged to a duel by Alexius, but both are relieved when Popoff intervenes and insists Bumerli marries Nadina. All ends happily, for Bumerli turns out to be the son of a rich businessman.

Music and Songs

A melodic score with the most popular songs being 'My hero' (Nadina), 'Sympathy' (Bumerli) and 'The letter song' (Nadina).

Did You Know?

✶ George Bernard Shaw, author of the original play, so regretted having given permission for the adaptation that he refused to let any other work be turned into a musical in his lifetime. He referred to it as 'The Chocolate Cream Soldier'. That's why we had to wait so long for what became *My Fair Lady*.

✶ The show was revived four times on Broadway up to the 1940s, and three times in England.

✶ The original production was given in Vienna in 1908 and it ran for only 60 performances.

Recommended Recording

Ohio Light Opera Company (CD) NPD 85650/2
This double CD set is the first full recording in English and it was recorded 'live' in actual performance. The recording quality is not as good as if it had been recorded in a studio, but the 'in performance' excitement makes up for that.

Film

MGM, 1941. Starring Rise Stevens and Nelson Eddy. Directed by Roy Del Ruth. As so often with MGM, the songs are retained in the context of a stage musical but the outer story is changed. This film is based on a 1931 version of *The Chocolate Soldier* called *The Guardsman*.

A Chorus Line

LYRICS ✳ Edward Kleban
MUSIC ✳ Marvin Hamlisch
BOOK ✳ James Kirkwood and Nicholas Dante, from a concept by Michael Bennett

First Performance

New York, Public Theatre (Newman Theatre), 21 May 1975
Transferred to the Shubert Theater on Broadway
(Shubert Theater run was 6137 performances)
London, Theatre Royal, Drury Lane, 22 July 1976 (903 performances)

Principal Characters

Zach ✳ The director/choreographer
Larry ✳ His assistant
Cassie, Sheila, Val, Diana, Kristine, Maggie, Connie, Mike, Paul, Al
✳ Potential members of a chorus line

Original New York Cast

Robert Lupone, Clive Clerk, Donna McKechnie, Carole Bishop, Pamela Blair,
Priscilla Lopez, Renée Baughman, Kay Cole, Baayork Lee, Wayne Cilento,
Sammy Williams, Don Percassi

Original London Cast

Eivind Harum, T. Michael Reed, Sandy Roveta, Jane Summerhays, Mitzi Hamilton,
Loida Iglesias, Christine Barker, Jean Fraser, Jennifer Ann Lee, Jeff Hyslop,
Tommy Aguilar, Steve Baumann

Plot

We are at an audition for singers and dancers. Zach is the (largely unseen) choreographer who has to choose a group of them for an upcoming show. After a series of tests, he has to eliminate down to a final selection. For this he takes a novel approach. He has seen their ability in song and dance. Now he wants more. Each dancer has to reveal his or her background, and convince Zach of his/her suitability. One of the candidates has found success through plastic surgery, there's a newly married couple and a young boy who was formerly a drag artiste and who, heartbreakingly, twists his ankle in the closing moments and loses the chance of the job. Another is a wisecracking dancer whose best years are behind her. The line also includes a waiter with a family to support, a confident young gay, a young girl who can't summon up false emotion, a youngster with nothing to offer but talent and ambition, an experienced older dancer who has suppressed his ethnic origin . . . and then there's Cassie. Some years before, Cassie and Zach had been together. They broke up when Cassie's ambition drove her to seek stardom in Hollywood or anywhere. It didn't happen. So now Cassie is auditioning for a job in the chorus line, where she started. Zach is yet to be convinced. But she needs the job. Finally, the eight performers are chosen, the rest dismissed. The search for a chorus line is over.

Music and Songs

One of the most evocative of Broadway scores, this one recalls all the showstoppers and all the classic numbers you'd expect in a successful Broadway musical. There are echoes of all the then-current Broadway favourites, from Kander and Ebb to Sondheim, with touches of Styne and Coleman. The songs include 'One' (the company), 'At the ballet' (Sheila), 'I can do that' (Mike) and 'What I did for love' (the company).

Did You Know?

✶ Michael Bennett assembled twenty-four dancers who reminisced about their backgrounds, and about when they auditioned for positions in various chorus lines for Broadway shows. He handed over the tapes to Nicholas Dante, himself a former dancer, to create the storyline for a show based on what they told him.

✶ *A Chorus Line* was the longest-running Broadway show until *Cats*.

✶ The show grossed over $140 million on Broadway.

✶ In tryouts Cassie was not chosen for the lineup but audience reaction was hostile, so the book was changed to allow her to be selected.

The Critics

A brilliantly packaged yet simple tribute to some of the hardest-worked folk in the theatre' – *The Daily Telegraph*
'If I could only keep half a dozen experiences from life and hand back all the rest, *A Chorus Line* would be one of the few keepsakes up for grabs' – *Daily Mail*

Recommended Recording

Original Broadway cast (CD) Sony SK 65282
A collection of song stories put over with the conviction of a highly-trained and involved company. Perhaps this is why there have been so few other recordings of the score.

Film

Embassy Films, 1985. Starring Michael Douglas, Alyson Reed, Cameron English, Greg Burge, Yamil Borges, Vicki Frederick, Charles McGowan and Audrey Landers. Directed by Richard Attenborough.

Chu Chin Chow

LYRICS ✱ Oscar Asche
MUSIC ✱ Frederic Norton
BOOK ✱ Oscar Asche

First Performance

London, His Majesty's Theatre, 1 August 1916 (2235 performances)
New York, Manhattan Opera House, 22 October 1917 (208 performances)

Principal Characters

Abu Hasan ✱ A robber
Zahrat Al-Kulub ✱ A slave
Marjanah ✱ A servant slave
Ali Baba ✱ Father of Nur
Nur Al-Huda ✱ Ali's son
Kasim Baba ✱ A rich trader
Alcolom ✱ Kasim's head wife, in love with Ali
Mahbubah ✱ Ali's wife

Original London Cast

Oscar Asche, Lily Brayton, Violet Essex, Courtice Pounds, J.V. Bryant,
Frank Cochrane, Aileen d'Orme, Sydney Fairbrother

Original New York Cast

Tyrone Power, Florence Reed, Henry E. Dixey, George Rasely, Kate Condon,
Albert Howson, Lucy Beaumont, Tessa Kosta

Plot

Chu Chin Chow is based on the tale of Ali Baba and the Forty Thieves. We're in
the magnificent Eastern palace of Kasim Baba who is welcoming the Chinese
merchant, Chu Chin Chow. In fact the latter is not who he seems, but is the
rascally Abu Hasan, a robber, come to glean information that will enable him to
rob his host. He has a slave, Zahrat, already spying in the palace. She has made
friends with Kasim's chief wife (Alcolom) who, in turn, is loved by Kasim's poor
brother, Ali Baba. Another friend is slave maid Marjanah who loves Ali's son, Nur
Al-Huda. The downfall of Kasim would solve a lot of problems. Marjanah
recognizes Abu Hasan and enlists him in a scheme to get rid of Kasim – she wants
her freedom and Alcolom wants to be with her beloved Ali. In exchange, Abu
Hasan's identity will not be disclosed. Kasim entertains his guest elaborately. Abu
Hasan tries to buy Marjanah as intended, but a drunken Ali Baba offers a fortune
(40,000 gold pieces, which he does not possess) to buy her for his son. The offer is
successful.

Next morning, Ali can't remember anything, but wakes up in a cactus grove
with a hangover. Meanwhile, Marjanah and Nur Al-Huda are preparing to escape

when they overhear Abu Hasan and his men coming out of a concealed rock entrance. When the robber band has left, Marjanah and Nur tell Ali about the concealed cave, its treasure and its password – 'Open O sesame'. Later, the incantation works for the three as well. Now they can acquire enough money to buy Marjanah from Ali. At the sale, Chu Chin Chow believes his identity has been revealed by Zahrat. He proposes to put Zahrat to death. She exposes his real identity and he leaves with her, his robbers and all the bid money.

Ali visits Kasim, his brother, tells him of the cave and brings the promised bid money for Marjanah, who can now wed Nur. The lovers return to the cave, where they discover Zahrat chained up. They can't release her. Kasim is ushered in and goes mad when he sees the treasure. He is captured and caught by Abu Hasan and put to death. Hasan has brought Zahrat's lover along to die with her. Eventually Zahrat is freed, the robbers are killed by boiling oil, and Hasan is stabbed to death. All that remains is for the young lovers to be united, and so are Ali and Alcolom.

Music and Songs

The score is typical of transitional early musical comedy of World War I, post-Gilbert and Sullivan but pre-Kern and Gershwin. Highlights include 'Any time's kissing time' (Alcolom), 'The cobbler's song' (the cobbler), 'The robbers' march' (Abu Hasan) and 'I love thee so' (Marjanah).

Did You Know?

✶ *Chu Chin Chow* was the first modern hit of the British musical theatre; its run lasted longer than World War I and it made a profit of £300,000 on an investment of £5000.

✶ The show remains one of the all-time long-runners of the British stage.

✶ Tyrone Power, star of the American production, was the father of the film star of the same name.

✶ A live camel used in the show fell down a manhole and had to be put to sleep. It was sold to a West End restaurant.

The Critics

'More navel than millinery' – Max Beerbohm
'Beyond all cavil, the thing is an immense success' – *The Times*

Recommended Recording

Studio/original cast (CD) EMI West End Angel 0777 7 89939 2 6
The studio cast recording featuring Inia Te Wiata is the only attempt at recreating the original score and is done professionally. The 'bonus' original cast tracks give a wonderful insight to the charm of the show.

Film

Gaumont British, 1934 . Starring Fritz Kortner, George Robey and Anna May Wong. Directed by Walter Forde.

City of Angels

LYRICS ✳ David Zippel
MUSIC ✳ Cy Coleman
BOOK ✳ Larry Gelbart

First Performance

New York, Virginia Theatre, 11 December 1989 (878 performances)
London, Prince of Wales Theatre, 30 March 1993 (263 performances)

Principal Characters

Stine ✳ Author
Stone ✳ Private eye
Buddy Fidler/Irwin S Irving ✳ Producer/director
Oolie/Donna ✳ Stone's secretary/Stine's secretary
Alaura Kingsley/Carla Haywood ✳ The husband-killing hirer of Stone
Gabby/Bobbi ✳ Stine's wife/Stone's girlfriend
Mallory ✳ Alaura's stepdaughter
Jimmy ✳ A nightclub singer

Original New York Cast

Gregg Edelman, James Naughton, Rene Auberjonois, Randy Graff, Dee Hoty,
Kay McClelland, Rachel York, Scott Waara

Original London Cast

Martin Smith, Roger Allam, Henry Goodman, Haydn Gwynne, Susannah Fellows,
Fiona Hendley, Sarah Jane Hassell, Maurice Clarke

Plot

We are in the world of the 1940s detective movies. Private eye, Stone, is in hospital with a bullet in his shoulder. A week earlier Alaura had come to his office to hire him to find her stepdaughter, Mallory. We are now introduced to Stine, the author, who is writing the screenplay we are witnessing. He, like Stone, adores women and, more than Stone, money. Gabby, his wife, wishes he would go back to writing novels. But back to the screenplay: Stone is in his bungalow listening to the radio when two hoods enter and beat him up. His ex-police partner tries to rouse him; he is a man who holds a grudge as Stone has got away with the murder of the Hollywood producer who took away his singer girlfriend, Bobbi. Angry because of the attack, Stone goes to Alaura and, once again, taken in by her charms (and cash) keeps on the case.

Stone at last finds Mallory – in his bed, naked. Stone does not take advantage of the situation while Stine, with his wife away, has dropped into the bed of Donna, his secretary. But back to the stepdaughter: a photographer has broken in and has taken a compromising photograph. Mallory has run off with Stone's gun that is subsequently used to kill a friend of Alaura's and this, of course, implicates Stone. Stone goes to jail but gets bail and has the two hoods on his tail.

Stine is having problems with his producer, Buddy, who is rewriting his script, and his wife, who has found out about his affair with Donna. He flies off to New York to see her but she does not accept what has happened. Stone, Stine's creation, has found Bobbi in a brothel, and also discovers that it is she who shot the producer. Oolie, Stone's secretary, discovers Alaura is a fortune hunter who has already removed one husband. Stone visits and tells her he knows all about her and, during a tussle for a gun, Alaura dies. Stone is now wounded and we are back to the beginning of the story. In real life Stine is without his wife and a script that has been rewritten: dejected, he gets himself sacked and the alter ego, Stone, rewrites the script. Finally, there is a happy ending with Gabby returning to Stine's side.

Music and Songs

Cy Coleman has come up with another inventive score. Songs which seem to fall out of the forties such as 'Ev'rybody's gotta be somewhere' (Angel City 4 Quartet) and 'Stay with me' (Jimmy Power) alongside point numbers 'I'm nothing without you' (Stine and Stone), 'You're nothing without me' (Stine and Stone) and 'The tennis song' (Stone and Alaura).

Did You Know?

✴ When the show went into the film script all the action was in black and white.

✴ It won best musical awards from the NY Drama Critics Circle, Outer Critics Circle, Drama Desk and Tony. It also won Tonys for James Naughton and Randy Graff and for best book, score and set design.

✴ While the reviews were raves in London an audience could not be found and the show was forced to close.

The Critics

'There's a miracle on Broadway – an American musical, with American jazz rhythms, American wisecracks, an original American script' – *Newsweek*
'The most brilliant of musical comedies' – *New York Daily News*

Recommended Recording

Original Broadway cast (CD) Columbia CK 46067
A recording that warrants many plays. Perfectly cast with Kay McClelland proving to have a powerful voice. The London cast was recorded and is excellent in its own way and does include the talented Martin Smith who died soon after. He played Stine to Roger Allam's Stone. On the Broadway cast CD these are Gregg Edelman and James Naughton.

Company

LYRICS ✳ Stephen Sondheim
MUSIC ✳ Stephen Sondheim
BOOK ✳ George Furth

First Performance

New York, Alvin Theater, 26 April 1970 (705 performances)
London, Her Majesty's Theatre, 8 January 1972 (344 performances)

Principal Characters

Robert ✳ A 35-year-old bachelor
Joanne, Sarah, David, Peter, Jenny, Harry, Susan, Larry
✳ His friends
Paul and Amy ✳ His about-to-be-married friends
April, Marta, Kathy
✳ His girlfriends

Original New York Cast

Dean Jones, Elaine Stritch, Barbara Barrie, George Coe, John Cunningham,
Teri Ralston, Charles Kimbrough, Merle Louise, Charles Braswell, Steve Elmore,
Beth Howland, Susan Browning, Pamela Myers, Donna McKechnie

Original London Cast

Larry Kert, Elaine Stritch, Marti Stevens, Lee Goodman, J.T. Cromwell,
Teri Ralston, Kenneth Kimmins, Joy Franz, Robert Goss, Steve Elmore,
Beth Howland, Carol Richards, Annie McGreevey, Donna McKechnie

Plot

Company has no real plot. It has a situation instead. Robert is a bachelor with five
sets of close friends who are married. Actually, that's not completely true. Paul
and Amy will get married during the course of the show. Otherwise we have
experienced, mature, much-married Joanne and her latest husband, Larry. Sarah
and Harry have, respectively, a food and a drink problem. Sarah is learning karate.
Harry is both sorry and grateful he got married. Susan and Peter seem happily
married. Even after their happy divorce they're planning to stay together . . .

Robert visits Jenny and David, a third married couple, and the three
experiment with marijuana – but to no great effect. We meet three of Robert's
girlfriends – the enchanting April, good friend Kathy about to move to Vermont,
and kooky, streetwise Marta, who diagnoses Robert as a very uptight person. Amy
and Paul are about to get married after a wedding breakfast of warm orange juice
and burnt toast. Amy panics. Robert, as best man, tries to sort it all out. He offers
to marry Amy himself ('and they'll leave us alone'). Wrong. You've got to want to
marry someone – not anyone.

Is Robert any further in his examination of marriage and his quest to sort out his own life? Well, no. He's not needed by his friends – without him they'd carry on with their lives as before. An evening with air stewardess April solves nothing. He argues strongly for her to stay overnight and she does. Finally, an evening with Larry and Joanne. While Larry's off paying the bill, Joanne propositions Robert – she'll look after him. But who will he look after? Robert is on his way at last. A surprise birthday party has been organised for him – but he's not there.

Note: The acclaimed revival in London at the Donmar suggested that the whole of the action is taking place in Robert's mind, and included 'Marry me a little' as the first act finale. This, together with other book changes, is now the accepted version.

Music and Songs

For immediate melody, wit, style and needle-sharp characterisation, Sondheim's score has few equals and no superior. Nearly every song is a classic, including 'Company' (Bobby and company), 'The little things you do together' (Joanne, Sarah and Harry), 'You could drive a person crazy' (Kathy, Marta and April), 'Someone is waiting' (Bobby), 'Another hundred people' (Marta) and 'The ladies who lunch' (Joanne).

Did You Know?

✱ Despite seeming to be anchored in time and place, *Company* has proved to be eminently revivable, on both sides of the Atlantic

✱ The show is based on a series of short playlets by George Furth, who would work with the composer again on *Merrily We Roll Along*.

The Critics

'It is extraordinary that a musical, the most trivial of theatrical forms [sic], should be able to plunge, as *Company* does, with perfect congruity into profound depths of human perplexity and misery' – *The Sunday Times*

Recommended Recording

Original Broadway cast (CD) Sony SK 65283
One of the great original cast recordings. The sessions were recorded and shown on American television and the programme is now available on video in the United States. The London cast recording utilised the Broadway cast recording with Dean Jones's voice replaced by Larry Kert.

A Connecticut Yankee

LYRICS ✶ Lorenz Hart
MUSIC ✶ Richard Rodgers
BOOK ✶ Herbert Fields, based on Mark Twain's novel
A Connecticut Yankee in King Arthur's Court

First Performance

New York, Vanderbilt Theater, 3 November 1927 (418 performances)
London, Daly's Theatre, 10 October 1929 (43 performances)

Principal Characters

Martin ✶ A Connecticut Yankee
Alice Carter ✶ His fiancée (Sandy in Camelot)
Fay Morgan ✶ A temptress
Merlin ✶ A magician
Gerald Lake
Evelyn
Arthur

Original New York Cast

William Gaxton, Constance Carpenter, Nana Bryant, William Norris,
Jack Thompson, June Cochran, Paul Evelyn

Original London Cast

Harry Fox, Constance Carpenter, Nora Robinson, J.G. Taylor,
Billy Holland, Gladys Cruickshank, Sam Livesey

Plot

It is the evening before Martin's wedding in Hartford, Connecticut, when a blow on the head from a champagne bottle delivered by his fiancée Alice (Sandy) sends him back in time to Camelot, the kingdom of King Arthur, where he's taken for an enemy, to be burnt at the stake. Just in time, good old yankee know-how (and remembering and exploiting an eclipse of the sun) wins Martin a prime position at court – as Sir Boss!

He's soon bringing 20th-century refinements to court – telephones, radio, time and motion, advertising and further delights. After outwitting a sorceress and winning his true bride, Martin is returned to the 20th century for a happy ending, where he discovers he is already married. The resourceful Sandy has arranged for a minister to marry them while Martin was repeating 'I do, I do' in his sleep.

Note: The 1943 revival had the cast in uniform in the modern scenes and Martin originally engaged to the wrong girl – Fay – before discovering that Alice was the girl for him. It featured five new songs.

Music and Songs

A lively Rodgers and Hart score, from their classic period, plus the last songs they wrote together for the revival; it includes the beautiful 'My heart stood still' (Martin and Alice), 'Thou swell' (Martin and Alice), 'Can't you do a friend a favor?' (Fay Morgan and Martin) and the deep, deadly humour of 'To keep my love alive' (Fay Morgan) (added 1943).

Did You Know?

✷ The revival contained Hart's last-ever lyric 'To keep my love alive'.

✷ The big hit, 'My heart stood still', had been introduced in a London revue by Jessie Matthews and Richard Dolman and had to be bought in for $5000 for the Broadway show in 1927.

✷ Hart died at the age of 48 three days after the 1943 revival of the show opened. He had generously praised the opening of Rodgers and Hammerstein's *Oklahoma!*

The Critics

The critics were kind:
'A novel amusement in the best of taste' – Brooks Atkinson
'It was Richard Rodgers, with his head full of tunes, who made the most valuable contribution . . . with so many fetching songs' – Alexander Woolcott

---

Recommended Recording

1955 television soundtrack (CD) AEI CD 043
A 'live' television production and it sounds like it. The cast is an interesting one with Boris Karloff as Arthur, Eddie Albert as Martin and Janet Blair as Alice. The songs are all here and it's worth putting up with the little imperfections to hear it.

Films

Fox, 1931. Starring Will Rogers, Maureen O'Sullivan and Myrna Loy. Directed by David Butler.
Paramount, 1949. Starring Bing Crosby, William Bendix and Sir Cedric Hardwicke. Directed by Tay Garnett. This film is based on the same Mark Twain story but has completely different music.

Dames at Sea

Lyrics ✶ Robin Miller and George Haimsohn
Music ✶ Jim Wise
Book ✶ Robin Miller and George Haimsohn

First Performance

New York (Off Broadway), Bouwerie Lane Theatre, 20 December 1968
(575 performances)
London, Duchess Theatre, 27 August 1969 (127 performances)

Principal Characters

Mona Kent ✶ A hardboiled leading lady
Joan ✶ A wisecracking hoofer
Hennessey ✶ A man of all work
Ruby ✶ Our little heroine
Dick ✶ The songwriter
Lucky ✶ His friend
The Captain ✶ (Played by the same actor as Hennessey)

Original New York Cast

Tamara Long, Sally Stark, Steve Elmore, Bernadette Peters,
David Christmas, Joseph R. Sicari

Original London Cast

Joyce Blair, Rita Burton, Kevin Scott, Sheila White,
Blayne Barrington, William Ellis

Plot

Take every Warner Brothers musical cliché then add a few from *Follow the Fleet*, and you've got the plot of *Dames at Sea*. Can innocent, talented little Ruby from Centerville find fame, fortune, a leading role in a musical and a love of her very own in 24 hours? Yes, of course she can! With star Mona Kent's Broadway show washed up before it opens due to lack of finance, isn't it lucky she has an old flame, a Captain of the Fleet, to lend her his ship on which to perform her show with the rest of the cast? With help from new friend Dick, a singer/dancer/ songwriter, his pal, Lucky, and his girl, Joan, it's a cinch for Ruby to take over the lead from Mona when the latter injures her foot.

Music and Songs

Throughout this amusing parody-musical there are plenty of opportunities for accurate send-ups of 1930s films. Highlights include the torch song 'That mister man of mine' (Mona), the exotic 'Singapore Sue' (Ruby) and of course the plaintive 'It's raining in my heart' (Ruby), plus 'It's you' (Dick and Ruby) and 'Dames at sea' (the company).

Did You Know?

✶ The names of the lead characters were chosen in tribute to Warner Brothers stars Ruby Keeler and Dick Powell.

✶ The show was, indirectly, the cause of many young acting hopefuls taking tap lessons.

✶ The star that can't perform because of leg injury is also evident in 42nd Street (one of the films used as the inspiration to the piece) and the film version of The Boy Friend.

The Critics

The critics enjoyed Dames at Sea:
'A real winner, a little gem of a musical . . . it is informed by a genuine love and knowledge for the period' – New York Times
Of Bernadette Peters: 'There is sheer perfection in her performance' – New York Post

Recommended Recording

Original cast (CD) Sony Broadway SK 48214
The young Bernadette Peters can be heard on this charming and amusing memory of one of the great pastiche shows, doing for the thirties what The Boy Friend did for the twenties. The freshness of this recording still stands above the other attempts.

Film

No film version, but the show was televised in 1971 with Ann Miller, Ann-Margret and Dick Shawn among the cast.

Damn Yankees

LYRICS ✶ Jerry Ross and Richard Adler
MUSIC ✶ Richard Adler and Jerry Ross
BOOK ✶ George Abbott and Douglas Wallop,
based on Wallop's novel *The Day The Yankees Lost the Pennant*

First Performance

New York, 46th Street Theater, 5 May 1955 (1019 performances)
London, Coliseum, 28 March 1957 (258 performances)

Principal Characters

Lola ✶ A temptress
Joe Hardy ✶ A baseball star
Mr Applegate ✶ A devil
Van Buren ✶ A manager
Meg Boyd ✶ Joe's wife
Rocky ✶ A baseball player
Gloria ✶ A reporter
Joe Boyd ✶ A baseball fan

Original New York Cast

Gwen Verdon, Stephen Douglass, Ray Walston, Russ Brown, Shannon Bolin,
Jimmy Komack, Rae Allen, Robert Shafer

Original London Cast

Belita, Ivor Emmanuel, Bill Kerr, Donald Stewart, Betty Paul,
Robin Hunter, Judy Bruce, Phil Vickers

Plot

Baseball fan Joe Boyd would sell his soul to the devil for the chance to play
baseball with the Washington Senators. Enter Mr Applegate, a devil in red socks.
Joe can become young Joe Hardy and help his favourite team to success in
exchange for his soul. Joe accepts and leaves home, emerging as the highly
talented and successful Hardy, even taking lodgings in his own home with his
wife, who, naturally, doesn't recognise him.

But Mr Applegate has, in a moment of weakness, allowed Joe an escape clause.
Joe can revert to his own self up to 9 pm on 24 September, the day before the end
of the season, and save his soul. He therefore enlists the help of the ageless Lola to
seduce Joe – but it doesn't work. Despite every trick in the devil's book, Joe helps
his team to win the championship and is changed back into his former elder self,
returning to his wife a wiser and happier man. Mr Applegate is defeated and
returns to Hell.

Music and Songs

A rousing, constantly inventive, richly melodic, rip-roaringly enjoyable score full of good old razzamatazz. What a pity that Jerry Ross died so soon afterwards. Alone, Richard Adler was never to scale the heights again. 'Heart' (the Players) was the big hit, followed by 'Whatever Lola wants' (Lola). 'Two lost souls' (Joe and Lola) and 'Shoeless Joe from Hannibal, Mo' (Gloria and the team) are other numbers from the show.

Did You Know?

✶ The *Faust* legend provided the plot for this, the most successful musical ever based on a sports story.

✶ The role of Lola which made Gwen Verdon a star was turned down by Mitzi Gaynor.

✶ The film version was originally launched in Britain under the title *Whatever Lola Wants*.

✶ Richard Adler and Jerry Ross enjoyed two hit shows in succession – this is the second (*The Pajama Game* was the first) – before Ross died tragically young.

The Critics

'Everything is fluid, everything moves . . . an artfully assembled design' – *Theatre Arts*
'The funniest thing about the show is that it does the toughest things best' – *New York Herald Tribune*
'*Damn Yankees* is a wonderful musical . . . an all-hitter under the lights' – *New York Daily News*

Recommended Recording

Original Broadway cast RCA Victor 3948-2-RG
Again the original cast recording wins out, even though there is a fine 1994 revival recording with Jerry Lewis and a terrific film soundtrack. Gwen Verdon's Lola and Ray Walston's Applegate are two of the great Broadway performances and, for once, they were brought to Hollywood to recreate their roles.

Film

Warner Brothers, 1958. Starring Gwen Verdon, Ray Walston and Tab Hunter. Directed by George Abbott..

The Dancing Years

LYRICS ✶ Christopher Hassall
MUSIC ✶ Ivor Novello
BOOK ✶ Ivor Novello

First Performance

London, Drury Lane Theatre, 23 March 1939 (187 performances)
Transferred to Adelphi Theatre, 14 March 1942 (969 performances)

Principal Characters

Rudi Kleber ✶ A young composer
Maria Ziegler ✶ An operetta star
Grete Schone ✶ A young friend
Cäcilie Kurt ✶ A singing teacher
Franzl ✶ A youngster
Prince Charles Metternich ✶ A noble

Original London Cast

Ivor Novello, Mary Ellis, Roma Beaumont, Olive Gilbert,
Peter Graves, Anthony Nicholls

Plot

It is 1938. Rudi Kleber has been imprisoned by the Nazis for complicity in the escape of Jews from Austria. A visitor to his cell is his former lover, Princess (Maria) Metternich, who arrives with her son, Otto, who does not know he is Rudi's son, too. Her husband, Prince Charles, has interceded to save Rudi's life. The son is, as Maria confirms, no Nazi himself either (this scene was sometimes cut, but was played as the final scene at Drury Lane).

The action moves back to the romantic period before World War I. The impoverished composer, Rudi Kleber, meets and falls in love with the great operetta star, Maria Ziegler, at a village inn. She installs him in a city flat where he is to write a new show for her and discards her former protector, Prince Charles Metternich. Rudi will marry her, but first there's his secret promise to Grete, the innkeeper's niece. A childhood promise meant that he would ask Grete to marry him when she grew up – she had first refusal. Grete returns from England, a successful musical comedy actress; Maria overhears Rudi's proposal and misunderstands – and doesn't even wait to hear Grete turning him down. Maria is already carrying Rudi's child and, in a jealous fit, marries Prince Charles. Much later, Rudi and Maria meet again – at a rendezvous at the inn. Maria brings Rudi's son, Otto. But Rudi cannot bring himself to break up Maria's family by disclosing his parenthood.

Music and Songs

Novello's deeply romantic scores are precursors of Lloyd Webber's music. The immediate appeal of the songs, many of them waltzes, owes much to Lehár, Kern and Johann Strauss, but with a style, sweep and Welsh passion that is Novello's own. *The Dancing Years* contains many enduring songs, including 'Waltz of my heart' (Maria), 'I can give you the starlight' (Maria), 'My dearest dear' (Maria), the musical comedy pastiche 'Primrose' (Grete) and 'Wings of sleep' (Maria and Cäcilie).

Did You Know?

✶ This was the first musical to cover the Nazi invasion of Austria and include references to concentration camps.

✶ This was the fourth successive successful musical by the composer to be mounted at Drury Lane – an unbeaten show record.

✶ The theatre management tried to reduce the Nazi story line but Novello insisted it remained as written.

The Critics

The critics pronounced:
'A most vivid and glamorous entertainment – perhaps the most vivid and glamorous he has ever accomplished' – *Evening Standard*
'And when in the last scene of all, in the captured Vienna of 1938, Mr Novello, now artistically decrepit, defies the conquerors . . . and brings the house down – why this is only to show that Mr Novello is astute enough to make the best of both worlds, the tinkles of 1911 and the tragedies of our own day' – *News Chronicle*
'Ivor Novello certainly has the Drury Lane touch' – *The Daily Telegraph*

Recommended Recording

Ivor Novello – The Classic Shows (CD) EMI Cedar CDP 7943682
Unfortunately there is little available on CD of Novello's shows, but this includes the original cast tracks with other Novello show tracks added, and does give the flavour of the show with some great performances by Roma Beaumont and Mary Ellis.

Film

Associated British Films, 1949. Starring Dennis Price, Patricia Dainton and Gisele Preville. Directed by Harold French.

The Desert Song

LYRICS ✶ Otto Harbach and Oscar Hammerstein
MUSIC ✶ Sigmund Romberg
BOOK ✶ Otto Harbach, Oscar Hammerstein and Frank Mandel

First Performance

New York, Casino Theater, 30 November 1926 (471 performances)
London, Drury Lane Theatre, 7 April 1927 (432 performances)

Principal Characters

Margot Bonvalet ✶ Our heroine
Pierre Birabeau (The Red Shadow) ✶ Son of the governor
Benny Kidd ✶ A newspaper correspondent
Azuri ✶ A dancing girl
Sid El Kar ✶ The Red Shadow's second-in-command
Captain Paul Fontaine ✶ A soldier
Clementina ✶ A Spanish courtesan
Susan ✶ Bennie's secretary

Original New York Cast

Vivienne Segal, Robert Halliday, Eddie Buzzell, Pearl Regay,
William O'Neal, Glen Dale, Margaret Irving, Nellie Breen

Original London Cast

Edith Day, Harry Welchman, Gene Gerrard, Phebe Brune,
Sidney Pointer, Barry Mackay, Maria Minetti, Clarice Hardwicke

Plot

Margot is increasingly frustrated by the unexplained absences of her studious, if foolish, friend Pierre, son of the governor of Morocco. She does not know that Pierre is also the Red Shadow, leader of the Riffs. Captain Fontaine, who is in love with Margot, has promised to bring the Red Shadow's head as a wedding gift. Benny Kidd is a war correspondent subsequently captured by the rebels. His life is spared by the Red Shadow, at the cost of spying for the Riffs at the French camp. Meanwhile, Captain Fontaine rides into the Riffs' camp when the band are out marauding. Azuri, a dancing girl, who is there, was formerly a lover of Captain Fontaine; she will do anything rather than let him marry Margot. She goes to Government House and offers to reveal the identity of the Red Shadow to Fontaine, if he forgets Margot. Her offer is rejected, and the wedding of Paul and Margot is arranged. However, the Riffs invade the house, and the Red Shadow sweeps Margot off her feet, kidnapping her and taking her to the Palace of Ali ben Ali.

The Red Shadow woos Margot, his captive – but she says her heart is Pierre Birabeau's. When Pierre appears as himself, Margot says she named him as her lover just to evade the Shadow's advances. The Governor now appears at the head of the troops and offers to fight the Red Shadow to free Margot. The Shadow refuses to fight him (his real father) and, as a result, is exiled to die in the desert. Benny escapes and Azuri turns up to tell the Governor that the Red Shadow is his son, whom Captain Fontaine is hunting down, as ordered by the Governor himself. Pierre, meanwhile, has escaped death and returns to his father dressed as the Red Shadow, whom he claims to have killed. His father now knows the truth, but the Red Shadow makes one final appearance to Margot, before claiming her for himself as Pierre.

Music and Songs

The apogee of romantic American musical comedy of the 1920s. A tuneful, often rousing, passionate Romberg score combining the best of the European tradition with the dynamic of American shows. The hits included 'Romance' (Margot), 'The desert song' (Red Shadow and Margot) and 'One alone' (Red Shadow).

Did You Know?

✳ The Riff uprising in Morocco of 1925/6 inspired the plot of *The Desert Song* (as did the adventures of Lawrence of Arabia).

✳ Such was the enduring popularity of the show that it was revived in London in 1931, 1936, 1939, 1943 and 1967.

✳ The original chorus lineup included Marjorie Robertson (better known later as Dame Anna Neagle).

The Critics

'The lyrics give indication that W.S. Gilbert had lived and died in vain' – *New York Herald Tribune*

Recommended Recording

Original London cast (CD) Pearl GEMM CD 9100
This is taken from 78s and the transfers are not as good as those found on the EMI issues, but it does make available all the tracks recorded by the original fine cast and there are also tracks from *The New Moon* and *Blue Train*. Edith Day and Harry Welchman are in fine form.

Films

Warner Brothers, 1929. Starring John Boles and Carlotta King and Myrna Loy. Directed by Roy Del Ruth.
Warner Brothers, 1943. Starring Dennis Morgan and Irene Manning. Directed by Robert Florey.
Warner Brothers, 1953. Starring Kathryn Grayson and Gordon MacRae. Directed by Bruce Humberstone.

Destry Rides Again

Lyrics ✳ Harold Rome
Music ✳ Harold Rome
Book ✳ Leonard Gershe, based on the story by Max Brandt

First Performance

New York, Imperial Theater, 23 April 1959 (472 performances)
London, Donmar Warehouse, 30 September 1982 (40 performances)

Principal Characters

Tom Destry ✳ The new deputy
Frenchy ✳ A saloon singer
Wash ✳ The town drunk, now sheriff
Mayor Slade
Kent ✳ A gambler
Clara

Original New York Cast

Andy Griffith, Dolores Gray, Jack Prince, Don McHenry,
Scott Brady, Rosetta Le Noire

Original London Cast

Alfred Molina, Jill Gascoine, Barrie Houghton, George Irving,
Ram John Holder, Nicola Blackman

Plot

Way out West in Bottleneck, there's a distinct lack of law and order. Gambler Kent runs the town from the Last Chance Saloon with his gang, helped by Frenchy and her saloon girls. Kent arranges for the sheriff, Keogh, to be killed over a land battle, and appoints the town drunk, Wash, in his place. The latter reforms and sends for the son of his old friend and sidekick, Thomas Destry. He'll help clean up this town. First impressions, however, are not too favourable – young Destry is shy and polite, and he doesn't carry a gun.

Still, he's persistent and intent on investigating Keogh's death. Perhaps Frenchy can delay him? Kent orders her to have a go. She doesn't succeed and finds herself falling for Destry despite herself. Destry is beginning to suspect Kent's hand in the murder, but refuses to use guns to force a showdown. Instead he tricks him into revealing the whereabouts of Keogh's body. Wash can now put the killer, Gyp Watson, in jail. A trial is to be held in the saloon, which will be a mockery of justice. Destry, feeling betrayed, puts on his father's guns and shows himself to be a virtuoso, before riding off to get Federal supervision for the trial. Meanwhile, Kent engineers Gyp's escape, during which Wash is killed. Destry returns and resolves to use his guns at last. In the ensuing battle the villains are killed but Destry's life is saved by Frenchy. Bottleneck is now a gunless town that wants law and order. And Frenchy and Destry are united.

Music and Songs

This was the first ever truly Western musical and the composer/lyricist rose to the occasion with a boisterous rip-roaring Country and Western-flavoured score. A bagful of strongly rhythmic, tuneful songs from Rome include 'Hoop de dingle' (townsfolk), 'Anyone would love you' (Frenchy and Destry), 'Once knew a fella' (Destry) and 'I say hello' (Frenchy).

Did You Know?

✷ In the original film with Marlene Dietrich and James Stewart, it is Frenchy who is killed in the crossfire at the end – unlike the stage musical.

✷ This was a second Western role for Dolores Gray. She had scored a notable personal success in the London run of *Annie Get Your Gun*, a run which was longer than Broadway's.

The Critics

The critics enjoyed *Destry Rides Again*:
'Destry is a rip-roaring rouser . . . A triumphant premiere for an exciting landmark in horse opera' – *New York Mirror*
'Yippee!' (the entire review) – *New York Daily News*
'It is faithful to the spirit and very nearly the letter of its source, and the songs and dances that have been added are right in the mood of the great American legend of the noble sheriff, the dastardly villain and the fancy lady with the heart of gold' – *Boston Herald*

Recommended Recording

Original New York cast (CD) Decca MCAD 11573
The performances of Dolores Gray and Andy Griffith make this the chosen one. There is an alternative, the scaled-down London version (**TER CDTER 1034**), but there is only one Dolores Gray.

Film

Universal, 1939. Starring James Stewart and Marlene Dietrich. Directed by George Marshall.

Do Re Mi

LYRICS ✳ Betty Comden and Adolph Green
MUSIC ✳ Jule Styne
BOOK ✳ Garson Kanin

First Performance

New York, St. James' Theater, 26 December 1960 (400 performances)
London, Prince of Wales Theatre, 12 October 1961 (169 performances)

Principal Characters

Hubie Cram ✳ A small-time operator
Kay Cram ✳ His wife
Tilda Mullen ✳ A waitress who sings
John Henry Wheeler ✳ Number One in the record and jukebox game

Original New York Cast

Phil Silvers, Nancy Walker, Nancy Dussault, John Reardon

Original London Cast

Max Bygraves, Maggie Fitzgibbon, Jan Waters, Steve Arlen

Plot

Hubie Cram is fed up with being one of life's all-time losers. Why can't he succeed like jukebox king John Henry Wheeler? Last night Hubie was thrown out of the Casacabana Club while John Henry was listening to one of his groups – and all because he moved his own table up to ringside! Hubie rounds up some of his old slot machine hoodlum friends. They'll start a new jukebox empire of their own. John Henry loses no sleep over this as they're bound to fail and they do. Hubie has another scheme. The waitress at the pancake parlour, Tilda, is surely a singing star in the making. For once Hubie is right. She opens at the Imperial Room – and meets John Henry. It's love.

Hubie's colleagues feel they're being elbowed out and robbed of their share in Tilda's success. They react in the violent, primitive way they've always done. Meanwhile, despite Kay's best efforts to break up Tilda and John's relationship, they go on to marry. Hubie's collection of former gangsters make a violent war of the jukeboxes and Hubie and Kay's marriage is also destroyed. At a Washington investigation of the violence, his former associates finger Hubie as the cause of the jukebox trouble. Hubie is delighted – fame at last! It doesn't last, of course, and the old Hubie is back as the failure he was before. Happily, Kay comes back and Hubie realises that life with her is the one big break he'd been looking for.

Music and Songs

Jule Styne, quintessential Broadway composer that he is, wrote this musical score in the middle of his career. It has a good, but not vintage, set of songs, full of Broadway confidence, including the hit 'Make someone happy' (John). Other memorable numbers include 'Cry like the wind' (Tilda), 'The late, late show' (Hubie) and 'All of my life' (Hubie).

Did You Know?

✶ The song 'Make someone happy' became Jerry Lewis' signature tune, after being a hit for Perry Como.

✶ Vaudevillian Phil Silvers went on to find TV fame as Sergeant Bilko.

✶ It was Max Bygraves's only musical, although he starred many times in the West End in large variety-style revues.

The Critics

The critics were happy:
'It's fun, loud fun, fast fun, old-fashioned fun, inconsequential fun, great fun' – *New York Herald Tribune*
Others lauded it as 'a great big razzle-dazzle of a musical' and 'a breezy and bountiful blockbuster'.

Recommended Recording

Original Broadway cast (CD) RCA Victor 09026-61994-2
Phil Silvers in great form and the wonderful Nancy Walker perfection in her support. A recent concert version was recorded but is disappointing when compared with the original.

Dreamgirls

LYRICS ✶ Tom Eyen
MUSIC ✶ Henry Krieger
BOOK ✶ Tom Eyen

First Performance

New York, Imperial Theater, 20 December 1981 (522 performances)

Principal Characters

Effie White, Deena Jones, Lorrell Robinson
✶ The Dreamgirls
Curtis Taylor Jnr ✶ An agent
James Thunder Early ✶ A singer
Michelle Morris ✶ A replacement singer

Original New York Cast

Jennifer Holliday, Sheryl Lee Ralph, Loretta Devine, Ben Harney,
Cleavant Derricks, Deborah Burrell

Plot

Three young singers from Chicago, Effie, Deena and Lorrell, join together to form a singing trio, the Dreams. Although a talent contest at the Apollo in New York brings no immediate success, it does bring them a livewire agent, Curtis, who teams them with a popular star, James Thunder Early. Curtis makes a play for Effie and they have a romance. Later on, the girls are promoted as a group, but Effie is not considered glamorous enough to be the lead. Deena gets the job. Effie rebels, but she's too late. The Dreams are on their way – without her.

The glamorous Michelle replaces Effie in the lineup, but the group has its problems. James Early is in love with Lorrell, but sees no reason to leave his wife for her. Deena envisages the chance of Hollywood stardom for herself. Meanwhile, Effie is making a career as a solo artiste. Curtis intends to spoil this with a cover version of her potential hit by The Dreams. He's thwarted and, instead, The Dreams come together at a farewell performance, with Effie as guest star, before each pursues her own individual career.

Music and Songs

Henry Krieger produced a pop score, comfortably arranged so as not to frighten seasoned Broadway theatregoers. It has been described as Motown and water, but that is unkind. There is genuine drama and fine melody here. 'And I am telling you I'm not going' (Effie) was the big hit, placed for high drama immediately before the end of the first act. Also effective are 'One night only' (Effie's comeback song) and 'Cadillac car' (The Dreams).

Did You Know?

✶ When *Dreamgirls* opened on Broadway it was described as 'a seismic jolt', and indeed its achievement was to link the popular music of America with what was recognised as the Broadway idiom. Not much dialogue, as such, was used, but there was a great deal of recitative (speaking with music).

✶ Although the show was widely believed to be a fictional representation of the trials and tribulations of the Motown group, The Supremes, the creators point to Etta James as a model for the heroine and to many other groups as inspiration for the show.

✶ Jennifer Holliday has gone on to personal fame and success – just as her theatrical counterpart did.

✶ The show won six Tony awards for the original Broadway production.

The Critics

'*Dreamgirls* may just be showbusiness, but it seems destined to be the musical of the 1980s' – Kevin Kelly, drama critic of *The Boston Globe*

Recommended Recording

Original Broadway cast (CD) Geffen 2007-2
The only recording of this show and it does not use the theatre orchestrations. Not surprisingly, the album sounds more like a pop concert and thus loses the atmosphere of the show on stage.

Dubarry was a Lady

LYRICS ✳ Cole Porter
MUSIC ✳ Cole Porter
BOOK ✳ Herbert Fields and B.G. DeSylva

First Performance

New York, 46th Street Theater, 6 December 1939 (408 performances)
London, His Majesty's Theatre, 22 October 1942 (178 performances)

Principal Characters

Louis Blore ✳ A lavatory attendant at the Club Petite
May Daly ✳ A singer
Alice Barton ✳ A singer/dancer
Charley ✳ Louis' potential successor
Alex Barton ✳ Louis' rival for May's hand
Harry Norton ✳ A singer/dancer

Original New York Cast

Bert Lahr, Ethel Merman, Betty Grable, Benny Baker,
Ronald Graham, Charles Walters

Original London Cast

Arthur Riscoe, Frances Day, Frances Marsden, Jackie Hunter,
Bruce Trent, Teddy Beaumont

Plot

Louis Blore is a rest room attendant at the Club Petite in New York. He wins $75,000 in the Irish sweepstake, and buys the club. Perhaps May, the singing star, will look favourably on him now? But she's also being pursued by Alex Barton. In desperation, Louis tries to doctor Alex's drink with a mickey finn – but by mistake drinks it himself. Louis is transported back to the time of Louis XV at the Petit Trianon in Paris. Louis takes his 20th-century manners and language with him, which jar on the polite diplomacy of the court. As King Louis, he pursues Madame Dubarry, who looks just like May. Alex is, meanwhile, a poet at the court who has written a song that's highly critical of May/Dubarry, and which all Paris is singing. He admits that he has loved Dubarry since he saw her in her carriage some time before. At the party to celebrate the opening of Le Petit Trianon, Alex is captured and Louis threatens him with execution. May/Dubarry, who has eluded Louis' advances while slyly accepting the gift of the odd chateau along the way, almost convinces the king that the song has been misinterpreted and that it is complimentary. Alex refuses May's protection and escapes through a window.

Alex returns to see Dubarry and is recaptured. To save him May/Dubarry agrees to admit Louis to her bed. Unfortunately the idiotic dauphin's arrow hits the king's bottom, incapacitating him. (The dauphin looks just like his assistant, Charley.) May refuses to extend her deadline – she's only his until midnight! A doctor from Paris

comes to extricate the arrow. In agony, Louis blacks out and returns to 1939.
It's now time for the epilogue which begins with May's clarion rendering of 'Katie went to Haiti'. Louis realises the hopelessness of his quest, and offers to lend Alex $10,000 of his sweepstake money to pay for his divorce and to marry May. The tax authorities will take the rest – so it's back to his job as lavatory attendant at the Club Petite for Louis Blore.

Music and Songs

This is a quintessential witty, catchy Porter score whose hits were 'Do I love you?' (May) and 'Friendship' (May and Louis). Others included 'It ain't etiquette' (May and Louis), 'But in the morning, No' (May and Louis), 'Well did you evah?' (Alice and Harry) and 'Katie went to Haiti' (May).

Did You Know?

✱ 'Well did you evah?' was revised for inclusion in the postwar film *High Society*.

✱ This is the Broadway show that catapulted Betty Grable (the second lead) towards her second and much more successful try at a Hollywood career as 20th Century Fox's supreme blonde singer/dancer of the 1940s.

✱ Betty Grable's dancing and singing partner, Charles Walters, became a distinguished film director in his own right, often working with Astaire and others on film musicals.

The Critics

'A rowdy, boisterous, high-spirited extravaganza which stops at just this side of nothing' – *New York Post*
Of Lahr's performance, Richard Watts wrote, 'He plays with the sort of spluttering, indignant violence and leering impudence that makes him one of the best comedians in the world.'

Recommended Recording

Ethel Merman compilation (CD) EMI CDAX 701561
There is no full recording of the show to date but 'Do I love you?' and 'Friendship' appear on this CD with songs from many of her other shows, such as *Girl Crazy, Anything Goes* and *Red, Hot and Blue*.

Film

MGM, 1943. Starring Lucille Ball, Gene Kelly and Red Skelton. Directed by Roy Del Ruth.

Evita

LYRICS ✶ Tim Rice
MUSIC ✶ Andrew Lloyd Webber
BOOK ✶ Tim Rice

First Performance

London, Prince Edward Theatre, 21 June 1978 (2900 performances)
New York, Broadway Theater, 25 September 1979 (1568 performances)

Principal Characters

Eva Duarte ✶ An actress with ambitions
Augustin Magaldi ✶ A performer
Juan Peron ✶ A politician
Mistress
Che

Original London Cast

Elaine Paige, Mark Ryan, Joss Ackland, Siobhan McCarthy, David Essex

Original New York Cast

Patti LuPone, Mark Syers, Bob Gunton, Jan Ohringer, Mandy Patinkin

Plot

This is the story of ambitious, charismatic Eva Duarte. The show opens in a Buenos Aires cinema, where the death of Evita is announced on 26 July 1952. At the funeral we meet the narrator, Che, who puts the case for the prosecution, mocking both the poor, deluded public and Eva herself as woman and politician. We move back in time to when Eva was 15 and hitching her star to that of the small-time tango singer, Magaldi. In the big city Eva moves upwards as an actress, notably on radio. When she meets the politician, Juan Peron, she enslaves him, eliminating his 16-year-old mistress, whom she replaces. As the new woman behind Peron, Eva pushes him towards supreme power.

In 1946 Peron becomes President of Argentina; Eva is now his wife. She is also his propaganda mouthpiece with the people, offering them a vision of the future that involves robbing the rich to pay the poor. By the age of 26, Eva is a folk heroine in her own right, a St Joan for Argentina. But that is not enough. She wants to be a figure on the world stage – hence the Rainbow Tour to Europe. Spain greets her but she is snubbed elsewhere, and she returns to Argentina to create the Eva Peron Foundation. This is very successful but Eva is not well. She insists on the position of Vice President but Peron cannot give it to her for political reasons. So she goes on the radio to turn the position down, even though it was never offered to her. She dies, hoping to be remembered by those who will succeed her.

Music and Songs

As with *Jesus Christ Superstar*, *Evita* was a bestselling record album before it was ever staged. The richly romantic music and witty lyrics ushered in a new age of musical theatre, not only influenced by Kern, Novello and Gershwin, but also by the English choral and classical tradition. There was also an underlying rhythm that came from contemporary pop – unlike most Broadway shows of the time. 'Don't cry for me Argentina' (Evita) was an instant hit, followed by 'Another suitcase in another hall' (Mistress and Evita). Other songs include 'Oh what a circus' (Che) and 'On this night of a thousand stars' (Magaldi).

Did You Know?

✶ *Evita* was one of the earliest of a tidal wave of British successes that would repeat their hit status throughout the world.

✶ *Evita* came after a rare Andrew Lloyd Webber flop, the show *Jeeves*.

✶ It was the last collaboration of Lloyd Webber and Tim Rice.

✶ The new song 'You must love me', written for the film version, won an Oscar.

The Critics

The critics were not as kind as the public:
'Though the Rice/Webber score sounds as if Max Steiner had arranged it for Carmen Miranda, there are waltzes and threatening polkas to keep us alert' – *New York Times*
'One of the most disagreeable evenings I have ever spent in my life, in or out of the theatre' – *The Times*

Recommended Recording

Original London cast (CD) MCA DMCG 3527
A remarkable tour de force by a remarkable cast. The concept album is also a wonderful recording with Julie Covington as Evita. She is excellent but cannot compare with the definitive Evita, Miss Elaine Paige.

Film

Warner Brothers, 1996. Starring Madonna, Jonathan Pryce and Antonio Banderas. Directed by Alan Parker.

Fanny

LYRICS ✷ Harold Rome
MUSIC ✷ Harold Rome
BOOK ✷ S N Behrman and Joshua Logan,
based on Marcel Pagnol's trilogy

First Performance

New York, Majestic Theatre, 4 November 1954 (888 performances)
London, Theatre Royal Drury Lane, 15 November 1956 (347 performances)

Principal Characters

Cesar ✷ Waterside café proprietor
Panisse ✷ A widower sail-maker
Fanny ✷ Honorine's daughter
Marius ✷ Cesar's son
Honorine ✷ Fish stall proprietor

Original New York Cast

Ezio Pinza, Walter Slezak, Florence Henderson, William Tabbert, Edna Preston

Original London Cast

Ian Wallace, Robert Morley, Janet Pavek, Kevin Scott, Mona Washbourne

Plot

Cesar runs a little café on the Marseilles waterfront. Fanny, Honorine's daughter, is in love with Cesar's son Marius and he with her – only he longs to see the world and signs a five-year contract on a ship. What he does not know is that Fanny is pregnant by him. He leaves and Panisse enters. Panisse has always loved Fanny; he is rich but is also middle-aged and has a weak heart. Honorine, however, sees him as the answer to her daughter's predicament; it would give the child a father and her daughter security. Fanny gives birth to a boy and he is named Cesario. Panisse and Fanny marry and on their wedding day Marius returns, claiming the child is his. However, Cesar sends him away, saying he is not up to fatherhood.

A few years go by and Marius returns once more. While he waits for a ship to take him to America he works in a garage. His son visits him and, not surprisingly, the lad wants to go to sea and wants to join Marius on his trip. Marius refuses and sails away on his own. On his deathbed Panisse writes to Cesar suggesting Marius marry Fanny, which he does, thus bringing together the younger loves and giving Cesario a new father.

Music and Songs

Harold Rome's score has a great deal of charm. Cherish 'Love is a very light thing' (Cesar), 'Why be afraid to dance' (Cesar), 'Fanny' (Marius) and 'Restless heart' (Marius).

Did You Know?

✱ Alexander Korda made a classic film trilogy of the stories in the 1930s, with a screenplay by the author.

✱ Walter Slezak won the outstanding musical actor Tony award for his performance.

✱ The producer, David Merrick, worked with many librettists on the project before asking Joshua Logan to assist. Logan brought Harold Rome as lyricist and composer as they had just finished working on *Wish You Were Here* together.

The Critics

'Audiences may go to Drury Lane to see a big musical; they will come away somewhat disappointed with the musical but quite charmed with the story that will not let itself be smothered. The music and dances are pleasantly old-fashioned in their tunefulness and leisurely rhythm' – *The Times*

'The principal players, Ian Wallace in a beard and Robert Morley in a beret, are so resolutely, unmistakably British. They reek of toothpaste. The have no garlic on their breath' – *Observer*

'It landed in London last night like a wet sack of sand' – *Daily Express*

Recommended Recording

Original Broadway cast (CD) RCA Victor 09026-68074-2
The only available recording, and none the worse for that. This is in glorious mono and it has been re-mastered beautifully. Ezio Pinza, following his Broadway debut in *South Pacific*, and Walter Slezak are at ease with the score, and the younger William Tabbert sings the title song wonderfully.

Film

Warner Bros, 1960. Starring Leslie Caron, Maurice Chevalier and Charles Boyer. It has no songs.

The Fantasticks

LYRICS ✶ Tom Jones
MUSIC ✶ Harvey Schmidt
BOOK ✶ Tom Jones, based on Edmund Rostand's play *Les Romanesques*

First Performance

New York (Off-Broadway), Sullivan Street Playhouse, 3 May 1960 (still running)
London, Apollo Theatre, 7 September 1961 (44 performances)

Principal Characters

El Gallo ✶ A professional abductor
Matt Hucklebee ✶ A boy
Luisa Bellamy ✶ A girl to whom he's attracted
Hucklebee ✶ Matt's father
Amos Babcock Bellamy ✶ Luisa's father
Henry Albertson ✶ An actor
Mortimer ✶ Another actor

Original New York Cast

Jerry Orbach, Kenneth Nelson, Rita Gardner, William Larsen,
Hugh Thomas, Thomas Bruce, George Curley

Original London Cast

Terence Cooper, Peter Gilmore, Stephanie Voss, Michael Barrington,
Timothy Bateson, John Wood, John Caton

Plot

A boy and a girl fall in love. Their respective fathers have built a wall between their adjoining properties to make their courtship that bit harder, and therefore more worthwhile in the end. In fact the parents, who seem to be sworn enemies, are plotting to ensure a happy outcome – there's nothing like forbidding children to do something to ensure they do exactly the opposite.

El Gallo, a visiting showman, organizes a fake abduction and the boy rescues the girl. All ends satisfactorily – or does it? The wall is pulled down, but when the bill for the abduction arrives, the lovers realise they've been tricked by their parents. The wall is rebuilt and the boy goes out into the real world of pain and heartache. Meanwhile, the girl has fallen for the ersatz charms of El Gallo, the bandit, himself. The latter has no desire for a long-term relationship and abandons her as the boy returns, less optimistic, more realistic and physically bruised by the outside world. Now Matt and Luisa are ready for a mature relationship. The fathers propose to dismantle the wall again. El Gallo advises against it – there should always be a wall.

Music and Songs

Jones and Schmidt hit the bullseye with their first show, a charming mixture of folk-like melody and artlessly simplistic ballads, spiced with up-tempo plot advancers. The hit song is 'Try to remember' (El Gallo), and others include 'Much more' (Luisa) and 'Soon it's gonna rain' (Luisa and Matt).

Did You Know?

✶ Some of the critics recognized what they were seeing – what would prove to be the longest-running musical attraction in our lifetime.

✶ Kenneth Nelson and Jerry Orbach of the original cast went on to further success in London and on Broadway respectively.

✶ The theatre where the show is playing in New York seats only 149.

✶ Like many off-Broadway hits it did not find success in London the first time it played, but since then it has been seen many times with a major revival playing the Regent's Park Open Air Theatre in London in 1990.

The Critics

'While the virtues it possesses are modest and less than exhilarating, it has freshness, youthful charm and imagination' – Richard Watts Jnr
'One of the happiest off-Broadway events in a season that has been happier off-Broadway than on' – *Saturday Review*

Recommended Recording

Original Off-Broadway cast (CD) TER CDTER 1099
With charm its greatest winning factor, this recording is the one to savour. Tom Jones, the book writer and lyricist, plays in a recording of a Japanese tour with the composer, Harvey Schmidt, at the piano which makes the recording of special interest. But, if you are only going for one, the original wins hands down.

Film

MGM/United Artists, 1996/7. Starring Jonathon Morris and Joel Gray. Directed by Michael Ritchie.

Fiddler on the Roof

LYRICS ✳ Sheldon Harnick
MUSIC ✳ Jerry Bock
BOOK ✳ Joseph Stein, based on stories by Sholom Aleichem,
including *Tevye's Daughters*

First Performance

New York, Imperial Theater, 22 September 1964 (3242 performances)
London, Her Majesty's Theatre, 16 February 1967 (2030 performances)

Principal Characters

Tevye ✳ A milkman
Golde ✳ His wife
Yente ✳ A matchmaker
Tzeitel ✳ Tevye's eldest daughter
Motel ✳ A tailor
Perchik ✳ A student
Hodel ✳ Tevye's second daughter
Lazar Wolf ✳ A rich merchant
Chava ✳ Tevye's youngest daughter

Original New York Cast

Zero Mostel, Maria Karnilova, Beatrice Arthur, Joanna Merlin, Austin Pendleton, Bert Convy, Julia Migenes, Michael Granger, Tanya Everett

Original London Cast

Topol, Miriam Karlin, Cynthia Grenville, Rosemary Nicols, Jonathan Lynn, Sandor Eles, Linda Gardner, Paul Whitsun-Jones, Caryl Little

Plot

In 1905, during the last years of Tsarist rule, the Russian village of Anatevka has a substantial Jewish population. Tevye is the local milkman and ekes out a living. He also strives to keep up the traditions of his race and culture. He has three daughters – making a good match for them is a constant worry. His eldest daughter, Tzeitel, rejects the rich butcher to whom Tevye has promised her. She has her heart set on a poor tailor, Motel. After Motel has asked for Tzeitel's hand, Tevye tells his wife, Golde, of a nightmare in which the butcher's deceased wife swore she would never let Tzeitel supplant her in her husband's bed.

Ominously, there's an anti-Jewish demonstration, orchestrated by the local chief of police – a portent of things to come. As the events obtrude, Perchik must return to Kiev. Hodel considers herself engaged to him. Her father refuses his permission, but to no avail. Perchik doesn't want permission, only Tevye's blessing. Later, Perchik is arrested and is to be deported to Siberia. Hodel will join him in exile. She promises to be properly married in traditional fashion as she bids her father farewell at a lonely railway halt.

What of Chava, the third daughter? She marries a Russian, Fyedka, who is not a Jew. This is something Tevye cannot accept – henceforth he has but two daughters. Meanwhile, Anatevka is itself under threat. Throughout Russia, Jews are being forced out of their villages and compelled to emigrate. Tevye and his wife will go to relatives in America. Motel and Tzeitel will join them. Chava and Fyedka can no longer live in Russia – they'll move to Poland. And the Fiddler on the Roof, the indomitable spirit of the Jewish people, will live on in all of them.

Music and Songs

An incredibly evocative tapestry of Jewish traditional music – perhaps Bock and Harnick's greatest achievement. Songs include 'If I were a rich man' (Tevye), 'Sunrise, sunset' (the company), 'Tradition' (Tevye), 'Matchmaker' (the daughters) and 'Anatevka' (the villagers).

Did You Know?

✶ Topol first appeared in an Israeli version of the show, then in London, then got the film part. He has since repeated his performance on stage throughout the world.

✶ *Fiddler on the Roof* won nine Tony Awards and went on to win awards around the world and in Hollywood.

✶ Beatrice Arthur, who became a television star in *The Golden Girls*, played Golde, Tevye's wife, on Broadway.

✶ Others who played in the original Broadway run include Julia Migenes and Bette Midler.

The Critics

Critical reaction was one of approval:
'A cinch to satisfy almost anyone who enjoys the musical theatre' – *Variety*
'An integrated achievement of uncommon quality' – *New York Times*

Recommended Recording

Original Broadway cast (CD) RCA Red Seal RCD1-7060
Zero Mostel created the role and is unsurpassed, even if Topol is now associated with the part because of the film and the many productions he has starred in. But all the performances are perfection.

Film

United Artists, 1971. Starring Topol, Norma Crane, Molly Picon, Rosalind Harris and Leonard Frey. Directed by Norman Jewison.

Finian's Rainbow

LYRICS ✳ E.Y. Harburg
MUSIC ✳ Burton Lane
BOOK ✳ E.Y. Harburg and Fred Saidy

First Performance

New York, 46th Street Theater, 10 January 1947 (725 performances)
London, Palace Theatre, 21 October 1947 (55 performances)

Principal Characters

Sharon McLonergan ✳ An Irish colleen
Finian McLonergan ✳ Her father
Woody Mahoney ✳ A sharecropper
Og ✳ A leprechaun
Susan Mahoney ✳ Woody's deaf-mute sister
Senator Billboard Rawkins ✳ A bigot

Original New York Cast

Ella Logan, Albert Sharpe, Donald Richards, David Wayne,
Anita Alvarez, Robert Pitkin

Original London Cast

Beryl Seton, Patrick J. Kelly, Alan Gilbert, Alfie Bass,
Beryl Kaye, Frank Royde

Plot

Rainbow Valley is in the mythical Southern state of Missituckey. Finian McLonergan has stolen a crock of gold from Og, a leprechaun, and brought it from Ireland to bury it in the fertile soil of Rainbow Valley where he thinks it will multiply, like a potato crop. This is because he had heard that the United States stored its gold in the ground at Fort Knox, and he believed it was this that made the country prosperous. He buys land from Woody and buries the gold. The gold has magical properties – it can fulfil three wishes. The first is quickly used when the bigoted, land-grabbing Southern senator, who has heard there is gold on the land, is transformed into a black man to teach him a lesson.

Meanwhile, Og, the leprechaun, has also come to America to rescue his gold, and has fallen in love with the dancer, Susan, who is deaf and dumb. But unless he becomes human, he has no chance of any real relationship. The second wish is used to restore Susan's speech and hearing. The third wish ensures Woody and Susan's happiness – he with Finian's daughter Sharon, and Susan with Og, the latter now completely human.

Music and Songs

Burton Lane never wrote finer music than this, and with Harburg's witty, politically alive lyrics, the result was a triumph – one of the greatest of all Broadway scores with a strong Irish tinge, and with echoes of the deep South. Hit songs include 'How are things in Glocca Morra?' (Sharon), 'If this isn't love' (Sharon and Woody), 'Look to the rainbow' (Sharon), 'Old devil moon' (Woody) and 'When I'm not near the girl I love' (Og).

Did You Know?

✳ Neither the London production, nor the film made 20 years later, were successful. The latter couldn't decide if it was romantic story or biting satire, and settled for neither. Audiences stayed away from both.

✳ E.Y.(Yip) Harburg was a man with strong political beliefs, and in the shows he wrote he managed to express his thoughts in his lyrics.

✳ In the first Tony Award celebrations *Finian's Rainbow* received two awards, one for David Wayne and the other for the choreographer Michael Kidd; it was an award he shared with Agnes de Mille for another fantasy show, *Brigadoon*.

The Critics

In his book, *Broadway*, Brooks Atkinson writes, '*Finian's Rainbow*, full of political satire and comic caprice, helped to redeem Broadway from drudgery.'
David Ewen described the score as, 'One of the best for the Broadway stage in the 1940s.'

Recommended Recording

Original Broadway cast (CD) Columbia CK4062
An original cast classic. Scot Ella Logan makes a fine Sharon and David Wayne is charm personified as Og. The score sounds new minted and fresh.

Film

Warner Brothers, 1968. Starring Fred Astaire, Petula Clark and Tommy Steele. Directed by Francis Ford Coppola.

Fiorello!

LYRICS ✳ Sheldon Harnick
MUSIC ✳ Jerry Bock
BOOK ✳ Jerome Weidman and George Abbott

First Performance

New York, Broadhurst Theater, 23 November 1959 (795 performances)
London, Piccadilly Theatre, 8 October 1962 (56 performances)

Principal Characters

Fiorello La Guardia ✳ A politician
Marie Fischer ✳ His secretary
Thea La Guardia ✳ His wife
Ben Marino ✳ Republican leader of the 14th District
Floyd Macduff
Morris Cohen ✳ Politician
Mitzi Travers ✳ A showgirl
Dora ✳ A helper
Neil ✳ A law clerk

Original New York Cast

Tom Bosley, Patricia Wilson, Ellen Hanley, Howard Da Silva, Mark Dawson,
Nathaniel Frey, Eileen Rodgers, Pat Stanley, Bob Holiday

Original London Cast

Derek Smith, Nicolette Roeg, Marion Grimaldi, Peter Reeves, Simon Oates,
David Lander, Patricia Michael, Bridget Armstrong, Peter Bourne

Plot

Ten years in the life of Fiorello (Little Flower) La Guardia, one of the best-loved
and best-remembered mayors of New York. Fiorello is a lawyer whose practice is
among the poor in Greenwich Village. He also plans to run for Congress – in a
district that never elects a Republican. As his election is plainly an impossibility,
the local political boss, Ben, agrees. Fiorello then helps striking garment workers
and falls in love with Thea, one of the strikers.

By mobilizing the ethnic workers of the district, Fiorello actually gets elected.
He's behind a draft act for call-up in World War I, and enlists himself. After the
war, married to Thea, Fiorello dedicates himself to fighting the corruption of the
incumbent mayor of New York, James J. Walker, surviving at least one murder
plot on the way. He loses the election and his wife dies. Meanwhile, there's
another corrupt target – the political bosses at Tammany Hall. When Tammany
Hall has been vanquished, Fiorello finally becomes New York's mayor and
marries his faithful secretary, Marie.

Music and Songs

Bock and Harnick wrote a warm, endearing, thoroughly Broadway score, full of rousing marches, stuffed with acute political comment and tender, simple love songs – a score Berlin would have been proud of. Apart from ''Til tomorrow' (Thea), there are the two political exposé numbers 'Little tin box' (politicians) and 'Politics and Polka' (politicians), and 'The name's La Guardia' (Fiorello) as representative of a fine varied score.

Did You Know?

✷ This is not the only musical about a mayor of New York. There's also *Jimmy*, about 'Gentleman Jimmy' – James J. Walker, and *Mayor* about Ed Koch.

✷ Sadly the show, despite its fine score, failed to succeed outside the borders of the United States.

✷ Tom Bosley, who starred as Fiorello, was to find television fame in the show *Happy Days*.

✷ *Fiorello!* shared the best musical Tony Award with *The Sound of Music*, and Tom Bosley won the Tony for his performance.

The Critics

The critics approved:
'It is exciting, it is enjoyable and it is decent' – *New York Times*
'One of the slickest, sassiest and most satisfying Broadway shows in years. *Fiorello* is so much fun that it looks easy' – *Newsweek*
'The whole show looks like La Guardia. It is solid, chunky, charging, electric and endearing' – *New York Herald Tribune*

Recommended Recording

Original Broadway cast (CD) Angel 2435-65023
The only available recording. Tom Bosley is superb as Fiorello and he had a marvellous cast to back him and to make this a Broadway score to cherish.

Florodora

LYRICS ✶ Ernest Boyd-Jones, Paul Rubens and Leslie Stuart
MUSIC ✶ Leslie Stuart
BOOK ✶ Owen Hall

First Performance

London, Lyric Theatre, 11 November 1899 (455 performances)
New York, Casino Theater, 12 November 1900 (549 performances)

Principal Characters

Lady Holyrood ✶ A widow
Dolores ✶ A working girl
Frank Abercoed ✶ A business manager
Anthony Tweedlepunch ✶ A charlatan
Cyrus Gilfain ✶ Owner of the island
Angela Gilfain ✶ His daughter

Original London Cast

Ada Reeve, Evie Green, Melville Stewart, Willie Edouin,
Charles E. Stevens, Kate Cutler

Original New York Cast

Christie MacDonald, Eleanor Painter, George Hassell, Walter Woolf,
John T. Murray, Margot Kelly

Plot

Florodora is a mythical island in the Philippines where the perfume named after it is manufactured. Cyrus Gilfain owns the island and the perfume's secret formula. His business manager is Frank Abercoed, a mysterious young Englishman. On Florodora Frank has fallen for Dolores, a flower picker. Gilfain, who also has hopes in that direction, pays Dolores double wages and has Frank lined up for his own daughter. Now a conman, Anthony Tweedlepunch, takes a hand. Lady Holyrood arrives from England. She's trying to marry her brother, Captain Donegal, to Gilfain's daughter, Angela. She also recognizes Abercoed, whose father has recently died, and he's now become Lord Abercoed. His jilted fiancée is already married to someone else. There's nothing to stop him declaring his love to Dolores. But the rascally Cyrus Gilfain has other ideas: Tweedlepunch will pair off couples according to their abilities as he sees them, and that means other partners for Abercoed and Dolores! The couples refuse to accept the judgment and Abercoed leaves for England in anger.

On his recent trip to England, Gilfain has bought Frank's family seat, Abercoed Castle, and has taken up residence there, with Lady Holyrood as social adviser. She invites her brother, the captain, to stay. Meanwhile, Frank and Dolores arrive in disguise, as does Tweedlepunch, who reveals to Lady Holyrood, after a £500 bribe, that Dolores is the missing heiress to the island; no wonder Gilfain wanted to marry her! Lady Holyrood persuades Tweedlepunch to tell the gullible Gilfain of a curse that will land on any man who tricks a young girl out of her inheritance. To add verisimilitude to the narrative, Lady Holyrood dresses up as a vengeful blood-bespattered ghost. Gilfain owns up to his evil deeds and all the lovers are properly united.

Music and Songs

A tuneful early score from a variety of hands in different styles. The hit song of the period was 'Tell me pretty maiden' (chorus – double sextet). Others included 'The fellow who might' (Angela), 'I want to be a military man' (Donegal) and 'The silver star of love' (Dolores).

Did You Know?

✱ The score was changed as different performers took over various roles.

✱ The show ran for 17 months in London – a most profitable run.

✱ New York saw a revival in 1902, and London revivals in 1915 and 1931.

✱ Owen Hall was the pseudonym of the solicitor and writer Jimmy Davis – the name is said to reflect his financial problems (owe 'em all).

The Critics

'Perhaps the most ingenious number is a so-called concerted piece in which a little scene of courtship is gone through by six couples at once; strange to say, this number 'Are there anymore at home like you' made a great hit' – *The Times* (The title of the song was actually 'Tell me pretty maiden')

'Tempestuous laughter [greeted] nearly every sally and topical allusion in Owen Hall's book full of that writer's mordant humour and insolently audacious cynicism' – *The Stage*

Recommended Recording

Original London cast (CD) Pearl Opal CD 9835
Billed as 'the world's first ever original cast album' this is the only recording available and it is a great pity the transfers from these very old 78s are not better. Through the often poor sound there are some moments of magic but it is not the best way to appreciate the score.

Flower Drum Song

LYRICS ✻ Oscar Hammerstein II
MUSIC ✻ Richard Rodgers
BOOK ✻ Oscar Hammerstein II and Joseph Fields,
based on Chin Y. Lee's novel

First Performance

New York, St. James' Theater, 1 December 1958 (600 performances)
London, Palace Theatre, 24 March 1960 (464 performances)

Principal Characters

Mei Li ✻ A recent arrival
Sammy Fong ✻ A bar owner
Madam Liang ✻ About to become a US citizen
Wang Ta ✻ A Chinese American
Linda Low ✻ Wang Ta's girlfriend
Wang Chi Yang ✻ Wang Ta's father
Helen Chao ✻ A nightclub singer
Frankie Wing

Original New York Cast

Miyoshi Umeki, Larry Blyden, Juanita Hall, Ed Kenney,
Pat Suzuki, Keye Luke, Arabella Hong

Original London Cast

Yau Shan Tung, Tim Herbert, Ida Shepley, Kevin Scott,
Yama Saki, George Pastell, Joan Pethers

Plot

Wang Ta lives in San Francisco's Chinatown in his father's home. Wang Ta is pulled two ways – between Chinese tradition and the newer, more relaxed, American customs. He tells Madam Liang that he's chosen a wife. Meanwhile, Sammy Fong, of the Celestial Bar, announces the arrival of his mail-order wife from China, Mei Li. But Sammy has other plans. He sells the contract on to Wang's father, Wang Chi Yang, for one of his sons. Wang Ta visits his girlfriend, Linda, and proposes marriage. He announces it at a party to celebrate Madam Liang's assumption of US citizenship. His father is angry and Mei Li is humiliated for she was to be Wang Ta's bride, as selected by his father. Sammy Fong is also in love with Linda and invites the Wangs to the Celestial Bar, where Linda sings. That will put a stop to Wang Ta's engagement, especially when Linda does a striptease. The bewildered Wang Ta seeks solace with an old flame, Helen Chao. The original contract was with Sammy; he must marry Mei Li. But now Wang Ta discovers, rather belatedly, that he really loves Mei Li and she finds an ingenious way out of all their problems. She entered the country illegally. The contract cannot be enforced! Happiness for all.

Music and Songs

Melodious Rodgers and Hammerstein score, including acute parodies of nightclub routines, plus Sino-American flavours, and including fine love songs such as 'Love look away' (Helen), 'Sunday' (Sammy and Linda) and 'You are beautiful' (Wang Ta and Madam Liang), as well as the up-tempo rousers 'I enjoy being a girl' (Linda) and 'Grant Avenue' (Linda).

Did You Know?

✶ This show was directed by Gene Kelly, veteran Hollywood dancer.

✶ Because of its need for Asians in its cast, *Flower Drum Song* has not proved a first choice for revival. But now, perhaps it will fare better after the success of *Miss Saigon*.

✶ *Flower Drum Song* was not an award-winning show and the best it did at the Tony Awards was one for the musical director.

The Critics

'Rodgers and Hammerstein have written a pleasant play' – *New York Times*
'*Flower Drum Song* is a big fat Rodgers and Hammerstein hit' – *New York Journal-American*
'Rodgers and Hammerstein's latest work is colorful, tuneful and lively . . . but with all its Oriental exoticism, it is extraordinarily lacking in distinction' – *New York Post*

Recommended Recording

Original Broadway cast (CD) Sony 7464–53536
While not one of the greatest of the Rodgers and Hammerstein scores, it still has that self-assuredness of the team, and there is no lack of charm and good performances in this memory of the show.

Film

Universal Pictures, 1961. Starring Nancy Kwan and Miyoshi Umeki. Directed by Henry Koster.

Follies

LYRICS ✴ Stephen Sondheim
MUSIC ✴ Stephen Sondheim
BOOK ✴ James Goldman

First Performance

New York, Winter Garden Theater, 4 April 1971 (522 performances)
London, Shaftesbury Theatre, 21 July 1987 (645 performances)

Principal Characters

Sally ✴ Ex-Follies girl
Phyllis ✴ Ex-Follies girl
Buddy ✴ Sally's salesman husband
Ben ✴ Phyllis' businessman husband
Dimitri Weismann ✴ Ex-producer of the Follies
Carlotta Campion ✴ A former star of the Follies

Original New York Cast

Dorothy Collins, Alexis Smith, Gene Nelson, John McMartin,
Arnold Moss, Yvonne De Carlo

Original London Cast

Julia McKenzie, Diana Rigg, Daniel Massey, David Healy,
Leonard Sachs, Dolores Gray

Plot

A party is being held to mark the demolition of the theatre where Dimitri Weismann mounted so many performances of his Follies. Some of the old stars are present and also two couples – Sally and Buddy, and Phyllis and Ben. They were all friends in the early days when the girls were members of the chorus, and Ben and Buddy were their stage-door beaux. They married, but Sally still yearns for Ben and lives unhappily with her salesman husband in a small town. Buddy for his part has a friend, Margie, in another town. Phyllis and Ben live a smart Fifth Avenue-type of existence – brittle, brilliant, self-destructive. Will this reunion solve anything for any of the four of them? And is there any hope of happiness?

There are no easy answers. By the end of the evening Sally is cured of her longing for Ben. He has undergone some sort of mental breakdown. Phyllis will probably leave him and he'll just have to pick up the pieces of his life as best he can. Buddy can't seem to do anything right, but at least as dawn breaks he accompanies Sally home, as the ghosts of their former selves flicker briefly before finally disappearing. The four may not have achieved much – except greater honesty and self-knowledge.

Music and Songs

A brilliant, melodically gorgeous Sondheim score showing his mastery of pastiche of Berlin, Gershwin, Kern, de Sylva, Brown and Henderson, but producing memorable melodies to move and stir listeners. 'I'm still here' (Carlotta) was the hit, with 'Broadway baby' (Hattie), 'Losing my mind' (Sally) and 'Could I leave you?' (Sally) close beind. The whole score is an iridescent tapestry of great songs.

Did You Know?

∗ The London edition, with completely revised book, will not be performed again – the official version is now the original Broadway script.

∗ The show was inspired by a photograph of Gloria Swanson standing in the wreckage of a theatre as it was about to be demolished.

∗ This was not the first time star Julia McKenzie had sung songs from the score on stage. She had sung some of them in *Side by Side by Sondheim* in London and New York. Millicent Martin, her co-star in that show, took over from Diana Rigg in London.

∗ The London version had five new songs and four of the original were cut.

∗ *Follies* won seven Tony Awards, including best score.

The Critics

The critical response was varied:
'*Follies* is a pastiche show, so brilliant as to be heartbreaking at times' – *New York Daily News*
'Sondheim's qualities as a theater composer can hardly be overstated' – Martin Gottfried, *The New York Sunday Times*
'*Follies* is intermissionless and exhausting' – Walter Kerr, *The New York Sunday Times*
'The man is a Hart in search of a Rodgers' – *New York Times*

Recommended Recording

Original Broadway cast (CD) Broadway Angel ZDM 7 64666 2 0
While frustrating because of the cuts made to issue it on a single LP, it is still the best recording and the most excitingly cast. One that should certainly sit in every collection. For those who want completeness and an exciting alternative there is the live concert version on RCA Red Seal (**RD87128 2**).

42nd Street

LYRICS * Al Dubin
MUSIC * Harry Warren
BOOK * Michael Stewart and Mark Bramble,
based on a novel by Bradford Ropes

First Performance

New York, Winter Garden Theatre, 25 August 1980 (3486 performances)
London, Theatre Royal Drury Lane, 8 August 1984 (1823 performances)

Principal Characters

Peggy Sawyer * The young hopeful
Billy Lawyer * The young male lead
Julian Marsh * The producer
Dorothy Brock * The star
Abner Dillon * The star's sugar daddy
Pat Denning * The star's boyfriend
Maggie and Bert * The show's writers

Original New York Cast

Wanda Richert, Lee Roy Reams, Jerry Orbach, Tammy Grimes, Don Crabtree,
James Congdon, Carole Cook, Joseph Bova

Original London Cast

Clare Leach, Michael Howe, James Laurenson, Georgia Brown, Ralph Lawton,
Bob Sessions, Margaret Courtney, Hugh Futcher

Plot

Julian Marsh, the Broadway producer, is rehearsing his new show, *Pretty Lady*.
One of the hopefuls, Peggy Sawyer, is direct from Allentown and late for
auditions. Billy introduces himself and she sings a number but is sent away
jobless, leaving her purse on the piano. We learn that Marsh was badly hurt by the
Wall Street crash and Dorothy Brock, his aging star, is there simply because her
sugar daddy, Abner, is putting up the money. Peggy returns looking for her purse
and Maggie, one of the show's writers, invites her out to lunch with three of the
chorus girls. They try to help the new girl in town by putting her through a
number. The dance director sees her and hires her as the extra girl. The rehearsals
continue, and Peggy faints from starvation. She is carried to the star's dressing
room where Pat, Dorothy's lover, tries to help, a gesture mistaken as a pass by
Dorothy. Pat has to leave so Abner does not see him. Without Pat, Dorothy is
lonely and bad tempered, and the girls have to ensure Abner does not realise the
true situation and take out his investment.

The show is out-of-town and going well until Dorothy comes on stage for the
Act I finale and Peggy accidentally knocks her down. She can't move and the
curtain comes down. Backstage, it is found she has broken an ankle and the show

either has to close or a replacement be found. The girls suggest Peggy, but she has gone to the station to catch the train home, believing showbusiness is not for her. The whole company turn up and talk her into staying on.

In New York, Peggy has thirty-six hours to learn the part and Julian keeps pushing her to her limits in order to get a performance out of her. Dorothy is wheeled into Peggy's room, wishes her luck and tells her she has married Pat. Peggy goes on stage and becomes a star overnight – Julian Marsh has a hit.

Music and Songs

The score is packed with hits: the title song (Peggy, Billy and ensemble), 'Go into your dance' (Maggie, Peggy and girls), 'You're getting to be a habit with me' (Dorothy, Billy and Peggy), 'Dames' (Billy and ensemble), 'We're in the money' (Peggy, Billy, girls and ensemble), 'Lullaby of Broadway' (Julian and company) and 'Shuffle off to Buffalo' (Maggie, Bert and girls).

Did You Know?

✴ The director of the show, Gower Champion, died the day the show opened in New York. The producer, David Merrick, made the announcement after the show won an amazing reception from its audience.

✴ It won the Tony and Olivier awards for best musical of the year. It also won a Tony for best choreography.

✴ The parts of Peggy and Billy are based on Ruby Keeler and Dick Powell, who starred in the film version, and many other similar films of the period.

The Critics

'The Hollywood musical with its innocent assumption that unknowns could warble or hoof their way to fame overnight delighted audiences who saw *42nd Street* in the early days of the all-singing, all-dancing, all-talking film and 50 years later it looks as though the same story and the same music will delight them all over again' – *The Standard*
'The father and mother of all musicals' – *Daily Mail*

Recommended Recording

Original Broadway cast (CD) RCA RCD1-3891
Record producer Thomas Z. Shepard gives us one of the most memorable recordings of a Broadway show. The dances come alive in an orgy of tap and there are bravura performances from Jerry Orbach and Carole Cook. The London production was not recorded, although the Australian was – but go for the original.

Film

Warner Bros, 1933. Directed by Lloyd Bacon and choreographed by Busby Berkeley, and starring Bebe Daniels, Ginger Rogers, Ruby Keeler and Dick Powell.

Free as Air

LYRICS ✶ Julian Slade and Dorothy Reynolds
MUSIC ✶ Julian Slade
BOOK ✶ Julian Slade and Dorothy Reynolds

First Performance

London, Savoy Theatre, 6 June 1957 (417 performances)

Principal Characters

Molly ✶ An islander
Mr Mutch ✶ Member of Parliament
Mr Potter ✶ Member of Parliament
Miss Catamole ✶ A friend of Lord Paul's
Lord Paul Postumous
Albert Postumous ✶ Lord Paul's nephew
Geraldine Melford ✶ A rich heiress
Ivy Crush ✶ Press reporter
Jack Amersham ✶ Geraldine's fiancé

Original London Cast

Patricia Bredin, Roy Godfrey, Howard Gorney, Dorothy Reynolds, Michael Aldridge, John Trevor, Gillian Lewis, Josephine Tewson, Gerald Harper

Plot

It's May on the Channel Island of Terhou. There's no young lady to be Carnival Queen in the Independence Day celebrations. Everyone eligible has already played the role. The monthly boat arrives from Jersey with a crowd of visitors. Perhaps Geraldine, a rich heiress just arrived by boat, could be the answer. She has run away from her fiancé, Jack Amersham. Unfortunately he's discovered she was in Jersey, where a press reporter, Ivy Crush, has been assigned to shadow her. Lord Paul meanwhile has fled to Jersey, after being rejected by Miss Catamole. He's enlisted by Jack and Ivy to take them to Terhou. Lord Paul finds himself admired by Ivy, and the island girls, led by Molly, find Jack very attractive. He in turn proposes to take Molly back to London.

Ivy wants to turn Terhou into a pleasure resort. Jack, Albert and Geraldine disagree. The islanders take drastic action and lock Ivy up. It's too late, however, because she's already told her newspaper where Geraldine is. The latter now goes back to Jersey to confront the reporters. But the islanders come too. They pose as Geraldine's relatives, among whom she's divided her money. The reporters now believe the heiress to be penniless. No story there, then. Geraldine can return safely to Terhou. Mr Potter proposes to Miss Catamole, after coaching by Geraldine, and is accepted. Ivy is forgiven, Lord Paul proposes and is accepted. Geraldine is crowned Carnival Queen. Molly decides to stay, too, while Jack returns to London.

Music and Songs

A wonderfully touching score that has both wit and humour – the musical equivalent of a charming Ealing comedy – and is proof of the composer's versatility. Songs include 'Let the grass grow under your feet' (Mutch, Potter and Lord Paul), 'I'm up early' (Molly and the islanders), 'Nothing but sea and sky' (Geraldine), 'A man from the mainland' (Molly), 'Free as air' (Albert, Geraldine and the islanders), 'Testudo' (Mutch, Molly, Bindweed and the islanders) and 'Terhou' (Molly and company).

Did You Know?

∗ The show, designed for the West End with full orchestra and elaborate production, consolidated Julian Slade's reputation, toured extensively and was also popular abroad, with successful productions in Australia and Holland (which produced an original cast recording).

∗ Julian Slade and Dorothy Fields went to the island of Sark to write the show, using the one piano on the island to compose on.

The Critics

'Those who were drawn by the originality, taste and unmalicious satire of the first show [*Salad Days*] will fill the Savoy for the second' – *The Stage*

'The tunes and delicious lyrics [are] all charming or witty or both . . ."Let the grass grow" is enchanting. It is Chekhov turned inside out' – *The Observer*

Recommended Recording

Sadly there is no CD issue of this show but it was originally released on LP by Oriole (**MG 20016**). So hopefully you have not thrown away your old record player and, perhaps, your local charity shop may well have a copy for you to pick up – you will not be disappointed.

Funny Girl

LYRICS ✳ Bob Merrill
MUSIC ✳ Jule Styne
BOOK ✳ Isobel Lennart

First Performance

New York, Winter Garden Theater, 26 March 1964 (1348 performances)
London, Prince of Wales Theatre, 13 April 1966 (112 performances)

Principal Characters

Fanny Brice ✳ An ambitious, young performer
Nick Arnstein ✳ A gambler
Eddie Ryan ✳ A dancer
Mrs Brice ✳ Fanny's mother
Mrs Strakosh ✳ A family friend
Florenz Ziegfeld ✳ The producer

Original New York Cast

Barbra Streisand, Sidney Chaplin, Danny Meehan, Kay Medford,
Jean Stapleton, Roger DeKoven

Original London Cast

Barbra Streisand, Michael Craig, Lee Allen, Kay Medford,
Stella Moray, Ronald Leigh-Hunt

Plot

A musical biography of Fanny Brice, the great comedienne, film and Broadway star.

The ambitions of young Fanny Brice know no bounds. She's going to be a bright Broadway star – the greatest – and star in the Ziegfeld Follies. As the show opens, Fanny is in her dressing room. Today is the day her gambler husband, Nick, is released from jail. Will they get together again? Fanny remembers her humble beginnings as a chorus girl, and the reaction of her friends and family. She recalls help from small-time hoofer, Eddie Ryan, and how she was introduced to Ziegfeld by Nick Arnstein, who would become her husband. Fanny's eye-catching comedy performances, including one as a heavily pregnant bride, set the seal on her success.

Marriage to Nick Arnstein is a mixed blessing. While he is doing his often shady deals, Fanny has to suffer emotionally both on stage and off. As her success grows, Nick's seems to shrink. At the end of the show Fanny makes her decision; the two, although still very much in love, must part.

Music and Songs

Tuneful Jule Styne score featuring the hit song 'People' (Fanny), plus 'I'm the greatest star' (Fanny), 'You are woman' (Nick and Fanny), 'Don't rain on my parade' (Fanny), 'Who are you now?' (Fanny) and 'The music that makes me dance' (Fanny).

Did You Know?

* The sequel to this musical was made on film as *Funny Lady*. It dealt with Fanny's marriage to Billy Rose, with new songs by John Kander and Fred Ebb, as well as a good sprinkling of songs made famous by Miss Brice. Barbra Streisand repeated her role as Fanny and Omar Sharif was again Nick Arnstein.

* Garson Kanin's book *Smash*, although fictional, is said to include insights on what it was like to be out on the road on a pre-Broadway tryout with the show.

* The film version included the song 'My Man' which Fanny Brice actually sang in the *Ziegfeld Follies*.

The Critics

The critics enjoyed the show and felt Miss Streisand's talent was 'very poignant and strong' – *New York Times*
'Bob Merrill's lyrics are light-miles above average' – *New York Times*
'*Funny Girl* is just this side of Paradise. Isobel Lennart's dialogue is vigorous and colourful' – *New York World Telegram & Sun*
'*Funny Girl* is comic, tuneful and enchanting. It is wonderful' – *Newsday*

Recommended Recording

Original Broadway cast (CD) Angel ZDM 7 64661 2 5
Barbra Streisand became a superstar because of this show and her fame tended to overshadow the show itself, making it one of the most underrated scores in Broadway history. Jule Styne was at his peak and Streisand was dynamic – certainly something to revisit.

Film

Columbia Pictures, 1968. Starring Barbra Streisand and Omar Sharif. Directed by William Wyler.

A Funny Thing Happened on the Way to the Forum

Lyrics ✶ Stephen Sondheim
Music ✶ Stephen Sondheim
Book ✶ Burt Shevelove and Larry Gelbart, based on Plautus

First Performance

New York, Alvin Theater, 8 May 1962 (964 performances)
London, Strand Theatre, 3 October 1963 (762 performances)

Principal Characters

Pseudolus ✶ Slave to Hero
Hysterium ✶ Slave to Senex
Marcus Lycus ✶ Dealer in courtesans
Philia ✶ A virgin
Senex ✶ An old man
Hero ✶ Senex's son
Miles Gloriosus ✶ A warrior

Original New York Cast

Zero Mostel, Jack Gilford, John Carradine, Preshy Marker,
Brian Davies, David Burns, Ron Holgate

Original London Cast

Frankie Howerd, Kenneth Connor, Jon Pertwee, Isla Blair,
John Rye, Eddie Gray, Leon Greene

Plot

It's 100 BC in Rome. While Senex goes to visit his wife's mother in the country, slave Hysterium is put in charge of the house and guardianship of the morals of their son, Hero. The latter, however, has already fallen for a courtesan from the house next door. His own servant, Pseudolus, wants to be free and will do anything to achieve that status. It turns out that the girl is already paid for by Miles Gloriosus, a warrior. Pseudolus gets to work and puts it about that this virgin comes from Crete, where there's a plague; she could infect everyone! Let Pseudolus look after her. With Hero's help the virgin is moved into Senex's house. Senex returns unexpectedly and is mistaken for her new master by the virgin, Philia, now living there. Before long event piles on event and Pseudolus ends up impersonating Lycus as the real Miles turns up for his bride.

Miles is entertained in Senex's house, which he thinks is the courtesan house. Senex's wife now returns and suspects her husband of sexual shenanigans. Pseudolus has to convince Miles his bride is dead and persuades Hysterium to dress up as a corpse. Now for the burning pyre! Hysterium is not best pleased at this turn of events

– and immediately returns to life! By the end of the evening Miles and Philia are revealed as brother and sister, long-lost children of Erronius, Hero and Philia are together and Pseudolus has his freedom!

Music and Songs

Sondheim's first full Broadway score, a dazzler with witty lyrics and good tunes, including 'Comedy tonight' (Pseudolus), 'Everybody ought to have a maid' (Senex and company), 'Love I hear' (Hero), 'Free' (Pseudolus) and 'Lovely' (Pseudolus, Hysterium, Philia and Hero).

Did You Know?

∗ Despite the title, no one goes to the Forum – or even tries to!

∗ Frankie Howerd scored such a personal success in the English production that he subsequently starred in a series of low comedy TV shows called *Up Pompeii!* that plainly owed a lot to Plautus.

∗ The role of Pseudolus was written for Phil Silvers, but he did not play the part until the show was revived on Broadway and on tour in the United Kingdom. When he played it on Broadway he won the Tony Award.

The Critics

'This is the funniest, bawdiest and most enchanting Broadway musical that Plautus, with a little help from Stephen Sondheim, Burt Shevelove and Larry Gelbart ever wrote . . . Mr Sondheim's music is original and charming, with considerable musical subtlety but a regard for the down-to-earth showbiz vigor that is precisely what is needed. And, as always, his lyrics were a joy to listen to. The American theater has not had a lyricist like this since Hart or Porter' – Clive Barnes

Recommended Recording

Original London cast (CD) West End Angel 077778906025
A sparkling original cast album. This is more complete than the original Broadway cast version and has a cast headed by Frankie Howerd in a part that could have been written for him. He is backed by a set of comedians who get every ounce of comedy out of their parts.

Film

United Artists, 1966. Starring Zero Mostel, Jack Gilford, Michael Crawford and Phil Silvers. Directed by Richard Lester.

Gentlemen Prefer Blondes

LYRICS ✶ Leo Robin
MUSIC ✶ Jule Styne
BOOK ✶ Anita Loos and Joseph Fields,
based on Miss Loos' novel

First Performance

New York, Ziegfeld Theater, 8 December 1949 (740 performances)
London, Princes Theatre, 20 August 1962 (223 performances)

Principal Characters

Lorelei Lee ✶ A blonde from Little Rock
Dorothy Shaw ✶ Her friend from the Follies
Gus Esmond ✶ A sugar daddy
Henry Spofford ✶ A wealthy Philadelphia benefactor
Ella Spofford ✶ His mother
Sir Francis Beekman ✶ A rich Englishman
Gloria Stark ✶ A girl from the Follies
Josephus Gage ✶ A manufacturer of zippers
Lady Phyllis Beekman ✶ Wife of Sir Francis
Robert Lemonteur ✶ A lawyer
Louis Lemonteur ✶ His son

Original New York Cast

Carol Channing, Yvonne Adair, Jack McCauley, Eric Brotherson, Alice Pearce,
Rex Evans, Anita Alvarez, George S. Irving, Reta Shaw,
Howard Morris, Mort Marshall

Original London Cast

Dora Bryan, Ann Hart, Donald Stewart, Robin Palmer, Bessie Love,
Guy Middleton, Valerie Walsh, Michael Malnick, Totti Truman Taylor,
John Heawood, Michael Ashlin

Plot

Gold-digging Lorelei Lee is off to Europe on the luxury liner *Île de France* with
her girlfriend, Dorothy, courtesy of her friend Gus Esmond, the button tycoon.
Lorelei believes, mistakenly, that Gus has lost interest, so she must find a new
protector. Both the liner and France seem to offer rich pickings. Dorothy has an
admirer of her own, Henry Spofford. He's wealthy, he's from Philadelphia and his
mother's on the ship, too. Lorelei loves diamonds and has her eyes on Lady
Beekman's tiara, getting the latter's son to lend her the $5000 needed to buy it.
Once in Paris, Lorelei turns her attention to Josephus Gage, manufacturer of
zippers. Unfortunately, Gus Esmond turns up, finds Lorelei with Gage and
misconstrues the situation. In addition, Lady Beekman decides to sue Lorelei for
the return of the tiara. Believing Lorelei to be unfaithful, Gus arranges for the

Paris nightclub debut of Gloria, a singer/dancer. However, they are soon reconciled; Gus gives Lorelei the money to repay Sir Francis for the tiara. Dorothy and Henry join Lorelei and Gus on the triumphant trip back to the USA.

Music and Songs

A tuneful Styne score in which the flapper age is recalled in adroit, chipper melodies, of which Styne is a past master. 'Diamonds are a girl's best friend' (Lorelei), 'Bye bye baby' (Gus and Lorelei) and 'It's delightful down in Chile' (Sir Francis and Lorelei)

Did You Know?

✶ The 1974 version, *Lorelei*, subtitled *Gentlemen Still Prefer Blondes*, still starred Carol Channing. The major change was adding a prologue and epilogue in which Lorelei, now Gus' widow, reminisces about her madcap youth.

✶ The film with Mesdames Monroe and Russell became one of the best-loved films of its era.

✶ Dora Bryan who played Lorelei in London also played the other great Carol Channing role of Dolly in *Hello, Dolly!*

The Critics

The critics roared:
'Happy days are here again' – *New York Times*
'Smash musical' – *New York Daily Mirror*
Critic David Ewen wrote, '*Gentlemen Prefer Blondes* was lively stage entertainment . . . it did succeed in bringing to life a decade symbolized by its heroine Lorelei Lee.'
In contrast, another London critic was to write, 'This brash, often vulgar and visually ugly recreation of the flapper era has an outmoded air. It hasn't the edge of sharp parody. It is a simply old-fashioned musical staged with little style or imagination.'

Recommended Recording

Original Broadway cast (CD) Sony Broadway SK 48013
Carol Channing at her overwhelming, innocent, gold-digging best with a top-notch cast of fellow professionals, and a resplendent, witty score.

Film

20th Century Fox, 1953. Starring Marilyn Monroe and Jane Russell. Directed by Howard Hawks. The film has a largely re-worked score.

Girl Crazy

LYRICS ✴ Ira Gershwin
MUSIC ✴ George Gershwin
BOOK ✴ Guy Bolton and John McGowan

First Performance

New York, Alvin Theater, 14 October 1930 (272 performances)

Principal Characters

Gieber Goldfarb ✴ A taxi driver
Danny Churchill ✴ A playboy
Molly Gray ✴ A postmistress
Slick Fothergill ✴ A gambler
Kate Fothergill ✴ His wife

Original New York Cast

Willie Howard, Allan Kearns, Ginger Rogers, William Kent, Ethel Merman

Plot

In order to toughen him up and remove him from the temptations of New York, Park Avenue socialite and playboy, Danny Churchill, is sent to Custerville, Arizona by his father. Danny travels there in Gieber Goldfarb's taxi (the fare, $742.30). Custerville offers few amenities apart from the bi-weekly assassination of the sheriff, so Danny decides to open a dude ranch there in his family's lodge, offering showgirls and gambling and run by the Fothergills, Slick, a gambler, and his wife, Kate. Luckily there's the local postmistress, Molly Gray, to teach Danny the error of his ways. And to fall in love with, despite the arrival of Tess Harding, an old girlfriend of Danny's. And the interference of one of Tess' old flames, who makes a play for Molly, and takes her off to San Luz with his gambling winnings. Meanwhile, Goldfarb becomes sheriff without knowing of the high mortality rate that goes with the office.

Danny is suspected of taking part in a robbery and injuring Sam, so Gieber and Molly race to the rescue. Poor Kate finds that Slick has been up to no good with señoritas in San Luz. The real criminals are arrested; Kate and Slick are reconciled – and so are Molly and Danny.

Music and Songs

A wonderful Gershwin score, with the unforgettable 'Embraceable you' (Molly), 'But not for me' (Molly), 'Sam and Delilah' (Kate) and 'I got rhythm' (Kate).

Did You Know?

✱ In 'I got rhythm' Ethel Merman electrified the audience by holding a high C note for sixteen bars!

✱ The original pit orchestra for the show included Benny Goodman, Glenn Miller, Red Nichols, Gene Krupa, Jack Teagarden and Tommy Dorsey – jazz and swing legends all.

✱ The smash revival or 'repackaging' for the 1990s of *Crazy for You* built on the skeleton of the story and score to create a fresh show, packed with other hits. It ran for over three years on Broadway and two in London.

✱ Ginger Rogers was the billed star but Ethel Merman got the reviews and became a star.

The Critics

The critics loved Ethel Merman in the show: 'She has the magnificent vitality of a steam calliope in red and gold loping down a circus midway playing "Entry of the gladiators" (or perhaps in her case "Sam and Delilah" or "I got rhythm")', as one unidentified critic, quoted by David Ewen, wrote.
'A smart and discriminating audience of first-nighters gave it a heartwarming welcome. They cheered Willie Howard when he impersonated an Indian, when he played a sheriff in a tough western town, and when he impersonated Jolson, Chevalier, Will Rogers and George Jessel the rafters fairly shook from the applause' – *Daily Mirror*

Recommended Recording

Studio cast (CD) Elecktra Nonesuch 7559-79250-2
A wonderful reconstruction of the score with Lorna Luft (Judy Garland's other daughter), Judy Blaze and David Carroll starring. This has the real authentic sound of the thirties and it is interesting to hear how integrated much of the score is to the plot.

Films

RKO, 1932. Starring Bert Wheeler and Robert Woolsey. Directed by William A. Seiter.
MGM, 1943. Starring Judy Garland, Mickey Rooney and June Allyson. Directed by Norman Taurog.
MGM, 1965. Starring Harve Presnell and Connie Francis. Directed by Alvin Ganzer. Called *When the Boys meet the Girls* and with an altered story.

Glamorous Night

LYRICS ✶ Christopher Hassall
MUSIC ✶ Ivor Novello
BOOK ✶ Ivor Novello

First Performance

London, Theatre Royal, Drury Lane, 2 May 1935 (243 performances)
Transferred to the Coliseum, 28 May 1936 (91 performances)

Principal Characters

Anthony Allen ✶ A young inventor
Militza Hajos ✶ A great singer
King Stefan
Lydyeff ✶ A politician
Cleo ✶ A stowaway

Original London Cast

Ivor Novello, Mary Ellis, Barry Jones, Lyn Harding, Elisabeth Welch

Plot

Instead of spending the £500 he's been granted to develop an improved version of television, Anthony Allen books himself on a cruise to Ruritania on the SS *Silver Star*. The ship docks at Krasnia, and Anthony treats himself to a night at the opera. It's the première of *Glamorous Night*. In the last scene a shot rings out. A marksman's aim has been deflected – by Anthony. The bullet was intended for King Stefan's mistress, the gypsy opera singer, Militza. The next day she offers her thanks. Rather than a signed photograph, he'd like a small cheque! Highly amused, Militza gives him one – for £1000. The anti-monarchist politician Lydyeff is her next visitor. She must leave the country immediately. She will – she is already booked on the *Silver Star* – but she will return for her next performances in the new opera.

On board, she finds that Anthony is unwilling to move out of the Royal Suite for her – or anyone else! At a ship's concert she sings and is again the target of a potential assassin. The ship is too dangerous for her. Anthony accompanies her on a ship's launch heading for the coast of her native province, Borovnik. They are only just in time. There's an explosion. The SS *Silver Star* has been attacked by the revolutionaries and is sinking fast.

At a gypsy encampment, Militza explains her relationship with the king to Anthony. Stefan is weak – only Militza helped him to stand up to Lydyeff. She is now strongly attracted to Anthony and he to her. They go through a form of gypsy wedding and Militza rallies the gypsies to the king's cause.

Back at the palace, Lydyeff pushes Stefan too far – the king will not sign abdication papers. Anthony kills Lydyeff in the armed struggle that follows, but the king refuses to let Militza leave his side and marry Anthony – she is needed to support her king. Stefan decorates Anthony and gives him enough money to complete his television project. In twelve months the first broadcast will be of the marriage of King Stefan to Militza Hajos. And so it is.

Music and Songs

This is Novello at his most opulently romantic, with magnificent soaring melodies, including 'Fold your wings' (Militza and tenor), 'Why is there ever goodbye' (Militza), 'Glamorous night' (Militza), 'Shine through my dreams' (tenor) and 'Shanty town' (Cleo).

Did You Know?

∗ This was the first musical at Drury Lane to be produced by a woman (Leontine Sagan).

∗ It was the last show seen by King George V before his death.

∗ Since Novello himself was no singer, the leading male role here, as in other musicals by Novello, has nothing to sing.

∗ The tradition of spectacular effects in British shows, attributed to the Mackintosh and Lloyd Webber shows of the 80s and 90s, dates back to Novello, whose own shows included such delights as train crashes and, as here, shipwrecks.

The Critics

'I lift my hat to Mr Novello. He can wade through trash with the straightest face . . . both as actor and author he can pursue adventures too preposterous even for the films and do it with that solemn fixity of purpose which romantic melodrama inexorably demands' – *The Observer*

'Highbrow authors . . . may pettishly suggest that the whole thing is punk. It may be so but it is inspired punk, and it is given to few to write it' – *The Bystander*

'Mr Novello has brought off the biggest achievement of his career. If it is nonsense, it is glamorous nonsense, and for those who are ready to be entertained it is the best show of its kind Drury Lane has had for years' – *The Daily Telegraph*

Recommended Recording

Ivor Novello – The Classic Shows (CD) EMI Cedar CDP 7943682

Film

Associated British Films, 1937. Starring Mary Ellis, Barry Mackay and Otto Kruger. Directed by Brian Desmond Hurst.

Godspell

LYRICS ✳ Stephen Schwartz
MUSIC ✳ Stephen Schwartz
BOOK ✳ John-Michael Tebelak,
based on the Gospel according to St Matthew

First Performance

New York (Off Broadway), Cherry Lane Theater, 17 May 1971 (2651 performances)
London, Wyndham's Theatre, 17 November 1971 (1128 performances)

Principal Characters

Jesus
Judas
The rest of the cast were not given specific identities

Original New York Cast

Stephen Nathan, David Haskell and including Herb Simon,
Sonia Manzano and Robin Lamont

Original London Cast

David Essex, Jeremy Irons and including Verity-Anne Meldrum,
Julie Covington and Marti Webb

Plot

A group of youngsters meet in a high school playground and enact in song and story the last days of Jesus Christ's life, largely as recorded in the Gospels. The leader of the group refers to Christ's mission to save the people. The kids relate a number of parables in their own words. These include 'The Good Samaritan', 'The Sermon on the Mount', 'The Importunate Widow' and 'The Sower and the Seed'. The first act ends with 'The Prodigal Son' and the cast inviting the audience on stage for a glass of wine.

In the second act, the leader takes on the role of Christ, the rest the role of Pharisees, to test his faith. They then become disciples at the Last Supper. One of them, as Judas, betrays Christ, who then hangs, arms outstretched, from the schoolyard fence. The show is over – Prepare ye the way of the Lord.

Music and Songs

A strong, beaty, melodic score with rock and roll, religious chants, gospel and country and western sounds predominating; a contemporary score for and of its time. Numbers include 'Prepare ye the way of the Lord' (leader), 'Save the people' (leader), 'Day by day' (the cast), 'Alas for you' (Jesus), 'Turn back o man' (the cast), 'We beseech Thee' (the cast) and 'On the willows' (Jesus).

Did You Know?

✶ The show was originally created as his degree thesis at college by John-Michael Tebelak.

✶ The British production featured many singers who would become major talents in their own right: David Essex a pop, film and stage star; Jeremy Irons a distinguished film and stage actor; Julie Covington was Evita on the original concept album and appeared as Sarah Brown in the Royal National Theatre *Guys and Dolls*. Marti Webb is the star of many West End shows and concerts, and a later replacement, Robert Lindsay, appeared in *Me and My Girl* as well as frequently on television.

✶ The show began at Carnegie Tech and was first presented at La Mama. It moved to the Cherry Lane Theater in May 1971.

✶ At one time seven different companies were touring the United States with the show.

The Critics

'*Godspell* has no bones, but it has many small sinews and darting reflexes. They serve beautifully to bean along its energy, its gaiety, its wit' – *New York Times*
'It is *Hair* with a haircut' – *New York Post*
'The Our Gang version of the Gospel according to St Matthew' – *Daily News*

Recommended Recording

Off Broadway recording (CD) Arista ARCD-8304
This was the first and it has intimacy, youthful fire and commitment. The original London cast album has yet to appear on CD, which is a pity as it has sparkling performances and gives the opportunity to hear some of today's stars at their youthful best.

Film

Columbia, 1973. Starring Victor Garber and David Haskell. Directed by David Greene.

The Golden Apple

LYRICS ✳ John Latouche
MUSIC ✳ Jerome Moross
BOOK ✳ John Latouche,
based on Homer's *The Odyssey* and *The Iliad*

First Performance

New York (Off Broadway), Phoenix Theater, 11 March 1954 (125 performances)

Principal Characters

Penelope ✳ Wife of . . .
Ulysses ✳ A soldier
Helen ✳ A farmer's daughter
Hector Charybdis ✳ The mayor
Paris ✳ A salesman
Menelaus ✳ The local sheriff

Original New York Cast

Priscilla Gillette, Stephen Douglass, Kaye Ballard, Jack Whiting,
Jonathan Lucas, Dean Michener

Plot

The plot relocates the mythical story of Penelope and Ulysses from legendary pre-Classical Greece to America, the state of Washington, in the first decade of the 20th century. The action is set in Angel's Roost, near the town of Rhododendron. Ulysses has been fighting in the Spanish/American War. He's now on his way back to his faithful wife, Penelope. Paris is a salesman who lands by balloon at the local county fair and falls in love with Helen, a farmer's daughter. They decide to elope to Rhododendron. Unfortunately she's already married to Menelaus, the local sheriff. Ulysses sets out to reclaim Helen in a search that takes ten years. Eventually he reaches Rhododendron, where its mayor, Hector, attempts to distract him with earthly pleasures, including the attentions of enchantresses Circe and Siren. Ulysses is not distracted. He beats Paris at boxing and returns at last to his wife, bringing back Helen to Angel's Roost – and to her husband.

Music and Songs

Moross is better known for his film music, notably the score for *The Big Country*, but this breezy, open-air score shows what Broadway has since missed – music of imagination, spark and memorability. The classic 'Lazy afternoon' (Helen and Paris) tops a score that has some fine choral work. 'Helen is always willing' (Ulysses's men) and 'It's the going home together' (Penelope and Ulysses) are other standouts.

Did You Know?

∗ The show was written with the proceeds of a Guggenheim fellowship several years before production.

∗ The eventual total cost of the staging was only $75,000, but the Broadway run, rather surprisingly, did not attract audiences, nor did the transfer run off-Broadway.

∗ The show was turned down by many prominent producers.

∗ It received the New York Critics and Donaldson awards as the Best Musical of the Season.

∗ This show established Kaye Ballard as a major comic talent.

The Critics

The critics enjoyed the show:
'A magnificent achievement . . . a sensational success . . . quite the most original and imaginative work of its kind to blaze across the theatrical horizon in many a moon' – Robert Coleman
'Easily the most satisfactory and original song and dance effort of the past several seasons and can be classed as an American Gilbert and Sullivan' – John McClain

Recommended Recording

Original New York cast (CD) RCA Victor 09026 68934
The only recording. For many years before the re-issue of this album on CD this was a rare LP to own. It became a cult show because of the quality of the score and now more people are able to appreciate it. So too can they appreciate the young cast which included Stephen Douglass, Kaye Ballard, Bibi Osterwald and Portia Nelson, who all went on to stardom. The show can be classed as a musical comedy opera and Moross said that his raw material for the show was derived from 'popular songs and dances of the period'.

Golden Boy

LYRICS ✷ Lee Adams
MUSIC ✷ Charles Strouse
BOOK ✷ Clifford Odets and William Gibson

First Performance

New York, Majestic Theater, 20 October 1964 (569 performances)
London, London Palladium, 4 June 1968 (118 performances)

Principal Characters

Tom Moody ✷ A manager
Roxy Gottlieb ✷ A co-manager
Joe Wellington ✷ A fighter
Lorna Moon ✷ His girlfriend
Mr Wellington ✷ Joe's father
Eddie Satin ✷ A gangster

Original New York Cast

Kenneth Tobey, Ted Beniades, Sammy Davis Junior, Paula Wayne,
Roy Glenn, Billy Daniels

Original London Cast

Mark Dawson, Louis Basile, Sammy Davis Junior, Gloria De Haven,
Al Kirk, Lon Satton

Plot

Joe Wellington wins his fights through points rather than knockouts. He's under contract to Tom Moody and Roxy Gottlieb who urge him to become a more dangerous fighter. Joe's family object to his fighting, but it's a passport out of the ghetto. Tom's mistress is Lorna Moon, and she and Joe discover a mutual attraction. If he changes his boxing style he can escape the poverty they both endure, she convinces him.

Joe attracts the attention of finger-in-every-pie gangster, Eddie Satin. He will get Joe into the big time – if Roxy and Tom sell him a share of the contract. Before Joe's debut at Madison Square Garden, his brother Frank warns Lorna that if Joe can't make it in her (white) world and can't live in his previous one, he's a man falling through space without anywhere to land – she should think carefully about their relationship. All this is swept aside when Joe wins the contest by a knockout. All are pleased, except Joe's father, brother and Lorna (who is a mass of confused emotion). Will Joe be able to cope?

Tom laments his weakening control over Joe. Tom's wife is off to Reno for a long-delayed divorce now Tom has money prospects – and Lorna and Tom can marry at last. But he needs another year of Joe's earnings to pay off his wife. Joe's brother returns to Joe the money he's sent their father – he'll have none of it. Eddie Satin's influence grows and grows. He gives Joe a new Ferrari at a party and sets up a fight he can't possibly win, against Pepe Lopez. Meanwhile, Lorna convinces Joe to keep Tom in the syndicate that is managing him, out of pity for Tom and for herself. Joe and Lorna admit their love, but next day Tom swears he'll cut his throat if Lorna leaves him for Joe.

Eddie and Joe announce the forthcoming bout. Lorna says she loves Tom. Just before the bout, Lorna tells Joe why. Both Tom and she are washed out has-beens. She doesn't have the strength for a relationship with Joe. Tom refers to Lorna as his wife, hoping this will incense Joe enough to make him tear into Lopez and finish him off. Eddie now makes a pass at Joe which is rebuffed. He tells his protegé to win or there will be a slab waiting for his carcass. Joe knocks out Lopez but the jubilation is cut short. Lopez is dead. Joe is horrified at what he has done. He flees into the night and is involved in a fatal crash in his new Ferrari.

Music and Songs

An electrifying collection of fight songs, tender ballads and show-stoppers, including 'Don't forget 127th Street' (Joe), 'This is the life' (Eddie), 'Stick around' (Joe), 'While the city sleeps' (Eddie), 'Can't you see it?' (Joe) and 'I want to be with you' (Lorna and Joe).

Did You Know?

✷ Three songs were restored for the London run, including 'Yes I can' (Joe), the title of Sammy Davis' autobiography. Despite its long Broadway run, the show did not make a profit.

✷ The original book had Joe as an Italian and not black as in the musical.

The Critics

The critical points scorecard:
'As crisp as a left jab and as jolting as a right uppercut . . . one can have nothing but admiration for the snap, speed and professionalism of the style of this musical' – *New York Times*
'Smart, taut, hard-eyed . . . the book packs so much basic weight that its scenes could go back into a straight play again. They are direct enough and believable for that' – *New York Herald Tribune*
'A knockout . . . a fascinating show' – *New York Journal American*
'A big fat musical hit' – *Cue*

Recommended Recording

Original Broadway cast (CD) Broadway Angel 2435-65024
Strouse and Adams supplied Sammy Davis with a set of knockout songs and he knew how to put them over. A good example of a star vehicle show that delivers what it promises.

Grease

LYRICS ✳ Jim Jacobs and Warren Casey
MUSIC ✳ Jim Jacobs and Warren Casey
BOOK ✳ Jim Jacobs and Warren Casey

First Performance

New York, Eden Theater, 14 February 1972
Transferred to Broadhurst, and later Royale, theatres after less than 4 months
(3388 performances)
London, New London Theatre, 26 June 1973 (236 performances)

Principal Characters

Sandy Dumbrowski ✳ A bright, young, innocent pupil
Danny Zuko ✳ A cool dude
Betty Rizzo ✳ Leader of the Pink Ladies
Roger ✳ A school kid
Doody ✳ Another school kid

Original New York Cast

Carole Demas, Barry Bostwick, Adrienne Barbeau, Walter Bobbie, James Canning

Original London Cast

Stacey Gregg, Richard Gere, Jacquie-Ann Carr, Stephen Bent, Derek James

Plot

The school kids are reassembling at Rydell High after a good 1950s summer. Newcomer Sandy enthuses about Danny, a holiday romance. Little does she know that Danny's a pupil there too. When they meet again, he seems curiously distant. He has a reputation as a tough guy. No matter. Sandy joins the Pink Ladies gang, thanks to her neighbour, Frenchy, but she has a lot to learn about being cool. She's aiming for the cheer leader squad and is coached by Patty, who is also keen on Danny and isn't averse to making Sandy jealous with a few well-chosen barbs. Betty Rizzo, the gang leader, mocks Sandy, who thinks Danny has put her up to it, and attacks Danny. The result: Danny asks Rizzo rather than Sandy to partner him at the school dance.

Sandy doesn't go to the dance, but Danny wins the dance contest partnered by Cha Cha, Kenickie's blind date. Later, Danny and Sandy go to a drive-in movie but she leaves when he gets fresh. Frenchy drops out of school, and also out of beauty school. Rizzo thinks she's pregnant. Sandy tries to help but fails. Sandy must do something about herself. Time for a complete makeover, supervised by Frenchy. Danny quits the athletics team and goes down to the burger palace with the boys. The Pink Ladies are there, including a newcomer in leather jacket and skintight jeans, complete with gum and cigarette. It's Sandy! She quickly disposes of Patty and wins Danny for herself. Rizzo isn't pregnant after all. A happy ending!

Music and Songs

Wonderful, often very funny, rock 'n' roll pastiche score, including 'Freddy, my love' (Pink Ladies), 'Greased lightnin'' (Kenickie and gang), 'Look at me, I'm Sandra Dee' (Rizzo), 'It's raining on Prom Night' (Sandy and Donna Sue) and 'We go together' (the company). The hit songs from the later film, 'Summer nights' and 'You're the one that I want', were interpolated into the 1990s revivals in the UK.

Did You Know?

✷ Two unsuccessful London productions preceded a highly-successful version in the 1990s featuring soap/pop star Craig McLachlan that incorporated extra songs written for the smash-hit film.

✷ A parallel, and also successful, American revival did not incorporate the film additions.

✷ The London home, originally, for *Grease*, starring Richard Gere, was known as an unlucky theatre – until *Cats* took up residence 'now and forever'.

✷ The New York run was for years the longest-running show after *The Fantasticks*.

The Critics

'A lively and funny musical that brings back the look and sound of the teenage world of the late 1950s with glee' – *New York Daily News*
'There is a cosy aggressiveness to the show' – *New York Times*

Recommended Recording

Original Broadway cast (CD) Polydor 827 548-2
This captures the original small-scale production and it is charming. Here is the gentle satire intended by the creators, a quality lost on the later revivals and in the film version.

Film

Paramount, 1978. Starring John Travolta, Olivia Newton-John and Stockard Channing. Directed by Randal Kleiser.

Guys and Dolls

LYRICS ✴ Frank Loesser
MUSIC ✴ Frank Loesser
BOOK ✴ Abe Burrows and Jo Swerling, based on Damon Runyon's
short story *The Idyll of Miss Sarah Brown*

First Performance

New York, 46th Street Theater, 24 November 1950 (1200 performances)
London, Coliseum, 28 May 1953 (555 performances)

Principal Characters

Sky Masterson ✴ A gambler
Miss Adelaide ✴ A singer and dancer
Nathan Detroit ✴ Her fiancé of fourteen years
Miss Sarah Brown ✴ A mission worker
Arvide Abernathy ✴ Another mission worker
**Big Jule, Nicely-Nicely Johnson,
Harry the Horse, Benny South Street**
✴ Gamblers

Original New York Cast

Robert Alda, Vivian Blaine, Sam Levene, Isabel Bigley, Pat Rooney Snr,
B.S. Pully, Stubby Kaye, Tom Pedi, Johnny Silver

Original London Cast

Jerry Wayne, Vivian Blaine, Sam Levene, Lizbeth Webb, Ernest Butcher,
Lew Herbert, Stubby Kaye, Tom Pedi, Johnny Silver

Plot

We're in Times Square, New York. Nathan Detroit, a small-time fixer, is trying to fend off the marriage plans of the featured attraction at the Hot Box Nightclub, Miss Adelaide. He's pretty good at it – they've been engaged for fourteen years. But organising the oldest-established floating crap game is always a good excuse for a postponement, isn't it? Especially when you haven't yet secured a location for your game. Then there's big-time gambler Sky Masterson – what won't he bet on? How about that he'll succeed in getting prim Sarah Brown, leading light of the Save a Soul Mission, to come with him to Cuba?

Sky succeeds, but the couple return to find that Nathan has organized his crap game in the mission itself. That doesn't look too good for Sky and Sarah's romance. Also, the mission is in trouble – not enough penitents. So Sky bets his biggest bet of all. If he wins, all the gamblers have to attend the next day's service when the mission's General comes by. Sky wins; the mission is crowded and penitence comes thick and fast! Sky joins the mission and Adelaide finally gets her wedding.

Music and Songs

A brilliant Loesser score, one of the finest ever written for Broadway, with style, wit and memorable tunes in traditional fashion, from intimate romance through streetwise New York ditties to rollicking gospel, including 'I'll know' (Sky and Sarah), 'A bushel and a peck' (Adelaide and the girls), 'Adelaide's lament' (Adelaide), 'If I were a bell' (Sarah), 'My time of day' (Sky), 'I've never been in love before' (Sky and Sarah), 'Luck be a lady' (Sky and the gamblers) and 'Sit down you're rockin the boat' (Nicely-Nicely and the congregation).

Did You Know?

✷ Recent revivals, including one at the Royal National Theatre, chosen by the retiring director, Richard Eyre, as his almost final production, have proved both popular and successful.

✷ The book of *Guys and Dolls* was completely rewritten by Abe Burrows after the score had been finished, because the original by Jo Swerling was not working.

The Critics

The critics realised what they had:
'The year's best musical' – *New York Daily Mirror*
'It has everything, as a top flight stake runner should. *Guys and Dolls*, the big, brash and bountiful musical comedy which is the town's newest hit' – *New York Post*
'It is a triumph and a delight and I think it will last as long as the roof remains on the Forty Sixth Street Theatre' – *New York Journal American*

Recommended Recording

Original New York cast (CD) MCA MCAD-10301
Not the most complete but certainly the best version with the best cast. This is Frank Loesser at his finest and this is an album that should be in the collection.

Film

Samuel Goldwyn, 1955. Starring Marlon Brando, Frank Sinatra, Jean Simmons and Vivian Blaine. Directed by Joseph Mankiewicz.

Gypsy

LYRICS ✶ Stephen Sondheim
MUSIC ✶ Jule Styne
BOOK ✶ Arthur Laurents, based on Gypsy Rose Lee's autobiography

First Performance

New York, Broadway Theater, 21 May 1959 (702 performances)
London, Piccadilly Theatre, 29 May 1973 (300 performances)

Principal Characters

Rose ✶ An ambitious stage mother
Herbie ✶ Her help along the way
Louise ✶ The elder daughter
Tessie Tura ✶ A stripper
Tulsa ✶ A young dancer
Uncle Jocko ✶ Runs talent contests
June ✶ The talented daughter, formerly Baby June

Original New York Cast

Ethel Merman, Jack Klugman, Sandra Church, Maria Karnilova, Paul Wallace,
Mort Marshall, Lane Bradbury/Jacqueline Mayro

Original London Cast

Angela Lansbury, Barry Ingham, Zan Charisse, Valerie Walsh, Andrew Norman,
George Moon, Debbie Bowen/Bonnie Langford

Plot

Mama Rose is going to put her daughter June on the stage. She enters her in a
'fixed' talent contest in Seattle and engages Herbie as manager of her troupe,
called Baby June and her Newsboys, to work on the Orpheum Circuit. Rose
dangles the prospect of marriage before Herbie as the years pass. Vaudeville is
dying, and Baby June leaves the act to elope with her sweetheart (and a separate
career as June Havoc on stage and screen).

Enter Madam Rose's Toreadorables led by the seemingly awkward and
talentless elder daughter, Louise. Making Louise a star is a full-time job for Rose.
They're booked into a low burlesque house, where strippers are the main item on
the bill. When one of them gets arrested, Louise takes her place. Rose still won't
marry Herbie, who leaves, finally. Meanwhile, Louise, as Gypsy Rose Lee, is a
sensation. Her fame leads her to the top and Minsky's in New York. She's witty,
elegant, self-confident – there's no longer an obvious place in Gypsy's life for the
archetypal stage mother. Rose becomes increasingly annoyed by her daughter's
intellectual pretensions. After a bitter quarrel, Rose shows what she could have
done herself – imitating Louise's stripping in the tremendous 'Rose's Turn', the
best 'eleven o'clock number' in Broadway history – and the two are reconciled.

Music and Songs

A brilliant Styne score – he never wrote anything better than this – including 'May we/Let me entertain you' (the children), 'Some people' (Rose), 'Small world' (Rose), 'Little lamb' (Louise), 'You'll never get away from me' (Rose and Herbie), 'If Mamma was married' (Louise and June), 'All I need is the girl' (Tulsa), 'Everything's coming up roses' (Rose), 'You gotta have a gimmick' (the strippers) and 'Rose's Turn' (Rose). Sondheim's lyrics are superlative.

Did You Know?

✶ The score contained 'You'll never get away from me', a song originally used in the TV show *Ruggles of Red Gap*, where it was introduced by Peter Lawford as 'I'm in pursuit of happiness' (lyric by Leo Robin). Ruggles, a butler, was played by Sir Michael Redgrave.

✶ *Gypsy* is a prime candidate for the greatest stage musical of all time.

✶ While based on Gypsy Rose Lee's autobiography, it is acknowledged that much of that was invented and the musical is almost completely fiction.

The Critics

The critics praised the show to the heights, calling Merman's performance the greatest of her career, and they were equally unanimous in praising Styne's score. A typical comment from a British critic: 'Jule Styne is the most persistently underrated of popular composers' – Kenneth Tynan

Recommended Recording

Original Broadway cast (CD) Columbia CK-32607
Just the overture is worth the price of this CD and this certainly helps make it the king of original cast recordings. As such it is a hard, if not impossible, act to follow. But it should be mentioned that Angela Lansbury's interpretation of the role of Rose on the London cast recording is, in its own way, remarkable and well worth having.

Films

Warner Brothers, 1962. Starring Rosalind Russell, Natalie Wood and Karl Malden. Directed by Mervyn LeRoy.
A television version on CBS in the United States during December 1993 starred Bette Midler.

Hair

LYRICS ✷ Gerome Ragni and James Rado
MUSIC ✷ Galt MacDermot
BOOK ✷ Gerome Ragni and James Rado

First Performance

New York, Public Theater, 29 October 1967 (94 performances)
Transferred to Biltmore Theater, 29 April 1968 (1472 performances)
London, Shaftesbury Theatre, 27 September 1968 (1998 performances)

Principal Characters

Claude, Berger, Sheila, Woof, Jeannie, Dionne, Crissy, Hud
✷ Hippies of the Age of Aquarius

Original New York (Public Theater) Cast

Walker Daniels, Gerome Ragni, Jill O'Hara, Steve Dean, Sally Eaton,
Jonelle Allen, Shelley Plimpton, Arnold Wilkerson

Original New York (Biltmore Theater) Cast

James Rado, Gerome Ragni, Lynn Kellogg, Steve Curry, Sally Eaton,
Melba Moore, Shelley Plimpton, Lamont Washington

Original London Cast

Paul Nicholas, Oliver Tobias, Annabel Leventon, Michael Feast, Marsha Hunt,
Linda Kendrick, Sonja Kristina, Peter Straker

Plot

Berger is a member of the Tribe, a collection of long-haired youngsters who look
for guidance and strength to his friend, Claude. There's also Sheila (who is in love
with both of them), Jeannie, who will protest against anything, and Woof who
hankers after Mick Jagger. Claude has received a draft notice. The group are dead
set against conscription, the Vietnam War and much else besides. Jeannie protests
against the polluted air of Manhattan. Meanwhile, Berger and Claude extol the
joys of drugs (Berger has been expelled from school on this account). Claude seeks
solace in marijuana. The group make a protest at a be-in, burn their draft cards,
and also the American flag for good measure.

Claude did not burn his draft card, however. He's decided to be conscripted and
wants Sheila to go with him on his final night of freedom. She won't, and is upset
that Claude isn't standing up in protest against the draft. Claude shares out his
possessions among his friends. On his last evening Sheila finally gives in. The
next day, Claude's hair is cut off and he's in the Army, off to war and probably
death.

Music and Songs

Tuneful, catchy and vibrant contemporary score that included the hits 'Aquarius' (the Tribe) and 'Good morning starshine' (the Tribe). Other songs included 'Ain't got no' (the boys), 'Frank Mills' (Crissy), 'Hare Krishna' (the Tribe), 'Where do I go?' (Claude), 'Easy to be hard' (Sheila), 'I got life' (Claude) and 'Let the sunshine in' (the Tribe).

Did You Know?

✶ The redirected, redesigned and recast Broadway version achieved a breakthrough of sorts, by having the cast totally nude at the first act finale.

✶ The London run was only forced to terminate when the roof of the Shaftesbury Theatre collapsed in July 1973. It reopened in June 1974 at the Queen's Theatre and ran for a further 111 performances.

✶ *Hair* is just one of a number of quintessentially American shows whose London West End runs exceeded their New York originals.

✶ *Hair*'s opening in London celebrated the end of stage censorship in the United Kingdom.

The Critics

'Masterly . . . new . . . subtle . . . the first Broadway musical in some time to have the authentic voice of today rather than that of the day before yesterday' – *New York Times*

'The first musical of the Love and Peace Generation epitomizing the hippy teaching on theology, war and sex' – Peter Knight Jnr

---

Recommended Recording

Original Broadway cast (CD) RCA Victor 1150-2-RC
Both the Broadway and a mix of two London casts (**Polydor 519 973-2**) have surfaced on CD, as well as a disappointing London revival cast version. The original Broadway cast have a freshness associated with a new show, but the score has not weathered well and only a few songs now seem to stand out – as indicated above.

Film

United Artists, 1979. Starring John Savage, Treat Williams and Beverly D'Angelo. Directed by Milos Forman.

Half a Sixpence

LYRICS ✶ David Heneker
MUSIC ✶ David Heneker
BOOK ✶ Beverly Cross, based on H.G. Wells' novel *Kipps*

First Performance

London, Cambridge Theatre, 21 March 1963 (677 performances)
New York, Broadhurst Theater, 25 April 1965 (512 performances)

Principal Characters

Arthur Kipps ✶ An apprentice who comes into money
Ann Pornick ✶ His sweetheart
Harry Chitterlow ✶ An actor/playwright
Helen Walsingham ✶ A member of society
Mrs Walsingham ✶ Helen's mother
Pearce ✶ Another apprentice
Sid Pornick ✶ A Socialist and Ann's brother
Buggins ✶ Another apprentice

Original London Cast

Tommy Steele, Marti Webb, James Grout, Anna Barry, Jessica James,
Anthony Valentine, John Bull, Colin Farrell

Original New York Cast

Tommy Steele, Polly James, James Grout, Carrie Nye, Ann Shoemaker,
Grover Dale, Will Mackenzie, Norman Allen

Plot

Arthur Kipps is a draper's apprentice in Folkestone at the turn of the century. He's smitten with Ann, sister of one of his fellow workers. He gives her a lover's token, half a sixpence. His employer, Mr Shalford, sends Kipps to the improving meetings of the Young Persons Association. On the way to see Ann, rather than attend one of the meetings of the YPA, he runs into (or is run into by) Chitterlow, a self-important actor and playwright. The latter is delighted for he's seen Arthur's name in a local paper and thinks he's inherited some money. They celebrate together, prematurely, and Arthur gets drunk, is seen by his employer and marched off to the YPA. There the boy puts his hand through a glass window, and is looked after by the teacher, Helen Walsingham. Next day, Ann is furious with Kipps. Enter Chitterlow with good news – Arthur has inherited £1200 a year! He resigns from the draper's shop and renews acquaintance with the Walsinghams, who invite him to the regatta. They're seen by Ann who throws the half a sixpence back at Kipps.

Arthur tries to fit into the Walsinghams' social round, but it just doesn't come naturally to him. Eventually he sees the error of his ways and returns to Ann, whom he courts and marries. He'll build her a large house. Unfortunately he's trusted his money to Helen's brother who plays the market and loses almost all of it. Luckily there's just enough to invest in a small bookshop and the Kipps family are happy. Even when Chitterlow returns, having made a success of his play in which Arthur had invested £200, they keep their heads screwed on. Money they have, but the Kipps family still enjoy a quiet Christmas at home rather than celebrating with their friend and, now, benefactor.

Music and Songs

The attractive and melodious score includes 'All in the cause of economy' (apprentices), 'Half a sixpence' (Arthur and Ann), 'Money to burn' (Arthur), 'She's too far above me' (Arthur), 'If the rain's got to fall' (Arthur), 'Flash! Bang! Wallop!' (Arthur) and 'I know what I am' (Ann).

Did You Know?

✶ The show was expressly written for Tommy Steele, confirmed his star status in Britain and gave him an international reputation which led to a substantial career in Hollywood.

✶ The score was altered for Broadway; the additions were by David Heneker. Steele not only got to take the show to Broadway, but of course made the film as well.

The Critics

'This gorgeous musical could pack them in anywhere in the world' – *Daily Sketch*
'Cor what a bloomin' triumph for Tommy Steele! It's a hit, hit, hit' – *Daily Mirror*
'A big blooming musical hit' – *New York Journal American*

Recommended Recording

Original London cast (CD) Deram 820 589-2
This has the vibrant and infectious performance of Tommy Steele captured beautifully. The Broadway cast recording, again with Steele heading the company, is dull in comparison. Another reason to go for the original London cast is the strong support given by the likes of Marti Webb.

Film

Paramount, 1967. Starring Tommy Steele and Cyril Richard, with Julia Foster. Directed by George Sidney.

Hello, Dolly!

LYRICS ✻ Jerry Herman
MUSIC ✻ Jerry Herman
BOOK ✻ Michael Stewart, based on Thornton Wilder's play *The Matchmaker*,
adapted from his *The Merchant of Yonkers*

First Performance

New York, St James' Theater, 16 January 1964 (2844 performances)
London, Drury Lane Theatre, 2 December 1965 (794 performances)

Principal Characters

Dolly Gallagher Levi ✻ A matchmaker
Horace Vandergelder ✻ A merchant
Irene Molloy ✻ A hat shop owner
Minnie ✻ Her assistant
Cornelius Hackl ✻ Horace's employee
Barnaby Tucker ✻ Another employee

Original New York Cast

Carol Channing, David Burns, Eileen Brennan, Sondra Lee,
Charles Nelson Reilly, Jerry Dodge

Original London Cast

Mary Martin, Loring Smith, Marilynn Lovell, Coco Ramirez,
Garrett Lewis, Johnny Beecher

Plot

It's New York in the 1890s. Dolly Gallagher Levi has been engaged by the rich Yonkers merchant, Horace Vandergelder, to matchmake for him. Irene Molloy, a hat shop owner, has been selected but Dolly decides to save Horace for her very own. Meanwhile, his two assistants have escaped from the drudgery of Vandergelder's store, determined to find girls and spend a night on the town in New York. They hide in the hat shop when they see Horace, meet Irene and one, Cornelius, falls in love with her, while Barnaby is quite attracted to her shop assistant, Minnie. These will be their dinner partners for the evening.

Meanwhile, Horace makes for the Harmonia Gardens Restaurant. So does Dolly, who is greeted with rapture by the staff there. It turns out that the assistants and their dates are also dining there, but with little possibility of paying the bill. Luckily Dolly ensures that Horace picks up the tab, but there's a little contretemps with the law that results in many of the protagonists finding themselves temporarily behind bars.

Back at Horace's grain store it takes little time for Dolly to convince Horace that they are made for each other, and with similar romantic alliances planned by the youngsters, all ends happily.

Music and Songs

A splendid Broadway score with waltzes, quicksteps, foxtrots and good old-fashioned marches. Highlights include the title song (Harmonia Gardens waiters), 'Before the parade' (Dolly), 'Elegance' (Cornelius and trio), 'Put on your Sunday clothes' (Cornelius and Dolly), 'Ribbons down my back' (Mrs Molloy) and 'So long dearie' (Dolly).

Did You Know?

✶ Most of the stars who originally turned down the leading role – Ginger Rogers, Mary Martin and Ethel Merman – went on subsequently to play it.

✶ When Ethel Merman inherited the role, two additonal songs were crafted for her, and issued as an EP on the Bar Mike label.

✶ The composer feels the film version is definitive.

✶ Bob Merrill helped with the songs 'Elegance' and 'Motherhood'.

The Critics

The critics, while recognizing the show's limitations, also realized its potential: 'A musical comedy dream . . . don't bother holding onto your hats; you'd be throwing them up in the air anyway' – *New York Herald Tribune*
'Qualities of freshness that are rare in the run of our machine-made musicals. It transmutes the broadly stylized mood of the mettlesome farce into the gusto and colors of the musical stage. What was larger and droller than life has been puffed up and gaily timed without being blown apart' – *New York Times*
'A handsome, big, turn-of-the-century musical which is at its ebullient best when director Gower Champion turns loose the finest Broadway dancers in the most exciting numbers I have seen since Jerome Robbins staged *West Side Story*' – *New York Daily News*

Recommended Recording

Original Broadway cast (CD) RCA 3814-2-RG
The original and the best – but there is a great deal of competition from the likes of Pearl Bailey in the all-black production, and Barbra Streisand in the film. Miss Channing re-recorded her role as Dolly when she brought the show back into New York over thirty years after she first played the part, but the excitement of the original is lost.

Film

20th Century Fox, 1969. Starring Barbra Streisand and Walter Matthau, with Michael Crawford. Directed by Gene Kelly.

High Spirits

LYRICS ✳ Hugh Martin and Timothy Gray
MUSIC ✳ Hugh Martin and Timothy Gray
BOOK ✳ Hugh Martin and Timothy Gray,
based on Noël Coward's *Blithe Spirit*

First Performance

New York, Alvin Theater, 7 April 1964 (375 performances)
London, Savoy Theatre, 3 November 1964 (93 performances)

Principal Characters

Madame Arcati ✳ A medium
Charles Condomine ✳ A haunted husband
Ruth ✳ His second wife
Elvira ✳ His first wife
Dr and Mrs Bradman ✳ Friends
Edith ✳ A maid

Original New York Cast

Beatrice Lillie, Edward Woodward, Louise Troy, Tammy Grimes,
Lawrence Keith, Margaret Hall, Carol Arthur

Original London Cast

Cicely Courtneidge, Denis Quilley, Marti Stevens, Jan Waters,
Peter Vernon, Ann Hamilton, Denise Coffey

Plot

Charles and Ruth, his second wife, entertain the Bradmans and the medium, Madame Arcati. At a seance later in the evening Madame Arcati finds there's someone desperate to contact Charles. It's Elvira, his first wife. She materializes and means to stay, although only Charles can see her. Ruth sulks but eventually is convinced. Ruth seeks out Madame Arcati and asks for her help in getting rid of her predecessor. Meanwhile, Charles and Elvira spend a pleasant evening together.

In fact, Elvira wants to kill Charles so he can join her in the after-life, and she makes several unsuccessful attempts to do so. One of these is to tamper with his car. Ruth drives it and is duly killed. A seance reveals the guilty party – and also summons up Ruth. Eventually with the help of the servant, Edith, a natural medium as it turns out, the two wives are duly exorcised, but they can still wreak havoc around the house. Charles has a farewell drink with Madame Arcati and toasts the ladies. Elvira has spiked it, however, and all three are happily reunited in heaven to enjoy a further existence.

Music and Songs

A determined effort to summon up the style and substance of Coward's own lyric and melodic writing. In the event, it is highly successful, as shown in 'Home sweet heaven' (Elvira), 'On my bike' (Madame Arcati), 'Was she prettier than I?' (Ruth), 'You'd better love me' (Elvira), 'Forever and a day' (Charles and Elvira) and 'If I gave you' (Charles).

Did You Know?

∗ Coward enjoyed the show so much he recorded some numbers from the score himself.

∗ The London production was not a success, perhaps because of Coward himself and his involvement, perhaps because of casting.

∗ Noel Coward directed the Broadway production and 'supervised' the London one.

∗ Marti Stevens stepped in to replace Fenella Fielding whom Coward described as 'synthetic'.

The Critics

Of Beatrice Lillie's performance: 'Overflowing with coziness, she begins to move like a ballerina. Her hands flutter as she takes little mincing steps, then they wave broadly as the afflatus of Terpsichore possesses her . . . the audience roars for more and won't let the show go on' – *New York Times*

Recommended Recording

Original Broadway cast (CD) Broadway Gold MCAD 10767
The one to have. It has bounce, confidence and Beatrice Lillie as well – a constant delight in every way. The London cast version does give the chance to hear the remarkable Cicely Courtneidge interpret the part of Madame Arcati, and there is the addition of four of the songs from the show sung by Noel Coward.

Hit the Deck

LYRICS ✳ Clifford Grey and Leo Robin
MUSIC ✳ Vincent Youmans
BOOK ✳ Herbert Fields,
based on Hubert Osborne's play *Shore Leave*

First Performance

New York, Belasco Theater, 25 April 1927 (352 performances)
London, Hippodrome, 3 November 1927 (277 performances)

Principal Characters

Loulou Martin ✳ A café owner
Bilge Smith ✳ A sailor
Charlotte Payne ✳ A rich young lady
Donkey
Battling Smith
Ensign Clark ✳ A friend of Charlotte
Toddy Gaie ✳ A friend of Charlotte

Original New York Cast

Louise Groody, Charles King, Madeline Cameron, Brian Donlevy,
Frank Woods, John McCauley, Bobbie Perkins

Original London Cast

Ivy Tresmand, Stanley Holloway, Mamie Watson, Reginald Sheridan,
Sydney Howard, Gerald Nodin, Dick Francis

Plot

Loulou Martin runs a dockside coffee bar. Her beau, Bilge Smith, turns up with a present, a foul-mouthed parrot. Charlotte Payne arrives with Ensign Clark and Toddy Gaie. They're slumming it, but Charlotte is intrigued by Loulou's jewelled elephant pendant. She'd like to buy it. Bilge returns and reveals he'd love to leave the navy and have his own vessel. Now Loulou decides to sell her pendant; it should pay for a small cargo ship.

Six months later, Loulou seeks out Bilge, but can't find him. So she arranges to invite loads of men surnamed Smith to a party run by a friend on the USS *Nebraska*. There's no Bilge though. In fact he's forgotten her – almost. He finally turns up at the party and he's so impressed he proposes marriage. Now she can offer him that ship. But the result is the reverse of what she'd hoped. If she's rich, she's not the girl for him. Battling Smith takes her part and has a fight with Bilge who ends up in the naval prison.

Bilge is off to China with the navy and Loulou decides to follow him, with Charlotte and company in tow. Once there they discover that Bilge has another girl, Rita, a brassy Chinese-speaking charmer who knows she's not Bilge's true love. Back in Newport, Rhode Island, Loulou reopens her café and hopefully sends out invitations to every Smith in town. Charlotte and Alan (Ensign Clark) pass through with their wedding certificate. Now a scruffy Bilge turns up – he's heard Loulou is poor. Soon Loulou is in his arms and after explaining that her money is tied up in a trust fund for her first child, they settle down to plan their marriage.

Music and Songs

Youmans at his best: attractive, zesty, melodically rousing songs, including 'Hallelujah' (Lavinia), 'Sometimes I'm happy' (Bilge), 'Join the navy' (Loulou), 'Why, oh why' (chorus) and 'Harbor of my heart' (Bilge).

Did You Know?

✱ 'Sometimes I'm happy' started life as 'Come on and pet me' for the show *Mary Lane McKane*, but was later dropped. Under its current title it appeared in the flop, *A Night Out*, and was cut when that show appeared out of town.

✱ 'Hallelujah' was written a decade earlier when Youmans was actually in the navy.

✱ In London some names were changed; the main setting was Plymouth and the USS *Nebraska* became the HMS *Inscrutable*.

The Critics

'Clean, pretty, bright and happy' – Percy Hammond
'If "Sometimes I'm happy" isn't sung all over the world until sometimes you'll be unhappy I'll eat my chapeau' – Alan Dale
'You can hit the deck for *Hit the Deck*, a musical a teeny weeny bit naughty, and an altogether friendly frolic by the beautiful sea' – *New York Times*

Recommended Recording

Compilation album: Through the years with Vincent Youmans (CD)
Audiophile ACD 89
This studio cast album follows the career of Vincent Youmans from 1921 and up to his score for the movie *Flying Down to Rio*. There are the three main hits of the show and an extra ('Keepin' myself for you'), which he wrote for the film version.

Films

RKO, 1930. Starring Jack Oakie and Polly Walker. Directed by Luther Walker.
RKO, 1936. Starring Fred Astaire and Ginger Rogers. Directed by Mark Sandrich. Filmed as *Follow the Fleet*, with new songs and an altered story.
MGM, 1955. Starring Jane Powell, Tony Martin and Debbie Reynolds. Directed by Roy Rowland. Again, an altered story.

House of Flowers

LYRICS ✱ Truman Capote and Harold Arlen
MUSIC ✱ Harold Arlen
BOOK ✱ Truman Capote

First Performance

New York, Alvin Theater, 30 December 1954 (165 performances)

Principal Characters

Madame Tango
Madame Fleur
Ottilie
Royal

Original New York Cast

Juanita Hall, Pearl Bailey, Diahann Carroll, Rawn Spearman

Plot

House of Flowers is a West Indies bordello run by the redoubtable Madame Fleur, whose girls are named after flowers. Madame Tango runs a rival establishment. An outbreak of mumps caught from visiting sailors closes the House of Flowers and Fleur faces ruin. Still, Ottilie, Fleur's protegée, has escaped the illness. Fleur is ready to sell her off to a wealthy shipowner, but Ottilie has other plans, namely a poor boy from the hills. Fleur has him kidnapped but he escapes from the ship, avoiding the odd shark. It's some time before he returns but he does, in the nick of time, to prevent Ottilie ending up with the shipowner. In addition, he's now the town's hero. Things haven't worked out exactly as Madame Fleur would have wished, but she has the satisfaction of knowing that Madame Tango has also had her problems. Her girls end up far away from the bordello on a world tour on a passenger cruise liner.

Music and Songs

Melodic Arlen at his peak. A rich bluesy score full of Caribbean overtones and subtle rhythms. It is one of the most distinguished of all Broadway scores, including 'A sleepin' bee' (Ottilie), 'House of Flowers' (Fleur), 'Two ladies in de shade of de banana tree' (the girls), 'Has I let you down?' (Fleur), 'I never has seen snow' (Ottilie) and 'Don't like goodbyes' (Fleur).

Did You Know?

∗ The tune of 'A sleepin' bee' had been written for, but not used in, *A Star is Born*.

∗ Truman Capote was not best pleased with the alterations to his stories and walked out after a series of rows. George Balanchine also resigned as director, handing over to Herbert Ross.

∗ Diahann Carroll later scored a major success in Richard Rodgers' *No Strings*.

∗ The show has been revived on a few occasions but commercial success continues to elude it.

∗ Because Harold Arlen had written songs for the Cotton Club shows and for other black shows, Truman Capote had assumed he was black too.

∗ Harold Arlen was in hospital during the troubled out-of-town tryout and Truman Capote had to work at his bedside.

The Critics

Although a few critics referred to the show as dull and dirty and mediocre, the true measure of it was summed up by George Jean Nathan: 'The most visually beautiful and in some respects the most exotically exciting evening I have encountered since I was last on the semitropical island in which it is laid.' *Variety* believed, 'The show is not bad, but by no means great.'
Others lauded it as 'a great big razzle-dazzle of a musical' and 'a breezy and bountiful blockbuster'.

Recommended Recording

Original Broadway cast (CD) CBS Special Products A2320
This delicious Harold Arlen score is well served by his original cast and is the only version that has reached CD. Arlen's gift to write 'black' music is heard to perfection here.

How to Succeed in Business Without Really Trying

LYRICS ✳ Frank Loesser
MUSIC ✳ Frank Loesser
BOOK ✳ Abe Burrows, Jack Weinstein and Willie Gilbert,
based on Shepherd Mead's book

First Performance

New York, 46th Street Theater, 14 October 1961 (1417 performances)
London, Shaftesbury Theatre, 28 March 1963 (520 performances)

Principal Characters

J. Pierrepont Finch ✳ Our hero
J.B. Biggley ✳ The president
Rosemary ✳ Finch's sweetheart
Smitty ✳ A secretary
Bud Frump ✳ The president's nephew-in-law
Miss Jones ✳ The president's secretary
Hedy La Rue ✳ The president's little friend
Mr Twimble ✳ A company man

Original New York Cast

Robert Morse, Rudy Vallée, Bonnie Scott, Charlotte Sutherland,
Charles Nelson Reilly, Ruth Kobart, Virginia Martin, Sammy Smith

Original London Cast

Warren Berlinger, Billy de Wolfe, Patricia Michael, Josephine Blake,
David Knight, Olive Lucius, Eileen Gourlay, Bernard Spear

Plot

An ambitious window cleaner, our hero, Finch, is at his work high up on the side of the World Wide Wicket Company. He's reading a manual, *How to Succeed in Business Without Really Trying*. Back on the ground he runs into the president, asks for a job, goes to personnel and begins his climb from the post room. He quickly makes friends but he's got an enemy, Bud, nephew of the president's wife. Mr Twimble, head of the post room, can choose his successor, and chooses Finch, who rejects the offer – in favour of Bud! Soon Finch is on his way himself, in Plans and Systems. He encounters the president, Biggley, when the latter pops in on Saturday and Finch is discovered asleep at his desk. Guess what, he went to the chairman's old school (oh yeah?). He is soon advancing up the ladder. And he's allotted Hedy, a shapely, but not too bright, close friend of Biggley's, as his secretary – better watch out. Meanwhile, Bud engineers Finch and Hedy into a seemingly compromising situation, but Finch's new friend Rosemary, a loyal secretary, helps him and Finch escapes unharmed. He's now vice president in charge of advertising! Unfortunately, incumbents usually don't last longer than a month in this job, so what can he do?

Rosemary is now the new vice president's secretary. But she's not happy – she wants to be more than this to Finch. Meanwhile, Bud offers Finch the idea of a TV treasure hunt (his uncle has already rejected this) and Finch sells this successfully. Hedy is the TV treasure girl giving out clues. Then disaster strikes. Hedy has got to swear on a Bible that she doesn't know where the treasure is. Only Finch and Biggley know, don't they? Well no, Hedy knows too, and the TV programme is a disaster. Enter the company chairman, Mr Womper. Who chose the treasure girl? Biggley did but Finch magnanimously manages to save the former's job. Womper marries Hedy and goes on a cruise. Finch is the new chairman, with Rosemary at his side.

Music and Songs

A wonderfully diverting set of songs by the old wizard, Frank Loesser, lyrically dextrous, melodically varied and memorable. The hit is 'I believe in you', a song sung to himself in a mirror by our hero. Also featured are 'Brotherhood of man' (Finch and company) and the witty 'The company way' (Twimble), with other tuneful highspots being 'Coffee break' (employees), 'Grand old Ivy' (Biggley and Finch), 'Paris original' (Rosemary and chorus) and 'Been a long day' (Finch and Rosemary).

Did You Know?

✴ This was Robert Morse's first Broadway starring role; he'd made his name previously in the play *Say Darling*, but not as the star.

✴ *How to Succeed* ... became the sixth longest-running Broadway show.

✴ Film favourite Billy de Wolfe took on the role in England created by Rudy Vallée on Broadway.

The Critics

'It stings mischievously and laughs uproariously . . . its irreverence is as bracing as a growth stock that matures into a nice capital gain' – *New York Times*
'Crafty, conniving, sneaky, cynical, irreverent, impertinent, malicious and lovely, just lovely' – *New York Herald Tribune*

Recommended Recording

Original Broadway cast (CD) RCA Victor 60352-2-RG
Robert Morse captured at his most sparkling best. One of the great scores of this golden Broadway period and a delight to own. The added attraction is the appearance of veteran performer Rudy Vallee showing a wonderful comic touch.

Film

United Artists, 1967. Starring Robert Morse and Michele Lee. Directed by David Swift.

I Do! I Do!

LYRICS ✶ Tom Jones
MUSIC ✶ Harvey Schmidt
BOOK ✶ Tom Jones,
based on the play *The Four-poster* by Jan de Hartog

First Performance

New York, 46th Street Theater, 5 December 1966 (561 performances)
London, Lyric Theatre, 16 May 1968 (115 performances)

Principal Characters

Michael ✶ A husband
Agnes ✶ A wife

Original New York Cast

Robert Preston, Mary Martin

Original London Cast

Ian Carmichael, Anne Rogers

Plot

Michael and Agnes are just married. *I Do! I Do!* charts their next fifty years together from their bedroom, which is dominated by an immense four-poster. As the years pass, Agnes bears two children and the couple realise how dependent they are on each other. This is not to say that their married life does not have its problems. Michael is a successful writer and Agnes exhibits understandable envy and jealousy – justified as it happens. Michael has had an extra-marital affair. Agnes decides that it's time for her to put on her gladrags, even if Michael is hurt and angered by her actions. Michael believes that men are in their prime in middle age, whereas women go to pieces. Agnes plans to leave and is only just dissuaded from doing so.

The years pass, and Michael finds it difficult to come to terms with his daughter's marriage. Her children now grown up, Agnes feels her life to be empty. Yet life has been good to them and Michael eventually realises the important role his wife has played in his creative life. The couple decide to move out of the house, leaving behind a small pillow embroidered with the words 'God is Love' for the young couple who are just moving in to begin their life together.

Music and Songs

A tender, lyrical, romantic score recalling Kern and Rodgers. Some of the better-known melodies are 'All the dearly beloved' (Michael and Agnes), 'I do! I do!' (Michael and Agnes), 'I love my wife' (Michael), 'My cup runneth over' (Michael and Agnes), 'Nobody's perfect' (Michael and Agnes), 'Flaming Agnes' (Agnes), 'The honeymoon is over' (Michael and Agnes) and 'When the kids get married' (Michael and Agnes).

Did You Know?

✳ This was the third musical version of *The Four-poster*, but the only successful one.

✳ As a two-parter the show was easily revived and mounted all over the world.

✳ Juliet Prowse and Rock Hudson revived the show for a limited London season in 1976.

The Critics

'A happy show generous with charm and lavish with love' – *New York World Journal Tribune*

'A work of remarkable consistency, fine musically, warm rhythms and fine performances. A warm and very original musical, Jones and Schmidt's work is lovely and strong' – *Women's Wear Daily*

'The whole performance has a choreographic pattern that only a dancer-singer of (Gower) Champion's demonstrated ability could design and carry out. The dancing, in other words, tends to be part of the action and dramatises the situation and the ideas and emotions of its stars' – *Variety*

Recommended Recording

Original Broadway cast (CD) RCA Victor 1128-2-RC
Two of Broadway's greatest performers at their best. This is a delightful album and it sounds as fresh today as it did back in the sixties.

Film

In 1982 *I Do! I Do!* was filmed for television, starring Lee Remick and Hal Linden.

I'd Rather Be Right

LYRICS ✶ Lorenz Hart
MUSIC ✶ Richard Rodgers
BOOK ✶ George S. Kaufman and Moss Hart

First Performance

New York, Alvin Theater, 2 November 1937 (290 performances)

Principal Characters

Franklin D. Roosevelt ✶ The President
Secretary Morgenthau ✶ A politician
Phil Barker ✶ A young man
Postmaster General Farley
Secretary Hull ✶ A politician
Judge's girl
Peggy Jones ✶ Phil's girl

Original New York Cast

George M. Cohan, Taylor Holmes, Austin Marshall, Paul Parks,
Marion Green, Mary Jane Walsh, Joy Hodges

Plot

Peggy Jones and Phil Barker can't get married. The problem is that he needs a hike in salary, and he is not likely to get one until the country's national budget is balanced. What to do? Phil dreams that he and Peggy are sitting on a park bench where they meet the president, Franklin D. Roosevelt. He agrees to help the young couple, but he's frustrated at every turn by political and social forces both within and outside Washington.

In one of his famous fireside chats the president suggests that women give up makeup for a year, and donate the savings to the national budget. No chance of that, as women throughout the land would rise up in protest. So how about using the gold stored in Fort Knox for the budget? The stock market won't hear of that either, and inevitably the result is that the budget can't be balanced. But the president is not done yet. He turns to Phil and Peggy and tells them that they should have faith in themselves – and in their country – and get married anyway! Phil wakes up and decides to take the president's advice.

Music and Songs

A score bound closely to the plot rather than consisting of numbers that can be picked out. However, some of them are 'A homogenous cabinet' (the Cabinet), 'Have you met Miss Jones?' (Paul), 'We're going to balance the budget' (the President) and 'Off the record' (the President).

Did You Know?

✴ George M. Cohan, an argumentative, embittered man, was hard to control. He'd been used to running his own shows and singing his own songs, yet he gave 'a performance of dimension and depth, a performance touched with warmth and humanity and wistfulness as well as mockery and gaiety' – David Ewen

✴ *I'd Rather be Right* remained the only Broadway book musical with a real president as its leading character, until the arrival of *Annie*, which also featured Roosevelt.

✴ *Mr President* and *1600 Pennsylvania Avenue* featured fictional presidents. *1776* featured at least two real, but future, presidents.

✴ An actor made up as Harry S. Truman took a curtain call in *Call Me Madam* but took no further part in the action.

The Critics

'It should swell our pride, in the freedom we enjoy and in the gift for laughter which must be counted among our natural assets. The more good-humoured liberties Mr Kaufman and Mr Hart's satire takes, the more liberty its mere performance bespeaks' – John Mason Brown, *New York Post*

Recommended Recording

While no recording of the score exists you can hear three numbers on *Ben Bagley's Rodgers and Hart Revisited, Volume IV* (Painted Smiles PSCD-126). The *Revisited* albums have long been a source for those rare Broadway songs by the master composers and lyricists of the last century, and these are well worth exploring.

I Love My Wife

LYRICS ✶ Michael Stewart
MUSIC ✶ Cy Coleman
BOOK ✶ Michael Stewart, from a play by Luis Rego

First Performance

New York, Ethel Barrymore Theater, 17 April 1977 (857 performances)
London, Prince of Wales Theatre, 6 October 1977 (410 performances)

Principal Characters

Alvin ✶ The nerd
Wally ✶ The brash, self-confident one
Cleo ✶ Alvin's wife
Monica ✶Wally's wife
Plus the band, which acts as a kind of Greek chorus, weaving in and out of the
action and accenting it where necessary

Original New York Cast

Lenny Baker, James Naughton, Ilene Graff, Joanna Gleason

Original London Cast

Richard Beckinsale, Ben Cross, Deborah Fallender, Liz Robertson

Plot

With a story vaguely reminiscent of the film *Bob and Carol and Ted and Alice*, *I Love My Wife* is set in Trenton, New Jersey. Alvin and Wally have been chums from high school, but their working lives are very different. Wally is a sophisticated public relations executive (well, semi-sophisticated, anyway). His pal Alvin is a furniture removal man, and that for him is the noblest job on earth. Over a beer in a local hostelry, Wally feels that a threesome in bed would improve his public relations no end! Alvin also feels that a further bed companion would indeed make the bedtime a bit warmer! There's an idea – Alvin suggests to Cleo that it would be nice to share their bed with Monica for once. Cleo thinks it would be nice to share a bed with Wally. In the end, whichever of the two comes in first will be their bedtime companion for the night. Of course, Wally and Monica come in at the same time! When Monica goes to visit her mother, the other three talk around the situation. Shall it be Wally and Cleo? Wally and both women? Or a foursome? They finally agree on the latter solution. Christmas Eve would be a nice night for it.

It's Christmas Eve. Wally and Monica open their presents at home. Wally hints that the real present is arriving at 9 pm for dinner – and then for the swap. Monica is livid with rage, but when Alvin and Cleo arrive she agrees to participate. Everyone is too excited to eat dinner, though. How about some 'pot' to help them relax (this *is* a 70s musical after all). They undress and all scramble into bed. Now Wally is hungry. Afterwards, Wally consults a sex manual, but all the routines seem too complex for beginners. They start with No.1, the Loop the Loop, but it's no good. Their hoped-for orgy has fizzled out. Never mind. Alvin and Wally will meet again after the festivities at their local bar, and Monica and Cleo will meet at the shops when they exchange the Christmas presents from their husbands for what they really want. The couples contentedly part, their friendship unimpaired.

Music and Songs

A gigantic shaggy dog story with a vibrant, catchy, heartily satisfying Coleman score full of light-hearted fun that screams Broadway at you. Songs include 'We're still friends' (the cast), 'Monica' (Wally), 'A mover's life' (Alvin and the band), 'Someone wonderful I missed' (Monica and Cleo), 'Hey there, good times' (the cast) and 'I love my wife' (Alvin and Wally).

Did You Know?

∗ The show won four Drama Desk awards and two Tonys.

∗ In an eerie parallel, both New York's and London's Alvins, among the brightest young comedians of their generation on each side of the Atlantic, died tragically young.

∗ Despite the potentially difficult subject, the authors managed to make the show genuinely funny, enjoyable and literate, with no prurience or, surprisingly, lack of taste.

∗ 'Hey there, good times' is one of Cy Coleman's 24 carat show-stoppers – once heard, never forgotten.

The Critics

'Bright, inventive, amusing and breezy' – *New York Times*
'I can't see the harm in a healthy, well adjusted, sentimental and cheerful musical about sex and marriage' – *New York Post*

Recommended Recording

Original Broadway cast (CD) DRG CDRG 6109
A cheerful recording of a Cy Coleman score that sits happily in its own seventies time capsule. It's all great fun.

Into the Woods

LYRICS ✶ Stephen Sondheim
MUSIC ✶ Stephen Sondheim
BOOK ✶ James Lapine

First Performance

New York, Martin Beck Theater, 5 November 1987 (764 performances)
London, Phoenix Theatre, 25 September 1990 (186 performances)

Principal Characters

Baker
Baker's wife
Witch
Jack the Giant-Killer
Cinderella
Rapunzel
Little Red Riding Hood
Mrs Giant
The Wolf/First Prince
A Prince
Jack's mother

Original New York Cast

Chip Zien, Joanna Gleason, Bernadette Peters, Ben Wright,
Kim Crosby, Pamela Winslow, Danielle Ferland,
Robert Westenberg, Chuck Wagner, Barbara Bryne

Original London Cast

Ian Bartholomew, Imelda Staunton, Julia McKenzie, Richard Dempsey,
Jacqueline Dankworth, Mary Lincoln, Tessa Burbridge,
Clive Carter, Mark Tinkler, Patsy Rowlands

Plot

The Baker and his Wife are cursed as barren by the neighbourhood Witch. They can overcome the spell only by acquiring Jack's cow, Cinderella's slipper, Rapunzel's hair and Red Riding Hood's cape. In so doing they bring untold mischief, not to mention death, to many of the main characters. However, as the first act ends, Cinderella has her Prince, Red Riding Hood has killed her Wolf, Rapunzel has her Prince too and has been rescued from the tower, and the Baker's Wife is newly pregnant. Happy ever after? Well, no.

In the second act the two princes develop wandering eyes and are back on the chase – after the Sleeping Beauty and Snow White respectively. After the death of her husband, Mrs Giant decides to do a little detective work to avenge her spouse and kill off his murderer. Jack's mother interposes herself between Jack and his pursuer, and is duly killed. The Baker's Wife dallies with a prince and is then crushed by the marauding giantess. Even the narrator is sacrificed. By the end, there's only the Baker and his child, Cinderella, Rapunzel, Jack and Red Riding Hood left to join together to fight and overcome their adversary, which they do with the help of Cinderella's friends, the birds. In the closing moments all characters past and present reassemble to offer optimism and reassurance to themselves – and to us.

Music and Songs

A vintage Sondheim score that includes both light and darkness, like all the best fairy tales. It includes 'No one is alone' (the company), 'No more' (Baker) and 'Children will listen' (Witch), plus 'Hello little girl' (Wolf), 'Agony' (Prince), 'Giants in the sky' (Jack) and 'Last midnight' (Witch).

Did You Know?

✷ The versions of the stories derive from Grimm rather than Perrault. Hence Cinderella goes to the ball more than once, and her sisters' eyes are pecked out by the birds (all absent in Perrault's gentler version).

✷ The highly interesting London version chose a radically different approach to staging and setting. The narrator and the old man were split, there was a new song, and the look was entirely different.

✷ *Into The Woods* won the best score, book and actress Tony Awards.

The Critics

The critics cast their verdict:
'*Into the Woods* has plenty of charm . . . a sparkling show with an ache at the center' – *Los Angeles Herald Examiner*
'The best show yet from the most creative mind in the musical theatre today' – *Time*
'Genuine musical theater. An evening of total enchantment' – *New York Daily News*
'[Sondheim's] new, placid musical leaves the unmistakable impression that his art is spoiling for a fresh fight' – *New York Times*

Recommended Recording

Original Broadway cast (CD) RCA Victor 6976-2 RC
This wins by a whisker. Julia McKenzie who, like Bernadette Peters, is a Sondheim favourite, heads the London cast. The London recording, however, seems darker in its attempt to make certain no one can mistake this for a pantomime.

Video

Original Broadway cast – Video and DVD (NTSC)

Irene

LYRICS ✴ Joseph McCarthy
MUSIC ✴ Harry Tierney
BOOK ✴ James Montgomery, based on his play *Irene O'Dare*

First Performance

New York, Vanderbilt Theater, 18 November 1919 (670 performances)
London, Empire Theatre, 7 April 1920 (339 performances)

Principal Characters

Irene O'Dare ✴ A simple colleen
Donald Marshall ✴ A son and heir
Madame Lucy ✴ A male couturier
Mrs O'Dare ✴ Irene's mother

Original New York Cast

Edith Day, Walter Reagan, Bobbie Watson, Dorothy Walters

Original London Cast

Edith Day, Pat Somerset, Robert Hale, Helen Kinnaird

Plot

Poor Irene O'Dare is an upholsterer from New York's Ninth Avenue, who is going into the piano-tuning business. She has just installed the new-fangled telephone to accept bookings. At Mrs Marshall's smart, Long Island home she meets Donald, the son and heir – he has arranged for her to tune all seven pianos scattered round the house. Donald's cousin, Ozzie, wants him to back a couturier, Madame Lucy (a middle-aged Irishman, in fact). Donald agrees to do so if Irene can be appointed the business manager. All goes well and there's a successful ball where Madame Lucy's creations are much admired – especially by Irene disguised as an Italian contessa! But Irene has something more permanent in mind for Donald and herself. What can she do?

Back home on Ninth Avenue, Irene maintains a strict business demeanour when Donald comes to visit her and kisses her. Of course, as she has resigned from the firm, and it wants her back, Donald's interest may be on several levels. She agrees to reappear at one last function as the contessa. And her mother comes too! The latter recognizes the couturier as a long-lost love, and Irene appears in an Alice-blue gown. Donald introduces her to the guests as his intended wife, Miss Irene O'Dare.

This synopsis is based on the revival. In the original Irene was an upholsterer-turned-shopgirl/mannequin who was involved with J.P. Bowden before her romance with Donald.

Music and Songs

'Alice-blue gown' (Irene) and the title tune 'Irene' (Donald) were the hits. The enduring score also included 'Skyrocket' (Irene), 'To be worthy of you' (Irene) and 'Castle of dreams' (Irene), the latter deleted in the revival. The revival incorporated 'I'm always chasing rainbows' (Donald) and 'You made me love you' (Irene).

Did You Know?

✳ The original Broadway run of *Irene* was the longest of any show there up to that time.

✳ The revival of the show transferred to open the Minskoff Theater in 1973.

✳ The London revival starring Julie Anthony was the world's longest-running production of *Irene*.

✳ Alice blue was a colour popularized in 1919 by Teddy Roosevelt's daughter, Alice Roosevelt Longworth, and both Roosevelts were the focus of a 1980s musical employing music by Sousa called *Teddy and Alice*.

The Critics

'Undemanding, raucous, frequently cheerful and the best 1919 musical in town' – *New York Times* of the 1973 revival

Recommended Recording

1973 Broadway cast (CD) Sony Broadway SK 32266
A fresh look at the score with wonderful orchestrations and rich performances. Debbie Reynolds is at her innocent best.

Films

First National, 1926 (silent). Starring Colleen Moore and George K. Arthur.
RKO, 1940. Starring Anna Neagle, Ray Milland, Alan Marshal and Roland Young. Directed by Herbert Wilcox.

Irma-la-Douce

LYRICS ✷ Julian More, Monty Norman and David Heneker
MUSIC ✷ Marguerite Monnot
BOOK ✷ Julian More, Monty Norman and David Heneker,
based on a French book and lyrics by Alexandre Brefford

First Performance

London, Lyric Theatre, 17 July 1958 (1512 performances)
New York, Plymouth Theater, 29 September 1960 (524 performances)

Principal Characters

Irma-la-Douce ✷ Girl of the boulevards
Nestor-le-Fripé ✷ Her man (also called Oscar)
Bob-le-Hontu ✷ Parisian bar owner
Polyte-le-Mou ✷ Pimp
Police Inspector
Frangipane

Original London Cast

Elizabeth Seal, Keith Michell, Clive Revill, John East,
Julian Orchard, Gary Raymond

Original New York Cast

Elizabeth Seal, Keith Michell, Clive Revill, Fred Gwynne,
George S. Irving, Stuart Damon

Plot

Bob-le-Hontu runs a small bar in Pigalle, Paris. He introduces us to his friends
and acquaintances, including Irma, a working girl (*poule*), selling time near her
beat, and taking the money (*grisbi*) back to her pimp (*mec*). Except Irma doesn't
have one any more. She's broken up with Polyte who treated her roughly, and a
young student, Nestor, came to her rescue. Nestor buys her a drink. Irma falls in
love. He moves in with her, and takes over the income. But then he becomes
jealous of the men she's going with. Perhaps he could get a job? Unheard of! *Mecs*
don't work. What Irma needs is a sugar daddy. Enter ageing, bearded, very sweet
Oscar. He'll pay 10,000 francs for her exclusive services – per day! Irma is pleased,
and the *mecs* are envious – Nestor is elected their chief. But Oscar *is* Nestor, and
he has to earn a living to make the money to pay himself with! That's an
exhausting prospect and he and Irma find themselves frequently quarrelling. He'll
have to kill Oscar off. He leaves Oscar's clothes beside the river, confesses his
'crime' and is promptly arrested.

There's a trial, and Nestor is convicted and sent off to Devil's Island in French
Guiana. The boys in the bar think Irma will return to her old freewheeling ways,
but not a bit of it. She's profoundly changed. She's pregnant, and the baby is

expected at Christmas. Nestor is not a success as a prisoner and decides to escape to attend the birth. Along with other *mecs*, he breaks out disguised as a prison warder following a drunken party. After his Atlantic voyage, Nestor has a beard again and looks like Oscar. Irma recognizes his previous deception, so it's off to the police to be cleared of his own murder! Later on the Christmas child Irma is expecting turns out to be twins, the first to be called Nestor and the second Oscar! Nestor and Irma get married – and sometimes even Oscar comes to visit!

Music and Songs

As gallic as garlic bread! The score is headed by 'Our language of love' (Irma and Nestor) and 'Dis-donc, dis donc' (Irma), but also includes 'Valse milieu' (Bob and Irma), 'The bridge of Caulincourt' (Irma and Nestor), 'She's got the lot' (Police Inspector), 'Le grisbi' (Bob, Nestor and company), 'Irma-la-Douce' (Irma and company), 'There is only one Paris for that' (Nestor and company) and 'Christmas child' (the company).

Did You Know?

✱ Madame Monnot was responsible for the worldwide hit 'Milord' and other songs for Edith Piaf.

✱ This is one of the very few Continental musicals to make a world impact in recent years – until *Les Miserables*, and that was another one-off. Both shows had London runs that exceeded the French originals.

The Critics

'Trust the French to make vice as innocent as a fable' – *New York Times*
'Its mixture of cynicism and romance is managed with such paradoxical charm that it all seems delightfully hearted' – *New York Post*
Miss Seal was described by a London critic as 'the brightest girl star of musical comedy to appear since the war'.

Recommended Recording

Original Broadway cast (CD) Sony Broadway SK 48018
The original London cast with the same three stars was recorded in mono and has not been re-issued on CD. So this stereo version was recorded two years after the first, and the performances are a little less spontaneous but not enough to take the enjoyment away.

Film

United Artists, 1963. Starring Shirley Maclaine and Jack Lemmon. Directed by Billy Wilder. The film has no songs.

Jamaica

LYRICS ✳ E.Y. Harburg
MUSIC ✳ Harold Arlen
BOOK ✳ E.Y. Harburg and Fred Saidy

First Performance

New York, Imperial Theater, 31 October 1957 (558 performances)

Principal Characters

Miss Savannah ✳ The belle of Pigeon Island
Koli ✳ A fisherman
Joe Nashua ✳ A city slicker
Grandma
Cicero ✳ Another fisherman
Ginger ✳ His sweetheart

Original New York Cast

Lena Horne, Ricardo Montalban, Joe Adams, Adelaide Hall,
Cicero Ossie Davis, Josephine Premice

Plot

Jamaica introduces us to the inhabitants of Pigeon Island, which lies just off the
shore of Kingston, Jamaica. Savannah is discontented. She has read all about the
delights of New York and heard more about it from the many tourists. A local
fisherman, Koli, is deeply in love with her, but there's no way she'll marry him
unless he accompanies her to New York – and he won't do that. But there's an
alternative: a recent visitor from Harlem is the smooth-talking Joe Nashua. He's
heard about the pearls lying offshore in the shark-infested waters that surround
Pigeon Island. He could be Savannah's passport to a brighter life.

But nature intervenes. There's a terrible hurricane, and Koli proves himself a
hero; he rescues Savannah's little brother, Quico. Savannah's hopes of a New York
visit are limited to a dream set in the Persian Room in New York. The hurricane
has given Cicero, another inhabitant, temporary hopes of ruling the island with
his sweetheart, Ginger. But all returns to normal, and Savannah, coming to her
senses, realises that the future holds a life on the island with Koli as her husband.

Music and Songs

An effective, Caribbean-influenced, Arlen-Harburg score with a smoky, bluesy
feel. There is a superb collection of fine songs but there are no classics among
them. They include 'Push de button' (Savannah), 'Little biscuit' (Savannah) and
'Ain't it de truth?' (Savannah), which was subsequently retained by Miss Horne in
her nightclub act, plus 'Cocoanut sweet' (Savannah), 'Pretty to walk with'
(Savannah), 'Leave the atom alone' (Ginger), 'For every fish' (Grandma) and
'Monkey in the mango tree' (Koli).

Did You Know?

✶ This show presented Lena Horne in her first Broadway starring role; she had made her professional debut in the *Cotton Club Revues*, with music by Harold Arlen.

✶ The show was originally planned for Harry Belafonte to play the lead. After Lena Horne was signed, Sidney Poitier was suggested for the role of Koli, but he was no singer. Montalban, a Mexican, was to receive hate mail for accepting the role.

✶ This is another Yip Harburg score with political comment.

✶ The set designer, Oliver Smith, won a Tony Award, but it was for *West Side Story*.

The Critics

'I'm afraid I've forgotten the book. I'm afraid Mr Harburg and Mr Arlen have also forgotten it . . . I believe she [Miss Horne] could survive any plot, including Guy Fawkes" – *Newsday*

'She shines like a tigress in the night, purring and preening and pouncing into the spotlight' – *Life*

'She stands as lithe as a willow at the center of the stage, sucks in her breath as though she were inhaling a windstorm and coos out the most imperturbable of mating pigeon sounds' – Walter Kerr

Recommended Recording

Original Broadway cast (CD) RCA 09026 68041-2
The CD is more complete than was either the original mono or stereo LP – each of which contained slightly different selections. It presents Miss Horne in top form, supported by equally vivid vocal characterisations from the rest of the talented cast.

Jesus Christ Superstar

LYRICS ✶ Tim Rice
MUSIC ✶ Andrew Lloyd Webber
BOOK ✶ Now unattributed, but previously credited (for the
New York production) to Tom O'Horgan, based on the New Testament

First Performance

New York, Mark Hellinger Theater, 12 October 1971 (711 performances)
London, Palace Theatre, 9 August 1972 (3358 performances)

Principal Characters

Jesus of Nazareth
Mary Magdalene
Judas Iscariot
King Herod
Pontius Pilate

Original New York Cast

Jeff Fenholt, Yvonne Elliman, Ben Vereen, Barry Dennen, Paul Ainsley

Original London Cast

Paul Nicholas, Dana Gillespie, Stephen Tate, John Parker, Paul Jabara

Plot

The last seven days of the life of Christ seen through the eyes of his betrayer, Judas Iscariot, who fears that the humanitarian movement with Jesus at its head has become a personality cult, with its leader's many statements taken up and twisted by his followers. Jesus must be stopped. He is regularly ministered to by a tramp from the streets, one Mary Magdalene. Still worse he is being hailed as the Messiah. Judas meets with Priests of Judaea and agrees to betray Jesus for thirty pieces of silver. Jesus preaches throughout the land offering riches in the afterlife – not here on earth.

Meanwhile, a Roman officer, Pontius Pilate, dreams of a strange Galilean whose path will cross his own and cause him, Pilate, to be despised. After casting out traders from the Temple, Jesus has a last supper with his disciples and lets Judas know he is aware of the coming betrayal. At Gethsemene, Jesus prays for strength for the coming ordeal, but also for a deliverance that he knows is not possible.

When Judas brings the soldiers to Gethsemene, Jesus does not resist. He is brought before Pilate who recognises the subject of his dream. Pilate refuses to convict him and sends Jesus to King Herod. Meanwhile, Judas has hanged himself. Back in Pilate's court (Herod has likewise refused to convict) a rabble insists; Jesus is convicted and crucified.

Music and Songs

A fine, hit-packed, red-blooded rock 'n' roll and music hall score. Rice and Lloyd Webber exposed their pop roots in songs such as 'Everything's alright' (Mary Magdalene), 'I don't know how to love him' (Mary Magdalene), 'Hosanna' (the disciples), 'Superstar' (Judas and company) and 'King Herod's song' (King Herod).

Did You Know?

∗ Until *Cats* finally overtook it, *Jesus Christ Superstar* held the record as the longest-running West End musical of all time.

∗ Andrew Lloyd Webber and Tim Rice are the only team to write successful musicals based on both Old and New Testament subjects.

∗ The latest revival opened the long-dark Lyceum Theatre in London at the end of 1996.

∗ This was written as a concept record album which became a huge hit almost everywhere other than in Great Britain. When live concert versions started to be produced it was realised that the show had theatrical possibilities, and so it was presented on Broadway.

∗ The original London version was a totally different production from that seen on Broadway.

The Critics

'Lyricist Tim Rice has found for the rock musical a personal and I think a persuasive tone of voice' – Walter Kerr
'A shattering theatrical experience unlike any other I can recall. It seems likely to be around for a long time to come' – *New York Daily News*

Recommended Recording

Original concept album (CD) MCA Records DMCX 501
A remarkable recording that is excellently sung and it is full of atmosphere (even Messrs Lloyd Webber and Rice join in with the chorus work). The 1997 London Revival cast recording is the best recording of a stage production and Steve Balsamo is thrilling.

Film

Universal Pictures, 1973. Starring Ted Neely and Carl Anderson. Directed by Norman Jewison.

Video/DVD

A video / DVD of latest revival stage version has been released in all country formats.

Joseph and the Amazing Technicolor Dreamcoat

LYRICS ✳ Tim Rice
MUSIC ✳ Andrew Lloyd Webber
BOOK ✳ Tim Rice

First Performance

London, Young Vic Theatre, 16 October 1972 (16 performances, plus 243
performances on transfer at the Roundhouse and Albery theatres)
New York, Entermedia Theater/Royal Theater, 18 November 1981
(747 performances)

Principal Characters

Narrator
Joseph
Pharoah

Original London Cast

Gary Bond, Peter Reeves, Gordon Waller

Original New York Cast

David James Carroll, Cleavon Little, Jesse Pearson

Plot

In the biblical land of Caanan, Joseph is the favourite son of Jacob. As such, he
encounters the jealousy of his brothers, who object to his dreams in which he is
the hero, with his brothers paying him homage. They arrange to have him killed
and show their father his multicoloured coat, spattered with blood, as proof of his
death. But this is not the truth. Joseph has been sold as a slave in Egypt and has
entered Potiphar's household, where he falls foul of his master who is jealous of
his wife's partiality for Joseph. Cast into jail, Joseph puts his interpretation of
dreams to use. He sees death ahead for a baker, and Pharoah's butler will be
restored to his master's side. Both dreams come true.

Pharoah starts having dreams. The butler remembers Joseph; he is hauled out
of jail to interpret Pharoah's dreams. Joseph foresees seven years of full harvests
followed by seven of famine. This is decoded as an instruction to stock up on
food. Pharoah wastes no time in putting Joseph in charge of the whole operation.
Everything prophesied comes to pass.

Back in Caanan, famine hits Jacob's family hard. The brothers travel to Egypt
to try to find work. They go to Joseph who recognises them, but they don't
recognise him, and they bow down before him (as in his earliest dreams). Joseph
loads them up with grain, but it's also time to settle old scores. He has a precious
goblet hidden in one sack and accuses Benjamin of theft (the goblet was in his

sack). As they plead with Joseph for Benjamin's freedom, the former relents and reveals himself as their brother. The ending is, of course, a happy one.

Music and Songs

A wide-ranging, hugely enjoyable, extremely eclectic collection embracing everything from country and western- and Elvis-inspired songs to French chanson and calypso. Jason Donovan scored chart successes with 'Any dream will do' (Joseph) and 'Close every door' (Joseph). Other songs are 'Those Caanan days' (the brothers) and 'One more angel in Heaven' (the brothers).

Did You Know?

✱ The show started as a 15-minute cantata for the pupils of Colet Court in 1968. However, it steadily grew and grew; the first recorded version was 35 minutes long. American productions from 1969 onwards preceded longer versions in Britain: in 1972 at the Edinburgh Festival and at the Old Vic. Coupled with *Jacob's Journey*, *Joseph* had a shortish run at the Albery the following year. A Brooklyn Academy of Music professional production in 1976 preceded a successful 1978 British production.

✱ The 1980 production became a provincial phenomenon in Britain, setting up a record as the longest-lived touring show of the postwar era, and making periodic appearances in London en route.

The Critics

The critics, originally hostile, changed their tune, the *New York Times* calling Lloyd Webber 'one of the most inventive artists in contemporary musical theatre'.

Recommended Recording

Studio Cast (CD) MCA DMCL 1906
This show has evolved over the years from a 15-minute piece to the full-length show it now is. This recording is from the early period and has charm. A more full-bodied and mature version can be heard of the London Palladium revival cast (**Really Useful Records 511 130-2**) with Jason Donovan playing Joseph and Linzi Hateley the narrator.

Video/DVD

A video / DVD of latest revival stage version has been released in all country formats.

The King and I

LYRICS ✷ Oscar Hammerstein
MUSIC ✷ Richard Rodgers
BOOK ✷ Oscar Hammerstein, based on Margaret Landon's novel *Anna and the King of Siam* and Talbot Jennings and Sally Benson's non-musical screen adaptation, both taken from Anna Leonowens' diaries, *The English Governess at the Siamese Court*

First Performance

New York, St James' Theater, 29 March 1951 (1246 performances)
London, Drury Lane Theatre, 8 October 1953 (926 performances)

Principal Characters

Anna Leonowens ✷ A governess
The King
Lady Thiang ✷ A principal wife
Tuptim ✷ A Burmese princess
Lun Tha ✷ Her escort
Prince Chulalongkorn ✷ The heir apparent
The Kralahome ✷ A principal minister at court

Original New York Cast

Gertrude Lawrence, Yul Brynner, Dorothy Sarnoff, Doretta Morrow, Larry Douglas, Johnny Stewart, John Juliano

Original London Cast

Valerie Hobson, Herbert Lom, Muriel Smith, Doreen Duke, Jan Mazarus, Timothy Brooking, Martin Benson

Plot

Anna, a young widow, has come to Bangkok as tutor to the 67 children of the King of Siam. She soon realises her task will not be easy as the king is pompous and dictatorial. She befriends Lady Thiang, the king's head wife, and the young couple Lun Tha, an emissary from Burma, and Tuptim whom he has brought as a gift from his own king. They are in love, a love destined to failure, but one that Anna understands.

Anna's first meeting with the king's children is a formal affair but they soon warm to her. The king is also eager to learn and he hosts a dinner and ball for a visiting British diplomat. During the entertainment, a Siamese version of *Uncle Tom's Cabin*, the young lovers try unsuccessfully to escape and Lun Tha is killed. Anna stops the king from punishing Tuptim, but this brings to a climax the king's own internal turmoil in trying to westernise Siam. He takes to his bed and dies, knowing his eldest son will continue his reforms. Anna, as a parting gesture, kisses the hand of the man she has come to respect and decides to stay to help the new king.

Music and Songs

One of the greatest of all Rodgers and Hammerstein scores, a dazzling meld of Eastern and Western elements, including 'I whistle a happy tune' (Anna), 'My lord and master' (Tuptim), 'Hello young lovers' (Anna), 'March of the Siamese children', 'A puzzlement' (The King), 'Getting to know you' (Anna and court), 'We kiss in a shadow' (Tuptim and Lun Tha), 'Something wonderful' (Lady Thiang), 'I have dreamed' (Lun Tha) and 'Shall we dance?' (King and Anna).

Did You Know?

∗ Both Gertrude Lawrence and Yul Brynner won Tony awards. It was also named as the year's outstanding musical and both costumes and scenic design won Tonys.

∗ It was Gertrude Lawrence who initiated the project and she wanted Cole Porter to write the score.

∗ Noël Coward was one of many who turned down the role of the King.

∗ This is the second musical to contain a ballet version of *Uncle Tom's Cabin* (the first was *Bloomer Girl*).

The Critics

'it is an original and beautiful excursion into the rich splendours of the Far East, done with impeccable taste, idiomatic lyrics and some exquisite dancing' – *New York Times*
'A distinguished musical play' – *New York Daily News*
'An East of frank and unashamed romance seen through the eyes of . . . theatrical artists of rare taste and power' – Richard Watts Jnr

Recommended Recording

Yul Brynner and Constance Cummings (CD) RCA Red Seal RD82610.
Despite there being a wonderful original Broadway cast recording, this revival cast is better sung and has Brynner playing again the role he originated, both on stage and in film, at his peak. Rodgers's score especially gains from this majestic recording.

Film

20th Century Fox, 1956. Starring Deborah Kerr and Yul Brynner. Directed by Walter Lang.

King's Rhapsody

LYRICS ✶ Christopher Hassall
MUSIC ✶ Ivor Novello
BOOK ✶ Ivor Novello

First Performance

London, Palace Theatre, 15 September 1949 (839 performances)

Principal Characters

King Nikki
Queen Elena ✶ The Queen Mother
Marta Karillos ✶ The king's long-time friend
Countess Vera Lemainken ✶ Marta's companion
Queen Cristiane ✶ The new queen
Count Egon Stanieff ✶ Marta's escort
King Peter ✶ Nikki's father
Vanescu ✶ The prime minister

Original London Cast

Ivor Novello, Zena Dare, Phyllis Dare, Olive Gilbert, Vanessa Lee,
Denis Martin, Victor Bogetti, Robert Andrews

Plot

It's the birthday of Princess Cristiane of Nordland, and she's just been told she is to marry Prince Nikki of Murania, currently in exile, at his own wish. For the last 20 years he's lived with his mistress, Marta, in Paris, after she had been expelled from Murania on the prompting of the royal family. Now his father is dying and his mother, Queen Elena, and the prime minister, Vanescu, are aiming to assure the succession. Nikki insists on Marta's recall to Murania as part of his price for returning. Nikki is not there when Cristiane arrives. Six weeks later, he turns up outside her window. She pretends to be her own maid. He does not recognise her, so when they meet at the grand ball it comes as a surprise. Marta turns up at the ball to everyone's consternation – although it is Cristiane who has invited her. Nikki, nevertheless, ignores Cristiane and dances with Marta.

Nikki marries Cristiane but returns to exile when a democratic bill he's sponsored is turned down. His young queen remains to bring up their son. At the age of fifteen the young man ascends the throne. His father is there in secret, and Queen Cristiane has dropped a rose that Nikki picks up, as he utters a prayer that his son can succeed where he, Nikki, has failed.

Music and Songs

Novello's swansong: his most yearning, lyrical score, packed with appealing, soaring melody, including the songs 'Someday my heart will awake' (Cristiane), 'Fly home little heart' (Vera), 'Mountain dove' (Cristiane), 'If this were love' (Cristiane) and 'A violin began to play' (Cristiane).

Did You Know?

✶ Ivor Novello, the creator and non-singing star of the show, fell ill during the run and died. His place was taken by Jack Buchanan.

✶ This was not Novello's last composed show. He wrote *Gay's the Word* (1951) for Cicely Courtneidge as a resting star turned drama teacher.

✶ Vanessa Lee's original name was Ruby Moule and under that name she had understudied in the third London revival of *The Dancing Years* in 1947. It was Ivor Novello who changed her name and she became an instant star.

The Critics

'It should run for years' – *Daily Mirror*
'The show will probably prove Novello's biggest hit of all. If so, it will do it not by new tricks, but by the simple infallible formula of lavish spectacle, Ruritanian pomp, lush, if faintly familiar, music, well sung, and a story that gives them every excuse' – *Daily Mail*

Recommended Recording

Ivor Novello – The Classic Shows (CD) EMI Cedar CDP 7943682

Film

British Lion, 1956. Starring Anna Neagle and Errol Flynn. Directed by Herbert Wilcox.

Kismet

LYRICS ✴ Robert Wright and George Forrest
MUSIC ✴ Robert Wright and George Forrest,
based on themes adapted from Alexander Borodin
BOOK ✴ Charles Lederer and Luther Davis,
based on a play by Edward Knoblock

First Performance

New York, Ziegfeld Theater, 3 December 1953 (583 performances)
London, Stoll Theatre, 20 April 1955 (648 performances)

Principal Characters

Hajj ✴ A public poet
Marsinah ✴ His daughter
Lalume ✴ Wife of the Wazir
Caliph
The Wazir ✴ Chief of Police
Omar Khayyam ✴ A poet
Princess Samaris ✴ A dancer

Original New York Cast

Alfred Drake, Doretta Morrow, Joan Diener, Richard Kiley, Henry Kalvin,
Philip Coolidge, Beatrice Kraft

Original London Cast

Alfred Drake, Doretta Morrow, Joan Diener, Peter Grant, Paul Whitsun-Jones,
Donald Eccles, Juliet Prowse

Plot

The story of *Kismet* centres on Hajj, a resourceful seller of rhymes and his
beautiful daughter Marsinah. As the show opens it is early morning and Hajj is
not having a good day. Marsinah has been sent off to steal food in the market, and
Hajj has set up at Baghdad's prime begging spot outside the main mosque using
the name of a beggar, also called Hajj. The use of this name soon brings problems
and he finds himself a prisoner of a bandit chief who many years before had been
cursed by the other Hajj. Resourcefully, in exchange for riches, he promises to lift
the curse and produce the bandit's long-lost son that day. With his new-found
fortune, he sends his daughter off on a spending spree, only to find himself in the
hands of the powerful Wazir, chief of police, for having stolen money on his
person.

The evil Wazir has financial problems and has promised a distant potentate,
through his scheming and voluptuous wife Lalume, that the young and handsome
Caliph will marry one of his daughters, in exchange for several camel loads of
gold. However, the Caliph has already set eyes on Marsinah and wants no other,
leaving the Wazir in a difficult position. During the Hajj's trial comes the

revelation that the Wazir is the son of the bandit, and that puts Hajj in a respected, but now more dangerous, position as a wizard. The Wazir's attempts to make the Caliph change his mind and to hide Marsinah from him are finally brought to an end by Hajj when he carries out the Caliph's death sentence on the Wazir. The happy ending brings Lalume with her own small fortune to Hajj and Marsinah to the Caliph. Surely, Kismet has brought all these things to pass.

Music and Songs

Adapted from the luscious classical melodies of the Russian classical composer Borodin, the show's songs include 'Fate' (Hajj) – based on Symphony No. 2 in B minor, 'Not since Ninevah' (Lalume) – based on *The Polovtsian Dances*, 'Baubles, bangles and beads' (tradesmen) – based on String Quartet in D, 'Stranger in paradise' (Caliph and Marsinah) – based on *The Polovtsian Dances,* and 'And this is my beloved' (quartet) – based on String Quartet in D.

Did You Know?

✳ A revised version of *Kismet* was created in 1978. Starring Eartha Kitt and entitled *Timbuktu*, it had an African setting and Afro-American cast.

✳ It opened on Broadway during a newspaper strike and so there were few reviews, yet it became a hit without them.

✳ 'Kismet' means your fate or destiny – the will of Allah.

The Critics

After the newspaper strike was over the *New York Times* declared, 'The show had been assembled from a storehouse of spare parts. Its rich massiveness was stupefying, making the show pretty heavy on its feet.' – *New York Times*
No matter; the rich, exotic settings and good word of mouth helped the show on its way.

Recommended Recording

Original Broadway cast (CD) Sony CK 32605
This mono original has the commanding Alfred Drake at the helm and no one has come up to him in the part. There have been a number of recordings of the show and recently a complete studio cast production was issued **(TER CDTER 1770)** which is a fine recording that allows the Borodin melodies to be heard in all their beauty.

Film

MGM, 1955. Starring Howard Keel, Ann Blyth and Dolores Gray. Directed by Vincente Minnelli.

Kiss Me Kate

LYRICS ✳ Cole Porter
MUSIC ✳ Cole Porter
BOOK ✳ Bella and Sam Spewack, based in part on Shakespeare's
The Taming of the Shrew

First Performance

New York, New Century Theater, 30 December 1948 (1077 performances)
London, Coliseum Theatre, 8 March 1951 (501 performances)

Principal Characters

Fred Graham ✳ A leading actor
Lilli Vanessi ✳ His estranged actress wife
Bill Calhoun ✳ A gambler
Lois Lane
Two Gangsters
Hattie
Paul

Original New York Cast

Alfred Drake, Patricia Morison, Harold Lang, Lisa Kirk, Harry Clark,
Jack Diamond, Annabelle Hill, Lorenzo Fuller

Original London Cast

Bill Johnson, Patricia Morison, Walter Long, Julie Wilson, Danny Green,
Sidney James, Adelaide Hall, Archie Savage

Plot

A new musical is in rehearsal at Ford's Theater in Baltimore. Unfortunately the show's director and main star, Fred Graham, starring opposite his ex-wife Lilli Vanessi, is paying a lot of attention to the girl playing Bianca, the cabaret star Lois Lane. Lois' friend, Bill Calhoun, is also in the show and he's going to cause Fred further trouble because Bill has signed Fred's name to his own gambling IOU for the sum of $10,000. The main backer of the show is Lilli's new boyfriend, the politician Harrison Howell.

Fred is accosted by two gangsters who are chasing up the IOU who say they will return later that night to collect. Lilli receives a bouquet, and thanks Fred through the dressing room wall. She's softening her feelings towards him. Fred, however, had intended the flowers for Lois. The rehearsal proceeds. The show is a version of *The Taming of the Shrew*, and all goes well until Lilli discovers a card addressed to Lois in the flowers. Pandemonium. Lilli flounces off, threatening to leave the show and marry Harrison without delay. The gangsters return. Fred tells them that if Lilli leaves the show he won't be able to repay the $10,000. Could the gangsters help? They can, and prevent her departure.

Harrison arrives and can't really believe Lilli is being held prisoner in the theatre. The situation develops rapidly; the gangsters' boss is deposed, so they don't need to chase the debt. Lilli is free. She sweeps off, leaving Fred to play the last act without her. Happily, when the end of the play approaches, she returns. Petruchio and Katharine are reunited!

Music and Songs

Cole Porter never wrote a more coruscatingly brilliant show than this. Wonderful Viennese waltzes, showbiz anthems, acute and witty point numbers, and tender, searing love songs, not to mention numbers of which Shakespeare himself would have been proud. This is one of the essential scores for any collection, and includes 'Another op'nin', another show' (the company), 'Why can't you behave?' (Lois and Bill), 'Wunderbar' (Lilli and Fred), 'So in love' (Lilli), 'I've come to wive it wealthily in Padua' (Fred), 'I hate men' (Lilli), 'Where is the life that late I led?' (Fred), 'Always true to you in my fashion' (Lois), 'Bianca' (Bill) and, of course, 'Brush up your Shakespeare' (the gangsters).

Did You Know?

✶ This was not the first time Patricia Morison and Alfred Drake had starred together. They had been in the ill-starred *The Two Bouquets* in 1938.

✶ One of the gangsters in the original London run was Sid James, later to be a stalwart of the 'Carry on' films. His partner, Danny Green, was a heavy in *The Ladykillers*.

✶ *Kiss Me Kate* was the first musical to win a Tony.

✶ BBC2 opened with a live production of *Kiss Me Kate* starring Howard Keel (who starred in the film), Patricia Morison (the original New York and Broadway star) and Millicent Martin.

The Critics

'One of the loveliest and most lyrical [scores] yet composed for the contemporary stage' – Walter Kerr
'If *Kiss Me Kate* isn't the best musical comedy I ever saw, I don't remember what the best musical comedy I ever saw was called' – *New York Daily Mirror*
'This new and festive musical comedy is the best song and dance show of the season' – *New York Sun*

Recommended Recording

Original Broadway cast (CD) Sony SK 60536 (re-mastered)
The original remains the definitive version even though it was only recorded in mono.

Films

MGM, 1953. Starring Howard Keel, Kathryn Grayson and Ann Miller. Directed by George Sidney. The film was made in 3D.
A US TV version was made in 1970 starring Robert Goulet and Carol Lawrence.

Kiss of the Spider Woman

LYRICS ✶ Fred Ebb
MUSIC ✶ John Kander
BOOK ✶ Terrence McNally

First Performance

London, Shaftesbury Theatre, 8 October 1992 (390 performances)
New York, Broadhurst Theater, 3 May 1993 (906 performances)

Principal Characters

Spider Woman/Aurora
Molina ✶ A convict
Valentin ✶ A prisoner
Marta ✶ His girlfriend
Gabriel
Prisoner Emilio
Esteban
Warden
Molina's mother
Marcos

Original London Cast

Chita Rivera, Brent Carver, Anthony Crivello, Kirsti Carnahan,
Jerry Christakos, Joshua Finkel, Philip Hernandez, Herndon Lackey,
Merle Louise, Michael McCormick

The same cast, originating with the Canadian production, transferred to open the
Broadway production.

Plot

Molina, a convict, is serving a sentence in a Latin American jail for allegedly
corrupting a minor. The conditions are dire, but Molina escapes into his own
imagination, where he's visited by his film star favourite, Aurora. But Molina is
not alone in the cell for long. Suddenly the door opens and the body of a political
prisoner, Valentin, is thrown in.

Valentin has been badly beaten up, but when he recovers consciousness, he
rejects Molina's offer of friendship and care. Molina is just the sort of friend he
doesn't need – flamboyant, camp, homosexual. Each combats his own personal
loneliness by thinking of a woman: for Molina it's his mother, for Valentin his
girlfriend, Marta. This helps Valentin when he is tortured again, at the very time
when the prison warden is busy denying the existence of torture in the prison.
Meanwhile, Molina continues to fantasise about Aurora in her many films, and in
her most telling portrayal as the Spider Woman. In the midst of the continuing
torture, Valentin tries to cope by remembering the love of Marta. Food now
offered to both prisoners makes them ill.

The warden tries to get Molina to betray his cell mate and discover the facts about his political associates' activities. Molina's mother is apparently ill too, and he is released and allowed to visit her. Valentin asks Molina to make some phone calls for him while he is out. Molina, despite his growing affection for Valentin, refuses. However, he capitulates next day after a kiss from Valentin during a carefully calculated seduction which he cannot resist. Molina leaves and is followed by the warden's men. He makes the call for Valentin.

Back in the prison, Valentin is tortured again. The warden threatens to shoot Molina, now back in jail, if Valentin doesn't reveal his associates. Molina, in a heroic gesture, proclaims his love for Valentin and refuses to allow him to betray his colleagues. The warden shoots Molina and, as he dies, Molina is embraced by Aurora and dances a final tango with the Spider Woman in all her glory. Finally she gives him her fatal kiss.

Music and Songs

A tough, gutsy score, as you'd expect from the toughest, most realistic writers for Broadway, including 'Prologue' (the inmates), 'Her name is Aurora' (Molina), 'Dear one' (Mother, Marta, Valentin and Molina), 'You could never shame me' (Mother and Molina), 'Russian movie/Good times' (Molina, Aurora, Valentin and warden), 'The day after that' (Valentin and families of the disappeared), 'Kiss of the Spider Woman' (Aurora) and 'Only in the movies' (Molina and the people in his life).

Did You Know?

✶ It was originally mounted in a workshop production in America where it was, in spite of the producers' protestations, reviewed. The show was then remounted, much changed, in Canada and embarked on an extensive tour, with a notable stay in London. The same cast took it to Broadway, when London received a replacement, also American, cast.

✶ The show won the Evening Standard Award for Best Musical, and six Tony awards on Broadway.

The Critics

'*Kiss of the Spider Woman* is far and away the best thing to have happened to the West End in three long years' – *The Spectator*
'Brave in principle' – *The Independent*

Recommended Recording

Original cast (CD) First Night Cast CD30 (issued in the USA on RCA Victor). An exciting recording of this powerful show.

Film

MGM, 1985. Starring William Hurt and Raul Julia. Directed by Hector Babenco. The film preceded the musical.

Lady, Be Good!

LYRICS ✳ Ira Gershwin
MUSIC ✳ George Gershwin
BOOK ✳ Guy Bolton and Fred Thompson

First Performance

New York, Liberty Theatre, 1 December 1924 (330 performances)
London, Empire Theatre, 14 April 1926 (326 performances)

Principal Characters

Dick Trevor ✳ Brother of . . .
Susie Trevor
J. Watterson Watkins ✳ A lawyer
Jeff ✳ An instrumentalist
Jack Robinson ✳ A rich young man

Original New York Cast

Fred Astaire, Adele Astaire, Walter Catlett, Cliff Edwards, Allan Edwards

Original London Cast

Fred Astaire, Adele Astaire, William Kent, Buddy Lee, George Vollaire

Plot

Dick and Susie Trevor are brother and sister scraping out an existence as orphans in a small town in New England. Luckily two youngsters as talented and charming as these have lots of kind friends they can visit when the rent becomes due. Dick loves Shirley (upper class, rich) but can't tell her. When the penniless pair are finally evicted by their landlord, it's time to visit a big party and get something to eat.

Susie takes up with a tramp (disinherited as it happens) who proposes marriage on the spot. Susie declines, regretfully, and it's off to the party. It turns out the party-giver is uncle of the Trevors' landlord. The tramp (Jack Robinson) turns up and Susie is very glad to see him again. Lawyer Watty Watkins engages Susie to impersonate a Mexican girl with claims on the estate of her 'late' husband (who turns out, later on, to be the very alive Jack).

Dick finds Susie at the Eastern Hotel, preparing for her deception. She pulls it off and then learns that the real Jack Robinson is alive! Jack comes in and is intrigued to find Susie pretending to be his own widow! When the police arrive he confirms that Susie (as Juanita) is his wife, as he has fallen in love with her. Later on, Jack and Susie get together at the Yacht Club Dance, and Dick finally gets to romance his Shirley – so all ends happily.

Music and Songs

Early but vintage Gershwin with all the fizzing vitality of rhythm and alertness of rhyme you'd expect. Classic songs include 'Fascinating rhythm' (Dick and Susie), 'I'd rather Charleston' (Susie and Dick), 'Oh lady be good' (Watty) and 'Swiss miss' (Dick and Susie).

Did You Know?

✴ This was the first of a few shows from which the song 'The man I love' was cut!

✴ The original title for the show was 'Black-eyed Susan'.

✴ The London run was only curtailed when the theatre was pulled down.

✴ The Astaire brother and sister partnership would end when Adele became Lady Cavendish and went to live in Ireland, giving up the stage for life.

The Critics

'The songs are consistently brisk, inventive, gay and nervous' – *New York Sun*
'George Gershwin wrote the score and this means that the tunes are tuneful, lively, gay and haunting' – *Brooklyn Times*

Recommended Recording

Studio cast recording (CD) Elektra Nonesuch 79308
A complete recording, one of a series authorised by the Gershwin estate, and conducted by Eric Stern using the original orchestrations. The sound is rich and it shows what a wonderful and hit-packed score it is. Fred and Adele did record a few tracks in London and these made it on to LP.

Film

MGM, 1941. Starring Eleanor Powell, Ann Sothern, Robert Young and Red Skelton. Directed by Norman Z. McLeod. This had a new story with added songs.

Lady in the Dark

LYRICS ✳ Ira Gershwin
MUSIC ✳ Kurt Weill
BOOK ✳ Moss Hart

First Performance

New York, Alvin Theater, 23 January 1941 (467 performances)
London, Royal National Theatre, 11 March 1997 (in repertory)

Principal Characters

Liza Elliott ✳ An editor
Kendall Nesbitt ✳ A publisher
Charley Johnson ✳ Advertising manager
Randy Curtis ✳ A film star
Russell Paxton ✳ The photographer
Dr Brooks ✳ A psychiatrist

Original New York Cast

Gertrude Lawrence, Bert Lytell, MacDonald Carey, Victor Mature,
Danny Kaye, Donald Randolph

Original London Cast

Maria Friedman, Paul Shelley, Adrian Dunbar, Steven Edward Moore,
James Dreyfus, Hugh Ross

Plot

The editor of *Allure* magazine, Liza Elliott, seeks psychological help from Dr Brooks:
she has been having an affair with publisher Kendall Nesbitt for many a year.
She's depressed, irresolute and is subject to disturbing dreams. And there's this
song, 'My ship', recalled from childhood, but she can't remember all of it.
The first dream: Liza's portrait is about to be unveiled. But the picture shows a
frumpish person. Liza is denying her femininity while editing a magazine that
encourages women to do the opposite. Back at the office of *Allure*, Randy Curtis is
visiting.

Publisher Kendall Nesbitt has arranged an expensive divorce from his wife so
he can marry Liza. In a dream he takes her to choose a ring, but Charley, her
colleague at work, is the salesman and offers her a dagger instead of a ring. Liza
realises she does not love Kendall, and wakes up. Dr Brooks attempts analysis: as
long as Kendall was safely married, everything was safe and all right. Now he's
getting divorced, he can't fit into Liza's life anymore. Back in the office Kendall
attempts to make Liza change her mind. Charley wants the Easter edition to have
a circus theme. (By the way, he's been offered a better job elsewhere.) Randy's
date for the evening is Liza – he finds her such a contrast to his usual glamorous
escorts. Liza is deeply upset at the thought and, grabbing a glamorous gown, is
determined to change her image.

Another dream: a circus where Liza is accused of indecision in a court set up in a circus ring where Charley is prosecutor and Randy is defence counsel. Before the case is over, Liza wakes up and later, at Dr Brooks' surgery, her past begins to unravel, and she remembers childhood humiliations. Each time, the song 'My ship' is there to underline any bad feelings she may have. Now Liza can deal with her past and her future. She can tell Kendall she won't marry him. She can also say no to Randy. Charley comes in to say goodbye, and Liza offers him joint editorship of *Allure*. He also knows the full words of 'My ship'. This is a relationship that can finally go somewhere.

Music and Songs

Weill at his most glowingly romantic. The score is packed with show-stoppers, including 'This is new' (Liza), 'My ship' (Liza), 'Jenny' (Liza) and the tongue-twister 'Tschaikowsky' (Russell).

Did You Know?

✶ The author of the book, Moss Hart, used his recent experiences undergoing psychiatric help in writing the scenario.

✶ The song 'This is new' was originally a duet for Randy and Liza. But the original Randy (Victor Mature) couldn't sing, so Liza sang it alone. In the London production it is back as a duet.

✶ This is the show that made Danny Kaye a star.

✶ Igor Stravinsky went on stage to congratulate the composer.

The Critics

'Your ship is trimmed with sails of gold' – George S. Kaufman
'[Weill is] the best writer of theater music this century' – Brooks Atkinson
'It is a bit more obvious in 1997 than it was in 1941. Liza is reacting to the father who thought her plain and the good-looking boy who snubbed her. She has been suppressing her femininity to avoid rejection' – *The Times*
'The ending comes a bit quickly and glibly; but this still seems an unusually sophisticated Broadway musical. Gershwin is capable of quoting from Herrick, then rhyming him with derrick and Weill's tunes, though bland at first, come into their own later' – *The Times*

Recommended Recording

Studio cast (CD) CBS Masterworks 07 464-62869-2
A fine re-issue of the Rise Stevens studio cast version with added tracks by Danny Kaye of songs from the show including the song that shot him to stardom, 'Tschaikowsky'.

Film

Paramount, 1944. Starring Ginger Rogers, Ray Milland and Warner Baxter. Directed by Mitchell Leisen. Almost all the songs were jettisoned. However, new ones, including 'Suddenly it's spring', not by the original team, were added.

Leave it to Jane

LYRICS ✶ P. G. Wodehouse
MUSIC ✶ Guy Bolton and P. G. Wodehouse
BOOK ✶ Jerome Kern, based on *The College Widow* by George Ade

First Performance

New York, Longacre, 28 August 1917 (167 performances)

Principal Characters

Jane Witherspoon ✶ Daughter of the president of the college
Billy Bolton ✶ A rival college football star
Stub Talmadge ✶ A football fan
Bessie Tanner ✶ A football fan
Bub Hicks ✶ A late developer
Flora Wiggins ✶ A landlady's daughter
Ollie Mitchell ✶ A sophomore
Hiram Bolton ✶ Billy's father and a friend of Jane's father

Original New York Cast

Edith Hallor, Robert Pitkin, Oscar Shaw, Ann Orr, Olin Howland,
Georgia O'Ramey, Rudolf Cutten, Will C. Crimans

Plot

Atwater College lacks good football players for their up and coming season. Stub, a football fan, seems to have saved the day by producing a new player. Stub is also interested in Bessie and they plan to marry, but he owes Flora's mother money for his digs. The popular-with-the-guys Jane is the daughter of the college president, who is being visited by his old friend, Hiram Bolton, a benefactor to the rival college, Bingham. Stub bets Bolton that Atwater will beat them at football – and then he finds that Bolton's son, Billy, is playing in the game and he is an all-American champ. Jane is called upon to help, and the plan is that she will flirt with Billy, and persuade him to change his name and side. Jane gets to work on Billy straight away and at that night's formal dance he agrees to become Billy Staples and change sides.

It's the day of the big game and it is not going too well for Atwater who have already lost one of their players. Hiram Bolton arrives; he hears that his son has not reached Bingham and that he has changed his name. He blames (rightly) Jane who pretends to faint while telling Stub to get the lads to kidnap Hiram. When Bolton escapes he finds his son and tells him that Jane only did what she did for Atwater and he is devastated – he plans to leave the college. In the meantime, Stub has won his bet, has paid off his debts, and has a job offer and the love of Bessie. Jane manages to find Billy just as he is about to leave and tells him she really does love him, and so there is a happy ending.

Music and Songs

Although not actually a Princess show, because it was presented at another theatre, it has all the hallmarks of one. Jerome Kern supplied a youthful, frothy score that includes a hypnotising title song (Bessie, Stub and ensemble), 'Cleopatterer' (Flora), 'Sir Galahad' (Flora), 'The siren's song' (Jane) and 'Just you watch my step' (Stub and Bessie).

Did You Know?

∗ The 1959 revival became the longest-running Off-Broadway revival of a Broadway show.

∗ The chorus were called 'Ladies and gentlemen of the ensemble'.

∗ American college football is a popular subject for musical comedies, with *Good News*, *All American* and *Too Many Girls* all being hit shows.

The Critics

'The old timers will soon begin to grieve sorely, to tear their hair and gnash their teeth, as they view the new form of rational musical comedy actually "getting over" and pushing the old style where it belongs. No more are we asked to laugh at the bottle-nosed comedian, as he falls down stairs; no longer is the heroine a lovely princess masquerading as the serving maid, and no more is the scene Ruritania or Monte Carlo. Today is rationally American, and the musical show has taken on a new lease of life' – *New York American*

Recommended Recording

Original Off-Broadway Revival cast (CD) DRG 15017
This is the recording of the successful revival that starred George Segal, Kathleen Murray and Art Matthews. On this CD it is coupled with a revival recording of *Oh, Kay!* so it is good value. It is also spirited and youthful and brings to life the score wonderfully. A chance to relive one of the first really American musical comedies.

Li'l Abner

LYRICS ✶ Johnny Mercer
MUSIC ✶ Gene de Paul
BOOK ✶ Norman Panama and Melvin Frank,
based on Al Capp's comic strip

First Performance

New York, St James' Theater, 15 November 1956 (693 performances)

Principal Characters

Daisy Mae ✶ A sweetheart
Abner Yokum ✶ Her feller
General Bullmoose ✶ A man of importance
Marryin' Sam
Mammy Yokum ✶ Abner's Ma
Appassionata von Climax ✶ A rival to Daisy
Stupefyin' Jones ✶ A temptation
Romeo Scragg, Clem Scragg, Moonbeam McSwine
✶ Denizens of Dogpatch, USA

Original New York Cast

Edith Adams, Peter Palmer, Howard St John, Stubby Kaye, Charlotte Rae,
Tina Louise, Julie Newmar, Marc Breaux, James Hurst, Carmen Alvarez

Plot

Daisy Mae is bent on capturing Li'l Abner for herself on the next Sadie Hawkins Day when the women literally make the running. But it's not as simple as that. Her rival, Appassionata von Climax, engages professional help, Evil Eye Fleagle, who in turn produces his own distraction in Stupefyin' Jones, a comely female. And that's not all. The US Government wants to use Dogpatch, where they all live, as the site for atom bomb experiments, because nothing important or historic ever took place there. In addition, Abner and the menfolk are taken away for scientific experiments that make them handsome, but completely uninterested in the opposite sex.

The men are eventually restored to their ugly, but potent selves, and Marryin' Sam unearths some salient facts about the founder of their town, the sensible but cowardly Jubilation T. Cornpone, and his whole catalogue of civil war disasters. The town is saved and even though the Sadie Hawkins Race does not lead to the expected conclusion (Earthquake McGoon catches Daisy and Appassionata von Climax gets Abner), by the end of the show Abner and Daisy Mae are married to each other – the ceremony performed by, of course, Marryin' Sam.

Music and Songs

The songs show Mercer's lyrics at their non-urban wittiest; de Paul's music is so good it makes us regret his small Broadway catalogue. Songs include 'If I had my druthers' (Abner), 'Jubilation T. Cornpone' (Sam and company), 'Namely you' (Abner and Daisy), 'The country's in the very best of hands' (Abner and townsfolk), 'Past my prime' (Daisy Mae), 'Put 'em back' (the wives) and 'The matrimonial stomp' (Sam and company).

Did You Know?

✶ This stage version of Al Capp's famous satirical comic strip is just one of many successful musical shows to come from comic strips. Others include *Annie* and *Peanuts*.

✶ The film version was one of the very few to used stylised rather than realistic sets following the concept seen on stage.

✶ The success of the Broadway version has not been replicated elsewhere in the world.

✶ The humorous and lively dance routines won Michael Kidd a Tony Award.

The Critics

'Motion is a better medium than words for animating this sort of drawing. All that happens is that the girls leg it after the boys at top speed. But Mr Kidd [director and choreographer] is the man who can see comic-strip humor in this primitive rite by varying the speed, by introducing low-comedy antics and by giving *Li'l Abner* its most exuberant scene' – Brooks Atkinson

Recommended Recording

Original Broadway cast (CD) CBS Special Products A 5150
The antics in Dogpatch, USA, come to life in this original cast recording that can boast of some fine performers – many of whom went on to make the film. 'Jubilation T. Cornpone' is one of the great show stopping songs that make this so enjoyable.

Film

Paramount, 1959. Starring Peter Palmer and Leslie Parrish. Directed by Norman Panama and Melvin Frank.

The Lion King

LYRICS * Elton John and Tim Rice
MUSIC * Elton John and Tim Rice
BOOK * Roger Allers and Irene Mecchi.
Additional music and lyrics by Lebo M, Mark Mancina,
Jay Rifkin, Julie Taymor, Hans Zimmer

First Performance

New York, New Amsterdam Theatre, 13 November 1997 (still running)
London, Lyceum Theatre, 19 October 1999 (still running)

Principal Characters

Rafiki * The wise one
Mufasa* The Lion King
Simba * His son
Nala * Simba's friend
Scar * Mufasa's brother
Zazu * The King's PA
Timon and Plumbaa * Simba's new friends

Original New York Cast

Tsidii Le Loka, Samuel E. Wright, Jason Raize, Heather Headley, John Vickery,
Geoff Hoyle, Max Casella, Tom Alan Robbins

Original London Cast

Josette Bushell-Mingo, Cornell John, Roger Wright, Paulette Ivory, Rob Edwards,
Gregory Gudgeon, Simon Gregor, Martyn Ellis

Plot

Rafiki, the wise one, watches over the kingdom. The young Simba has been presented by his proud father, the Lion King Mufasa, to the animals of the kingdom who share their lives in a delicate balance. Father takes his son to Pride Rock and he is taught that everything he can see is the king's kingdom and Simba will one day be king. There is one place, the shadowy place, where Simba is told he should not go and Simba learns from his uncle Scar the place is an elephant graveyard – Scar makes it their little secret and has deliberately made the place an enticement for Simba. Simba goes off to play with Nala, the girl cub he is destined to marry, and he wants to take her to the forbidden place. But the faithful Zazu goes with them and they have to lose him. Finally, they get there, with Zazu in hot pursuit, but it is too late – the hyenas are after them and only just in time they are saved by the king.

The hyenas are visited by Scar – he has a plan to kill both Mufasa and Simba and to become king. As a surprise for Mufasa, Scar gets Simba to wait on a rock in the gorge. But the surprise is not the pleasant one he was expecting when the hyenas start a stampede of wildebeest. Mufasa hears that Simba is in the gorge and comes to save him. Simba is holding onto a tree and his father helps him, only to be swept away. In an attempt to climb up and save himself, Mufasa is pushed back by Scar. The king is dead. Scar makes Simba believe it is his fault and he runs away to what should be his death. Simba is found by the unlikely pairing of Timon and Plumbaa and he settles down with the hakuna matata reflection on life to become their friend.

Simba is now a fully-grown lion and one day another lion attacks looking for food. Simba starts to fight and then he recognises her – it is his old friend Nala. They fall in love and she wants him to come back to Pride Rock and take his position as king. Under Scar and the hyenas there is no food and water. But he is too full of guilt to return. Re-enter Rafiki who brings him to the water where he sees the reflection of his father and hears him too, for his father lives within him. Fired with a new strength he returns, using Timon and Plumbaa as decoys. Face to face Scar and Simba fight, but it is the hyenas that kill Scar. The nightmare over, the land returns to its past beauty and there is a new cub to be taught how to be king.

Music and Songs

The sound is that of Africa and its authenticity blends beautifully with the rock score by Elton John and Tim Rice. The score was extended for the show and includes the infectious 'Hakuna matata' (Timon, Pumbaa and Simba) and 'Circle of life' (Rafiki). There is the amusing 'The morning report' (Zazu and Mufasa) and the villain's song 'Be prepared' (Scar).

Did You Know?

✶ *The Lion King* won the best musical Tony Award.

✶ The director, Julie Taymor, also designed the costumes, masks and wigs.

✶ Elton John and Tim Rice followed this hit with a totally new Disney show and not one based on a film – the show is *Aida*.

The Critics

'The beast that is *The Lion King* has come to London, and a beautiful thing it is, too' – *Variety*
'Stunning proof of the unmatchable potency of live theatre' – *The Times*

Recommended Recording

Original Broadway cast (CD) Disney 60802–7
The excitement of the stage production can be relived through this excellent recording. There are some wonderful performances from the villain Scar (John Vickery) and Mufasa (Samuel E. Wright). The old favourite 'The lion sleeps tonight' blends in beautifully with the magic of Sirs John and Rice.

Little Me

LYRICS ✶ Carolyn Leigh
MUSIC ✶ Cy Coleman
BOOK ✶ Neil Simon, based on the novel by Patrick Dennis

First Performance

New York, Lunt Fontanne Theatre, 17 November 1962 (257 performances)
London, Cambridge Theatre, 18 November 1964 (334 performances)

Principal Characters

Miss Poitrine ✶ Mother of . . .
Belle ✶ Our heroine
Lady Eggleston ✶ Mother of . . .
Noble Eggleston ✶ Our hero*
Mr Pinchley ✶ A well-known miser*
Val du Val ✶ The entertainer*
Fred Poitrine ✶ A First World War private*
Otto Schnitzler ✶ An admirer of Belle*
Prince Cherny ✶ Another admirer*
George Musgrove ✶ A friend
*Played by the same performer

Original New York Cast

Nancy Andrews, Virginia Martin, Nancy Cushman, *Sid Caesar, Swen Swenson

Original London Cast

Avril Angers, Eileen Gourlay, Enid Lowe, *Bruce Forsyth, Swen Swenson

Plot

Little Me is the autobiography of the optimistic, yet spectacularly accident-prone, Hollywood star, Belle Poitrine (born Schlumpfert), who rises from the wrong side of the tracks to wealth, culture and and position in society. Born in Venezuela, Illinois, she lives with her highly dubious Momma beside the railway tracks.

Fellow urchin, George Musgrove, is in love with her, but Belle has higher ambitions – Noble Eggleston – and the attraction is mutual. But Noble is a scion of society. He invites her to his sixteenth birthday party, but his mother despatches Belle with speed – she's not the right match for her son. Belle next encounters the miserly landlord Amos Pinchley who soon sets her up in a flat. What a pity that in a close embrace, a gun he keeps in his pocket goes off and kills him. Belle stands trial for his murder. Noble comes to her rescue and she is acquitted and sets off on a vaudeville tour. War comes. Belle does her bit.

There follows a parade of lovers, friends and patrons – Val du Val (she helps him recover his memory on the battlefield), private Fred Poitrine (she marries him before his untimely death as a result of lodging a finger in a typewriter), George Musgrove and, of course, Colonel Noble Eggleston (nine times VC).

Eventually Belle sails home to America on the SS *Gigantic* with her current husband Val and encounters Noble with his wife Ramona. The ship sinks and Noble organises the saving of all passengers – except, unfortunately, Val. Belle sues the steamship company, and is at last rich. Hollywood claims her for its own.

Unfortunately disaster continues to strike. Her director, Otto, impales himself on a trick dagger, that wasn't a trick dagger at all! Then it's off to Monte Carlo where Prince Cherny wagers all on a number that Belle chooses – and loses everything. Belle nurses him through the resulting heart attack. He makes her the Countess Zoftig and at last she has social class!

Now she could marry Noble, couldn't she? Well, no. He's become a hopeless alcoholic. So she marries George. Her daughter meets Noble Junior and marries him. But Noble's mother blames Belle for the reversal in her son's fortunes and plans to kill her. Just in the nick of time Noble Senior, dried out, reappears in Belle's life. His mother takes aim and fires. Noble falls but he is unhurt – the bullet killed George. So Belle ends up with Noble at long last. A happy ending as the happy couple walk off into the sunset.

Music and Songs

Cy Coleman at his zesty best. A beautiful, witty, bounteous score full of fine touches, with wonderful lyrics that fit like a glove, from the sorely missed Carolyn Leigh. Numbers include 'The truth' (Belle), 'The other side of the tracks' (Belle), 'I love you' (Noble), 'Deep down inside' (Pinchley), 'Boom boom' (Val du Val), 'I've got your number' (George), 'Real live girl' (soldiers) and 'Little me' (Belle).

Did You Know?

✶ 'Here's to us' was a Judy Garland favourite. It was played at her funeral.

✶ *Little Me* proved (not once, but twice) to be much more popular in London than on Broadway. Perhaps Russ Abbot's engaging performance in the lead had something to do with it (just like Bruce Forsyth in the original London cast).

✶ Patrick Dennis, the author, appears as a character here (the ghost writer of the autobiography). He also takes part in the stage version of another of his books, *Mame*.

✶ The only Tony Award the show won was for Bob Fosse's inventive choreography – the other big shows of the season, *Oliver!* and *A Funny Happened on the Way to the Forum* scooped up most of the other musical awards.

The Critics

'It gleams with show-business savvy' – *New York Times*

Recommended Recording

Original London cast (CD) DRG 13111
While the Broadway version with Sid Caesar is an enjoyable issue, it is the London version that is recommended. It features a wonderful performance by Bruce Forsyth and the rest of the cast. It also has more music than the Broadway version.

A Little Night Music

LYRICS ✶ Stephen Sondheim
MUSIC ✶ Stephen Sondheim
BOOK ✶ Hugh Wheeler,
based on Ingmar Bergman's film *Smiles of a Summer Night*

First Performance

New York, Shubert Theater, 25 February 1973 (601 performances)
London, Adelphi Theatre, 15 April 1975 (406 performances)

Principal Characters

Desirée Armfeldt ✶ A touring actress
Fredrik Egerman ✶ A lawyer
Madame Armfeldt ✶ A former courtesan
Anne Egerman ✶ Fredrik's child bride
Count Carl-Magnus Malcolm ✶ A soldier
Countess Charlotte Malcolm ✶ His wife
Henrik Egerman ✶ Fredrik's son
Fredrika Armfeldt ✶ Desirée's daughter
Petra ✶ A maid
Frid ✶ A butler

Original New York Cast

Glynis Johns, Len Cariou, Hermione Gingold, Victoria Mallory,
Laurence Guittard, Patricia Elliot, Mark Lambert, Judy Kahan,
D. Jasmin-Bartlett, George Lee Andrews

Original London Cast

Jean Simmons, Joss Ackland, Hermione Gingold, Veronica Page,
David Kernan, Maria Aitken, Terry Mitchell, Christine McKenna,
Diane Langton, Michael Harbour

Plot

In Sweden at the turn of the last century, lawyer Fredrik has taken his young wife Anne to the theatre, where his old flame Desirée is the star of the show. Anne intercepts a glance between the former lovers and demands to be taken home. There they interrupt her maid Petra helping Henrik, Fredrik's son, make a voyage of sexual discovery. In fact Henrik is in love with his new stepmother who, like him, is still a virgin.

That night Fredrik pays a clandestine visit to Desirée's lodging, where they are interrupted by the arrival of her current lover, Count Carl-Magnus, who orders Fredrik to leave. To try to explain his presence Fredrik is said to be Desirée's mother's lawyer and attending to some legal papers. Even the Count does not believe this and he sends his wife, Charlotte, on a spying visit to Anne who happens to be an old acquaintance. Charlotte is aware of the 'decrepit Desirée's' hold on her husband but is prepared to be humiliated for his sake and informs Anne of the previous night's shenanigans. An invitation arrives from country home of Madame Armfeld, Desiree's mother. Upon hearing this Charlotte and Carl-Magnus decide to gatecrash the party.

Madame Armfeldt is not impressed. A former courtesan, she finds modern manners very shabby and unstylish. Nevertheless, she entertains regally. Henrik disgraces himself, Anne runs to comfort him and, after a botched suicide attempt, they run off together. Petra finds romance with a butler and Madame Armfeldt peace, as she passes over under the summer moon. Fredrik finally realises his love for Desirée and plays a game of Russian roulette with the count in which he is grazed on the temple. The excitement also rekindles the affection between the count and his wife. Desirée and Fredrik will live together, along with her daughter Fredrica whose father is Fredrik.

Music and Songs

The ghosts of Lehár, Strauss and other great waltz kings can be glimpsed in this sometimes joyous, but always deeply satisfying, score. Well-known numbers include 'Send in the clowns' (Desirée), 'You must meet my wife' (Fredrik and Desirée), 'Liaisons' (Madame Armfeldt), and 'The miller's son' (Petra).

Did You Know?

✶ The music is all written in 3/4 time or multiples of it. The essence of the waltz permeates every bar of this magical score.

✶ In the Royal National Theatre's successful revival, Laurence Guittard moved up from his original Broadway role as the count to play Fredrik.

✶ *A Little Night Music* won the best musical, score, book and costume Tonys. In addition, both Glynis Johns and Patricia Elliott won Tonys.

The Critics

'Heady, civilized, sophisticated and enchanting. It is Dom Perignon. It is supper at Lasserre. Yet the real triumph belongs to Stephen Sondheim . . . breathtaking lyrics . . . good God! an adult musical' – *New York Times*
'I wish I could wrap up this beguiling operetta just as it is and fling it onto the West End stage' – *The Daily Telegraph* (from New York)

Recommended Recording

Original Broadway cast (CD) Sony SK 65284 (re-mastered)
Glynis Johns is unforgettable as Desirée and the entire recording is perfection. Hermione Gingold can also be heard on the excellent London cast recording together with a vibrant Diana Langton (Petra) and a perfectly cast David Kernan (Count Carl-Magnus).

Film

Sacha Films, Vienna, 1977. Starring Elizabeth Taylor, Diana Rigg, Lesley-Anne Down, Len Cariou and Hermione Gingold. Directed by Harold Prince.

Little Shop of Horrors

LYRICS ✳ Howard Ashman
MUSIC ✳ Alan Menken
BOOK ✳ Howard Ashman, based on the script of the film by Charles Griffith

First Performance

New York (Off Broadway), WPA Theater, 6 May 1982
Transferred to Orpheum Theater, 27 July 1982 (2209 performances)
London, Comedy Theatre, 12 October 1983 (813 performances)

Principal Characters

Seymour ✳ A nerd
Audrey ✳ His beloved
Orin ✳ An evil dentist
Mr Mushnik ✳ A florist
Audrey II ✳ A carnivorous plant

Original New York Cast

Rick Moranis, Ellen Greene, Franc Luz, Hy Anzell,
Ron Taylor/Martin P. Robinson

Original London Cast

Barry James, Ellen Greene, Terrence Hillyer, Harry Towb,
Anthony B. Asbury/Michael Leslie

Plot

On 21 September not so long ago, creatures from outer space invaded our galaxy intent on world domination. Some of them took the form of plants (just like in *The War of the Worlds*). One such landed in Mr Mushnik's flower shop on skid row, where it was tended by Seymour who named it Audrey II, after his fellow assistant Audrey.

As you might gather, Seymour is very fond of Audrey, and Audrey II proves a major draw in the shop, attracting many visitors. The trouble is, Audrey II's plant food is fresh blood. Audrey has a sadistic boyfriend, Orin, who is a dentist – she knows she doesn't deserve such a sweet and kind friend as Seymour (in thinking this, she's wrong of course). As the fame of the shop grows, Audrey II also increases in size. Mushnik offers Seymour a partnership.

Meanwhile, Seymour grows faint from the loss of his own blood, with which he's been feeding Audrey II, who now starts to talk – her insistent cry is 'Feed me'. In exchange for regular supplies of nice fresh blood, Seymour will be granted his heart's desire by Audrey II. Orin gets Seymour in his dentist's chair and prepares to go to work on him. The dentist decides to give himself a good dose of laughing gas. However, he overdoes it and he laughs himself to death – Audrey II has her first human victim.

Mushnik begins to suspect the worst, so he becomes the next victim. Audrey II is now growing rapidly. She entraps Audrey but Seymour rescues her. Yet Audrey is now dying from malnutrition. Seymour tells her the full story of Audrey II and her victims. Audrey wants to join them – and does. Next day Seymour is visited by representatives of World Botanical Enterprises. They want to propagate Audrey II. When they've gone, Seymour tries to kill off the bloodsucking plant but is pulled into its heart. The representatives return and take cuttings. World domination – here come Audrey II, and III, and IV . . .

Music and Songs

A merry rock 'n' roll score full of grand guignol zest and fun, and including 'Little shop of horrors' (the company), 'Somewhere that's green' (Audrey), 'Feed me' (Audrey II), 'Suddenly Seymour' (Audrey) and 'Suppertime' (Audrey II).

Did You Know?

✳ This was the first successful show by Menken and Ashman, which would be followed by further successes, especially in Hollywood.

✳ Ellen Greene – what a trouper – appeared in the New York, London and film versions of the show!

✳ Cameron Macintosh was one of the American producers – it was the first time he had started off a project in the United States.

The Critics

'Wow! Totally entrancing . . . totally hilarious' – *New York Post*
'Zany, fun-filled and thoroughly delightful . . . a winner' – *Variety*
'A musical comedy that is both musical and comic . . . and that hits just the right tone of mockery without ever slipping into camp . . . with a witty book and witty lyrics' – *The New Yorker*
'Madly entertaining, full of side-splitting laughs . . . the show's a hoot' – *Gannett Westchester Newspapers*

Recommended Recording

Original Off-Broadway cast (CD) Geffen GEFD 2020
This is a joyous recording that is packed with fun. Ellen Greene is one of those unique performers who match her visual persona with that of her voice. No wonder she performed in the London production and the film.

Film

Warner Brothers, 1986. Starring Ellen Greene, Rick Moranis and Vincent Gardenia, with a special appearance by Steve Martin. Directed by Frank Oz.

Lost in the Stars

LYRICS ✳ Maxwell Anderson and Alan Paton
MUSIC ✳ Kurt Weill
BOOK ✳ Maxwell Anderson,
based on Alan Paton's novel *Cry the Beloved Country*

First Performance

New York, Music Box Theater, 30 October 1949 (293 performances)

Principal Characters

Stephen Kumalo ✳ A preacher
James Jarvis ✳ Father of the murdered man
Absolom Kumalo ✳ Stephen's son

Original New York Cast

Todd Duncan, Leslie Banks, Julian Mayfield

Plot

Reverend Stephen Kumalo is a preacher in the South African town of Ndorsbeni.
There's been no word for some time from his son, Absolom, who left to seek his
fortune in Johannesburg. The Kumalos pool their savings and go to
Johannesburg, but their search is initially fruitless. In fact, their son is living in a
rundown part of the city, and has taken part in a gang robbery in order to get
funds to support his unborn child. Unfortunately, a white man is killed during the
robbery. Absolom is arrested and visited in prison by his father, who feels
deserted by his God and questions his own faith.

The trial proceeds. Absolom's fellow robbers are acquitted through their own
perjured testimony. Absolom alone is condemned to hang for the crime. His father
returns to his flock, broken in spirit, yet understanding how Man is born in and
dies in darkness. Before the execution, the Kumalos receive an unexpected visitor.
This is James Jarvis, the formerly racist father of the murdered man. Together the
two fathers seek understanding, as they are united in a common bond of tragedy
– the loss of both of their sons – and they pray for forgiveness and tolerance.

Music and Songs

Deeply personal and evocative, this memorable score includes 'Lost in the stars'
(Stephen), 'Trouble ma' (Inna) and 'Stay well' (Inna), all of which have achieved a
separate musical life, plus 'The hills of Ixopio' (leader), 'Thousands of miles'
(Stephen), 'The train to Johannesburg' (leader), 'The little gray house' (Stephen),
'Cry the beloved country' (leader) and 'Bird of passage' (villager).

Did You Know?

∗ Kurt Weill and Maxwell Anderson, the major playwright, had collaborated before on *Knickerbocker Holiday* and had been anxious to find a suitable vehicle that repeated their views on social prejudice.

∗ The show was an artistic but not a financial success. This had a detrimental effect on Weill's health.

∗ *Lost in the Stars* was Weill's last Broadway score. It has since been adopted into their repertoire by many opera companies (as his *Street Scene* has).

The Critics

'Most of *Lost in the Stars* is good, some of it is excellent. But the beauty and simplicity of Paton's book infrequently comes through' – *New York Journal American*

Recommended Recording

Original Broadway cast (CD) MCA Classics Broadway Gold MCAD-10302
This remains a powerful recording with the wonderful Todd Duncan on top form.

Film

AFT Films, 1974. Starring Brock Peters and Melba Moore. Directed by Daniel Mann.

Mack and Mabel

LYRICS ✶ Jerry Herman
MUSIC ✶ Jerry Herman
BOOK ✶ Michael Stewart

First Performance

New York, Majestic Theater, 6 October 1974 (65 performances)
London, Piccadilly Theatre, November 1995 (270 performances)

Principal Characters

Mack Sennett ✶ A film-maker
Mabel Normand ✶ A silent-movie star
Lotte ✶ Mack's assistant

Original New York Cast

Robert Preston, Bernadette Peters, Lisa Kirk

Original London Cast

Howard McGillin, Caroline O'Connor, Kathryn Evans

Plot

The early days of movie-making. Mack Sennett recalls the hurly-burly of the silent screen and his greatest star, Mabel, first encountered as a sandwich lady from the local deli. Mack fashions Mabel into a star, not averse to chucking custard pies around. But Mabel has ambitions and moves on to a film-maker who can offer her bigger roles in longer films. No matter – Mack invents a troupe of Sennett bathing beauties, and for good measure, the Keystone Cops as well. He can exist without Mabel – as she can without him. He'd never shown her the affection she craved; he never sent her roses after all.

Mabel, meanwhile, drifts into bad company. She's implicated, however peripherally, in scandal when director William Desmond Taylor, her lover, is shot dead. Her career is over. Mabel drifts down a sorry path aided by drugs. Mack, in 1928, can just remember her as once a bright, luminous star of his own creation. (In the revised version Mabel is visited by Mack, bearing roses and the promise of a new film career and rehabilitation.)

Music and Songs

A superb score. Top-notch Herman at his brightest and best, including the songs 'Movies were movies' (Mack), 'I won't send roses' (Mack), 'Time heals everything' (Mabel), 'Tap your troubles away' (Lotte) and 'I promise you a happy ending' (Mack).

Did You Know?

✶ *Mack and Mabel* has one of the finest of all musical comedy overtures. It is a thrilling potpourri of great tunes made famous as the music for a classic ice-dance routine by Torvill and Dean.

✶ Of the recent London version, its composer said, 'Not many people have a second chance twenty years later to fulfil a dream, but this *Mack and Mabel* working as I knew it could be is that dream come true.'

✶ The blame for its short Broadway run was put on its unhappy ending. However, other shows have overcome this handicap, such as *West Side Story* and *Blood Brothers*. The difference is that the others have not classed themselves as musical comedies, while this has.

The Critics

'A big sentimental musical – tuneful songs and witty dances. All are to be congratulated' – *The New Yorker*
'A splendid, superb, terrific, enthralling musical' – *Associated Press*
'Jerry Herman's songs are excellent – the most tuneful and lyrically suitable in years' – *Variety*

Recommended Recording

Original Broadway cast (CD) MCA Broadway Gold MCAD-10523
Once that famous overture ends there is much enjoyment in the performances of Bernadette Peters and Robert Preston. They have a strong lead on both a concert version and the London cast, even though the latter is the most complete.

The Maid of the Mountains

LYRICS ✶ Harry Graham, F. Clifford Harris and (Arthur) Valentine
MUSIC ✶ Harold Fraser-Simson. Additional music by James W. Tate
BOOK ✶ Frederick Lonsdale

First Performance

London, Daly's Theatre, 10 February 1917 (1352 performances)
New York, Casino Theater, 11 September 1918 (37 performances)

Principal Characters

Teresa ✶ The Maid
Baldassare ✶ Chief brigand
Beppo ✶ A brigand in love with Teresa
Tonio ✶ A comic foil in Beppo's band
Vittoria ✶ Companion of the governor's daughter, Angela
General Malona

Original New York Cast

José Collins, Arthur Wontner, Thorpe Bates, Lauri di Frece,
Mabel Sealby, Mark Lester

Original London Cast

Sidonie Espero, William Courtney, Carl Gantvoort, Bert Clark,
Miriam Doyle, William Danforth

Plot

Baldassare, the chief of a robber band, has announced his retirement from plundering and his men are about to disperse. The band pleads with the lovely Teresa to ask Baldassare to reconsider his decision, but she has little influence over the man she's in love with. As they divide the booty, a knocking is heard at the door of the fortress. It's the governor's daughter Angela, and her companion, Vittoria, lost in the fog. Angela recognises a stolen brooch that Baldassare is wearing. She demands to be released – and is. Teresa has been captured by government forces. The price of her freedom is Baldassare himself. The latter has a plan. A new governor is expected the next day. The brigands will capture him, Baldassare will assume his identity and rescue Teresa himself.

In the town square, General Malona boasts that he will capture Baldassare, who now enters as Count Orsino, the new governor. The latter suggests that Teresa leads them to the mountain retreat to capture the brigand. They run into Angela and Vittoria. Baldassare's disguise passes muster but Tonio is Vittoria's husband! For him she has turned down twenty-six proposals from the general. Not any more – especially when Tonio refuses to acknowledge his own identity. What will he do?

Baldassare is much taken with Angela, and Teresa jealously reveals his true identity. He is seized as Teresa sinks to the earth in regret, and Angela is repelled by the bandit Baldassare has been revealed to be.

The action moves to the prison island of Santos where Teresa pleads for Baldassare's life and Vittoria tries to do the same for Tonio with her money as a bribe. Baldassare finds a new friend, Lieutenant Rugini, banished to the island. He's planning to desert. He compares the flighty Angela with the honest and sincere Teresa – but Baldassare can only remember the latter's betrayal of him. Here's a test: Teresa would release Baldassare given the chance, even if she knew the bandit would run away with Angela. That would demonstrate her love, thinks Rugini. He hands over the key, and Teresa duly releases Baldassare at night. There's a boat waiting, manned by Vittoria and Tonio. Baldassare can flee with his beloved while Teresa will return to the mountains. At last Baldassare's eyes are opened and he leaves with Teresa and the others for happiness elsewhere.

Music and Songs

A magnificent, opulent, romantic score with wonderful tunes and stirring sentiments. 'Live for today' (Beppo), 'Love will find a way' (Teresa), 'A paradise for two' (Beppo and Teresa) and 'A bachelor gay' (Beppo) have all remained as concert hall ballads which are still performed today.

Did You Know?

✸ Original cast recordings of shows were a regular part of musical life in Europe from long before World War I. The extensive coverage of *The Maid of the Mountains* with José Collins (from 1917) is just one of many examples.

✸ The show had the longest London run of any show between *Chu Chin Chow* and *Me and My Girl*.

✸ It was very successful in original runs and on frequent revivals in Australia, starring the redoubtable Gladys Moncrieff.

✸ The 1972 revival did not prove successful, but it was disfigured by the addition of several unlikely tunes from many years later, including 'Pedro the fisherman' and 'Song of the vagabonds', which had no business there.

The Critics

'Praise and congratulations to everybody for what is surely the most brilliant, tasteful show of its kind yet seen' – *Eros*
'*The Maid of the Mountains* is as pleasing a musical entertainment as has been seen in London for some years' – *The Times*

Recommended Recording

Studio cast (CD) Hyperion CDA 67190
The second reconstruction by Hyperion of a historically important musical (the first was *The Geisha*). Janis Kelly plays the maid with a solid performance and Christopher Maltman is Beppo the brigand. It is well performed and it shows off the fine score well.

Mame

LYRICS ✴ Jerry Herman
MUSIC ✴ Jerry Herman
BOOK ✴ Robert E. Lee and Jerome Lawrence, based on their play *Auntie Mame*,
adapted from the novel by Patrick Dennis

First Performance

New York, Winter Garden Theater, 24 May 1966 (1508 performances)
London, Drury Lane Theatre, 20 February 1969 (443 performances)

Principal Characters

Mame Dennis Burnside ✴ Our heroine
Vera Charles ✴ Her bosom buddy
Agnes Gooch ✴ Patrick's nurse and Mame's protegée
Patrick Dennis ✴ Her nephew
Dwight Babcock ✴ Patrick's trustee
Beauregard Burnside ✴ A Southern gentleman

Original New York Cast

Angela Lansbury, Beatrice Arthur, Jane Connell, Willard Waterman,
Frankie Michaels/Jerry Lanning, Charles Braswell

Original London Cast

Ginger Rogers, Margaret Courtenay, Ann Beach, Guy Spaull,
Gary Warren/Tony Adams, Barry Kent

Plot

It's 1928 in New York and party-giving, fun-loving Mame Dennis is about to receive a surprise package – her newly orphaned nephew, Patrick, and his nurse, Agnes Gooch. Mame has rather unconventional ideas about schooling which are eventually scotched by Patrick's trustee, the strait-laced Mr Babcock and, after a few false starts, Patrick has a conventional schooling. The Wall Street Crash wipes out all Mame's resources and she takes a series of disastrous jobs, not to mention a swift entry into, and exit from, showbiz courtesy of her oldest and dearest friend, Vera Charles, who was the star of a new *Moon* musical that Mame comprehensively torpedoes.

Back in Beekman Place, the servants decide they need Christmas *now*, and in the middle of the premature celebrations one of Mame's ex-customers turns up – a victim of her manicurist skills. This is Beauregard Burnside, and he invites Mame down to visit his Mama in the South. Mame tries valiantly to fit in, and is given a dangerous horse to ride in a fox hunt by a jealous rival for Beau's hand, only to emerge the heroine of the hunt.

Mr and Mrs Burnside (yes, that's Mame!) take a world trip, but Beau falls off a mountain and Mame returns to New York a rich, though sad, widow. She encourages Agnes to 'live, live, live' life and in doing so she gets pregnant.

Mame visits the Upsons, the now grown up Patrick's intended parents-in-law, but has a thoroughly uncomfortable time. She returns the compliment when the Upsons visit Beekman Place. The apartment is packed with Mame's zany crowd, and the star turn is Agnes, who comes out with her own little surprise! Also present is a young decorator, Pegeen, who has made the apartment over. After the Upsons leave, Patrick realises his lucky escape and notices her.

Ten years later Patrick and Pegeen pay Mame a visit with their young son. Within minutes, young Peter and his Great Auntie Mame are planning a round-the-world trip – and who can resist Mame?

Music and Songs

Vintage Herman on peak form, with numbers including 'Open a new window' (Mame), 'It's today' (Mame), 'My best girl' (Patrick), 'We need a little Christmas' (Mame and the servants), 'Mame' (the hunt), 'Bosom buddies' (Vera and Mame) and 'If he walked into my life' (Mame).

Did You Know?

✱ The London production ran only as long as Ginger Rogers was in it (apart from a short holiday when Juliet Prowse scored a success in the leading role).

✱ The original stage play had featured Rosalind Russell, who also appeared in the non musical film.

✱ Beatrice Arthur recreated the role of Vera in the film but had her number with Mame ('Bosom Buddies') trimmed.

✱ The three Tony Awards won by the show were all for actors.

The Critics

'The whopping musical comedy hit that everyone was waiting for . . . a song and dance blockbuster' – *Variety*
'The star vehicle deserves its star and vice is very much versa' – *New York Times*
'In this marathon role she [Miss Lansbury] has wit, poise, warmth' – *New York Times*

Recommended Recording

Original Broadway cast (CD) Columbia CK 3000
Angel Lansbury in sparkling form singing this top-notch Herman score with an energy that makes a true star. All other Mames shrink when they are put by the side of Miss Lansbury.

Film

Warner Brothers, 1974 . Starring Lucille Ball, Robert Preston and Beatrice Arthur. Directed by Gene Saks.

Mamma Mia!

LYRICS ✳ Benny Andersson and Bjorn Ulvaeus
MUSIC ✳ Benny Andersson and Bjorn Ulvaeus
BOOK ✳ Catherine Johnson.
Additional songs with Stig Anderson

First Performance

London, Prince Charles Theatre, 6 April 1999 (still running)

Principal Characters

Donna ✳ Sophie's mother and lead singer with the Dynamos
Sophie ✳ A girl about to be married
Sky ✳ A boy about to be married
Rosie ✳ An ex-member of the Dynamos
Tanya ✳ An ex-member of the Dynamos
Harry Bright ✳ The possible father
Bill Austin ✳ The possible father
Sam Carmichael ✳ The possible father

Original London Cast

Siobhan McCarthy, Lisa Stoke, Andrew Langtree, Jenny Galloway, Louise
Plowright, Paul Clarkson, Nicolas Colicos, Hilton McRae

Plot

On a tiny Greek island, a wedding is about to take place. Donna settled there some
years before and has run a successful little café. It is her daughter Sophie who is
getting married to the handsome Sky. Donna has never told her daughter who her
father is and now is the time for her to find out. The three possible fathers have
been invited and they have arrived. Also, two ladies who used to be in a pop
group with Donna are here, and they are only too happy to remember the old
days and the songs they sang.

Against this wafer-thin plot line there is ample time for pleasant memories of
the past, and each prospective father believes it is he who is the real father, and
each wants to give his daughter away. What is the outcome? Well, it would be
wrong to divulge the end of the story – it would be like knowing the butler did it!

Music and Songs

The songs of Abba are universally known and loved and, as such, this show is a
glorious bathe in nostalgia. Cleverly, the songs have been set in the story so that
they do not seem out of place. The title song is given to Donna, 'Dancing queen'
and 'Super trouper' bring the girl group back together (Donna, Rosie and Tanya)
and the young bride gets 'I have a dream' and 'The name of the game'.

Did You Know?

✶ The film *Buona Sera Mrs Campbell* has a very similar story line and so has the Broadway musical *Carmelina* by Alan Jay Lerner, which was based on it.

✶ The play and film *Shirley Valentine* has an English lass moving to a Greek island to start a new life.

✶ The first production of the show out of London was at the Alexander Theatre in Toronto, Canada, where it opened on 23 May 2000 and became an immediate hit.

The Critics

'Sheer heaven' – *Daily Telegraph*
'One can hear the roar all the way across the Great Lakes to Toronto and across the great Atlantic from London. The word is out and it is 'smash hit'. The show is *Mamma Mia!* And it's one of the most enjoyable evenings on both continents' – *New York Newsday*

Recommended Recording

Original London cast (CD) Polydor 543 115-2
These well-known songs are given a refreshing new lease of life in this original cast recording that brings back all the zest and fun of the stage show.

Man of La Mancha

LYRICS ✳ Joe Darion
MUSIC ✳ Mitch Leigh
BOOK ✳ Dale Wasserman, based on his television play *I, Don Quixote*,
adapted from the novel by Miguel de Cervantes Saavedra

First Performance

New York, Washington Square Theater, 22 November 1965 (2328 performances)
London, Piccadilly Theatre, 24 April 1968 (253 performances)

Principal Characters

Don Quixote ✳ A knight out of his time
Aldonza ✳ A serving wench
Sancho Panza ✳ His squire
Innkeeper
Padre
Dr Carrasco
Housekeeper

Original New York Cast

Richard Kiley, Joan Diener, Irving Jacobson, Ray Middleton, Robert Rounseville,
Jon Cypher, Eleanor Knapp

Original London Cast

Keith Michell, Joan Diener, Bernard Spear, David King, Allan Crofoot,
Peter Arne, Olive Gilbert

Plot

During the Spanish Inquisition author Miguel Cervantes whiles away the time, until called from the prison cell, by telling tales of his most famous creation, Don Quixote. The latter, a country squire, decides to take up his lance against man's inhumanity to man, accompanied by his dim, loyal and willing squire, Sancho Panza. The first target turns out to be a windmill (Quixote's eyesight is not of the best). Quixote believes that the adventure failed because he had not been properly dubbed a knight, so he needs to find somebody who will knight him. He sees a castle (an inn actually). Inside is Aldonza, being attacked by muleteers. Don Quixote hails her as a sweet lady and dubs her his fair Dulcinea. From now on she has her champion – him. Let her give him a token to carry into battle; she contemptuously throws him a dishcloth. Meanwhile, a clutch of Quixote's friends arrives – his doctor and padre.

Quixote sallies forth for new adventure. Aldonza now softens at hearing about Quixote and the gentle being he is. Although he and Sancho Panza lay out a whole band of muleteers, Aldonza still gets assaulted by them after Quixote has preached forgiveness, has been dubbed a knight by the innkeeper, and is spending time in prayer. Quixote takes to the road and is robbed of his possessions by

Moorish gypsies. Back at the inn, Aldonza tells him the full sordid story of her life, but Quixote can only see beauty. Suddenly Quixote is faced by his most feared opponent, the Great Enchanter, whose weapon is a mirror which he holds up to Quixote so he can see the reality behind his illusions. Beaten, the knight sinks to the floor. His opponent reveals himself as Quixote's doctor, whose ploy was intended to restore the knight to his senses. It has, but at what cost. Quixote lies mortally ill at home, where Aldonza visits him – he has altered her life for the better. Happy at last, Quixote rises for one final attempt at the Impossible Dream – and dies.

It is time for Cervantes' own final trial. He is called before the Inquisition, and the governor and prisoners wish him well as he ascends the steps out of the prison cell.

Songs

Rich, powerful Iberian-flavoured score surmounted by the powerhouse hit 'The impossible dream' (Quixote). Other songs include 'Man of La Mancha' (Quixote), 'Dulcinea' (Quixote), 'I'm only thinking of him' (Quixote's family), 'I really like him' (Sancho Panza) and 'What do you want of me?' (Dulcinea).

Did You Know?

✴ The show received ecstatic reviews and has been mounted with success all over the world, including East Berlin. Jacques Brel took the lead in Paris.

✴ When it finally closed on Broadway, *Man of La Mancha* was the fourth longest-running Broadway show.

✴ *Man of La Mancha* won five Tony Awards including those for best musical and best score.

The Critics

'As Dale Wasserman has written him, Albert Marre has directed him and Richard Kiley has played him, he [Don Quixote] is a mad, gallant figure who has honestly materialized from the pages of Cervantes. At its best, *Man of La Mancha* is audacious in its conception and tasteful in execution' – Howard Taubman

Recommended Recording

Original Broadway cast (CD) MCA Records MCAD 1672
A powerful score best served by this recording. Richard Kiley as Don Quixote is perfection. The complete London cast recording has not made it onto CD and nor has an excellent studio cast with Marilyn Horne and Jim Nabors, which gives the original a tight run.

Film

United Artists, 1972. Starring Peter O'Toole, Sophia Loren and James Coco. Directed by Arthur Hiller.

Martin Guerre

LYRICS ✶ Edward Hardy and Stephen Clark,
with additional lyrics by Herbert Kretzmer and Alain Boublil
MUSIC ✶ Claude-Michel Schönberg
BOOK ✶ Alain Boublil and Claude-Michel Schönberg, based on folk tales

First Performance

London, Prince Edward Theatre, 10 July 1996
Revised version Prince Edward Theatre, 11 November 1996 (700)

Principal Characters

Martin Guerre ✶ A villager
Arnaud du Thyl ✶ A soldier
Bertrande de Rols ✶ Their bride
Guillaume ✶ A villager in love with her
Benoît ✶ A villager
Hortense, Celestine, Ernestine
✶ Wise villagers
Madame de Rols ✶ Bertrande's mother
Pierre Guerre ✶ Martin's uncle
Father Dominic ✶ A priest
Catherine ✶ A local Protestant

Original London Cast

Matt Rawle, Iain Glen, Juliette Caton/Rebecca Lock, Jérôme Pradon,
Michael Matus, Ann Emery, Sheila Reid, Julia Sutton, Susan Jane Tanner,
Martin Turner, Marcus Cunningham, Stephanie Putson

Plot

The action is set in the French village of Artigat during the 16th century. As the
Roman Catholic villagers work in the fields a group of Protestants pass by and are
jeered at. Bertrande is to wed Martin Guerre and join their lands and property,
ensuring a Roman Catholic heir. Only Guillaume objects; he's in love with
Bertrande himself. In the following year there's no sign of a pregnancy and,
burdened with shame, Martin abandons family and home. Seven years later in a
battle against the Protestants, Martin is wounded and believed dead by his friend,
Arnaud, who journeys to Artigat and claims to be Martin, thwarting the plans of
Guillaume who plans to marry Bertrande and name any heir Guerre. Bertrande
feels isolated. Only a local Protestant, Catherine, offers her any comfort and
invites her to the secret Protestant services. Bertrande accepts Arnaud as her
husband; soon they are expecting a child. Bertrande, now a Protestant, takes
Arnaud to the secret services. Unfortunately they are followed and spied on by
Guillaume, who then foments an inter-denominational riot in the village. This
results in the revealing of Arnaud's real identity and his arrest and trial.

At the trial there is a surprise witness – Martin Guerre himself, back from the dead. Arnaud is imprisoned. There is a slaughter of Protestants in the village organised by the vengeful Guillaume. Martin visits Bertrande and Arnaud in prison, recognises the depth of their love, and helps them to escape. Guillaume gets wind of this and aims a fatal dagger thrust at Martin – now the object of his hatred. The dagger is intercepted by Arnaud, who dies in his friend's place. The villagers gather to beg forgiveness of Bertrande. She leaves the village with the Protestants, but perhaps will return some day. Martin understands and at last assumes the leadership of Artigat; the villagers will now work on the land again.

Music and Songs

The third of Boublil and Schönberg's Cameron Mackintosh-produced shows takes a well-worn story and enrobes it in rustic French ballads, stirring marching songs and the odd tender love song. Recognisably by the composers of *Les Miserables* is the title tune, sung by Martin. Other fine numbers include 'Here comes the morning' (Arnaud and Bertrande), which is a charming love ballad, 'Sleeping on our own' (old ladies), 'Tell me not to go' (Arnaud and Bertrande) and 'The land of the fathers' (Father Dominic and the villagers).

Did You Know?

✴ *Martin Guerre* is based on a true story. It is the third of three musicals by the Boublil/Schönberg team to be mounted in English (the others are *Les Miserables* and *Miss Saigon*). Its producer closed the show after five months to revise and tighten it up, and employed an additional lyricist, reopening almost immediately.

✴ Iain Glen, the RSC actor, made an impressive West End singing debut in the leading role.

✴ A third version played in the United States but did not reach Broadway.

The Critics

'A musical masterpiece; for the third time in a decade, Boublil and Schönberg have written a great and classic musical' – *International Herald Tribune*
'The triumph of the evening . . . is Bob Avian's choreography' – *Daily Express*

Recommended Recording

London revised version cast (CD) First Night Cast CD59
While you can hear the Boublil and Schönberg touches, this score does not have the same magnitude as their previous offerings. Even so, there are some powerful moments. This recording was the first issued and is of the show after the changes made in November 1996.

Films

Palace Films, 1982. Starring Gérard Dépardieu.
Warner Brothers, 1993. Starring Richard Gere and Jodie Foster. Called *Sommersby*. Both these films preceded the musical, but are based on the same story.

Me and My Girl

LYRICS ✶ L. Arthur Rose and Douglas Furber
MUSIC ✶ Noël Gay
BOOK ✶ L. Arthur Rose and Douglas Furber

First Performance

London, Victoria Palace Theatre, 16 December 1937 (1646 performances)
New York, Marquis Theater, 10 August 1986 (1420 performances)

Principal Characters

Bill Snibson ✶ A chirpy Cockney
Sally Smith ✶ His girl
Parchester ✶ The family solicitor
Sir John Tremayne
The Duchess
Lady Jacqueline ✶ A vamp

Original London Cast

Lupino Lane, Teddie St Denis, Wallace Lupino, George Graves,
Doris Rogers, Betty Frankiss

Original New York Cast

Robert Lindsay, Maryann Plunkett, Timothy Jerome, George S. Irving,
Jane Connell, Jane Summerhays

Plot

Who turns out to be the long-lost heir to the Barony of Hareford, its 17th Baron
and 8th Viscount? Lambeth's own Cockney sparrow, Bill Snibson, that's who. He
has his own girlfriend, Sally, but that won't stop gold-digger Lady Jacqueline. She
ditches her dumbfounded boyfriend, Gerald, when Mr Parchester, the family
solicitor, presents Bill to the flabbergasted family as the new son and heir. But Bill
has still to win the family's approval to inherit the title – and the money. If he
doesn't, he'll be given an annuity and sent away. The formidable Duchess is
determined Bill should stay, insisting that all will be well and, with a little
grooming, Bill will be suitable to inherit. There will be an official reception to
introduce him to the county set. But Sally is not to be invited. Bill faces up to the
Duchess – no Sally, no Bill. But Sally doesn't want to come anyway – not to a posh
party. The party goes ahead and Sally turns up in full Cockney get-up complete
with a posse of pearly kings and queens who perform the 'Lambeth walk' to prove
Bill doesn't belong. But they are all invited to the reception and go into dinner.

Next day there's croquet on the lawn. The Duchess has persuaded Sally to tell
Bill she no longer loves him, in an effort to make him stay and take up his
inheritance. She does this, and slips out to an unknown destination. Bill, helped
by Sir John and Parchester, determines to find Sally (whom he still loves), urged
on by a *Ruddigore*-like gallery of ghostly portraits of his ancestors.

Back at her landlady's Sally decides to move on. She's got a telegram from Bill and must escape. However, Sir John arrives and has a cunning plan for her. When Bill arrives, her landlady says she's not there, but Bill waits. He expends all his energies on locating Sally and bringing her back. Sir John makes the Duchess soften her attitude towards Bill's beloved. Bill finally rejects Lady Jacqueline and she returns to Gerald. Bill is making to leave when Sir John enters with a new Eliza Doolittle – it's a posh Sally! The Duchess is delighted and Bill has his girl!

Music and Songs

Music hall, popular song and Gilbert and Sullivan all contributed to the style of this catchy musical comedy. Noël Gay was renowned for his novelty numbers, too, and there's a fair crop of them here. 'The Lambeth walk' (Sally, Bill and company) and 'Me and my girl' (Bill and Sally) have never been neglected, and 'Once you lose your heart' (Sally) is an affecting ballad. The final score, as used for the revival, also includes the George Formby success 'Leaning on a lamppost' (Bill) that may have originally been planned for the show.

Did You Know?

✶ The original nine-song version was so short it played twice nightly and was the 1930s' longest-running musical, emerging frequently for revival during World War II.

✶ The show's success was assured when a BBC radio unit was forced to cancel a visit elsewhere and decided, instead, to relay a live broadcast from the Victoria Palace. When the audience at home heard 'The Lambeth walk' it made an immediate impact. From next day, the bookings were up.

✶ The show was bombed out of two theatres during the war.

✶ The celebrated revival starring Robert Lindsay and Emma Thompson opened in London on 4 February 1985 at the Adelphi Theatre, and ran for more than 4000 performances. Lindsay headed the Broadway cast and won a Tony Award for his performance.

The Critics

'Lupino Lane has seldom found better material for his well-known gifts of genial and genuine humour' – *The Stage*
'A new and fairly durable comedy' – *The Times*

Recommended Recording

Original London revival cast (CD) Manhattan Records CDP 7 46393
Robert Lindsay and Emma Thompson head the robust cast in this rip roaring revitalised version and it is a joy from start to finish. Lindsay repeated his success on Broadway where the show was recorded again with a distinctive Broadway sound. The London version wins!

Film

MGM, 1939. Starring Lupino Lane, Sally Gray and Seymour Hicks. Directed by Albert De Courville. This version was called *The Lambeth Walk*.

Merrily We Roll Along

Lyrics ✷ Stephen Sondheim
Music ✷ Stephen Sondheim
Book ✷ George Furth, based on the play by George S. Kaufman and Moss Hart

First Performance

New York, Alvin Theater, 16 November 1982 (16 performances)
London, Donmar Warehouse, 1 December 2000 (limited season)

Principal Characters

Franklin Shepard ✷ A composer
Charley Kringas ✷ A lyricist and playwright
Mary Flynn ✷ Their friend
Beth ✷ Franklin's first wife
Gussie ✷ Joe's wife, who will marry Franklin
Joe ✷ A producer

Original New York Cast

Jim Walton, Lonny Price, Ann Morrison, Sally Klein,
Terry Finn, Jason Alexander

Original London Cast

Julian Ovenden, Daniel Evans, Samantha Spiro, Mary Stockley,
Anna Francolini, James Millard

Plot

There's a class reunion in 1980 at which Frank gives the speech and then remembers the failure of his last picture and the disastrous reception afterwards. (The revised version opens at the film's reception where the film has been a success.)

Now the plot goes back in time. It's 1979 and Frank's new friend, Meg, has a part in the film. Frank's long-time friend, Mary, tells Meg exactly what she thinks of the film, and her performance. Frank's wife Gussie hurries Mary out of the party and out of Frank's life for ever; she's also made the mistake of bringing up the subject of former close friend, Charley, and his fine new play.

Back in 1975 Mary and Charley are drinking in the Polo Lounge. Can Mary bring Charley and Frank back together? No. Frank comes in and snubs Charley. He simply doesn't exist any more. Charley asks Frank for his autograph and they fight. What had happened?

In 1973 the Frank and Charley writing team is being interviewed for TV and Charley shoots his mouth off – Frank's virtually a corporation, too busy to write any more. He is humiliated on air by Charley, and their partnership dissolves in acrimony.

It was all so different in 1968. The collaborators are in Frank's new apartment. Charley pleads with Frank not to give up writing for record producing. Enter producer Joe and his wife, Gussie. It becomes evident Frank and Gussie are having an affair, and Joe is powerless to stop it. We understand that Mary is still hopelessly in love with Frank.

Now it's 1966. Outside a courthouse Frank has just endured a messy divorce from Beth. Outside the Alvin Theater (actual first home of *Merrily* itself), you can just hear a massive hit inside. It's Joe's production of Charley and Frank's show.

Back in 1962 in Joe's apartment we glimpse the show's genesis. Gussie, Joe's wife, makes a play for Frank and he and his partner sing a potential song for the show – twice.

Two years earlier Frank and Charley are at their Greenwich Village revue. The years 1958 and 1959 find Frank, Charley and friend Mary engaged in a series of writing and performing jobs. There's a slot for a hastily put-together revue in Greenwich Village. They write it and one of the girl singers they audition is to become Frank's first wife, Beth. She'll be pregnant before they eventually marry in 1960.

October 1957 finds Mary, Frank and Charley on their roof looking at the Sputnik that will change all their lives for ever – won't it? (This is where the revised version ends.) The action now jumps from 1956 to 1980 and the graduation. Frank is left with the memory of the collapse of his dreams and ideals as a song he and Charley wrote together rings out.

Music and Songs

Sondheim in his most straightforward, Broadway style. A brilliant collection of passionately felt sentiments expressed in music, including 'Old friends' (Charley, Frank and Mary), 'Not a day goes by' (Mary, Frank and Beth) and 'Our time' (Mary, Frank and Charley). There are also the fine graduation hymn (dropped in the revised version) 'The hills of tomorrow' (the class), the revue number to end all revue numbers 'Bobby and Jackie and Jack' (Charley, Frank and Beth), and the classic ballad recorded by Frank Sinatra 'Good thing going' (Frank and Charley).

Did You Know?

✱ This show has one of the finest of all scores of the 1980s, as much anthologised and performed as any of the period.

The Critics

Critical reaction on Broadway was mixed:
'A dud' – *New York Daily News*
'Far too good a musical to be judged by those twin kangaroo courts of word of mouth and critical consensus' – Clive Barnes

Recommended Recording

Original Broadway cast (CD) RCA Red Seal RCD1-5840
A relaxed Sondheim in tuneful Broadway style with great songs performed wonderfully on this disc. As the show plays backwards you may want to hear it chronologically and that is easy on a CD player. Whatever way you choose, the score will almost certainly grow on you.

The Mikado, or The Town of Titipu

LYRICS ✳ W.S. Gilbert
MUSIC ✳ Arthur Sullivan
BOOK ✳ W.S. Gilbert

First Performance

London, Savoy Theatre, 14 March 1885 (672 performances)
New York, Fifth Avenue Theatre, 19 August 1885 (250 performances)

Principal Characters

The Mikado of Japan ✳ The number one man
Nanki-Poo ✳ His son
Ko-Ko ✳ Lord High Executioner
Pooh-Bah ✳ Lord High of everything else
Pish-Tush ✳ Noble Lord
Yum-Yum ✳ Ko-Ko's ward
Katisha ✳ An elderly Lady, in love with Nanki-Poo

Original London Cast

Richard Temple, Durward Lely, George Grossmith, Rutland Barrington, Frederick Bovill, Leonora Braham, Rosina Brandram

Original New York Cast

F. Federici, Courtice Pounds, George Thorne, Fred Billington, Charles Richards, Geraldine Ulmar, Elsie Cameron

Plot

Nanki-Poo, the Mikado's son, who is disguised as a wandering minstrel, arrives to see Yum-Yum whom he loves, but who is engaged to her guardian, Ko-Ko. However, Ko-Ko has been arrested for the capital offence of flirting, and because he holds the post of Lord High Executioner it makes it impossible for him to carry out his own execution. Yum-Yum and her sisters are out of school and she is resigned to the marriage to Ko-Ko that is now set for that afternoon. Nanki-Poo tells her who he is and that he has run away from court to escape an enforced marriage with Katisha.

The lack of executions has come to the notice of the Mikado and he orders that there should be one during the month. Ko-Ko has the choice – either behead himself or find a substitute. In his unhappy state, Nanki-Poo is set to commit suicide but, instead, agrees to be the substitute if he can marry Yum-Yum and live with her for the month. Unfortunately, Katisha arrives, sees her Nanki-Poo and rushes off to the Mikado.

As the arrangements continue for the wedding it is discovered that by law, when a man is executed for flirting, his wife must be buried alive. This puts Yum-Yum in a quandary and, as the Mikado approaches, Ko-Ko uses the power of one of his many titles to sign a death certificate in the name of Nanki-Poo and, under his title of archbishop, to marry Yum-Yum and Nanki-Poo. But when the Mikado discovers his son has been 'executed', Ko-Ko has to persuade him to return to life – but that would mean marriage to Katisha and Nanki-Poo would prefer death to her. The answer is simple: Ko-Ko courts Katisha and she agrees to marry him. So, Nanki-Poo and Yum-Yum can live happily ever after.

Music and Songs

One of the best loved Gilbert and Sullivan scores with 'A wandering minstrel I' (Nanki-Poo), 'Three little maids from school are we' (Yum-Yum and sisters), 'I've got a little list' (Ko-Ko) and 'Here's a how-de-do!' (Yum-Yum, Nanki-Poo and Ko-Ko).

Did You Know?

✳ American producers rushed to present *The Mikado* prior to D'Oyly Carte opening their production. When the English company opened in New York, an American company opened the next day and both productions ran successfully.

✳ *The Mikado*, the story of its creation and the problems between Gilbert and Sullivan form the basis of the film *Topsy-Turvey*.

✳ There has been a *Black Mikado*, a *Hot Mikado*, a *Swing Mikado* and a *Cool Mikado*.

The Critics

'The story on which Mr Gilbert's libretto is founded is extremely slight, and, if the truth be owned, so childish that on being compelled to sum it up on paper one blushes at the remembrance of many a hearty laugh it has excited' – *The Times*

Recommended Recording

Studio cast (CD) Telarc CD-80284
Sir Charles Mackerras and the orchestra and chorus of the Welsh National Opera give a fine, full-throated version which is nearly complete. But there are many to choose from, some being more traditional, such as the excellent D'Oyly Carte version (**TER CDTER2 1178**) that can boast the complete score.

Films

GFD/G and S, 1939. Starring Martyn Green and Kenny Baker. Directed by Victor Schertzinger.
1960. *Bell Telephone Hour* on television with Groucho Marx, Helen Traubel, Stanley Holloway and Dennis King.

Les Miserables

LYRICS ✶ Herbert Kretzmer (French lyrics by Alain Boublil)
MUSIC ✶ Claude-Michel Schönberg
BOOK ✶ Alain Boublil and Jean-Marc Natal, after Victor Hugo

First Performance

Paris, Palais des Sports, 17 September 1980 (107 performances)
London, Barbican Centre, 30 September 1985 (63 performances)
Transferred to Palace Theatre, 4 December 1985 (still running)
New York, Broadway Theater, 12 March 1987 (still running)

Principal Characters

Jean Valjean ✶ A felon
Javert ✶ An officer of the law
Fantine ✶ A factory girl
Cosette ✶ Her daughter
Monsieur and Madame Thenardier ✶ A couple of opportunists
Marius ✶ A student
Eponine ✶ A girl of the streets

Original London Cast

Colm Wilkinson, Roger Allam, Patti LuPone, Zoe Hart, Alun Armstrong,
Susan Jane Tanner, Michael Ball, Frances Ruffelle

Original New York Cast

Colm Wilkinson, Terrence Mann, Randy Graff, Judy Kuhn, Leo Burmester,
Jennifer Butt, David Bryant, Frances Ruffelle

Plot

Jean Valjean is released from prison on parole and chooses to run away. To get money he steals candlesticks from a bishop who forgives him, and thus makes Valjean eager to help others. An implacable policeman, Javert, pursues him.

Through the years Valjean rises in power and responsibility, becoming mayor in Montreuil, a town in the French provinces. He looks after Cosette, the daughter of Fantine, a former employee whom he once loved but who had died after being reduced to prostitution. Valjean rescues Cosette from her corrupt foster parents, the Thenardiers and they move to Paris, but it is far from being a safe haven.

As Cosette grows up she becomes part of a student crowd and falls in love with Marius. The students are leading an anti-government riot and Marius is among them. Valjean is determined to keep a watchful eye on Marius, and look after him. The barriers go up and Valjean joins the fighters, eventually saving a wounded Marius. The revolution fails and many die, including the urchin Eponine. In Valjean and Marius's retreat they encounter Javert, who has been captured and bound by the rebels, and set him free. Javert cannot understand this act of mercy. He cannot live with the idea that he will always be beholden to Valjean and commits suicide in the Seine, unknown to Valjean. The Thenardiers encounter the unconscious bodies of Valjean and Marius in the sewers, overcome by exhaustion, and rob Marius of a ring.

Back in safe surroundings, Marius grieves for his friends, and grows well under the care of Valjean and Cosette. Valjean reveals his secret former life to Marius, who is to marry Cosette, and he decides to vanish, so as not to bring shame and disgrace on them. At the wedding, the Thenardiers try to blackmail Marius because of his father-in-law. They had seen Valjean leave the barricades with a body on his shoulder, and they bring out the ring that Marius recognises as his own. He now realises it was Valjean who rescued him. He races with Cosette by his side to find Valjean, and does so just in time for Valjean is dying, and about to rejoin his beloved Fantine in the next world

Music and Songs

Thoroughly Gallic in inspiration and feeling, the dramatic through-sung score includes the hits 'I dreamed a dream' (Fantine), 'Empty chairs and empty tables' (Marius), 'One day more' (the company) and 'Bring him home' (Jean), plus among many others, 'Soliloquy' (Jean), 'Master of the house' (the Thenardiers), 'Do you hear the people sing?' (the company), 'A heart full of love' (Marius and Cosette) and 'On my own' (Epinome).

Did You Know?

∗ The show was originally mounted in part-subsidised form by the RSC, which still gets a royalty from the Cameron Mackintosh productions.

∗ There have been well over 20 international productions.

∗ It won eight Tonys on Broadway, including one for Frances Ruffelle repeating her London triumph as Eponine.

The Critics

'A dose of alkaline amid the engulfing acids, a refreshing antidote to contemporary cynicism; but it's also a thumping good story, and at the Barbican, a superbly staged one too' – *New York Times* (London correspondent)

Recommended Recording

Original London cast recording (CD) First Night Encore CD1
The first English version was recorded while the production was still at the RSC at the Barbican. It has all the freshness and excitement of a young show out to prove itself and includes 'Little people' which was cut before the show transferred to the Palace Theatre. It is also interesting to hear the original French concert version (also on First Night) and the 10th anniversary concert.

Video

Videos of the making of the show and of the 10th anniversary concert are available.

Miss Saigon

LYRICS ✷ Alain Boublil and Richard Maltby Jnr
MUSIC ✷ Claude-Michel Schönberg
BOOK ✷ Alain Boublil

First Performance

London, Drury Lane Theatre, 20 September 1989 (4246 performances)
New York, Broadway Theater, 11 April 1991 (4063 performances)

Principal Characters

Kim ✷ A young girl
The Engineer ✷ An entrepreneur
Chris ✷ An American soldier
John ✷ His friend
Ellen ✷ Chris' eventual wife
Thuy ✷ Kim's cousin

Original London Cast

Lea Solonga, Jonathan Pryce, Simon Bowman, Peter Polycarpou,
Claire Moore, Keith Burns

Original New York Cast

Lea Solonga, Jonathan Pryce, Willy Falk, Hinton Battle,
Liz Callaway, Barry K. Bernal

Plot

Kim is a new recruit to the Saigon brothel run by the Engineer. The American
army is soon to move away, but meanwhile the joint is full of American soldiers
who tonight include young Chris and his friend John. The Engineer wants an all-
important American visa on his passport so he can spread his operations. Perhaps
Chris can help him – through Kim? Chris and Kim meet, the attraction is more
than physical and they leave for her home where they make love. Chris is really
smitten. He rings John. Can he have all his leave at once to spend the time with
Kim? After some time her door bursts open. It is Kim's cousin, Thuy, her intended
husband. Kim will not leave Chris and is cursed by Thuy. The American army is in
retreat and Chris gets a pass for Kim to be transported out of Saigon but she
misses the last helicopter.

Three years pass. Vietnam is reunified and the people are celebrating. The
Engineer still hasn't got a visa for America. Kim is living in a shanty village with
her two-year-old son by Chris. Thuy comes and menaces her; she shoots him with
a pistol.

And Chris? He's back in America, with his new wife Ellen. But he hasn't told her
everything about his past. Kim arrives in Bangkok and visits an organisation run
by John for the repatriation of half-American babies, 'bu doi'. John contacts
Chris, who determines to go and see his son. He arrives in Bangkok. Kim goes to

246

his hotel and meets Ellen, Chris' wife, who tells her the precise situation. There will be help, but Chris has a new life with Ellen. There's no room in it for Kim or the child. Kim is devastated. She won't believe any of this unless Chris tells her himself. Chris comes to her room backstage at the club. Kim dresses her son in his best clothes, slips behind a curtain and shoots herself. Now Chris will have to take his son to America – and the American Dream.

Music and Songs

The team, including the fine American lyricist Richard Maltby, came up with a stirring, dramatic score with universal immediate appeal, at times tenderly romantic, at others brutally realistic, and led by 'The movie in my mind' (Kim), 'I still believe' (Kim), 'The last night of the world' (Chris) and the bitter 'The American dream' (Engineer).

Did You Know?

✶ The original plot was inspired by the libretto for Puccini's opera *Madama Butterfly*, which also inspired the play *The World of Suzie Wong*.

✶ For the American production Cameron Mackintosh, the producer, insisted on repeating his English cast, with Lea Salonga and Jonathan Pryce as the leads. US Equity objected to the latter. However, the producer insisted, threatening to cancel the entire production. He won.

✶ Jonathan Pryce had a great personal success with his role as the engineer and won awards both in New York and London.

The Critics

'Musicals come and go. This one will stay' – *The Sunday Times*
'An unusually intelligent and impassioned piece of popular theatre, revamped Puccini with a sharp political edge' – *The Guardian*
'The best of the new school of British musicals' – *The Independent*

Recommended Recording

Original London cast (CD) Geffen 7599-24271-2
This is one of the best scores to materialise from the wave of spectacular musicals in the eighties. It is a powerful story with a commanding and passionate score that is captured magnificently on this recording.

Mr Cinders

LYRICS ✶ Leo Robin, Clifford Grey and Greatorex Norman
MUSIC ✶ Vivian Ellis and Richard Myers
BOOK ✶ Clifford Grey and Greatorex Norman

First Performance

London, Adelphi Theatre, 11 February 1929
(529 performances; final eight months at the Hippodrome Theatre)

Principal Characters

Jim Lancaster ✶ Our hero, a male Cinderella
Jill Kemp ✶ Our heroine
Guy Lancaster ✶ Ugly brother No. 1
Lumley Lancaster ✶ Ugly brother No. 2
Henry Kemp ✶ A millionaire
Lady Lancaster ✶ A dominant mother
Sir George Lancaster ✶ Her husband

Original London Cast

Bobby Howes, Binnie Hale, Basil Howes, Jack Melford, Charles Cautley,
Ruth Maitland, Sebastian Smith

Plot

Lady Lancaster is firmly in control at Merton Chase. She concentrates on pursuing the fortunes of her sons from her first marriage – Guy and Lumley. Her adopted orphan nephew by marriage, Jim, is good natured, amenable and therefore bullied by Lady L and her brood. (Sir George Lancaster, her husband, is big in the glue industry, whereas Lady L is descended from the Plantagenet dynasty.) A bedraggled millionaire, Henry Kemp, has been rescued from the river. Surely Henry can do something for Guy's prospects? Guy tries to point out that Jim was the rescuer but his mother shuts him up as usual, and when Jim turns up, fetchingly clad in a barrel, he's ordered to keep quiet. It turns out that Kemp has a daughter, Jill.

On the way to pick up her father, Jill has a little motor accident and knocks off a policeman's hat. Jill changes clothes with a servant and emerges at the Towers, unrecognisable, where she meets and is attracted to Jim, busy with his chores. As 'Sarah', Jill finds herself the new maid and gives Miss Kemp's name as her reference! Meanwhile, Minerva is greeted effusively as the real heiress. The family soon receives an invitation from Mr Kemp to attend a ball. Jim is not considered part of the family by Lady L – no ball for him – but he helps the brothers into their elaborate costumes. However, 'Sarah' comes to the rescue with an invitation for Jim and produces a spare costume as a South American explorer. At the party Jim finds himself in hot water when his fictional South American adventures are being questioned by a real South American, Donna Lucia d'Esmeralda. When he meets Jill he's dumbfounded – what is 'Sarah' the maid doing here, and with an expensive diamond necklace (her father's twenty-first birthday present) round her neck? Lumley proposes to Minerva and is accepted. Meanwhile, the necklace disappears and is found by the butler in Jim's coat. A policeman tries to arrest Jim but then it's discovered that the butler has disappeared with the necklace. Jim and Jill give chase on Lumley's motorbike, which duly runs out of petrol. In fact the butler is in the sidecar and is now captured – together with the necklace. The next morning Lady L finds that Lumley is adamant about marrying Minerva, and Guy is fixed up with his girlfriend, Phyllis. Jill returns as 'Sarah' and tells Lady L exactly what she thinks about the family's treatment of Jim and Sir George. When Lady L protests, Jim stoutly defends 'Sarah', and the latter is thrilled. PC Marks turns up with a hat. It was worn by whoever captured the butler. Lady L pushes her sons forward, but to no avail. Enter Jill in her proper clothes; it was Jim, who it turns out is the Earl of Ditcham! Jim wins the reward and also Sarah/Jill. There can be a triple wedding!

Music and Songs

A typical musical comedy of the period, with sweet, uncomplicated songs to match, including 'Spread a little happiness' (Jim), 'She's my lovely' (Jim) (added for the 1980s revival, from *Hide and Seek* originally), 'Every little moment' (Minerva and Lumley), 'I've got you' (Jim and Jill), 'On the Amazon' (Jim) and 'One-man girl' (Jill).

Did You Know?

✶ *Cinderella* is usually a lucky plot for a musical and this role-reversal example was no exception.

✶ Bobby Howes and Binnie Hale made this one of the most popular shows of its time. The small-scale revival in 1982 was even more successful. It even reached the Goodspeed Opera House in New York.

✶ The original writers of the basic score, Vivian Ellis and Greatorex Norman, wrote an additional song, 'Please, Mr Cinders', in 1986 – a record 58 years after the original score was completed!

The Critics

'A little happiness spread very thinly' – *Daily Mail*
'As delicious, nonsensical and intoxicating as pink champagne' – *The Times*

Recommended Recording

London revival cast (CD) TER CDTER 1069
This is the recording of an excellent small-scale revival starring Denis Lawson. It has charm and is well sung. Vivian Ellis was one of best composers to come out of the twentieth century and this is a great tribute to him.

Film

Wardour 1934 starring Clifford Mollison, Zalma O'Neil and the Western Brothers.

Mr Wonderful

LYRICS ✶ Jerry Bock, Larry Holofcener and George Weiss
MUSIC ✶ Jerry Bock, Larry Holofcener and George Weiss
BOOK ✶ Joseph Stein and Will Glickman

First Performance

New York, Broadway Theater, 22 March 1956 (383 performances)

Principal Characters

Charlie Welch ✶ A young entertainer
Ethel ✶ His girlfriend
Fred and Lil Campbell ✶ Two showbusiness friends
Rita Romano ✶ A dancer/singer

Original New York Cast

Sammy Davis Jnr, Olga James, Jack Carter, Pat Marshall, Chita Rivera.
Also the Will Mastin Trio, the group with which Davis' family, and Sammy
himself, had worked.

Plot

There wasn't that much of a plot, but what there was was this:

Charlie Welch is a struggling song and dance man in Union City, New Jersey,
where the nearest he gets to exotic locales is a Miami beach setting. He also plays
drums, and does impressions as well. He has a girlfriend, Ethel Pearson, and loyal
friends in the Campbells. Fred Campbell has discerned a real talent in Charlie, and
urges him to try his hand in the big lights and big city showbusiness of New
York's Broadway. Charlie is diffident, but is evidently persuaded by Fred, his wife
Lil, and his girlfriend, Ethel, to try his luck.

In the second act, Charlie eventually plucks up the courage to clamber up on
the stage of the nightclub of his choice, together with his musicians, and scores a
big success. Mr Wonderful is on his way – he's a star.

As suggested, there isn't a great deal of plot, and what little there is is happily
elbowed aside to enable the star to perform at length, as his many fans would
wish.

Music and Songs

Basically the songs were devised as being suitable for the variety needed in a
nightclub act and they exhibit strong rhythm and easy-to-assimilate melodies.
The main hits were 'Too close for comfort' (Charlie), 'Sing you sinners' (Charlie)
and 'Mr Wonderful' (Ethel).

Did You Know?

✳ Not only was this Sammy Davis Jnr's Broadway debut in a book show, but it was also a watershed show for Chita Rivera, whose previous outing had been in the flop, *Seventh Heaven*.

✳ Of the three collaborators, Jerry Bock became one of the major Broadway creators of the 1950s and '60s, in partnership with Sheldon Harnick.

✳ Larry Holofcener became known as a writer of off-beat subjects.

✳ The song 'Mr Wonderful' became a hit sung by Peggy Lee and 'Too close for comfort' one for Eydie Gorme.

The Critics

The critics were impressed:
'Davis does just about everything . . . and everything he does is right . . . he manages in addition to display his spectacularly varied talents to act a role with complete sincerity. I'm for Davis' – *New York Daily News*
'The youthful Davis is by all odds one of the most versatile and stupendous singer-dancer-musician-impersonators on view anywhere in the world today' – *New York Journal American*

Recommended Recording

Original Broadway cast (CD) MCA MCAD 10303
A great star vehicle for Sammy Davis captured excellently on this CD.

The Most Happy Fella

LYRICS ✶ Frank Loesser
MUSIC ✶ Frank Loesser
BOOK ✶ Frank Loesser, based on Sidney Howard's
play *They Knew What They Wanted*

First Performance

New York, Imperial Theater, 3 May 1956 (676 performances)
London, Coliseum, 23 April 1960 (288 performances)

Principal Characters

Tony ✶ A middle-aged winegrower
Rosabella ✶ A mail-order bride
Joe ✶ A handsome foreman
Cleo ✶ A waitress
Marie ✶ Tony's sister
Herman ✶ A farm-hand

Original New York Cast

Robert Weede, Jo Sullivan, Art Lund, Susan Johnson, Mona Paulee, Shorty Long

Original London Cast

Inia Te Wiata, Helena Scott, Art Lund, Libi Staiger, Nina Verushka, Jack de Lon

Plot

Amy and Cleo are waitresses in a San Francisco diner. One day Amy receives a piece of jewellery from an admirer who calls her Rosabella – the girl he'd like to marry. He is Antonio (Tony) Esposito, a wine grape grower in the Napa valley. She doesn't know what he looks like. They exchange letters, and soon it's the talk of Tony's town that he's conducting a love affair by post. Amy, acting as Rosabella, sends a photo and then Tony makes a big mistake. His sister Marie mocks his pretensions – a fat fifty-year-old Italian and this beautiful girl? No way. So he sends a picture of his handsome foreman, Joe, who has also helped Tony with the letters, instead.

Soon Rosabella accepts Tony's marriage proposal, but she only discovers what he looks like when she arrives in town, and realises she has been tricked. She plans to leave, but Tony has been injured in his truck. He pleads with Rosabella for the marriage to go ahead. Joe's still around. He had originally planned to leave during the marriage service, but who will look after Tony's vineyard? Rosabella appears at the church door. She's weeping. Joe sweeps her into his arms, and one thing leads to another . . . Yet she still marries Tony.

A month later in the vineyard, Rosabella and Joe are ignoring each other. In fact, nothing has happened between them since her wedding night. Tony is gradually improving after his accident, though he is still confined to a wheelchair. Tony has arranged for Cleo to visit and has promised her a job. What a kind, sweet man Tony is, Rosabella realises. Cleo refuses to help Marie break up Tony and Rosabella's marriage. She's discovered farm-hand Herman who, like her, is from Texas. Tony, getting better by the minute, is treating Rosabella like a child. Soon, all is fine between them and they declare their love. They dance and Rosabella faints – she is pregnant!

Rosabella and Cleo plan to leave. It is obvious who the father really is. Rosabella admits everything to Tony, who is understandably heartbroken. Joe is already at the station. Tony grabs a pistol and makes off after the two girls. Joe doesn't know that Rosabella is also leaving. Tony arrives, and discovers that Joe has left on the train alone and that Rosabella is leaving by bus for San Francisco with Cleo, who is saying goodbye to Herman. Marie, always one for trouble, kicks away Tony's cane so he can't reach Rosabella. Cleo comes to help Tony and a ranch-hand comes to help Marie. Now timid Herman weighs in on Cleo's side. Tony gets Rosabella and her things off the bus. The baby will be Tony's baby.

Tony urges her not to be scared and regrets that he sent Joe's picture and that he never actually introduced himself. They put that right and we learn that her real name is Amy – he gives her back the pin and they embrace while their friends and neighbours rejoice for them.

Music and Songs

A score on an almost operatic scale. It is full of soaring romantic melodies and catchy show-stoppers, including 'Standing on the corner' (bystanders), the duet 'My heart is so full of you' (Tony and Rosabella), 'Big D' (townsfolk), 'Ooh, my feet' (Cleo), the plaintive 'Somebody somewhere' (Rosabella), 'The most happy fella' (Tony), 'Joey, Joey, Joey' (Joe) and 'Warm all over' (Rosabella).

Did You Know?

✶ This was the most elaborate, ambitious and original of all Loesser's shows and the one that showed his almost limitless imagination at full stretch.

✶ Frank Loesser married Jo Sullivan who starred in the show.

The Critics

'A profoundly moving dramatic experience . . . a rare moment for the theatre. Broadway is used to heart. It is not accustomed to evocations of the soul' – *New York Times*

'The show was heavy in its own inventiveness . . . there is a surplus on that farm and something should be plowed under. I was hoping that Mr Loesser had written six shows in the six years since *Guys and Dolls* instead of packing all the energy of the six into one' – *New York Herald Tribune*

Recommended Recording

Studio cast (CD) TER CDTER3 1260
The first complete stereo version recording starring Frank Loesser's daughter, Emily, with the late Louis Quilico as Tony. With Frank's wife, Jo Sullivan Loesser, also appearing and overseeing the project, this is a faithful reconstruction of the original. It is excellent in every way and has bonus tracks of cut songs.

Music in the Air

LYRICS ✳ Oscar Hammerstein II
MUSIC ✳ Jerome Kern
BOOK ✳ Oscar Hammerstein II

First Performance

New York, Alvin Theater, 8 November 1932 (342 performances)
London, His Majesty's Theatre, 19 May 1933 (275 performances)

Principal Characters

Cornelius ✳ A bird seller
Frieda Hatzfeld ✳ An operetta star
Bruno Mahler ✳ A composer
Sieglinde Lessing ✳ A young singer
Dr Walther Lessing ✳ Her composer and music teacher father
Karl Reder ✳ Her lyricist friend, the local schoolteacher
Ernst Weber ✳ A publisher
Lili Kirschner ✳ Wife of the producer

Original New York Cast

Reinhold Werrenrath, Natalie Hall, Tullio Carminati, Katherine Carrington,
Al Shean, Walter Slezak, Nicholas Joy, Ivy Scott

Original London Cast

Lance Fairfax, Mary Ellis, Arthur Margetson, Eve Lister,
Horace Hodges, Bruce Carfax, Herbert Ross, Muriel George

Plot

This musical adventure takes place in Bavaria in the mountain town of Edendorff,
where music teacher, Dr Walther Lessing, has a beautiful daughter called
Sieglinde. She is in love with Karl Reder, the local schoolmaster. Karl and
Sieglinde go to Munich to try to get a song published. It was written by Karl and
Walther. Once there, Karl is taken up by an operetta star, Frieda Hatzfeld.
Meanwhile, Sieglinde becomes friendly with the operetta librettist, Bruno Mahler.
He wants her to appear in his new work, *Tingle Tangle*. Frieda moves out of
Bruno's apartment, and takes up residence in a hotel where she can regularly see
Karl.

Bruno takes Sieglinde to the zoo. Once there, Sieglinde is warned by Cornelius,
a bird seller, that she and Karl are country people and it is not wise to stay in
town. She fends off a pass from Bruno, and Frieda finds Karl equally
unresponsive. Frieda now plans to leave for Berlin and a new film. She warns Karl
that Bruno will cast Sieglinde aside when he's used her. Later on Karl has to tell
the producer and composer that Frieda has left. No matter, Sieglinde can assume
the lead in the operetta. Karl is horrified. Nevertheless, Sieglinde is given her

chance. Her father, however, interferes with the orchestration and gets on everyone's nerves.

The dress rehearsal, and a few facts become evident. Sieglinde is far too inexperienced for the principal role. Bruno's affection for her vanishes. Walther and Sieglinde are brutally told that the theatre is no place for amateurs – they should go back to their mountain home. And they do. The operetta, with Frieda in the lead, is a success. Karl returns to Edendorff and Sieglinde – they have both learned valuable lessons.

Music and Songs

A classic Kern score, including 'The song is you' (Karl and Sieglinde), 'I've told every little star' (Karl and Sieglinde), 'There's a hill beyond a hill' (Trekkers), 'I am so eager' (Karl and Sieglinde), 'When the spring is in the air' (Sieglinde), 'And love was born' (Cornelius), 'In Egern on the Tegern See' (Frieda) and 'I'm alone' (Sieglinde).

Did You Know?

✷ This was Kern's thirty-third musical and the fourth of five times he would work with Oscar Hammerstein II.

✷ The show is a gentle send-up of an operetta but this was not always recognised; many audiences were so used to the operetta-style storylines that they took it seriously.

The Critics

The critics across the years:

'Almost every moment is full of mesmeric airs' – Percy Hammond

Originally Brooks Atkinson wrote, 'Sentiment and comedy that are tender and touching without falling into the clichés of the trade. At last musical comedy has been emancipated.' In 1951 he would add, 'Although ours is a graceless world, the lovely Kern score is full of friendship, patience, cheerfulness and pleasure.'

Recommended Recording

Cast recording (CD) AEI CD 024
Taken from a radio broadcast the sound quality is not perfect but there is an attempt to tell the tale. Two Mark Ellis tracks from the original London cast are added ('I've told every little star' and a medley of 'I'm alone' and 'The song is you').

Film

20th Century Fox, 1934. Starring Gloria Swanson, John Boles and Al Shean. Directed by Erich Pommer.

The Music Man

LYRICS ✶ Meredith Willson
MUSIC ✶ Meredith Willson
BOOK ✶ Meredith Willson, from a story by Willson and Franklin Lacey

First Performance

New York, Majestic Theater, 19 December 1957 (1375 performances)
London, Adelphi Theatre, 16 March 1961 (395 performances)

Principal Characters

Harold Hill ✶ A musical instrument salesman
Marian Paroo ✶ A librarian
Mayor Shinn
Mrs Paroo ✶ Marian's mother
Marcellus Washburn ✶ A friend of Harold's
Eulalie Shinn ✶ The Mayoress
Winthrop Paroo ✶ Marian's brother

Original New York Cast

Robert Preston, Barbara Cook, David Burns, Pert Kelton,
Iggie Wolfington, Helen Raymond, Eddie Hodges

Original London Cast

Van Johnson, Patricia Lambert, C. Denier Warren, Ruth Kettlewell,
Bernard Spear, Nan Munro, Denis Waterman

Plot

It's 4 July 1912 in River City, Iowa. Harold Hill (who has single-handedly given the profession of travelling salesmen a bad name), has arrived to sell musical instruments to parents for their children. He will teach their kids to play – or will he? He runs up against opposition from straight-laced Marian Paroo, the local librarian, and Mayor Shinn, who quite rightly smell several rats. However, Harold is a master salesman. He befriends Marian's young brother, Winthrop, a withdrawn, listless child with a speech impediment. And the mayor isn't pleased when our hero pairs his daughter off with the local layabout, Tommy. Harold also creates an instant barber shop quartet out of four local councillors. So, on to his Think System for learning music. This involves just thinking the notes, and eventually out they come.

Marian decides to look up Harold's credentials for herself. He doesn't have any. But by now, she's under Harold's spell too, and tears the appropriate page out of the register. The instruments arrive. Little Winthrop is thrilled with his cornet – and speaks! Festivities are under way and Marian finds she is falling in love, while fully realising what a charlatan Harold Hill is. Now another salesman arrives, prepared to spill the beans about our hero. Harold gets wind of this, but this time he's going to stay and face the music. Winthrop is brokenhearted – his hero has feet of clay, he wishes Harold had never come to their city – but Marian recognises the changes Harold has made, and she stands up for him against the mayor, as – one by one – do the rest of the citizens. Then the new band comes in, kitted out in their bright uniforms and with their shiny new instruments, led by young Tommy and the mayor's daughter. Marian gives Harold a blackboard pointer for a baton and he conducts the band. The result is only just barely recognisable as music, but music it is! The parents are delighted and only Schubert is turning gently in his grave! For once 'The Music Man' has delivered the goods.

Music and Songs

As betokens a former member of Sousa's band, Willson's music has the flavour of a big parade, with stirring marches as well as a couple of fine barber shop quartets, witty patter numbers and fine ballads. '76 trombones' (Harold) was the big success, but 'Till there was you' (Marian and Harold) is an equally famous ballad, and 'Ya got trouble' (Harold) is a wonderful patter song.

Did You Know?

∗ The tunes of '76 trombones' and 'Goodnight my someone' are the same, only the speeds are different.

∗ The original title for the show was 'The Silver Triangle'.

∗ The Beatles included one show tune in their recorded repertoire; it was 'Till there was you' from *The Music Man*.

∗ It took Meredith Willson ten years to get the show produced.

∗ The 2000 Broadway revival has proved to be a hit all over again.

∗ *The Music Man* won the Most Outstanding Musical award at the Tonys.

The Critics

'Not in recent memory has a Broadway audience been so spectacularly carried away. Something happened in that theater on opening night which was without precedent: in the touching finale, the audience broke out spontaneously into applause to the even rhythm of the music. Nothing like it has even been seen on Broadway' – *Variety*

Recommended Recording

Original Broadway cast (CD) Broadway Angel ZDM 7 64663 2 3
Robert Preston and Barbara Cook on one disc has to be good, and when you add Willson's inventive and unique score you have a masterpiece. Certainly this is a recording to own.

Film

Warner Brothers, 1962. Starring Robert Preston, Shirley Jones and Hermione Gingold. Directed by Morton DaCosta.

My Fair Lady

LYRICS ✶ Alan Jay Lerner
MUSIC ✶ Frederick Loewe
BOOK ✶ Alan Jay Lerner, after George Bernard Shaw's play *Pygmalion*

First Performance

New York, Mark Hellinger Theater, 15 March 1956 (2717 performances)
London, Drury Lane Theatre, 30 April 1958 (2281 performances)

Principal Characters

Professor Henry Higgins ✶ An expert in phonetics
Eliza Doolittle ✶ A flower girl who wants to better herself
Colonel Pickering ✶ Lately returned from India
Alfred Doolittle ✶ Eliza's father
Freddy Eynsford-Hill ✶ A young man about town

Original New York Cast

Rex Harrison, Julie Andrews, Stanley Holloway,
Robert Coote, John Michael King

Original London Cast

Rex Harrison, Julie Andrews, Stanley Holloway,
Robert Coote, Leonard Weir

Plot

Professor Henry Higgins listens to a flower girl speaking and knows exactly where she is born; it is a meeting which leads to an introduction to Colonel Pickering, himself a student of Indian dialects, and a bet that Higgins can pass her off as a lady at an Embassy Ball later in the year. Eliza is cleaned up and lives in his house while the transformation takes place. Her father, hoping to make some money out of the liaison, visits and leaves with cash and introductions as an original moralist.Eventually he has to get married .

Eliza learns her vowels and is tested at Ascot as a guest of Higgins's mother. She looks radiant and speaks 'correctly', although she uses Cockney terminology. It makes Freddy fall in love with her. At the Embassy Ball she passes the test allowing Higgins to win his bet. After her triumph she is ignored and, upset, she goes back to Covent Garden where no one recognises her. Eliza has only one friend, Mrs Higgins, who takes her part. Unable to make Higgins understand why she left she swears she will marry Freddy.

Back home, Higgins now admits he misses Eliza and, as he listens to one of her early recordings, she enters speaking as she once did. He looks up and, without showing emotion, asks for his slippers.

Music and Songs

Frederick (Fritz) Loewe was one of the very last operetta composers, and *My Fair Lady* was his masterpiece. Its musical style combined the warmth of Lehár, Strauss and Stolz with the boisterous exuberance of the English music hall. For the first time, the hero, Higgins, was not a full-throated tenor or baritone. As created by Rex Harrison, he virtually spoke his way through his songs. 'Why can't the English?' (Higgins), 'Wouldn't it be loverly?' (Eliza), 'With a little bit of luck' (Doolittle), 'The rain in Spain' (Eliza, Higgins and Pickering), 'I could have danced all night' (Eliza) and 'On the street where you live' (Freddy) are all well known.

Did You Know?

✶ At least one song intended for *My Fair Lady* was used in the film *Gigi* instead. It was 'Say a prayer for me tonight'.

✶ Although the lyricist received part of his education in England, at Bedales, there are still a few phrases in the show which seem American. For instance, 'on' rather than 'in' the street where you live. And would Higgins refer to a wedding band rather than a wedding ring?

✶ Almost every major Broadway writer had attempted to make *Pygmalion* into a musical and it took two tries for Alan Jay Lerner to come up with the way to do it.

✶ *My Fair Lady* walked away with awards all over the world and the film followed in its footsteps with the Oscars.

The Critics

The critics were very happy:
'One of the best musicals of the century . . . in taste, intelligence, skill and delight, *My Fair Lady* is the finest musical in years' – Brooks Atkinson

Recommended Recording

Studio cast (CD) TER CDTER2 1211
It would be surprising to find anyone interested in the musical without the original mono Broadway cast recording in their collection. So it is remarkable when a new recording comes along that challenges the original. The real star here is Alec McCowen who allows Henry to sing a little more than Harrison's. Bob Hoskins plays Alfred to perfection and Tinuke Olafimihan is a charming Eliza.

Film

Warner Brothers, 1964. Starring Rex Harrison, Stanley Holloway, Audrey Hepburn (sung by Marni Nixon), Wilfred Hyde-White and Jeremy Brett (sung by Bill Shirley). Directed by George Cukor.

The Mystery of Edwin Drood

LYRICS ✳ Rupert Holmes
MUSIC ✳ Rupert Holmes
BOOK ✳ Rupert Holmes, based on the novel by Charles Dickens

First Performance

New York, Delacorte Theater, 4 August 1985
(25 performances at the New York Shakespeare Festival)
New York, Imperial Theater, 2 December 1985 (608 performances)
London, Savoy Theatre, 7 May 1987 (68 performances)

Principal Characters

Cartwright ✳ The chairman
Edwin Drood ✳ Our hero
John Jasper ✳ His rival
Rosa Bud ✳ A sweetheart
Neville Landless ✳ An orphan
Helena ✳ His sister
Princess Puffer ✳ A gin house proprietor

Original New York Cast

George Rose, Betty Buckley, Howard McGillin, Patti Cohenour,
John Herrera, Jane Schneider, Cleo Laine

Original London Cast

Ernie Wise, Julia Hills, David Burt, Patti Cohenour/Sarah Payne,
Mark Ryan, Marilyn Cutts, Lulu

Plot

It's a fine evening at the Royale Music Hall in London in 1873. Instead of the usual variety bill, there's a story to tell tonight. Edwin Drood (a principal boy role) is engaged to lovely Miss Rosa Bud. Edwin's uncle, John Jasper, is a somewhat unstable character. Does he approve of the forthcoming wedding? Edwin meets two newcomers from Ceylon, brother and sister Neville and Helena Landless, and, in addition, he and his bride-to-be break off their engagement – not for lack of affection, but so that they can rekindle their romance from the beginning. Enter the proprietress of an opium den, Princess Puffer, and a mysterious, bearded man, Dick Datchery. After a stormy dinner party at John Jasper's, Edwin leaves wearing Neville's overcoat – at the latter's insistence – and is never seen again. Neville is accused of his murder and John Jasper proposes to Rosa, who rejects him.

The audience is asked to vote on whether Edwin is dead, and then whether they know who is the mysterious Dick Datchery? Then there is a vote on who killed Edwin Drood?

So to the conclusion. Rosa flees to the London train and is met by Princess Puffer. Does she not recognise her old nurse? Now, regardless of the audience's vote, Dick Datchery is revealed as Uncle John Jasper, who confesses to having murdered Edwin. But he didn't and Durdles, a worker in the churchyard, reveals that the murderer was whoever the audience chose – unless they chose John Jasper of course. And yet, it's time for a happy ending, and Edwin is proved to be still alive, stunned but not killed in the murderous attack.

Music and Songs

An evening at the music hall with melodramatic and rousing Victorian melodies and a couple of tender, sweet ballads, all with a strong touch of mystery and suspense. Songs include 'A man could go quite mad' (Jasper), 'The name of love/Moonfall' (Rose and Jasper), 'Perfect strangers' (Drood and Rosa), 'Never the luck' (Bazzard), 'Don't quit while you're ahead' (Puffer), 'The garden path to Hell' (Puffer) and 'Out on a limerick' (the company).

Did You Know?

✷ Although Rupert Holmes is one of America's most distinguished popular composers, he was born in Britain.

✷ Dickens' original story remains incomplete – hence the opportunity to enable the audience to complete it for him.

✷ The show won five Tonys on Broadway. It did not succeed during a short run at the Savoy Theatre in London, alas.

✷ Ernie Wise took the role of Cartwright after his partner, Eric Morecambe, died.

✷ *The Mystery of Edwin Drood* won five Tony Awards including best musical, best score and best book.

The Critics

'Drood from the neck up . . . woefully unfunny' – *The Independent*
'Panto parody is Dickens of a disaster' – *Evening Standard*

Recommended Recording

Original Broadway cast (CD) Varese 30206 5597
A fun recording with the added attraction that you can choose the ending you want to hear – one of the great advantages the CD has over the LP.

Naughty Marietta

LYRICS ✶ Rida Johnson Young
MUSIC ✶ Victor Herbert
BOOK ✶ Rida Johnson Young

First Performance

New York, New York Theater, 7 November 1910 (136 performances)

Principal Characters

Marietta d'Altena ✶ An escaped countess
Captain Dick Warrington ✶ A dashing soldier
Etienne Grandet ✶ The acting governor's son
Adah ✶ An old servant

Original New York Cast

Emma Trentini, Orville Harrold, Edward Martindel, Marie Duchene

Plot

Etienne Grandet, the acting governor's son, has just returned to New Orleans. It is the 18th century and the locals are full of stories of the notorious buccaneer, Bras Piqué, who is terrorising the town. In fact the pirate is Etienne himself. A group of Tennessee and Kentucky volunteers now arrives, led by Captain Dick Warrington and his lieutenant, the Irishman, Harry Blake. They've been commissioned by the King of France to seek out and destroy the pirate. But they certainly don't expect to find him among New Orleans society. All they need is the governor's signature on their arrest warrant. They don't know that Etienne has captured the real governor during his father's absence. Suddenly a mysterious melody arises from a fountain – the singer is Marietta. She can only love the man who can complete her plaintive song. She already knows dashing Dick, who arranges for her to pose as a relative of puppeteer Rudolfo, and work as his boy assistant.

News from France is that the Countess d'Altena has run away, and all the facts point to her being Marietta. After a battle between Etienne and Dick's forces, Marietta escapes with Rudolfo. Etienne is still convinced she's the countess; they'll meet at the upcoming ball. Etienne proposes marriage, but repels Marietta with his talk of slavery. He sells off an old servant, Adah, and Marietta ensures that Dick makes the highest bid for her and frees her on the spot. In gratitude she tells Dick of the tattoo on Etienne's arm that will prove him to be Bras Piqué. But Etienne has powerful protection. Marietta refuses to marry Etienne. Locked in a room by him, she hears Dick outside complete the melody, appears at the window and they fall into each other's arms. As the couple are rescued by Dick's motley crew, the pirates escape to rob another day.

Music and Songs

A high-spirited, zesty, full-blooded score with romantic overtones, including the songs 'Tramp! Tramp! Tramp!' (Dick), ''Neath the southern moon' (Marietta), 'Italian street song' (Marietta), 'I'm falling in love with someone' (Dick) and 'Ah! sweet mystery of life' (Dick and Marietta).

Did You Know?

✳ The operetta was originally titled 'Little Paris' (incidentally, the city of New Orleans was under Spanish, not French, rule at the time in which *Naughty Marietta* is set).

✳ The refusal of Emma Trentini during subsequent performances to encore one of the numbers so incensed the composer that he refused to compose her next project, *The Firefly*, which was taken up by Rudolf Friml instead.

✳ While there was a tour in 1945 that advertised the show as 'prior to the West End', *Naughty Marietta* has never played there.

✳ The 1935 film version with Jeanette MacDonald and Nelson Eddy re-popularised the score and the show became a firm favourite with amateur societies.

The Critics

The critics acclaimed the show and its star:
'Victor Herbert has written one of his most tuneful scores for the piece and the orchestra is always effective. It is difficult to accord sufficient praise to Victor Herbert's score, much of which ranks among the best of his career' – Edward Waters
'For the soprano it is a fearfully cruel score . . . whereas Melba is proud if she hands an audience two high Cs in the course of an evening, this little Italian [Trentini] scatters them about with largesse' – *New York Evening Sun*

Recommended Recording

A collection of operetta favourites (CD) Newport Classics NPD 85654
Elizabeth Futral and Steven White sing the songs sung in the films by Jeanette and Nelson and among the all-time favourites Victor Herbert and Sigmund Romberg melodies is Herbert's 'Ah, sweet mystery of life' from *Naughty Marietta*.

Film

MGM, 1935. Starring Jeanette Macdonald and Nelson Eddy. Directed by W.S. van Dyke.

The New Moon

LYRICS ✶ Oscar Hammerstein II
MUSIC ✶ Sigmund Romberg
BOOK ✶ Oscar Hammerstein II, Frank Mandel and Laurence Schwab

First Performance

New York, Imperial Theater, 19 September 1928 (509 performances)
London, Drury Lane Theatre, 4 April 1929 (148 performances)

Principal Characters

Marianne Beaunoir ✶ Daughter of a shipowner
Robert Mission ✶ A nobleman wanted for murder
Alexander ✶ His servant
Philippe ✶ Robert's friend
Julie ✶ Alexander's girlfriend

Original New York Cast

Evelyn Herbert, Robert Halliday, Gus Shy, William O'Neal, Marie Callahan

Original London Cast

Evelyn Laye, Howett Worster, Gene Gerrard, Ben Williams, Dolores Farris

Plot

The setting is New Orleans in 1792 where Robert Mission, a French aristocrat, is in exile. He's in disguise as a servant to Monsieur Beaunoir, a shipowner. Robert is in love with Beaunoir's daughter, Marianne. A ship, *The New Moon*, has docked. It carries Ribaud, whose task is to recapture Robert and bring him back to France. Robert ignores the advice of his friend Philippe that his love is dangerous. He goes to a masked ball to steal a kiss from his beloved. He gets it, but is arrested by the ship's captain. Ribaud claims that Marianne was responsible for him being caught.

On *The New Moon*, Marianne manages to leave a note for Robert assuring him of her love, having got on board under disguise of affection for the captain. There's a mutiny en route for France and the crew decamp on an island, the Isle of Pines, where they plan to set up a free government. Marianne doesn't hold with the mutiny, but her love for Robert is stronger. The captain and Ribaud try, and almost succeed, in turning Robert's men against him and so gaining control. All seems lost when two French ships arrive at the island. But they bring good news for Robert. France is now a republic and Ribaud is condemned as a criminal and monarchist. Meanwhile, Robert and Marianne can get on with their life on the island in Utopian freedom and prosperity.

Music and Songs

An enduring musical comedy/operetta score full of red-blooded rousing songs, by the masters of the genre. Highlights include 'Marianne' (Robert), 'The girl on the prow' (Marianne), 'Softly as in the morning sunrise' (Philippe), 'Stouthearted men' (Robert), 'One kiss' (Marianne), 'Wanting you' (Robert and Marianne) and 'Lover come back to me' (Marianne).

Did You Know?

✷ **The show combined the creative and production talents of** *The Desert Song* **and also featured the same original leading man.**

✷ **Although New Orleans is shown under French rule at the time, it was in fact ruled by Spain (as in** *Naughty Marietta*, **where the same mistake was made).**

The Critics

The critics were pleased: 'full-blooded', 'stirring', 'seductive' and 'tuneful' were some of the words they used.

Of a 1944 revival the *New York Times* wrote: 'There is no denying that when he [Romberg] set it down he was writing the hit parade of 1928 as well as writing songs that have not been forgotten.'

'The most charming and fragrant of its sort that I have seen in a long time' – *New York World*

Recommended Recording

1998 Media Theatre cast (CD) Rockwell Productions IND90152
The only modern recording of Romberg's powerful score. For those wanting to hear how the show originally sounded, then there are historic recordings on **AEI CD 052** with both the Broadway and London casts represented. The quality of the new issue, however, is far superior.

Film

MGM, 1940. Starring Jeanette Macdonald and Nelson Eddy. Directed by Robert Z. Leonard.

Nine

Lyrics ✶ Maury Yeston
Music ✶ Maury Yeston
Book ✶ Arthur Kopit, based on the screenplay *8½* by Federico Fellini

First Performance

New York, 46th Street Theater, 9 May 1982 (732 performances)
London, Donmar Theatre, 6 December 1996 (limited season)

Principal Characters

Guido Contini ✶ A film director
Luisa ✶ His wife
Carla ✶ A mistress
Claudia Nardi ✶ A film star
Guido's mother
Liliane Le Fleur ✶ The producer
Sarraghina ✶ A prostitute

Original New York Cast

Raul Julia, Karen Akers, Anita Morris, Shelley Burch, Taina Elg,
Liliane Montevecchi, Kathi Moss

Original London Cast

Larry Lamb, Susannah Fellows, Clare Burt, Eleanor David, Dilys Laye,
Sara Kestelman, Jenny Galloway

Plot

Guido Contini is a famous film director at a mid-life crisis point. He's almost forty years old, and he seems washed up artistically. His last three films have not set the box office alight and his marriage is crumbling. He goes to Venice for a refreshing stay at a spa. His wife, Luisa, is there and also his current mistress, Carla. Then there's his protegée, Claudia Nardi, the well-known actress. How to choose between them? An added complication is the vivacious producer, Liliane, who wants him to create a new film. Guido retreats into memories from the past: his mother remembered from when he was nine years old; his sexual initiation with the prostitute, Sarraghina; and subsequent school punishment for visiting her on the beach.

Guido is having a mental block about an idea for Liliane's picture. Claudia Nardi arrives in Venice from Paris, at Luisa's urging, and suddenly the ideas start flowing. How about a musical about Casanova? But Guido's private life is still in disarray; he betrays Luisa's affection with vulgar script references to real-life situations, and alienates Carla and Claudia for good measure. They abandon him and he abandons the film. He contemplates suicide, but is saved by a vision of himself as a nine-year-old who appears, seizes the gun and urges him to grow up and go after his real love – his wife Luisa. He does.

Music and Songs

A highly evocative, subtle, most melodic, Mediterranean-flavoured score, including 'My husband makes movies' (Luisa), 'In an unusual way' (Claudia), 'Bells of San Sebastian' (the company), 'Be on your own' (Luisa) and 'Ti voglio bene' (Sarraghina).

Did You Know?

∗ *Nine* won the Tony Award for the Best Musical of 1982, plus four others. The show took fourteen years to achieve fully-staged, continuous performances in Britain.

∗ Another, later, show to which the composer/lyricist contributed, *Grand Hotel*, reached London ahead of it. Yet *Nine* is the finer show.

∗ The show owed a great deal to the concept of Tommy Tune, the director and choreographer who stamped his own style on what was already a stylish show.

∗ *Nine* won the Tony Award for best musical and best score. Tommy Tune also won for his direction.

The Critics

The critics rhapsodised in America (the British were more mixed):
'*Nine* is a gloriously enchanting musical, tender, funny and provocative . . . sleek, slick and elegant' – *Gannet Today*
'Maury Yeston's score is dazzling with zestful, inventive and thoughtfully imaginative music and lyrics' – *New York Post*
'Anyone who cares about the progress of the Broadway musical has to see *Nine*' – *New York Times*

Recommended Recording

Original London cast (CD) TER CDTER2 1193
The cast of a star-studded charity show went into the recording studio the next day and produced this outstanding recording. Jonathan Pryce plays Guido and Elaine Paige makes a guest appearance. This has the freshness of the original and becomes the recommended version because it delivers beautifully the complete score.

No, No, Nanette

LYRICS ✻ Irving Caesar and Otto Harbach
MUSIC ✻ Vincent Youmans
BOOK ✻ Otto Harbach and Frank Mandel,
based on the play *My Lady Friends* by Frank Mandel and Emile Nyitray,
adapted from the novel *Oh James* by May Edgington

First Performance

London, Palace Theatre, 11 March 1925 (665 performances)
New York, Globe Theater, 16 September 1925 (321 performances)

Principal Characters

Nanette ✻ Jimmy's protegée
Jimmy Smith ✻ A Bible publisher
Lucille Early ✻ Wife of . . .
Billy Early ✻ A lawyer
Tom Trainor ✻ Their nephew
Sue Smith ✻ Jimmy's wife
Pauline ✻ The Smiths' cook

Original London Cast

Binnie Hale, Joseph Coyne, Irene Browne, George Grossmith,
Seymour Beard, Marie Hemingway, Grace Leigh

Original New York Cast

Louise Groody, Charles Winninger, Josephine Whittell, Wellington Cross,
Jack Barker, Eleanor Dawn, Georgia O'Ramey

Plot

Jimmy Smith is a successful Bible publisher who relies on his punctilious and houseproud wife, Sue, to help him in his work and run his home with just a cook, Pauline, as help. The latter dislikes her mistress, but is very fond of Nanette, an orphan, who lives with them. Nanette has been brought up very strictly by Sue, but now wants freedom and fun. Friends of the family are lawyer, Billy Early, his extravagant wife, Lucille, and their nephew and Billy's assistant, Tom. Tom is bit of a stuffed shirt, but his intentions towards Nanette are pure, true and honourable. Jimmy gives Nanette some money to go shopping, but when Tom finds out he insists on asking Nanette where the cash came from, and they quarrel. Sue, scenting something wrong, decides to have detectives investigate Jimmy.

Nanette, meanwhile, is off to the seaside to stay at Jimmy's cottage. Three young ladies also arrive at the cottage. Betty, Winnie and Flora are protegées of Jimmy (he's their sugar daddy) but all is relatively innocent. Now Lucille arrives; Flora has turned up at Jimmy's home and demanded to marry Jimmy. Enter Sue, who discovers the girls talking to Billy and immediately jumps to the wrong conclusion – these are Billy's girls, aren't they? She believes Billy is the philanderer and has been using Jimmy's name. She is horrified when the threesome tell her about a fourth girl there – Nanette.

Billy has been damned unfairly, and Lucille won't talk to him. Meanwhile, Betty, Winnie and Flora just want a settlement and to be quit of the whole situation. Eventually Lucille realises her mistake – the playboy is, and always was, Jimmy. The girls have advice for Sue. Let Jimmy spend his money at home – and on her! Sue takes the advice and it's spend, spend, spend for her. Jimmy is horrified. Tom and Nanette solve their little local difficulty and all ends happily.

Music and Songs

A vintage Youmans score full of spice, verve and rhythm, including 'Too many rings around Rosie' (Lucille), 'I've confessed to the breeze' (Nanette), 'I want to be happy' (Nanette), 'No, no, Nanette' (Nanette), 'Tea for two' (Nanette and Tom) and 'Take a little one step' (Pauline and company).

Did You Know?

✱ The original American production spent so much time touring and being altered that the London production reached the West End ahead of the Broadway version. It ran longer, too.

✱ The lavish revivals starred much-loved movie stars – Broadway had Ruby Keeler and London had Anna Neagle. Busby Berkeley's name was associated with the staging of both revivals.

The Critics

'The first expression of high spirits London has had for years' – *ERA*
'The zest, brio and go of the performers . . . the liveliness and entrain [sic] of the music' – *The Stage*

Recommended Recording

Broadway Revival cast (CD) Columbia CK 30563
A feel-good show and a feel-good recording of it. The American cast version is far superior to its London revival and the presence of Ruby Keeler, sounding exactly the way she did in the thirties, is an added bonus.

Films

Warner Brothers, 1930. Starring Alexander Gray, Bernice Claire and ZaSu Pitts. Directed by Clarence Badger. The film included miscellaneous songs from the show.
RKO, 1940. Starring Anna Neagle, Victor Mature and ZaSu Pitts. Directed by Herbert Wilcox.

Nymph Errant

LYRICS ✶ Cole Porter
MUSIC ✶ Cole Porter
BOOK ✶ Romney Brent, based on the novel by James Laver

First Performance

London, Adelphi Theatre, 6 October 1933 (154 performances)

Principal Characters

Evangeline Edwards ✶ An experimenter
Haidée Robinson ✶ An American
Miss Pratt ✶ A teacher
Constantine ✶ A Greek businessman
André de Croissant ✶ A theatre owner
Ben Winthrop ✶ A plumber
Count Hohenalderborn-Mantalini ✶ A suitor
Alexei ✶ A morose Russian

Original London Cast

Gertrude Lawrence, Elisabeth Welch, Moya Nugent, David Burns,
Austin Trevor, Walter Crisham, Morton Selten, Alexander Ivo

Plot

We're in the garden of Aunt Ermyntrude's house. The year is 1933 and the old girl who is getting quite forgetful, is expecting her niece, Evangeline, back from her Swiss finishing school.

Over to Switzerland. Evangeline is about to take a train to Calais. Miss Pratt, her chemistry teacher, urges her to experiment with life. In the railway carriage Evangeline meets André, who owns the Folies de Paris; he assures her he can make her a star of the Folies. Eventually his offer is refused, and Evangeline, now at Neufville-sur-Mer, is wooed by a Count and also by the doleful Russian, Alexei. The latter's choice seems to be suicide or a trip to Paris! So they go to Paris and starve until the Count turns up.

Next it's Venice, where Evangeline dumps the Count and leaves on a yacht to the Orient, in the company of Constantine, a Greek businessman. On the way, there's a stopover at the Acropolis in Athens, before journeying to Smyrna. The timing is not ideal. The Turks are sacking the city. Constantine is killed and Evangeline is carried off by the fierce Kassim Mahmud Hadji. He offers her two choices: to be taken to the British consulate, or on a trip round town to see the local statues! Evangeline has another idea – a two-day camel ride to the slave market (she's already been deemed unacceptable as a slave locally).

We next find our heroine in a harem where a new member is an American, Haidée Robinson, who becomes a friend. Then, up through the floor comes an American plumber, Ben Winthrop, with whom Evangeline escapes to the desert. Ben will put her on the Paris express.

Next, a different kind of harem. This one is on stage at the Folies de Paris. Miss Pratt is there, and Evangeline explains all the trouble her advice to experiment has caused. Eventually Evangeline decides to go back to Oxford, and Aunt Ermyntrude. It is one year to the day since Evangeline was expected back from school. She arrives as virginal as she left and catches the eye of Joe, a good-looking gardener, who offers her an apple as the curtain falls. Perhaps now she will be able to 'experiment'.

Music and Songs

A fine mid-period Cole Porter score, with 'Experiment' (Miss Pratt), 'It's bad for me' (Evangeline), 'How could we be wrong?' (Evangeline), 'Nymph errant' (Evangeline), 'The physician' (Evangeline), 'Solomon' (Haidée) and 'If you like les belles poitrines' (the company).

Did You Know?

✷ Elizabeth Welch scored a big hit with 'Solomon'. She had also introduced Cole Porter's 'Love for sale' in New York in the show *The New Yorkers*.

✷ This is Cole Porter's only score written for the English stage which was not professionally taken up at the time by Broadway. Porter felt this was his best score.

✷ Celebrated choreographer, Agnes de Mille, did her first work on musicals in this show.

The Critics

'Mr Porter's songs are certainly amongst the cleverest elements of the piece; he is one of the few lyricists who really make one want to hear the words' – *Manchester Guardian*
'The trouble with the play was that there was no strong dramatic interest . . . the play consisted of a series of dramatic sketches – at times the show resembled a revue . . . I wonder if Mr Cochran [the impresario Charles B. Cochran] chose wisely in selecting this piece for his big Autumn show' – *Manchester Evening Chronicle*

Recommended Recording

1989 concert recording (CD) EMI CDC 7 54079 2
An all-star international cast recorded live in concert at the Theatre Royal, Drury Lane. The excitement of the moment is captured on this recording.

Of Thee I Sing

LYRICS ✶ Ira Gershwin
MUSIC ✶ George Gershwin
BOOK ✶ George S. Kaufman and Morrie Ryskind

First Performance

New York, Music Box Theatre, 26 December 1931 (441 performances)
London, Bridewell Theatre, 8 August 1999 (limited season)

Principal Characters

John P. Wintergreen ✶ The President
Mary Turner Wintergreen ✶ His wife
Alexander Throttlebottom ✶ The Vice-President
Sam Jenkins
French Ambassador
Diana Devereaux ✶ A Southern beauty
Emily Benson
Matthew Arnold Fulton ✶ The Chief Justice
Senator Carver Jones

Original New York Cast

William Gaxton, Lois Moran, Victor Moore, George Murphy, Florenz Ames,
Grace Brinkley, June O'Dea, Dudley Clements, Edward H. Robbins

Original London Cast

Gavin Lee, Fiona Benjamin, Michael Winsor, Jonjo O'Neill, Peter Gale,
Sarah Redmond, Sarah Bayliss, Ian Burford, Roger Martin

Plot

After sixty-three ballots, John P. Wintergreen is chosen to run for President of the United States and what's-his-name for Vice-President. Wintergreen is unmarried. There will be a contest for First Lady, run in Atlantic City, in which Diana Devereaux is a front-runner in every sense. John, however, prefers his secretary, Mary, since she can cook, sew and generally look after him. Meanwhile, Diana wins the contest, and John rejects her; she can't make corn muffins (Mary can). Mary and John set off on the campaign trail. But Diana comes up with a breach of promise suit. No contest; the judges rule in favour of corn muffins. John and Mary are set for the White House.

Diana continues to stir up trouble and gains a countrywide following which includes the French ambassador, who claims Diana to be an illegitimate descendant of Napoleon. John refuses to have his marriage annulled or to resign. At the enquiry, where the Vice-President is trying to impeach the President, John is beginning to lose support when Mary rushes in – she's pregnant! The French ambassador tries a different tack. France must be given the baby to help the birthrate. John refuses. Twins are born – a boy and girl. War is then threatened by

France. There's a solution, though. Alexander Throttlebottom (the Vice-President) will take on the obligation of marriage to Diana Devereaux. A happy ending!

Music and Songs

Although most songs here exist to service the plot, there are also a number of Gershwin classics to be discovered. Wit, satire and strong, rhythmic melody combine to create a most pleasing effect in 'Wintergreen for president' (chorus), 'The dimple on my knee' (Diana), 'Never was there a girl so fair/Some girls can bake a pie' (Diana and the Wintergreen Committee), 'Love is sweeping the country' (Jenkins and Miss Benson), 'Of thee I sing' (John and Mary), 'A kiss for Cinderella' (John) and 'Who cares?' (Mary and John).

Did You Know?

✳ This musical had the longest run of any book musical of the thirties. It was the first musical to win a Pulitzer Prize for its libretto.

✳ It took almost seventy years for the show to reach London.

✳ Its revival in 1952 in New York only ran 72 performances.

✳ There was a sequel, *Let 'Em Eat Cake*, with the same characters that ran for only 90 performances in 1933.

✳ There was a third Gershwin political show called *Strike Up the Band*.

✳ The show is often mounted in America in election years.

The Critics

Critical approval included:
'The happiest and most successful native music-stage lampoon to come the way of the American stage' – George Jean Nathan

Recommended Recording

Studio Recording (CD) CBS M2K 42522
A lovingly recreated studio cast version of this and another of the Gershwin's political shows *Let 'Em Eat Cake*. The Gershwin brothers at their best and it is a delight to hear these scores in their complete state.

Film

No film version, but the show was televised in 1972 with Carroll O'Connor, Jack Gilford, Cloris Leachman and Michele Lee among the cast.

Oh, Kay!

LYRICS ✳ Ira Gershwin
('Oh, Kay!' and 'Heaven on earth' with help from Howard Dietz)
MUSIC ✳ George Gershwin
BOOK ✳ Guy Bolton and P.G. Wodehouse

First Performance

New York, Imperial Theater, 8 November 1926 (256 performances)
London, His Majesty's Theatre, 21 September 1927 (214 performances)

Principal Characters

Lady Kay ✳ Sister of the Duke of Durham
Jimmy Winter ✳ A Long Island playboy
Shorty McGee ✳ A bootlegger
Larry Potter ✳ Another bootlegger
Phil and Dolly Ruxton ✳ Twins
The Duke ✳ An aristocratic bootlegger
Constance Appleton ✳ One of Jimmy's wives
Revenue Officer
Molly Morse

Original New York Cast

Gertrude Lawrence, Oscar Shaw, Victor Moore, Harland Dixon,
Marion and Madeleine Fairbanks, Gerald Oliver Smith, Sascha Beaumont,
Harry T. Shannon, Betty Compton

Original London Cast

Gertrude Lawrence, Harold French, John Kirby, Claude Hulbert,
Beth and Betty Dodge, Eric Coxon, April Harmon, Percy Parsons, Rita McLean

Plot

It's 1924 in the Long Island home of playboy Jimmy Winter. Prohibition is in full swing and the coast is home to rum-runners. A group of smugglers, who have been using the house for storage, are led by an English Duke, whose team includes his sister, Lady Kay, and two Americans, Shorty and Larry. At the moment the house is empty, but the owner is shortly to take up residence there.

The night's rum-run is cancelled, and the alcohol already in the house is to be removed. A customs and excise officer visits the house, but the owner arrives with his latest bride, Constance, so Shorty passes himself off as the new butler. A telegram brings shocking news: Jimmy's previous marriage has not been annulled, so he's not married to Constance after all. Constance leaves, and Jimmy is left alone.

Later that night a bedraggled waif arrives; it's Lady Kay who, as it turns out, had rescued Jimmy from drowning the previous summer. Jimmy hides her from the customs officer, but when the officer catches them together, they claim to be man and wife.

Next morning the Duke arrives, looking for his sister. One thing leads to another, and Kay ends up dressed as the maid to allay the suspicions of both the Duke and of Constance, who still wants to marry Jimmy, but Kay now has similar ideas.

The wedding of Jimmy and Constance is about to take place, despite everything Kay can do to try to prevent it. As the ceremony proceeds, the revenue officer arrives to arrest Jimmy for harbouring illicit alcohol. Everyone is arrested, but there's a surprise – the revenue officer is himself a bootlegger. The Blackbird, a major rum-runner, has been thwarted. He thinks he'll have his revenge; Lady Kay is an illegal immigrant and he'll have her deported. Too late; a few hours earlier Lady Kay became the wife of Jimmy Winter – legitimately.

Music and Songs

A vintage height-of-their-powers Gershwin score, packed with catchy and enduring songs that have helped to establish the legend of the Gershwins as master songwriters of the twenties and thirties. The score includes 'Dear little girl' (Jimmy), 'Maybe', (Jimmy and Kay), 'Clap yo' hands' (Potter), 'Someone to watch over me' (Kay), 'Fidgety feet' (Larry), 'Do, do, do' (Kay and Jimmy) and 'Oh, Kay!' (chorus).

Did You Know?

✳ Gertrude Lawrence had become a Broadway star when she appeared with Beatrice Lillie and Jack Buchanan in the *Andre Charlot Revue of 1924*.

✳ The musical, which was at various times during its preparation called 'Mayfair', 'Miss Mayfair' and 'Cheerio!', was the first of two (the other was the unsuccessful *Treasure Girl*) that the Gershwins wrote for Miss Lawrence.

The Critics

'An outstanding example of how taste, talent and affection can be combined to the best effects' – *New York Herald Tribune*
'Rich, melodic, lovely, rhythmical, out of the ordinary and unforgettable' – *New York Times*

Recommended Recording

Studio Recording (CD) Nonesuch 79361-2
A superb recording of this wonderful Gershwin brothers' score. It is authentic, complete and beautifully performed.

Film

First National, 1928 (silent). Starring Colleen Moore, Lawrence Gray, Ford Sterling and Alan Hale.

Oklahoma!

LYRICS ✴ Oscar Hammerstein II
MUSIC ✴ Richard Rodgers
BOOK ✴ Oscar Hammerstein II, based on Lynn Riggs' *Green Grow the Lilacs*

First Performance

New York, St James' Theater, 31 March 1943 (2212 performances)
London, Drury Lane Theatre, 29 April 1947 (1548 performances)

Principal Characters

Eller Murphy ✴ A farmer
Curly McLain ✴ A cowboy
Laurey Williams ✴ His girl
Jud Fry ✴ A hired hand
Ali Hakim ✴ A pedlar
Ado Annie Carnes ✴ A young girl
Will Parker ✴ A cowhand
Andrew Carnes ✴ A rancher

Original New York Cast

Betty Garde, Alfred Drake, Joan Roberts, Howard Da Silva, Joseph Buloff,
Celeste Holm, Lee Dixon, Ralph Riggs

Original London Cast

Mary Marlo, Harold (Howard) Keel, Betty Jane Watson, Henry Clarke,
Marek Windheim, Dorothea Macfarland, Walter Donahue, William S. McCarthy

Plot

It is the turn of the century and Oklahoma is still Indian territory. Aunt Eller Murphy
has a pretty niece, Laurey, who is loved shyly by her cowboy, Curly – and also by the
sinister Jud Fry, a ranch-hand employed by Aunt Eller. There's a social evening
coming up but Curly muffs his chances of taking Laurey, and it is Jud who ends up
escorting her to the dinner and dance, while Curly escorts Aunt Eller. Before they all
set off there's a freshen-up party for the young girls going to the social. Ado Annie
has two suitors – Will Parker, newly back from Kansas City, and the rascally pedlar,
Ali Hakim. Gertie Cummings, a visitor, has her eyes set on Curly. Laurey is not best
pleased. Meanwhile, Curly tries to warn Jud to keep away from Laurey and vice-
versa; Laurey leaves for the box social (in which the men bid for picnic hampers and
the girls who made them) with Jud after a disturbing dream.

The farmers and cowhands are gathering at the Skidmore ranch. Will is angry
with Ali for robbing him of Ado Annie's company – if only he had enough money to
ask for Ado Annie's hand. Ali sees a way out of a wedding between Annie and
himself – he buys back all the gifts he's sold Will at exaggerated prices. Meanwhile,
bidding is going strong on the picnic hampers. Jud menaces Laurey and she fires him.
Later on, after the social, Laurey and Curly are married. But at the 'shivaree' wedding

celebration, Jud turns up with a knife and challenges Curly to a fight in which Jud falls on his own weapon. But this is Curly and Laurey's wedding night and a tricky situation must be resolved. An impromptu trial organised by Aunt Eller results in justice in double-quick time, and the happy pair set off on their honeymoon.

Music and Songs

One of the finest collaborations of all, Rodgers and Hammerstein came up with a score of such freshness and vitality that it changed the direction of musical comedy forever. From 'Oh what a beautiful morning' (Curly) through a succession of wonderful hits to the final rousing chorus of 'Oklahoma!', this is a musical treat in a million. 'Many a new day' (Laurey), 'People will say we're in love' (Laurey and Curly) and 'Out of my dreams' (Laurey) are just examples of its great richness of texture and contrast, offering the romantic sweep of a *Show Boat*, the accumulated folk melodies inherited from the pioneers, plus the freshness and verve of the best of American musicals of the past.

Did You Know?

✶ This was Rodgers and Hammerstein's first collaboration.

✶ The show was known as *Away We Go* in tryouts.

✶ Shirley Jones had been a chorus girl; then she won a beauty contest and the leading roles in the films of *Oklahoma!* and *Carousel*.

✶ For fifteen years the show held the record as the longest-running Broadway musical (it was beaten by *My Fair Lady*).'

The Critics

The show virtually crept into New York. However, the critics were ready:
'Jubilant and enchanting' – *New York Herald Tribune*
'Beautifully different, the most thoroughly attractive musical comedy since *Show Boat*' – *New York Daily News*

Recommended Recording

Original Broadway cast (CD) MCA Classics MCAD 10798
The first Broadway cast recording still sparkles today with its virile-voiced hero and sweet-toned heroine. This was one of the first full recordings of a Broadway show and so is of historical interest as well as a joy to listen to. The 1980 London revival cast **(TER CDTEM 1208)** was recorded live and has a freshness to it that is pleasing.

Film

Todd-AO, 1955. Starring Gordon Macrae, Shirley Jones and Rod Steiger. Directed by Fred Zinnemann.

Video/DVD

The Royal National Theatre production was recorded in a studio after the show closed and was broadcast on television. It has been released on video and DVD.

Oliver!

LYRICS ✶ Lionel Bart
MUSIC ✶ Lionel Bart
BOOK ✶ Lionel Bart, based on Charles Dickens' novel *Oliver Twist*

First Performance

London, New Theatre, 30 June 1960 (2618 performances)
New York, Imperial Theater, 6 January 1963 (744 performances)

Principal Characters

Fagin ✶ A thiefmaster
Nancy ✶ A young girl
Oliver Twist ✶ An orphan
Mr Bumble ✶ A beadle
Mrs Corney ✶ His friend who runs the workhouse
Bill Sikes ✶ A thief and murderer
Mr Brownlow ✶ An old gentleman
The Artful Dodger ✶ A young pickpocket
Sowerberry ✶ An undertaker

Original London Cast

Ron Moody, Georgia Brown, Keith Hamshere, Paul Whitsun-Jones,
Hope Jackman, Danny Sewell, George Bishop, Martin Horsey, Barry Humphries

Original New York Cast

Clive Revill, Georgia Brown, Bruce Prochnick, Willoughby Goddard,
Hope Jackman, Danny Sewell, Geoffrey Lumb, David Jones, Barry Humphries

Plot

It's mealtime at the grim, Victorian workhouse. The boys come in for their gruel but it is not enough for orphan Oliver, who asks for more. He is locked up as a punishment and finally sold to an undertaker, as a mute for funeral processions. Next morning he runs away and is picked up by the Artful Dodger, one of a gang of youthful pickpockets run by the thiefmaster, Fagin. In Fagin's kitchen Oliver meets Nancy, the girlfriend of the local felon, Bill Sikes, along with her friend Bet. After a good meal, Oliver is tucked up in bed. Next morning he is sent off on a pickpocketing expedition with Dodger, and is unfortunately caught, just for looking guilty.

At a local inn, The Three Cripples, we hear that Oliver's innocence has been established and he's currently being looked after by Mr Brownlow at his town house. Bill Sikes is worried that Oliver might give away details of Fagin's organisation. He must be kidnapped and silenced. And indeed that's what happens when Oliver steps outside his new home for the first time. Bumble and Mrs Corney have now discovered that Oliver comes from a rich family and try to recover him. The scheme fails. Nancy is wracked with guilt; she'll return Oliver to Mr Brownlow at midnight. But Bill Sikes discovers her intentions, and kills her. After an exciting chase, Sikes is himself killed and Oliver returns to the bosom of his new family. Fagin lives to rob another day.

Music and Songs

One of the finest scores for a British show, combining the sounds of folk, music hall and other popular song forms, and led by the international hit 'As long as he needs me' (Nancy). The score also includes 'Food, glorious food' (workhouse boys), 'Where is love?' (Oliver), 'Consider yourself' (Artful Dodger and company) and 'Who will buy?' (vendors and Oliver).

Did You Know?

✶ The show was an instant hit with audiences and critics alike, and Bart won a Tony Award on Broadway for the vibrant music and lyrics.

✶ Barry Humphries, a cast member for the London/Broadway runs, was to find enduring fame as Dame Edna and Sir Les Patterson. He has recently played Fagin in the London revival.

✶ The show became the longest-running British musical seen on Broadway up to that time.

✶ The recent large-scale revival at the London Palladium has proved the durability of the show.

The Critics

'This importation from England has enormous energy' – *New York Herald Tribune*
'Its beauty, melodiousness, humor and occasional pathos are shrewdly combined in apattern that isn't ashamed to be good fun' – *New York Post*
'Simply scrumptious. It represents a breakthrough for the British in a field which has for so long been dominated by Americans' – *New York Journal American*

Recommended Recording

Original London cast (CD) Deram 820 590-2
One of the first British stereo recordings of a show. The original cast has never been bettered and it is a perfect memory of one of the most durable of all shows. While there are many recordings to choose from with this show, there really is no choice – none comes anywhere close to it.

Film

Columbia, 1968. Starring Ron Moody, Harry Secombe, Shani Wallis and Oliver Reed. Directed by Carol Reed.

On a Clear Day You Can See Forever

LYRICS ✷ Alan Jay Lerner
MUSIC ✷ Burton Lane
BOOK ✷ Alan Jay Lerner

First Performance

New York, Mark Hellinger Theater, 17 October 1965 (280 performances)
London, Bridewell Theatre, 10 January 2000 (limited season)

Principal Characters

Daisy Gamble ✷ A student with extra-sensory powers
Mark ✷ A psychiatrist
Warren ✷ Daisy's boyfriend
Edward Moncrief ✷ An 18th-century painter
Themistocles Kriakos ✷ A shipping magnate

Original New York Cast

Barbara Harris, John Cullum, William Daniels, Clifford David, Titos Vandis

Original London Cast

Jenna Russell, Harry Burton, Charles Baker, Maurice Clarke, Julian Duncan

Plot

At a lecture on hypnotism at the Bruckner Clinic, Mark discovers that Daisy, one of his students, is highly susceptible to hypnosis. Afterwards she stays on and tells Mark of her special powers: she can make flowers grow, she can see into the future – but she can't stop smoking. Perhaps Mark can help?

At various sessions Daisy is hypnotised, and Mark gradually realises that she is remembering a marriage to a painter in the 18th century. Her name then was Melinda Wells. Later, Mark takes her out for a river trip, and she quite forgets a previous engagement with her boyfriend Warren.

At subsequent sessions Mark discovers more about Melinda's adventures in the 18th century - and how the painter Moncrief rescued her from the Hell Fire Club and married her. Mark is determined to discover whether such people and events existed. He files a medical report on the case in a journal. One day Daisy arrives early and discovers that she is the subject of the now-famous regression sessions. She rushes out of his office, determined to lead a normal life with Warren. But Mark decides to take matters into his own hands. He discovers extra-sensory powers of his own and wills Daisy to come to his office – she does. It is obvious that their future will be together.

Music and Songs

All of the Broadway scores written by Burton Lane are musically superb. The songs have a confidence, style and melodic memorability that have given them life long after the shows have closed. *On a Clear Day* is no exception. 'What did I have?' (Daisy), 'She wasn't you' (Moncrief), 'Melinda' (Mark) and the title song 'On a clear day you can see forever' (Mark) are especially satisfying.

Did You Know?

✶ Alan Jay Lerner had tried to collaborate with Richard Rodgers to make a musical of this story, tentatively titled 'I Picked a Daisy'.

✶ The director, Herb Ross, was often asked to help doctor (improve) incoming Broadway musicals. His wife, ballerina Nora Kaye, was known to enquire that if he was such a good doctor, why did so many of his patients die?

✶ It was Alan Jay Lerner's interest in the subject of extra sensory perception that brought the idea for the show.

The Critics

'The songs have bright, charming lyrics . . . more melodic grace and inventive distinction than has been heard in some years' – *New York Times*

Recommended Recording

Original Broadway cast (CD) RCA 09026 60820 2
An interesting score as it changes from one century to another and this is indicated in Burton Lane's beautiful music as well as in the well-formed lyrics of Alan Jay Lerner. Barbara Harris is at her most appealing and John Cullum gives splendid support. The film version cut many songs and, even with the magic of Barbra Streisand, the loss is too great.

Film

Paramount, 1970. Starring Barbara Streisand and Yves Montand. Directed by Vincente Minnelli. The songs, some old, plus two new ones for Miss Streisand, were concentrated on the principals, and the 18th-century scenes were curtailed and changed, as was the ending.

Once on this Island

LYRICS ✳ Lyn Ahrens
MUSIC ✳ Stephen Flaherty
BOOK ✳ Lyn Ahrens, based on the novel *My Love, My Love* by Rosa Guy

First Performance

New York, Friday Playwrights Horizons (Off Broadway), 6 May 1990
(60 performances)
Transferred to Booth Theater (Broadway), 18 October 1990 (487 performances)
London, Island Theatre (aka Royalty Theatre), 28 September 1994
(145 performances)

Principal Characters

Ti Moune ✳ A young peasant girl
Daniel ✳ A rich young man
Euralie ✳ Moune's guardian
Asaka ✳ A goddess

Original New York Cast

La Chanze, Jerry Dixon, Andrea Fierson, Kecia Lewis-Evans

Original London Cast

Lorna Brown, Anthony Corriette, P.P. Arnold, Sharon D. Clarke

Plot

There's a violent storm whipping around a small Caribbean island, as storytellers calm the fears of a frightened child. The island is inhabited by light- and dark-skinned people, the light-skinned being rich landowners, the others poor peasants scraping a living. Ti Moune, an orphan, has been saved for a special destiny by Asaka, mother of the earth.

Now a grown-up, Ti Moune sees the handsome Daniel Beauxhomme passing in his fine car. In the storm the car crashes and Ti Moune rushes to his rescue. By cheating the demon of death, Papa Ge, Ti Moune saves Daniel's life, but at a terrible price – her soul. (We now learn some history. In the 19th century, Armand, a Frenchman, has a son, the original Beauxhomme. The latter rises up and expels his father and his compatriots from the island. He and his future descendents are then cursed by Armand.) Ti Moune wants to marry Daniel but Euralie, who brought her up, points out the impossibility of this as they are of different classes. Nevertheless, the pair become lovers. As Daniel recovers he realises his responsibilities; his bride-to-be is the rich Andrea Devereux and the announcement is made at a grand ball.

Papa Ge arrives to claim Ti Moune; only by killing Daniel herself can she escape the devil's bargain. She can't, of course. The newly-married couple come to the front of the hotel and throw coins to the peasants. Daniel gives a coin to Ti Moune, but she's dying. Her life and untimely death nevertheless leave a positive ending, in that the power of love conquers the terror of death.

Music and Songs

A delicious collection of West Indian rhythms, fine melodies and plot-advancing ditties, proving the composer/lyricist's versatility and talent. Songs include 'We dance' (storytellers), 'One small girl' (Euralie , Tonton Julian, Ltttle Ti Moune and storytellers), 'Waiting for life' (Ti Moune), 'Forever yours' (Ti Moune, Daniel and Papa Ge), 'Mamma will provide' (Asaka and storytellers), 'Ti Moune' (Euralie, Tonton and Ti Moune), 'When we are wed' (Andrea, Ti Moune and Daniel) and 'Why we tell this story' (storytellers).

Did You Know?

✳ This was the Broadway breakthrough show for these two fine, new writers, authors of *My Favorite Year* and *Lucky Stiff* – and in 1997, *Ragtime*.

✳ For the London performances the Royalty Theatre was made over as the Island Theatre, offering West Indian food and drink and creating a carnival atmosphere. Unfortunately the show had a short run.

The Critics

'The evening is carried along fully 90 minutes on a heat haze of pure enjoyment' – *Daily Mail*
'In its straightforward feel-good way it is tremendous fun' – *Evening Standard*
'A delightful evocation of West Indies folklore and songs' – *The Herald*

Recommended Recording

Original Broadway cast (CD) RCA Victor 60595-2-RC
The original version, sung with verve and relish, and conjuring up a never-never land of colourful exoticism. The London cast recording may have a more authentic Caribbean-sounding cast, but the original has the edge.

One Touch of Venus

LYRICS ✷ Ogden Nash
MUSIC ✷ Kurt Weill
BOOK ✷ S.J. Perlman and Ogden Nash, based on *The Tinted Venus* by F. Anstey

First Performance

New York, Imperial Theater, 7 October 1943 (567 performances)

Principal Characters

Venus ✷ A goddess
Rodney Hatch ✷ A barber
Gloria ✷ Rodney's fiancée
Whitelaw Savory ✷ A millionaire art patron
Molly Grant ✷ His assistant
Taxi Black ✷ A private detective
Stanley

Original New York Cast

Mary Martin, Kenny Baker, Ruth Bond, John Boles, Paula Laurence,
Teddy Hart, Harry Clark

Plot

Art patron, Whitelaw Savory, is awaiting the arrival of a 3000-year-old statue of Venus, whose features resemble those of an old girlfriend. It's being smuggled in from Anatolia by a private detective. Savory's barber, Rodney Hatch, is immune to the statue's undoubted charms, preferring the looks of his girlfriend, Gloria Kramer. Nevertheless, something makes Rodney slip the engagement ring he's bought for Gloria on Venus' finger. There's a clap of thunder and Venus, suddenly all woman, gets down from her plinth to follow the man who has awakened her.

On her travels she dresses herself from a shop window's dummy. This naturally arouses the interest of the police, but Savory turns up and rescues her. Venus is only interested in the owner of the ring, and quickly leaves the millionaire alone. He hires detectives to find her. Rodney's girlfriend is also getting suspicious, especially when Venus turns up in Rodney's apartment. Savory turns up as well and offers to help Venus, but he merely locks Rodney up in the basement. For good measure Gloria is bound and gagged as well. Venus then unties Gloria, but packs her off out of the way to the North Pole. Savory accuses Rodney of Gloria's murder, but this mischief is foiled when Venus insists on accompanying Rodney to jail.

Some Anatolians arrive to persuade Venus to return to her native land. She refuses, and has Rodney released; they go to a luxury hotel suite, but Rodney is still preoccupied with the absence of Gloria. So Gloria is returned, but sees the situation in the hotel room and flees. Now Rodney can contemplate life with his new love. But it transpires that his idyll of a suburban life is not what Venus has in mind. She disappears into the sky. Rodney is now alone, but not for long. A young girl comes in to enrol at the art class. Rodney has no need to ask her name ...

Music and Songs

The score includes the standards 'Speak low' (Venus and Rodney) and 'That's him' (Venus). Others include 'How much I love you' (Rodney and Gloria), 'I'm a stranger here myself' (Venus), 'West wind' (Venus) and 'Foolish heart' (Venus).

Did You Know?

∗ The original star approached to head the show was Marlene Dietrich.

∗ This was Mary Martin's first starring role. She had turned down *Oklahoma!* and would do the same to *Kiss Me Kate*, *My Fair Lady* and *Mame*.

∗ This was Kurt Weill's longest-running Broadway show. His revival of *The Threepenny Opera* became his longest-running off-Broadway show.

∗ This is another version of the Pygmalion story.

The Critics

The critics were divided:
'Venus and Broadway come to life' vied with 'At long last a hit' and even '*One Touch of Venus* proves a disappointment', but they loved Miss Martin, rating her acting and singing as 'lovely and assured' and declaring her to be 'worthy of her star part'.

Recommended Recording

Original Broadway cast (CD) MCA MCAD-11354
This has just the Mary Martin numbers and also includes her songs from *Lute Song*. It is Hobson's choice but Mary Martin can never disappoint and the songs are glorious.

Film

Universal Pictures, 1948. Starring Ava Gardner, Robert Walker and Dick Haymes. Directed by William A. Seiter..

On the Town

LYRICS ✶ Betty Comden and Adolph Green
MUSIC ✶ Leonard Bernstein
BOOK ✶ Betty Comden and Adolph Green, from an idea by Jerome Robbins

First Performance

New York, Adelphi Theater, 28 December 1944 (463 performances)
London, Prince of Wales Theatre, 30 May 1963 (53 performances)

Principal Characters

Ivy Smith ✶ Miss Turnstiles, the girl of the month
Brunhilde Esterhazy (Hildy) ✶ A cab driver
Claire de Loon ✶ An anthropologist
Ozzie ✶ A sailor
Gabey ✶ Another sailor
Judge Pitkin W. Bridgework
Chip Offenbloch ✶ A sailor
Lucy Schmeeler ✶ Brunhilde's friend

Original New York Cast

Sono Osato, Nancy Walker, Betty Comden, Adolph Green, John Battles,
Robert Chisholm, Cris Alexander, Alice Pearce

Original London Cast

Andrea Jaffe, Carol Arthur, Gillian Lewis, Eliott Gould, Don McKay,
Franklin Kiser, John Humphrey, Rosamund Greenwood

Plot

Three sailors, Gabey, Chip and Ozzie, have just 24 hours shore leave in New York. At 6 am they leave Brooklyn Navy Yard, determined to have a day packed with fun and frolic. Chip has a guidebook to help, but it's out of date and many of the attractions listed aren't there any more. Gabey falls for Miss Turnstiles of the Month, as depicted on the walls of the subway, and wants to find her. Ozzie doesn't care – he just wants to meet some girls. Chip is soon taken up with a cab driver, Hildy, who also says she'll help in the search. But first, up to her place . . . Ozzie ends up in the Natural History Museum and meets anthropologist, Claire de Loon, a victim of her own sensuality, as Ozzie soon finds out!

Gabey goes to Carnegie Hall. Ivy Smith, Miss Turnstiles, is actually there taking lessons, using her earnings as a carnival dancer to train as a dancer and singer. Gabey recognises her and manages to arrange a date in Times Square that evening. Ozzie and Claire are back at her apartment where they meet Claire's friend, a judge. Gabey waits for Ivy in Times Square, but she's been waylaid by her boozy singing teacher, Madame Dilly, who insists she earn her fees at Coney Island. Meanwhile, Gabey is alone, and his friends arrive and try to comfort him. Now for a night on the town, and Gabey has a replacement partner, cold-ridden Lucy Schmeeler, Hildy's flatmate.

The six pay whirlwind visits to a variety of nightclubs and in the last they strike lucky. Madame Dilly is there and tells Gabey where Ivy is. The group make off for Coney Island, the gaudy carnival centre for jaded Manhattan-ites and others. A little tussle with the police, a spell in jail and the three friends are returned to their ship, but their three girls, Ivy, Hildy and Claire, are there to accompany them. What a wonderful day they've had; now it's time for a fresh batch of shipmates to be 'On the Town'.

Music and Songs

This was Bernstein's first Broadway show, and it tingles with life, imagination, unusual and attractive melodies and daring. It is threaded through with the vitality of New York. The score includes the memorable songs 'New York, New York' (the sailors), 'Come up to my place' (Hildy), 'Lonely town' (Gabey) and 'Some other time' (the sailors and their girls), as well as three fine dance episodes choreographed in New York by Jerome Robbins and in the long-delayed London production by Joe Layton.

Did You Know?

✴ The original idea of three sailors out on the town in New York was previously employed in Jerome Robbins' ballet, *Fancy Free*, with music by Bernstein.

✴ What is never stated, but lies behind the mad make-the-most-of-the-shore-leave core to the flimsy plot, was the fact that the guys were going off to war.

The Critics

Critical reaction was favourable:
'One of the freshest, gayest, liveliest musicals I have ever seen' – Louis Kronenberger, *PM*
'The most original and engaging musical to hit New York since *Oklahoma!*' – *Newsweek*

Recommended Recording

Concert recording (CD) Deutsche Grammophon 437 516-2
Michael Tilsson Thomas created this recording in conjunction with a videoed concert version. It is a rare example of an all-star celebrity version being the best, and the most complete, of the available options. A must!

Film

MGM, 1949. Starring Frank Sinatra, Gene Kelly, Vera-Ellen and Betty Garrett. Directed by Stanley Donen. The film features mostly new songs.

Video

A video of the concert recording was issued and has been broadcast.

On The Twentieth Century

LYRICS ✳ Betty Comden and Adolph Green
MUSIC ✳ Cy Coleman
BOOK ✳ Betty Comden and Adolph Green, based on the plays by
Ben Hecht, Charles MacArthur and Bruce Millholland

First Performance

New York, St James Theatre, 19 February 1978 (460 performances)
London, Her Majesty's Theatre, 19 March 1980 (165 performances)

Principal Characters

Oscar Jaffee ✳ A director
Lily Garland ✳ A star
Letitia Primrose ✳ A religious heiress
Bruce Granit ✳ A Hollywood star
Owen O'Malley ✳ Oscar's henchman
Oliver Webb ✳ Oscar's henchman

Original New York Cast

John Cullum, Madeline Kahn, Imogene Coca, Kevin Kline, George Coe,
Dean Dittman

Original London Cast

Keith Michell, Julia McKenzie, Ann Beach, Mark Wynter, David Healy,
Fred Evans

Plot

It is Chicago in the 1930s and we are at the closing moments of a play about Joan of Arc, Oscar Jaffee's latest flop. He is out of money and can't pay what he owes, so he escapes on the 'Twentieth Century' train bound for New York. He has taken a certain compartment for he knows that Lily Garland is to join the train. He had made her a success and they had been lovers until their egos got in the way. Lily is now a Hollywood star and he needs her back. When she boards the train she is with her latest co-star, Bruce Granit, who is just as eager to keep her by his side. Oscar's henchmen tell Lily that he needs her, but she is adamant she will never go back.

Also on board is Mrs Primrose, an escapee from an asylum, who is a religious fanatic; she puts stickers up everywhere and gives out dud cheques. The stickers give Oscar an idea for a play, which includes Lily portraying Mary Magdalen. Mrs Primrose offers to back the production.

Oscar gets a cheque for $200,000 from Mrs Primrose, and Lily signs the contract when Mrs Primrose says she will also back the film of the play. It all goes wrong when they find out the truth about Mrs Primrose and Oscar sees his plans disappear. Lily is furious because she thinks she has been made to look a fool. Oscar wants to end it all and seizes a gun, whereupon Mrs Primrose goes for it, it goes off but no one is hurt. However, Oscar sees a chance and pretends to be fatally wounded, thus persuading Lily to sign the contract – only she signs it 'Peter Rabbit'. They can both play the game and they seem so suited to each other, that it is no surprise to see them in an embrace as the curtain falls.

During the show there are flashbacks showing Lily becoming a star and highlights of her past relationship with Oscar.

Music and Songs

A fine score with a touch of burlesque. There are the send-ups of operetta in 'Veronique' (Lily and Oscar) and 'Babette' (Lily), Broadway magic with the title song (company) and 'Life is like a train' (Porters), and comedy in 'Repent' (Mrs Primrose) and 'She's a nut' (company).

Did You Know?

✴ It won Tonys for the best book and best score. Both John Cullum and Kevin Kline won Tonys.

✴ The score requires a female star with an operatic range and with a comic ability – not an easy combination. On Broadway Madeline Kahn was soon replaced by Judy Kaye and in London it was Julia McKenzie in a part that could have been written for her.

The Critics

'Funny, elegant and totally cheerful ... Miss Comden, Mr Green, Mr Coleman, Mr Prince (the director) and their dazzling crew have brought back what seemed dead or at least endangered: the comedy in musical comedy' – *The New York Times*

Recommended Recording

Original Broadway cast (CD) Sony Broadway SK 35330
An inventive, fun and demanding score given good treatment here. The partnership of Comden, Green and Coleman worked magic and most of the performances are worthy of the score. It is indeed sad that the London production was not recorded. However, this is a gem well worth owning.

On Your Toes

LYRICS ✶ Lorenz Hart
MUSIC ✶ Richard Rodgers
BOOK ✶ Richard Rodgers, Lorenz Hart and George Abbott

First Performance

New York, Imperial Theater, 11 April 1936 (315 performances)
London, Palace and Coliseum Theatres, 5 February 1937 (123 performances)

Principal Characters

Junior Dolan ✶ A young dancer
Vera ✶ A Russian dancer
Peggy Porterfield ✶ A patron of the arts
Sergei Alexandrovitch ✶ An impresario
Frankie Frayne ✶ Junior's pupil and friend
Vassilli
Sidney Cohen ✶ A student composer
Konstantine Morrosine ✶ A principal dancer

Original New York Cast

Ray Bolger, Tamara Geva, Louella Gear, Monty Woolley, Doris Carson,
David Morris, Robert Sidney, Demetrios Vilan

Original London Cast

Jack Whiting, Vera Zorina, Olive Blakeney, Vernon Kelso, Gina Malo,
Dick Taylor, Eddie Pola, Jack Donohue

Plot

The Dolans are a vaudeville act touring the American theatre circuits. The family pack Junior off to school. Fifteen years pass and Junior is teaching music at Knickerbocker University. His students include Frankie, who has had a song published, and Sidney Cohen, who has written a jazz ballet. No one knows Junior's background until Frankie catches him dancing to Sidney's music. A family friend and arts patron, Peggy Porterfield, has decided to back a production of this jazz ballet. Meanwhile, the ballet's star, Vera, is throwing a tantrum; she believes her co-star Morrosine is unfaithful. She is, however, intrigued over the new ballet. The impresario, Sergei, won't agree to mount the new work. There's the Scheherezade-like ballet, *Princess Zenobia*, to concentrate on now. When a dancer is jailed, Junior, hanging round the company, is pressed into service as a company member. Although everything goes wrong, the audience is delighted.

   Junior invites Sergei and Peggy to his class in an attempt to reverse Sergei's decision on the new ballet, which is to be called *Slaughter on 10th Avenue*. Vera comes too and, to Frankie's discomfiture, Junior must look after her. Peggy tells Sergei she'll withdraw her funding unless he puts on the new ballet. Bowing to the inevitable, Sergei acquiesces. Morrosine goes berserk and Junior inherits the leading role. By opening night Vera and Morrosine are reconciled, and the latter is upset at Junior's participation. Vera plays a stripper and Junior a dancer who gets involved with her. Morrosine arranges for a gangster to shoot Junior from front of house, but he's unable to as Junior keeps moving until the police can arrest the gunman. All ends happily; Junior is with Frankie, Morrosine with Vera and possibly even Peggy ends up with Sergei – or is that too much to ask?

Music and Songs

A superb collection of top-quality Rodgers and Hart masterpieces, including 'It's got to be love' (Junior and Frankie), 'Too good for the average man' (Sergei), 'There's a small hotel' (Junior and Frankie), 'Glad to be unhappy' (Frankie), 'Quiet night' (Hank J. Smith), 'On your toes' (Frankie, class and dancers) and, of course, the ballet score for *Slaughter on 10th Avenue*.

Did You Know?

✶ One of the world's greatest choreographers, George Balanchine, later of the New York City Ballet, made his Broadway debut creating the dances for this show.

✶ When revived, the part of the show that still made the greatest impression was the jazz ballet, *Slaughter on 10th Avenue* – and it did the same in the film version and the film biography of Rodgers and Hart, *Words and Music*.

✶ The London revival run of 539 performances two years after Broadway's 1983 version made up for the poor showing of the prewar original, and exceeeded the runs of both the Broadway original and of any other revival!

The Critics

'The songs are mildly hearable' [!] – Percy Hammond
'A definite milestone in musical theater' – *Time*

Recommended Recording

1983 Broadway Revival cast (CD) TER CDTER 1063
This revival was a faithful reconstruction using the original orchestrations. It is a near-perfect recording of this score, and has wonderful performances and beautifully recorded ballet sequences.

Film

Warner Brothers, 1939. Starring Vera Zorina and Eddie Albert. Directed by Ray Enright. The film features only a limited number of songs.

Pacific Overtures

LYRICS ✶ Stephen Sondheim
MUSIC ✶ Stephen Sondheim
BOOK ✶ John Weidman and Hugh Wheeler

First Performance

New York, Winter Garden Theater, 11 January 1976 (203 performances)
London, Coliseum Theatre, 10 September 1987 (in repertoire)

Principal Characters

The Reciter
Abe ✶ The first councillor
Manjiro
The Shogun's mother
Kayama ✶ The third councillor
Tamate ✶ Kayama's wife
Commodore Matthew Galbraith Perry, The Shogun's wife, The Shogun's companion, The Shogun, Madam, American Admiral, British Admiral, Dutch Admiral, Russian Admiral, French Admiral

Note: Many of the performers doubled or tripled their parts. The principal performers are shown below.

Original New York Cast

Mako, Yuki Shimoda, Sab Shimono, James Dybas,
Alvin Ing, Freddy Mao, Isao Sato, Soon-Tech Oh, Ernest Abuba/Mark Hsu Sayers,
Haruki Fujimoto, Ricardo Tobia, Jae Woo Lee, Tim Fujii, Conrad Yama,
Larry Hama, Haruki Fujimoto

Original London Cast

Richard Angas, Leon Berger, Christopher Booth-Jones, Edward Byles,
John Cashmore, Gordon Christie, Ian Comboy, Graham Fletcher, Terry Jenkins,
John Kitchener, Simon Masterton-Smith, Harry Nicoll, Malcolm Rivers,
Eric Roberts, Michael Sadler

Plot

The title has a number of meanings, of course – Pacific meaning both the ocean and the opposite of warlike. The evening is threaded through with the experiences of two Japanese, a humble fisherman and a Samurai warrior, who observe the opening up of trade and cultural barriers between Japan and the West. One becomes Westernised as a result. The other makes a cultural and warlike stand against the invasion of his country by trade, by culture and by values to which he has no aspiration.

The action springs from the visit of warships (Four Black Dragons) to the coast of Japan in 1865, under the American, Commander Perry. His arrival is watched, appalled, by local residents. Despite a rearguard action by the local dignitaries, the industrialisation of Japan is about to begin. Traditionalists try desperately to turn back the tide – but to no purpose. There are soon trade emissaries from America, Europe and Russia who bring goods, backed up with fire power.

Finally there's a scene in modern-day Japan, now the king of industrial nations, showing the power and expertise that give it primacy not merely among Asian nations, but also in world trade.

Music and Songs

There is a conscious and successful attempt to recall traditional Japanese forms of verse such as the haiku and, by the use of instruments and orchestration, the sound of Japanese music. In addition, there are brilliant parodies of Gilbert and Sullivan and other styles in 'Please, hello' (admirals) and also a Japanese idea of an American attempt to do a Japanese musical. 'Someone in a tree' (observers) is one of Sondheim's major achievements, and comments on how someone can see everything and understand nothing! Other highlights are 'The advantages of floating in the middle of the sea' (The Reciter), 'Welcome to Kanagawa' (Madam), 'Pretty lady' (English sailors) and 'Next' (the company).

Did You Know?

✴ The brilliant original production was partly staged in the very formal Japanese kabuki style.

✴ This was the first Sondheim show to enter the repertoire of a British opera house, in this case ENO at the Coliseum.

✴ The European premiere of the show took place at Wythenshaw, Manchester.

✴ The original Broadway production was recorded on video and shown in Japan but not in the United States.

The Critics

The critical reaction was mixed:
'A triumph of sophistication, taste and craft . . . the most original, profound, the most theatrically ambitious of the Prince [producer Hal Prince]-Sondheim collaborations. It is also, for this viewer, the production in which the team that sets Broadway's highest standards most fully meets the astonishing objectives they set themselves' – Howard Kissel
'Sometimes it only floats, sometimes it actually sinks, but it tries to soar. And the music and lyrics are as pretty and as well formed as a bonsai tree. *Pacific Overtures* is very, very different' – *New York Times*

Recommended Recording

Original Broadway cast (CD) RCA RCD1-4407
Although not as complete a recording as that of the English National Opera double set (TER CDTER 1152), this is still one of the essential Sondheim recordings. It has the excitement of musical theatre at its edgy and dangerous best.

The Pajama Game

LYRICS ✴ Jerry Ross and Richard Adler
MUSIC ✴ Jerry Ross and Richard Adler
BOOK ✴ George Abbott and Richard Bissell,
based on Bissell's book $7^{1/2}$ Cents

First Performance

New York, St James' Theater, 13 May 1954 (1063 performances)
London, Coliseum Theatre, 13 October 1955 (588 performances)

Principal Characters

Babe Williams ✴ A pajama factory worker
Sid Sorokin ✴ A new manager
Vernon Hines ✴ A time-study man
Gladys ✴ A secretary and bookkeeper

Original New York Cast

Janis Paige, John Raitt, Eddie Foy Jnr, Carol Haney

Original London Cast

Joy Nichols, Edmund Hockridge, Max Wall, Elizabeth Seal

Plot

The setting is the Sleep Tite pajama factory in Iowa where the employees are after a $7^{1/2}$ cent an hour pay rise. However, Hines, the time and motion man, wants more productivity and the new-to-town factory superintendent Sid Sorokin is out to prove himself in his new job. Not surprisingly, he is annoyed when an employee will not help mend a machine and Sid shoves him aside – an action that brings down the wrath of the grievance committee, led by the attractive Babe. Sid attempts to date Babe but she is against management and workers mixing. However, at the annual union picnic she thaws and he is invited to her home. Their happiness is short-lived, for there is more friction between management and workers when the union orders a slowdown and Babe literally puts a spanner in the works to make it so.

The slowdown is working – orders are late and some sizes are mixed. Sid unsuccessfully tries to get the boss to make a compromise and is forced to look for another solution. He gets Gladys, the boss's secretary, drunk in a nightclub, takes the key to the company ledgers, and finds the boss has already been charging the extra $7^{1/2}$ cents on the orders. With this knowledge Sid is able to change the boss's mind and the union win their $7^{1/2}$ cents rise. And, of course, Sid gets Babe.

Music and Songs

A superb score that included the big hit 'Hey there' (Sid). With the help of the film many other songs became popular: 'Hernando's Hideaway' (Gladys), 'I'm not at all in love' (Babe), '$7^{1}/_{2}$ cents' (company), 'Once a year day' (company), 'I'll never be jealous again' (Hines) and the infectious 'Steam heat' (Gladys and dancers).

Did You Know?

✶ Having written the original book about the factory, Richard Bissell then wrote another about his experiences with the making of the musical (*Say, Darling*), that was itself turned into a play with full musical score by Jule Styne, and lyrics by Comden and Green.

✶ Shirley MacLaine was the understudy to Carol Haney, went on to play the part and was noticed by a Hollywood agent – film stardom followed.

✶ *The Pajama Game* won the Tony Award for outstanding musical and Bob Fosse won it for his choreography. Carol Haney took one home too.

The Critics

The critics enjoyed the show:
'Bright, brassy and jubilantly sassy. Has a fresh and winning grin on its face from the outset. It is gay, contemporary, wonderfully innocent and wonderfully sly all at once' – *New York Herald Tribune*
'A funny and frisky musical comedy . . . the plot is about labour trouble in a pajama factory' – *New York Daily News*
'A riot of fun . . . a deliriously daffy delight! A royal flush and a grand slam rolled into one' – *New York Daily Mirror*
'Fast, raucous and rollicking . . . the story is told with incredible delight and ingenuity' – *New York Journal American*

Recommended Recording

Original Broadway cast (CD) Sony Columbia CK 32606
A wonderful original cast album (the Original London cast is pretty good too). The cast is exceptional and virtually all except Miss Paige went into the film version. (There is a more complete recording of the show with a studio cast on **TER CDTER2 1232**.)

Film

Warner Brothers, 1957. Doris Day, John Raitt, Eddie Foy Jnr and Carol Heney. Directed by Stanley Donen.

Pal Joey

LYRICS ✷ Lorenz Hart
MUSIC ✷ Richard Rodgers
BOOK ✷ John O'Hara, based on his short stories

First Performance

New York, Ethel Barrymore Theater, 25 December 1940 (374 performances)
London, Princes Theatre, 31 March 1954 (245 performances)

Principal Characters

Vera Simpson ✷ A rich socialite
Joey Evans ✷ A dancer
Gladys Bumps ✷ A chorus girl
Linda English ✷ An innocent
Ludlow Lowell ✷ A gangster
Melba Snyder ✷ A newspaper reporter

Original New York Cast

Vivienne Segal, Gene Kelly, June Havoc, Leila Ernst, Jack Durant, Jean Casto

Original London Cast

Carol Bruce, Harold Lang, Jean Brampton, Sally Bazeley, Lou Jacobi, Olga Lowe

Plot

Joey Evans is working as a song-and-dance man at a run-down Chicago nightclub. Though he has a sweet, but empty-headed, girlfriend called Linda, Joey always has an eye for the main chance. When the bored, rich and powerful local socialite, Vera Simpson, drops by and shows interest in him, he sees a chance. He wagers she'll come back to the club where he works; he loses and loses his job too. But she does eventually turn up at closing time on the very last night of his employment, picks him up and offers him his own nightclub. The deal includes clothes and his own apartment, courtesy of Vera. Poor Linda, who is on the staff of his outfitters, just looks on helplessly.

Joey opens his own club, and is miffed to discover the reviews concentrate on the social niceties and the atmosphere of the place, rather than on his talent. Meanwhile, gangster Ludlow Lowell and his girlfriend, Gladys, plan to blackmail Vera over Joey (since she is married). Linda overhears them and tries to warn Vera and Joey. Eventually she succeeds and the police commissioner has a nice surprise awaiting the blackmailers – himself.

The experience makes Vera realise that things with Joey have gone far enough. She dismisses him and cuts off his credit. Later, Linda's looking in the window of a pet shop and Joey comes along. Will he come to dinner with her sister? Well no, he's off to New York to try out for a new musical. Perhaps next time?

Music and Songs

Rodgers and Hart at their peak. The score has a clutch of classics, including 'You mustn't kick it around' (Joey), 'I could write a book' (Joey and Linda), 'Chicago' (chorus girls), 'What is a man?' (Vera), 'Bewitched' (Vera), 'Zip' (Melba), 'In our little den' (Vera and Joey) and 'Take him' (Vera and Linda).

Did You Know?

✶ The run of the 1952 production was, at the time, the longest of any revival in American theatre history.

✶ The hit was expected to be 'I could write a book'. In fact, thanks to Bill Snyder's postwar recording, the hit turned out to be 'Bewitched'.

✶ Gene Kelly was whisked off to Hollywood after his appearance in this.

✶ When first seen in 1940 audiences were not used to seeing characters in musicals as unpleasant, and the success of the revival showed it was before its time.

✶ The songs written for the nightclub show-within-a show were purposely second rate, although they have a charm of their own when listened to in their context.

The Critics

The show enjoyed mixed notices. Brooks Atkinson complained, 'Although *Pal Joey* is expertly done, can you draw sweet water from a foul well?', but had the grace to revise his verdict with the 1952 revival: 'Brimming over with good music and fast on its toes, it renews confidence in the professionalism of the theater.'

Recommended Recording

Studio cast (CD) Columbia CK 4364
This recording led to the hugely successful 1952 revival of this Rodgers and Hart classic. Vivienne Segal and Harold Lang went into the revival for good reason as can be heard on this recording. There is a pleasant later recording of the London 1980 revival with Denis Lawson and a glorious singing debut by Sian Phillips.

Film

Columbia, 1957. Starring Frank Sinatra, Rita Hayworth and Kim Novak. Directed by George Sidney. Because of screen censorship at the time, the plot was bowdlerised.

Passion

LYRICS ✶ Stephen Sondheim
MUSIC ✶ Stephen Sondheim
BOOK ✶ James Lapine, based on the 1981 film *Passione d'Amore*

First Performance

New York, Plymouth Theater, 9 May 1994 (280 performances)
London, Queen's Theatre, 13 March 1996 (232 performances)

Principal Characters

Giorgio ✶ A young soldier
Clara ✶ His Milanese mistress
Fosca ✶ Cousin of his commanding officer
Doctor Tambourri
Colonel Ricci ✶ The station commander

Original New York Cast

Jere Shea, Donna Murphy, Marin Mazzie, Tom Aldredge, Gregg Edelman

Original London Cast

Michael Ball, Maria Friedman, Helen Hobson, Hugh Ross, David Firth

Plot

Passion is set in Italy in 1863. Giorgio, a young soldier, is bidding farewell to his mistress, Clara. He is to join his new regiment in the outposts of northern Italy and must leave her. They will keep in touch through their correspondence in future. Giorgio seems set for a bright future. He has the confidence of his new commanding officer, Colonel Ricci. The regimental doctor, Doctor Tambourri, has a special patient, the commander's cousin, Fosca, a black-clad recluse for whom reading is her only passion. Giorgio lends her some of his books – which include poetry; Giorgio is a dreamer. Fosca is frail, and her illness manifests itself in hysterical convulsions. She is in pain and desperate for intellectual companionship, fastening onto Giorgio with the strength of a leech.

In letters Clara warns Giorgio to keep Fosca at arm's length. But Fosca has already gone far. At dinner she grabs Giorgio's leg under the table, refusing to let go, and gives him a letter. Giorgio immediately asks for leave, to which the colonel reluctantly agrees. Fosca turns up as Giorgio is leaving and gets him to write to her in his absence. On his return, Fosca discovers that Giorgio's mistress is married, and retires to her bedroom. Weeks pass without contact, but then the doctor asks Giorgio to visit Fosca. She asks the soldier to take down a letter she dictates. He does so. It is a love letter from him to her.

Colonel Ricci tells Giorgio about Fosca's marriage to a worthless count, which made her ill and penniless. Giorgio takes walks on the desolate mountain nearby. Fosca follows on one occasion. It rains and he carries her fainting body back to camp. He falls ill himself and is granted sick leave in Milan. Fosca is on the train.

He begs her to give him up, and returns her to the camp, where the doctor insists he take the leave. He does, but curtails the time involved. His former mistress will devote her time to bringing up her family, and her romance with Giorgio is over.

Back in camp, a transfer notice arrives for Giorgio, arranged secretly by the doctor. Fosca rushes to her room in distress. The colonel discovers Giorgio's love letter and challenges him to a duel. That night Giorgio visits Fosca's room, acknowledges his whole-hearted love for her and they make love. Next morning he is injured in the duel. Months later a letter from the doctor reveals Fosca's death, three days after the duel she never knew about, and a small box of her possessions is delivered to Giorgio in hospital. He is now finally alone.

Music and Songs

Sondheim has written nothing more impressive than this sustained lyrical and passionate rhapsody of life that recalls Ravel and Rachmaninov at their finest. While there are sections that stand out, these are not songs as such. Nevertheless, 'Happiness' (Clara and Giorgio), 'I wish I could forget you' (Fosca), 'Is this what you call love?' (Giorgio), 'Loving you' (Fosca) and 'No one has ever loved me' (Giorgio) are all memorable elements of this glowing score.

Did You Know?

✷ The show won awards on both sides of the Atlantic: Tony awards for Best Musical, and for best score, book and musical actress (Donna Murphy), and the London Evening Standard Award for Best Musical.

The Critics

'Stephen Sondheim's new musical drama is one of his darkest but also one of his most exciting; a hard, stormy, unsettling and spellbinding piece of theatre' – *The Sunday Times*
'Sondheim's gorgeous, insinuating music' – *Variety*
'Fosca is perhaps the most irritating heroine ever devised for a musical' – *New York Times* (reviewing the TV version)

Recommended Recording

Original Broadway cast (CD) EMI Angel 72435 55251 23
A passionate recording of Sondheim's deepest score. It is not easily accessible and requires repeated listenings.

Film

The Broadway production was filmed and shown on American television. This has been released on video in American (NTSC) format.

Peter Pan

LYRICS ✶ Carolyn Leigh, Betty Comden and Adolph Green
MUSIC ✶ Mark Charlap and Jule Styne
BOOK ✶ Based on the J.M. Barrie play

First Performance

New York, Winter Garden Theater, 29 October 1954 (152 performances)
London, Aldwych Theatre, 29 December 1985 (73 performances)

Principal Characters

Peter Pan ✶ The boy who never grew up
Wendy, John, Michael, Liza
✶ The Darling children
Nana ✶ The dog
Mrs Darling
Mr Darling/Captain Hook ✶ A pirate
Smee ✶ His mate

Original New York Cast

Mary Martin, Kathy Nolan, Robert Harrington, Joseph Stafford, Heller Holiday,
Norman Shelley, Margalo Gillmore, Cyril Ritchard, Joe E. Marks

Original London Cast

Bonnie Langford, Annabelle Lanyon, Grant Olding/Ross Dawes/
Matthew McNeany, Martin Harvey/Julian Wright/Alexander Wright, Lisa Kent,
Tim Flannigan, Judith Bruce, Joss Ackland, Edward Phillips

Plot

Mr and Mrs Darling go out, leaving their children under the protection of their dog, Nana. Nana sees a young boy appear in the middle of the room, but before she can catch him, he flies out of the window. She did grab his shadow, however, which Mrs Darling tucks away in a dresser drawer. Mr Darling insists that Nana be kennelled downstairs.

When the children are asleep a fairy, Tinkerbell, and Peter Pan fly in. They recover the shadow (which belongs to Peter) but Peter can't stick it back on. Wendy wakes up and sews it in place.

Peter invites Wendy and the boys back to his home in Never Never Land, to meet his followers, the Lost Boys. Unfortunately the Lost Boys' enemies, the Pirates led by Captain Hook, intend to kill Peter. Hook has discovered the boys' secret hideout and is about to do his worst, when he hears the tick-tock of a clock from within his own sworn enemy, the Crocodile. Now the Indians appear, led by Tiger Lily. The boys are urged to shoot down a strange bird in the sky. They do, and it turns out to be Wendy. They bring her inside to make her well. They build her a house. Tinkerbell becomes jealous of Wendy, though the latter is now homesick. The boys wish they had parents too and Wendy offers her own. They all want to go to Wendy's home – except Peter. Wendy plans to come back to Never Never Land once a year to spring clean for him. Hook captures the boys one by one and poisons Peter's drink, which Tinkerbell swallows instead. She can only be restored to health if all who believe in fairies clap their hands. On board the pirate ship, Peter rescues the boys and Wendy, and Hook is finally consumed by the crocodile.

Back home the Darlings and Nana have been waiting for the return of the children. One night they all return through the open window, and their parents joyfully adopt the Lost Boys.

Years pass and Peter reappears at the window. He wakes Wendy, who is now grown up with her own child, Jane, and can't come to spring clean. But Jane can, however, and she flies away with Peter as the curtain falls.

Music and Songs

A fine selection of dramatic children's songs for a well-loved children's story provided by two sets of contributors, including 'I've gotta crow' (Peter and Wendy), 'Never Never Land' (Peter and Wendy), 'I'm flying' (Peter, Wendy and the Lost Boys), 'Hook's tango' (Hook), 'I won't grow up' (Peter and the Lost Boys) and 'Oh my mysterious lady' (Peter and Hook).

Did You Know?

✻ This was the fourth musical version of *Peter Pan* to be seen on Broadway (including one starring Jean Arthur, with music by Leonard Bernstein and featuring Boris Karloff as Hook).

✻ London had produced, virtually every year, its own staging of the play, with proceeds going to the Great Ormond Street Hospital for sick children.

✻ The name Wendy was created by J.M. Barrie. A young girl referred to the author as 'My (f)Wendy'.

✻ Both Mary Martin and Cyril Ritchard won Tony awards for their performances in the original production.

✻ Traditionally Peter has been played by a girl (until an RSC production of the original play in recent times).

The Critics

'Its air of high spirits keeps away the curse of excessive sentimentality' – *New York Post*
'It's the way *Peter Pan* should have been and wasn't' – *New York Herald Tribune*
'Inventiveness and delight' – *New York Times*

Recommended Recording

Original Broadway cast (CD) RCA Victor 3762-2-RG
Mary Martin made this part her own on stage and television and she performs beautifully on this disc. However, it is in glorious mono and if you want stereo then Cathy Rigby is America's newest Peter and there is a fine recording of her performance on **JAY CDJAY 1280**.

The Phantom of the Opera

LYRICS ✱ Charles Hart
MUSIC ✱ Andrew Lloyd Webber
BOOK ✱ Richard Stilgoe, based on the novel by Gaston Leroux

First Performance

London, Her Majesty's Theatre, 9 October 1986 (still running)
New York, Majestic Theater, 26 January 1988 (still running)

Principal Characters

Christine Daae ✱ A young soprano
The Phantom of the Opera
Messrs Firmin and André ✱ Lessees of the theatre
Carlotta ✱ A principal soprano
Raoul de Chagny ✱ Christine's admirer

Original London Cast

Sarah Brightman, Michael Crawford, John Savident, David Firth,
Rosemary Ashe, Steve Barton

Original New York Cast

Sarah Brightman, Michael Crawford, Cris Groendaal, Nicholas Wyman,
Judy Kaye, Steve Barton

Plot

We're at an auction of items from the Paris Opera House. Here is a musical box, there a chandelier that featured in a famous accident. Suddenly it rises up to the top of the theatre, and the action moves back several decades.

Christine Daae is a young member of the chorus of the Paris Opera. Unbeknown to all, she is helped by a Svengali, a vocal coach whom she has never seen. She believes him to be the spirit of the Angel of Music, promised to her as a guardian by her late father. The voice belongs to a phantom, the Phantom of the Opera, a facially disfigured genius who lives in the hidden passages of the opera house. He's fallen in love with his young student. He terrorises the theatre's administrators into mounting a production of the opera, *Don Juan Triumphant*. He also frightens the leading soprano, Carlotta, and causes the gigantic chandelier to crash into the auditorium.

But the Phantom cannot accept the mutual affection between Christine and a young nobleman, Raoul de Chagny. He kidnaps Christine, taking her down to his secret apartments beneath the theatre, on its underground lake. By this time he has committed murder, as well as terrorising the theatre and its inhabitants. A party of avengers, led by Raoul, is searching for him. Christine tears off the

Phantom's mask and, though appalled by the wreck of his face, shows him compassion and tenderness. The Phantom now has it in his power to kill Raoul, but her action has melted his spirit and he disappears, leaving Christine safely reunited with her lover as the show ends.

Music and Songs

A sumptuous score with elements conjuring up the glories of Meyerbeer and Puccini. It includes among its hits the title song (The Phantom), 'All I ask of you' (Raoul and Christine) and 'Music of the night' (The Phantom), plus 'Think of me' (Christine), 'Angel of music' (Christine and The Phantom) and 'Wishing you were somehow here again' (Christine).

Did You Know?

∗ *The Phantom of the Opera* has proved to be one of the most successful musicals of all time, in terms of audience numbers.

∗ There have been at least four films of the original story, and three other musical adaptations, of which that by Maury Yeston is the most current.

∗ Andrew Lloyd Webber started working on a collaboration with Ken Hill who had produced his own version of the story. When Lloyd Webber went on his own the Ken Hill version toured successfully all over the world.

The Critics

The critics were, in general, not too kind:
'A romantic lyric spectacle with nothing abrasive about it and all ironies, such as they are, are carefully concealed' – *The Observer*
'For every sumptuously melodic love song in this score, there is an insufferably smug opera parody that can't match its prototype (Meyerbeer? Salieri?), a thrown-in pop number that slows the action or a jarring anachronistic descent into the vulgar synthesizer chords of *Starlight Express*' – *New York Times*
'The final moments as Christine rips off the mask and the lovers' triangle is resolved in a descent to the lair and an emotional farewell that are almost unbearably moving' – *The Guardian*

Recommended Recording

Original London cast (CD) Polydor 831 273-2
The original and best recording, with the thrill of fresh-voiced Sarah Brightman and her electric partnership with Michael Crawford. Rosemary Ashe as Carlotta is a formidable plus.

Pickwick

LYRICS ✶ Leslie Bricusse
MUSIC ✶ Cyril Ornadel
BOOK ✶ Wolf Mankowitz, based on Charles Dickens'
Posthumous Papers of the Pickwick Club

First Performance

London, Saville Theatre, 4 July 1963 (694 performances)
New York, 46th Street Theater, 4 October 1965 (56 performances)

Principal Characters

Pickwick ✶ Our hero
Mrs Bardell ✶ An amorous widow
Jingle ✶ A peculiar fellow
Rachel Wardle ✶ A young girl
Sam Weller ✶ A jack of all trades

Original London Cast

Harry Secombe, Jessie Evans, Anton Rodgers, Hilda Braid, Teddy Green

Original New York Cast

Harry Secombe, Charlotte Rae, Anton Rodgers, Helena Carroll, Roy Castle

Plot

As the original story was offered in instalments in magazine form, its episodic nature has not given rise to a structured narrative. The backbone, if one exists at all, is formed by the entertaining characters who take part in the action.

The jolly, jocund Mr Pickwick is at the centre of a group of friends who experience a series of adventures in the early Victorian era. Mr Pickwick himself is the subject of a case for breach of promise, brought by the amorous Mrs Bardell, who is over-optimistic as to Pickwick's intentions, but yet she wins her case in the courts. We first meet Pickwick in prison where he remembers events from his life so far, including his first meeting with his servant, Sam Weller.

A friend, Mr Jingle, 'a bit of a character', gets involved with Rachel Wardle. There's an ice-skating party which brings its own share of spills and excitement. The characters, some of Dickens' most richly comic, come vividly to life in this Christmas card of a musical, and none more so than Sam, Mr Pickwick's eager and endlessly inventive servant.

The Eatanswill election is the location for the show's principal song, 'If I ruled the world'. By the end of the show, Mr Pickwick and his friends have solved all the problems for themselves and others, and can settle back into the happy and companionable fellowship for which the Pickwick Club was formed, even if the club itself is now dissolved.

Music and Songs

The score's popular hit is 'If I ruled the world' (Pickwick), and it also includes a fine bundle of ballads and old music hall-type ditties to keep the evening alive. The composer was a prominent conductor of musicals, and he learned a lot in the process. Other telling numbers are 'Business is booming' (the debtors' lament), 'That's what I'd like for Christmas' (Pickwick and friends), 'You never met a feller like me' (Sam and Pickwick) and 'The trouble with women' (the Wellers).

Did You Know?

✶ One critic described the show as 'Comic Strip Dickens', but since the original stories were in instalments anyway, perhaps this was not such a bad thing.

✶ The pre-Broadway tour featured Davy (The Monkees) Jones as Sam Weller.

✶ The hit song 'If I ruled the world' spent 17 weeks in the British top 20.

✶ Lyricist Leslie Bricusse also wrote the film and subsequent stage musical *Scrooge*, another adaptation from Dickens. On that occasion he also provided the music.

The Critics

'Mr Secombe sings, does two cartwheels and often looks very like the Pickwick of the original illustrations' – *The Guardian*
'Cyril Ornadel has written lively music to effective lyrics by Leslie Bricusse' – *The Daily Telegraph*
'What the musical fails to do – and it is a serious flaw in a Dickens adaptation – is to bring the main characters to life' – *The Times*

Recommended Recording

1993 revival cast (CD) TER CDTER 12
The original cast version of this show has not been issued on CD. However, this Chichester cast version also starred Harry Secombe (now more the correct age for the part) and it is difficult to picture anyone else playing it. He sounds little different than he did thirty years before and this recording has an excellent supporting cast. It is, therefore, a good substitute for the original.

Film

A BBC television adaptation starring Harry Secombe was shown in Great Britain and the United States.

Pippin

LYRICS ✶ Stephen Schwartz
MUSIC ✶ Stephen Schwartz
BOOK ✶ Roger O. Hirson

First Performance

New York, Imperial Theater, 23 October 1972 (1944 performances)
London, Her Majesty's Theatre, 30 October 1973 (85 performances)

Principal Characters

Charles (Charlemagne)
Catherine ✶ Pippin's love
Fastrada ✶ His stepmother
Berthe ✶ His grandmother
Leading Player
Pippin ✶ The young king

Original New York Cast

Eric Berry, Jill Clayburgh, Leland Palmer, Irene Ryan,
Ben Vereen, John Rubinstein

Original London Cast

John Turner, Patricia Hodge, Diane Langton, Elisabeth Welch,
Northern J. Calloway, Paul Jones

Plot

A Leading Player, a master of ceremonies, at the head of a group of *commedia dell'arte* players, tells the story of the son of King Charlemagne. This son is Pippin, and he goes out on a journey of self-enlightenment. Naturally he encounters many of the seven deadly sins on the way, and is scarred and influenced by them. They include War, Sins of the Flesh, Revolution and Insurrection and, indeed, stepmothers. Incidentally, his own stepmother has a narcissistic son whose cause she promotes vehemently. Pippin hopes to bring honour, justice and freedom to his own kingdom. Of course he fails.

He seeks advice from his old grandmother but, in the end, even though he gets a wife and a child, Pippin appears to paint himself into a corner. Nothing gives him any satisfaction. Is Death the ultimate satisfaction? This is a situation from which he can only be extricated by stopping the plot and having the scenery disappear. The show closes with Pippin, his wife and child alone before the Leading Player.

Music and Songs

A highly catchy score, flavoured with what was then current pop, that confirmed Schwartz's fine talent, first shown in *Godspell*, that has yet to realise its full potential. Numbers include 'Magic to do' (Leading Player), 'Corner of the sky' (Pippin), 'No time at all' (Berthe), 'Glory' (Leading Player and soldiers) and 'I guess I'll miss the man' (Catherine).

Did You Know?

∗ The show seemed to stand or fall because of Bob Fosse's dazzling staging of the numbers, which proved more successful in America than in Britain.

∗ However, the composer established an important principle, when an Australian production was allowed by law to differ markedly from Fosse's original.

∗ This was one of the first shows to use a TV advertising campaign effectively and efficiently in the USA.

∗ The show won five Tony awards.

∗ Irene Ryan of the original Broadway cast played the grandmother in *The Beverly Hillbillies* television series.

The Critics

'The staging by Bob Fosse. This is fantastic. It takes a painfully ordinary little show and launches it into space' – *New York Times*

Recommended Recording

Original Broadway cast (CD) Motown MCD 09088 MD
Stephen Schwartz at his best with a great cast. Close your eyes and the wonderful Bob Fosse staging comes back right before them.

Video

A video of the Broadway production has been issued. It stars William Katt as Pippin and Chita Rivera as Fastrada.

The Pirates of Penzance, or A Slave to Duty

LYRICS ✶ W.S. Gilbert
MUSIC ✶ Arthur Sullivan
BOOK ✶ W.S. Gilbert

First Performance

Paignton (England), Bijou Theatre, 30 December 1879 (1 performance)
London, Opera Comique, 3 April 1880 (363 performances)
New York, Fifth Avenue Theatre, 31 December 1879 (three seasons within five months)

Principal Characters

Frederic ✶ An apprentice pirate
Mabel ✶ A young lass
Pirate King ✶ The leader of the pirates
Major-General Stanley ✶ Mabel's father
Ruth ✶ Frederic's nurse

Original New York Cast

Hugh Talbot, Blanche Roosevelt, Sgr. Broccolini, J.H. Riley, Alice Barnett

Original London Cast

George Power, Marion Hood, Richard Temple, George Grossmith, Emily Cross

Plot

The pirates are on a Penzance beach, their ship anchored while they toast Frederic on his twenty-first birthday and the end of his pirate apprenticeship. Frederic has no intention of remaining a pirate for he never intended to be one – his apprenticeship had been a mistake made by Ruth, his nurse, who had confused the word pirate with pilot. Ruth tries to convince him that she is a perfect example of womanhood, a lie soon exposed when pretty young maidens arrive. The last to come is Mabel and she, unlike her sisters, approves of the young man and shows it. When the pirates see the girls they want to make them their wives but their father, the major-general, declares himself an orphan, and as orphans themselves the pirates will do no harm to a kindred fellow, so they are all set free.

In the ruins of their Gothic mausoleum home the major-general and his daughters worry that the lie will be detected. Frederic is out to capture the pirates with the local police force but he is visited by the Pirate King and Ruth who announce that, in fact, his apprenticeship is not yet finished for, as his birthday is on the 29 February, he has had only four birthdays. As a pirate apprentice once more he is again a 'slave of duty' and tells of the major-general's lie.

The police know about the pirates and surround the mausoleum awaiting their arrival. They do not have long to wait and once the Pirate King has his sword at the ready to kill the major-general they attack, only to lose the fight. The sergeant has the winning hand, however, and charges them to yield in the name of Queen Victoria. The pirates are, of course, loyal British pirates and they indeed yield. It is then their turn to be released as Ruth announces they are noblemen who can return to society – which they do, each with one of the major-general's daughters.

Music and Songs

A major Gilbert and Sullivan score discovered by many when Broadway decided to give it an update. There is a wonderful mix of patter songs, ballads and rousing chorus numbers, including 'I am the very model of a modern major-general' (Major-General), 'With cat-like tread' (Samuel and chorus of Pirates) and 'Poor wand'ring one' (Mabel).

Did You Know?

∗ The first performance at Paignton was for copyright reasons and to stop an American production opening first; the show opened the next day in New York.

∗ The American revival with new orchestrations and a slightly augmented score ran 787 performances, which was longer than any other G&S production. The London run of that production in 1983 was 601 performances.

The Critics

'Taken as a whole the music to *The Pirates of Penzance* did not seem quite equal to that of the *Pinafore*. The libretto, for of this alone we are now speaking, is as full of drolleries and amusing conceit as anything that has proceeded from the same pen' – *The Times*

'On the first night the satisfaction of the crowded audience was boundless, culminating in the call before the curtain of the performers including the four and twenty maidens and the authors. Of the rendering we can speak in brief and highly favourable terms' – *The Times*

Recommended Recording

Revival Broadway cast (CD)
This re-orchestrated version may not be for the purist but it made the show accessible to a whole new generation of theatregoers, and could well have been the way Gilbert and Sullivan would have wanted it to sound. For those who prefer a move to the traditional, then Welsh National Opera under Sir Charles Mackerras do a fine job (**Telarc CD 80353**).

Plain and Fancy

LYRICS ✳ Arnold B. Horwitt
MUSIC ✳ Albert Hague
BOOK ✳ Joseph Stein and Will Glickman

First Performance

New York, Mark Hellinger Theatre, 27 January 1955 (461 performances)
London, Theatre Royal Drury Lane, 25 January 1956 (315 performances)

Principal Characters

Ruth Winter ✳ A New York sophisticate
Dan King ✳ A New York writer
Papa Yoder ✳ An Amish elder
Katie ✳ His daughter
Ezra Reber ✳ The suitor to Katie
Peter Reber ✳ His brother
Hilda Miller ✳ A young impressionable girl

Original New York Cast

Shirl Conway, Richard Derr, Stefan Schnabel, Gloria Marlowe, Douglas Fletcher
Rodgers, David Daniels, Barbara Cook

Original London Cast

Shirl Conway, Richard Derr, Malcolm Keen, Grace O'Connor, Reed de Roven,
Jack Drummond, Joan Hovis

Plot

On a road outside Lancaster, Pennsylvania, Ruth and Dan, two New Yorkers, are
lost. Dan is a writer and he is there to sell his grandfather's farm. They get
directions to Bird-in-Hand, a small Amish community, and pass Papa Yoder and
his daughter Katie in their buggy. She is to marry Ezra Reber in two days' time
and the farm Dan is selling is to be the wedding present. In town the preparations
for the wedding are underway. Peter Reber has returned after two years (he was
thrown out because of a fight) to see his brother wed. Peter had been pledged to
Katie before his exile and they are still in love.

Ruth is missing her creature comforts while Dan makes the mistake of telling
the young, impressionable Hilda that she is nice, a comment she mistakes for a
declaration of love. And, on that subject, Dan has a chat with Papa Yoder telling
him that Katie is in love with Peter and that they should be allowed to marry. Papa
does not agree. The brothers meet and Ezra jokes about Peter's past relationship
with Katie, whereupon Peter starts another fight. The barn on Dan's farm is struck
by lightning and burns down; to Yoder this is a sign that Peter should go and the
community turn their backs on him.

The community builds another barn and Peter pleads with Katie to leave with
him, but she can't. Ruth thinks she is helping Ezra by giving him a drink, and in

his drunken state he runs off to a carnival playing in the next town. Hilda now understands that Dan does not love her and so she follows her heart and runs after Ezra. At the carnival Ezra gets into a fight and Peter saves him. Yoder is no longer happy about Katie marrying Ezra and sees that Peter was trying to help both his brother and the community. Peter is forgiven and he takes Katie's hand. At the wedding Dan, who at last has been able to voice his love for Ruth, passes the key of the farm to the young couple.

Music and Songs

This show successfully compared modern life (represented by the New Yorkers) with the simple beliefs of the Amish without making fun of it. The score does the same. The hit song was 'Young and foolish' (Peter and Katie) and other charm songs include 'Plain we live' (Papa Yoder and Amish men) and 'It wonders me' (Katie). The New York side is represented with 'It's a helluva way to run a love affair' (Ruth) and 'City mouse, country mouse' (Emma and Amish wives).

Did You Know?

✶ An Amish couple assisted as advisers on the show but were unable to see it as their religion does not allow theatre visits.

✶ Barbara Cook took another step forward in her career with this, the first show in which she originated a part.

✶ The composer Albert Hague is better known now as the older male teacher in the television series *Fame*.

The Critics

'A remarkably pleasant score' – *New York Times*
'A completely captivating musical hit ... one of the most original musicals ... it has everything – the best of everything' – *Daily Mirror*

Recommended Recording

Original Broadway cast (CD) Broadway Angel ZDM 7 64762 2 3
Maybe not the greatest Broadway score but one with many pleasures, not least the performances of Shirl Conway, Richard Derr and Barbara Cook. A pleasant addition to any collection.

The Producers

LYRICS ✳ Mel Brooks
MUSIC ✳ Mel Brooks
BOOK ✳ Mel Brooks and Thomas Meehan, based on
the film *The Producers*

First Performance

New York, St James Theater, 19 April 2001 (still running)

Principal Characters

Max Bialystock ✳ A Broadway producer
Leo Bloom ✳ His accountant
Roger de Bris ✳ The director
Carmen Ghia ✳ The director's boyfriend
Ulla ✳ The secretary
Franz Liebkind ✳ A playwright

Original New York Cast

Nathan Lane, Matthew Broderick, Roger Bart, Gary Beach,
Cady Huffman, Brad Oscar

Plot

It is 1959 and the show opens on Broadway's Shubert Alley where Max Bialystock's latest flop has opened. A few days later, Max's books are being audited by his timid accountant, Leo Bloom, who comments that it would be possible to make more money out of a flop than a hit by raising more money than needed. It is not long before he is not just dreaming of becoming a producer but has become Max's business partner.

Max and Leo set about finding the worst play ever written and they find it in Franz Liebkind's *Springtime for Hitler, a Gay Romp with Adolf and Eva at Berchtesgaden*. The search for the worst director brings them to the extravagantly camp Roger de Bris and his boyfriend Carmen. Now they need a secretary and they cannot resist the physical charms of the blonde Swedish Ulla. Max starts his hunt for show angels to raise two million dollars and for this he throws himself into 'Little Old Lady Land'.

We move on. Max has successfully raised the money and it is opening night. He is doing everything possible to bring bad luck to the production and even their star breaks his leg and the director has to go on in his place. It all goes awry and *Springtime for Hitler* is an instant critical and financial success. Max is arrested and Leo runs off with Ulla and the money to Rio. But, at Max's trial Leo returns and they are each sentenced to five years in Sing Sing, where they produce their new musical *Prisoners of Love*. For this they get a pardon and, back on Broadway, they present the non-convict version starring, once again, Roger de Bris. It is a hit and Leo and Max are happy, as well as being Broadway's most successful producers.

Music and Songs

No stage version of this popular film could omit 'Springtime for Hitler' and 'Prisoners of love', the two over-the-top songs from the film. The rest of the score is new with Leo and Max duos 'We can do it' and 'Where did we go wrong?', Leo's 'I wanna be a producer' and Max's 'Betrayed' showing the talent of Mel Brooks to write a traditional old-style-of-Broadway score. As Max and Leo, Nathan Lane and Matthew Broderick prove to be the perfect foil for each other. But the laughs are not only with them; the questionable taste of songs such as 'In old Bavaria' and 'Keep it gay' make this a unique score and the Swedish sex goddess's 'When you got it, flaunt it' tends to prove it's not art we're listening to but good old-fashioned naughtiness.

Did You Know?

★ *The Producers* holds the record for the number of Tony awards, having received 12 from a record 15 nominations.

★ Mel Brooks originally asked Jerry Herman to write the score but Herman persuaded Brooks to write it himself.

★ *The Producers* is Broadway's biggest critical and financial success since *The Lion King*.

★ Originally Mike Ockrent and his wife Susan Stroman were to direct and choreograph the show, but when he died she took over the direction.

The Critics

'*The Producers* is a cast-iron, copper-bottomed, superduper, mammoth old-time Broadway hit' – *New York Post*
'No new musical for ages has offered so much imagination, so much sheer pleasure' – *New York Daily News*
'Whether *The Producers* should be classified as a Broadway musical or a party exploding eight times a week at the St James Theater can be debated. However you choose to describe it, the show is a rip-roaring, gut-busting, rib-tickling, knee-slapping, aisle-rolling (insert your own compound adjective here) good time' – *Variety*

Recommended Recording

Original Broadway Cast (CD) Sony Classical SK 89646
An outlandishly comic, and sometimes adult, musical that brings back to Broadway one of those scores which, although not brilliant in musical and lyrical content, is just plain fun. If you've been asking 'Whatever happened to musical comedy?', the answer is 'Waiting for this to arrive.'

Film

Embassy, 1968. Starring Zero Mostel, Gene Wilder and Dick Shawn. Directed by Mel Brooks.

Rent

LYRICS ✷ Jonathan Larson
MUSIC ✷ Jonathan Larson
BOOK ✷ Jonathan Larson,
inspired by Puccini's *La Bohème*

First Performance

New York, Theater Workshop, 23 February 1996
Transferred to Nederlander Theater, 29 March 1996 (still running)
London, Shaftesbury Theatre, 12 May 1998 (614 performances)

Principal Characters

Roger Davis ✷ A songwriter
Mark Cohen ✷ A film maker
Angel Schunard ✷ A musician
Tom Collins ✷ A friend of Mark's
Benjamin Coffin III (Benjy) ✷ A property developer
Joanne Jefferson ✷ Maureen's new friend
Mimi Marquez ✷ A junkie
Maureen Johnson ✷ Mark's ex-girlfriend

Original New York Cast

Adam Pascal, Anthony Rapp, Wilson Jermaine-Heredia, Jesse L. Martin,
Taye Diggs, Fredi Walker, Daphne Rubin-Vega, Idina Menzel

Original London Cast

Adam Pascal, Anthony Rapp, Wilson Jermaine Heredia, Jesse L. Martin,
Bonny Lockhart, Jacqui Dubois, Krysten Cummings, Jessica Tezier

Plot

It's Christmas Eve in an East Village loft in New York, and Roger Davis is trying to write a song. His flatmate, Mark, a film maker, taunts Roger about his writer's block. Mark has his problems – he's lost his girlfriend, Maureen, an actress, to a woman. A friend, Collins, rings from a payphone downstairs – he's being mugged. Then it's their former flatmate, now landlord, Benjy, demanding rent. Mark agrees to help Maureen with her performance piece that night. Collins is rescued by Angel, a street musician, and they discover that both are HIV positive. Roger is too, and takes his AZT (an AIDS drug).

The doorbell rings – it's Mimi, a junkie from downstairs. She and Roger are instantly attracted to each other. Mark returns with Collins, Angel, food and money. Now Benjy arrives; can they stop Maureen's performance? If they can, then he'll forget the rent. Mark meets Maureen's lover Joanne, and they find they can get on together. Angel buys Collins an overcoat.

The performance piece protesting against Benjy's commercial development goes ahead, and Benjy is livid. Mimi reveals to Roger that she also has to take AZT as she and Roger share the same illness. A riot breaks out and Benjy has Roger and Mark locked out of their building.

On New Year's Eve they break back into the building, and Mark films it. Benjy turns up with new keys for Mark and Roger, implying that he's softened his attitude since Mimi, an old flame, has slept with him. Roger doesn't believe Mimi's protestations of innocence.

By Valentine's Day, Roger and Mimi are living together, but Roger is still jealous. Throughout the spring, summer and autumn the couples split and come together again. Angel dies. Mark accepts a TV job and Roger decides to leave New York for Santa Fe. Benjy offers to pay for Mimi's drug rehabilitation. She runs away. Benjy pays for Angel's funeral and finds a new friend in Collins.

It's another Christmas Eve. Roger is back, finishing the same song that he started a year earlier. Maureen and Joanne arrive, bringing a desperately ill Mimi with them. Roger sings his new song to her and she drifts away, only to return to life. She believes she's been steered back through a warm, white light by Angel. Love is the strongest force and there is 'No day but today'.

Music and Songs

The whole score is written in a soft rock idiom – nothing out of the way that might frighten off conventional Broadway patrons – and includes 'Rent' (Mark and Roger), 'Seasons of love' (the company), 'Out tonight' (Mimi), 'Another day' (Roger and Mimi), 'I should tell you' (Roger and Mimi), 'Take me or leave me' (Mark and Mimi), 'Your eyes' (Roger), 'Over the moon' (Mark and Maureen) and 'No day but today' (the company).

Did You Know?

✶ The author/composer died on 25 January 1996, just as *Rent* was about to open; he was never to know the huge success it would achieve.

✶ The show has been awarded a Pulitzer Prize and several Tonys.

✶ *Rent* was to prove Broadway's hottest ticket of the 1996 season.

✶ Although New York critical opinion was good, the London *Daily Mail*'s Jack Tinker, in one of the last reviews he filed, did not agree with the consensus.

The Critics

'*Rent* is ready to bring down the house' – *Toronto Sun*
'*Rent* is brilliant and messy all at once' – *The New York Sunday Times*

Recommended Recording

Original Broadway cast (CD) Dreamworks DRD 50003
This soft rock score is served well by the original Broadway cast. The London production was not recorded.

The Rink

LYRICS ✳ Fred Ebb
MUSIC ✳ John Kander
BOOK ✳ Terrence McNally

First Performance

New York, Martin Beck Theater, 9 February 1984 (294 performances)
London, Cambridge Theatre, 17 February 1988 (38 performances), following a
short run at the Manchester Library Theatre earlier that year

Principal Characters

Anna Antonelli
Angel ✳ Her daughter

Original New York Cast

Chita Rivera, Liza Minnelli

Original London Cast

Josephine Blake, Diane Langton

Plot

It's fifteen years since Angel Antonelli has been to the broken-down roller rink run
by her mother, Anna, at the seaside. But she's back now. It's the late '70s and Anna
has hugely resented Angel's absence. They quarrel, of course.

In flashback, the ill-assorted pair recall events in their life: the drifter, Angel's
husband, who gives his wife blue crystal; her fifth birthday, when Daddy Dino
returns from Vietnam. He's not at all the same man who went off to war – now he's
drunk and moody.

Back in the present Angel realises her mother is selling the rink, and has forged
Angel's signature on the necessary documents. Angel can stop it, perhaps. But
things have changed. The area is being bulldozed and rebuilt. And it's revealed that
Anna has been raped and robbed by teenage hoodlums. But Angel won't give up her
dreams of coloured lights and magic.

Angel shares some marijuana with her mother. Who will be Anna's companion
on a trip to Rome? Will it be good old reliable Lenny who hangs around in hope?
Anna remembers how her husband, Dino, walked out on her and his child. Angel
was told he had died, although he hadn't. And in the early '60s her drunken uncle
told Angel the truth. At that point Angel left home.

Now it's the present. There's a small child in the entrance to the rink – Angel's
young daughter. Her name is Anna. And she's fatherless. The generations forgive
each other and embrace as the last vestiges of the old rink are removed for ever.

Music and Songs

Kander and Ebb provide an alert, witty, gutsy score, tingling with rhythm, that fits the trenchant and hard-edged story of two survivors. Numbers include 'Coloured lights' (Angel), 'Blue crystal' (Dino), 'We can make it' (Anna and Angel), 'Marry me' (Lenny) and 'Wallflower' (Anna and Angel).

Did You Know?

∗ The adult members of the cast, apart from Anna and Angel, of whatever sex, were played by the male gang of wreckers – all on roller skates.

∗ The show was originally intended as a vehicle for Chita Rivera, but when Liza Minnelli (another Kander and Ebb favourite) was signed as well, the flavour and emphasis changed.

∗ Members of the British cast chipped in with their savings when it was proposed to bring the production they were in to London. Unhappily they lost their investment.

∗ Chita Rivera won a Tony Award for her performance.

The Critics

'The show explodes like a small hand grenade in a bag of cookies' – *The Sunday Times*
'Two hours of big tunes and outsize emotions' – *Time Magazine*

Recommended Recording

Original Broadway cast (CD) Polydor 823 125-2 Y-1
Two great stars, a fabulous score and a terrific recording. The London recording has style and good performances but lacks the verve of the original.

Rio Rita

LYRICS * Joseph McCarthy
MUSIC * Harry Tierney
BOOK * Guy Bolton and Fred Thompson

First Performance

New York, Ziegfeld Theater, 2 February 1927 (494 performances)
London, Prince Edward Theatre, 3 April 1930 (59 performances)

Principal Characters

Rio Rita Ferguson
Captain Jim Stewart * A Texas ranger
Chick Beam * A comic relief
Ed Lovett * Another one
Dolly * A friend of Chick and Ed
General Romero Joselito Esteban

Original New York Cast

Ethelind Terry, J. Harold Murray, Bert Wheeler, Robert Woolsey,
Ada May, Vincent Serrano

Original London Cast

Edith Day, Geoffrey Gwyther, Leslie Sarony, George Gee,
Rita Page, Bernard Nedell

Plot

Texas ranger, Captain Jim Stewart, is at work south of the border in Mexico, hunting the notorious bandit known as the Kinkajou. He also has more than a passing eye for the charms of Rio Rita Ferguson. What he doesn't know, is that she is also the object of the attentions of General Esteban (who will do anything to break up any incipient romance). The general attempts to persuade Rita that her brother is the bandit – and, for good measure, convinces Jim of it too. He also tries to make Rita believe that Jim's only interest in her is to use her to capture her brother.

As the general moves in on Rita, he tries to make her pretend that he, the general, is Jim. This only makes Rita realise how much she is in love with the real Jim. There's just the little problem of her brother to solve. By the closing curtain, however, the real bandit is unmasked. It is the general himself who is the Kinkajou; her brother is released, and Rita is finally united with her Jim.

Music and Songs

A lusty score of its period that today sounds charmingly old-fashioned and a little four-square, including the songs 'Rio Rita' (Jim), 'The rangers' song' (the chorus), 'The Kinkajou', (Dolly and the chorus), 'If you're in love you'll waltz' (Rita) and 'You're always in my arms' (Rita).

Did You Know?

✳ This was the show chosen by Florenz Ziegfeld to open the new Broadway theatre he'd named after himself. *Rio Rita* represented an old-fashioned contrast to the more up-to-date *Irene*, with which the creative collaborators had just had a great success.

✳ *Rio Rita* also had the distinction of being the first show at the newly-built Prince Edward Theatre in London's Soho.

✳ Because the first film was released in Britain ahead of the first London stage presentation, the show suffered badly and only achieved 59 performances.

✳ Ziegfeld had originally wanted *Show Boat* to open his new theatre but then changed his mind, and so *Show Boat* was not produced for another year.

The Critics

'Just a convenience for the display of handsome scenes and glamorous costumes' – Donald Ewen
'The music is tuneful and taking enough' – *The Stage*

Recommended Recording

At the time of writing there has been no CD issue of this score and on LP only two short versions exist (**World Record Club LZ 7063** which couples with *The Great Waltz* and **RCA Victor LK 1026** with *A Connecticut Yankee*).

Films

RKO, 1929. Starring Bebe Daniels, John Boles, and Wheeler and Woolsey. Directed by Luther Reed.
MGM, 1942. Starring Bud Abbott and Lou Costello, with Kathryn Grayson. Directed by Sylvan Simon.

The Roar of the Greasepaint, the Smell of the Crowd

LYRICS ✶ Leslie Bricusse and Anthony Newley
MUSIC ✶ Leslie Bricusse and Anthony Newley
BOOK ✶ Leslie Bricusse and Anthony Newley

First Performance

Nottingham, Theatre Royal, 3 August 1964 , then Liverpool,
Newcastle and Manchester to 30 October 1964
New York, Shubert Theater, 16 May 1965 (232 performances)

Principal Characters

Cocky
Sir
The Kid
The Girl
The Negro
The Bully

Original Nottingham Cast

Norman Wisdom, Willoughby Goddard, Sally Smith, Dilys Watling,
Cy Grant, Bruce Wells

Original New York Cast

Anthony Newley, Cyril Ritchard, Sally Smith, Joyce Jillson,
Gilbert Price, Murray Tannenbaum

Plot

There are always winners and losers. In this show it's Sir who wins and Cocky
who loses. Sir insists that the 'haves' must always retain their position in charge,
even if the rules of the game need to be stretched to accommodate them and their
stratagems. Each time Cocky tries to win, he's frustrated by new rules – he'll never
be a gentleman! Not if Sir has anything to do with it, anyway.

And each time he loses there are new rules to be written in the rule book. In a
mock ceremony Cocky is crowned King, but it's only so that he can be mocked by
Sir and the attendant urchins; the Girl he thinks he's won is taken over by Sir. In
order to heap on further humiliation, Sir urges Cocky to play the game over and
over again – perhaps he'll win next time?

A Negro enters and wants to play the game. Has Cocky found someone worse
off than himself? Cocky becomes even more overbearing than Sir. This gives

Cocky a confidence he's able to use against Sir who, for the first time, backs down. Cocky wins the game at last and proposes new rules – his own – for the game. Yet each needs the other. The way ahead lies in sharing the load as they work towards a future with a mutual understanding.

Music and Songs

The Newley/Bricusse partnership has always produced great, full-impact, romantic and show-stopping songs. 'Who can I turn to?' (Cocky), 'Feeling good' (Negro), 'A wonderful day like today' (Sir and Cocky) and 'Look at that face' (Cocky) are just four standards from a superb score that also includes 'The joker' (Cocky) and 'Nothing can stop me now' (Cocky).

Did You Know?

✷ The failure of the British try-out, where audiences were unwilling to accept Norman Wisdom in the principal role, meant no London run. David Merrick took it to Broadway, but insisted on co-author Anthony Newley taking the lead.

✷ The second Broadway hit for the Bricusse/Newley partnership. And again they composed a score where the numbers could be lifted from the score so that they could have a recording life all of their own. Because of this they ended up with four new song standards.

The Critics

The critics were varied in their response:
'A delightful, freshly imaginative show with a most haunting score' – *New York Post*
'There is so much exuberance in this show especially amongst its chorus of small female urchins that you'd feel like a traitor if you didn't enjoy yourself' – *New York World Telegram & Sun*
'A rousing hurrah! Everything about the show is imaginative' – *New York Daily News*
'Third-rate commerce masquerading as art' – *New York Herald Tribune*

Recommended Recording

Original Broadway cast (CD) RCA Victor 60351-2-RG
The only complete recording of this score and the definitive version. Anthony Newley and Cyril Ritchard are perfectly balanced in their roles as Cocky and Sir.

Roberta

LYRICS ✳ Otto Harbach
MUSIC ✳ Jerome Kern
BOOK ✳ Otto Harbach,
based on Alice Duer Miller's novel *Gowns by Roberta*

First Performance

New York, New Amsterdam Theater, 18 November 1933 (295 performances)

Principal Characters

Clementina Scharwenka ✳ An actress
Huckleberry Haines ✳ An actor
Aunt Minnie ✳ Owner of a dress shop
Stephanie ✳ A designer
Billy Boyden
Lord Henry Delves ✳ An Englishman
John Kent ✳ Our hero
Sophie Teal ✳ His fiancée

Original New York Cast

Lyda Roberti, Bob Hope, Fay Templeton, Tamara, George Murphy,
Sydney Greenstreet, Raymond Middleton, Helen Gray

Plot

When American footballer, John Kent, inherits a Parisian modiste's shop after a visit to his old Aunt Minnie, whose professional name was 'Roberta', he moves to Paris to take up the reins, especially as he's just been jilted by his debutante fiancée, Sophie. Once there he makes a number of mistakes due to the clash of cultures between America and Europe. Meanwhile, he has become close to the incumbent principal designer, Stephanie, who turns out to be a Russian princess in exile.

Aided and abetted by two American theatrical friends, Huckleberry Haines and Clementina Scharwenka, John and Stephanie battle through misunderstandings. John's American ex-girlfriend comes to Paris to make up with him, but by this time John is on his way to a final reunion with Stephanie. The show culminates in a gigantic fashion parade which cements the fortunes of 'Gowns by Roberta', and gives John and Stephanie a real reason to celebrate.

Music and Songs

The score features the florid romanticism of middle-period Jerome Kern, a style that still harks back to operetta, with zippy numbers that also point forward to the golden age that Kern was helping to inaugurate. Instant standards from the show include 'Smoke gets in your eyes' (Stephanie) and 'Yesterdays' (Stephanie and Aunt Minnie), plus 'The touch of your hand' (John), 'I'll be hard to handle' (Clementina) and 'You're devastating' (Huckleberry and Stephanie).

Did You Know?

✳ The veteran Fay Templeton, who played 'Roberta', who dies shortly after the show opens, was so heavy that her part was written to enable her to spend most of the role seated.

✳ The tune of 'You're devastating' had turned up previously as 'Do I do wrong?' in the British musical *Blue Eyes* about Bonnie Prince Charlie. 'I won't dance', added to the 1935 film, came from the British show *Three Sisters*.

✳ Bob Hope, George Murphy and Fred MacMurray all made their Broadway debuts in *Roberta*.

The Critics

'Kern may have abandoned some of the more unusual methods adopted in early musical plays, but his melodic touch had lost none of its magic' – David Gwen

Recommended Recording

Studio cast (CD) CBS Special Products A 7030
The only CD issue. The cast is Joan Roberts, Jack Cassidy, Kaye Ballard, Portia Nelson and Stephen Douglass. With a cast like this it has to be good, and it is.

Films

RKO, 1935. Starring Irene Dunne, Fred Astaire and Ginger Rogers. Directed by William A. Seiter.
MGM, 1952. Starring Kathryn Grayson, Howard Keel, Red Skelton, and Marge and Gower Champion. Directed by Mervyn LeRoy. The film was retitled *Lovely To Look At.*

Robert and Elizabeth

LYRICS ✶ Ronald Millar
MUSIC ✶ Ron Grainer
BOOK ✶ Ronald Millar, based on the unproduced musical *The Third Kiss*
by Fred G. Moritt, adapted from the play *The Barretts of Wimpole Street*
by Rudolph Besier

First Performance

London, Lyric Theatre, 20 October 1964 (948 performances)

Principal Characters

Edward Moulton-Barrett
Elizabeth Barrett ✶ His daughter
Robert Browning ✶ A poet
Henrietta
Captain Surtees Cook

Original London Cast

John Clements, June Bronhill, Keith Michell, Angela Richards, Jeremy Lloyd

Plot

London in 1845 is not a happy place for Elizabeth Barrett, an invalid confined to bed in a house where her widowed father rules his large young family with severity. She has, however, established a correspondence with a fellow poet, Robert Browning. When he walks into her room and talks to her of love, she gains a new strength to live a fuller life, and to rise from her bed. Her father will have none of this. An invalid she is, and an invalid she shall stay, totally dominated by his somewhat extreme and unnatural concern for her. He has Browning's visits stopped. Elizabeth is heartbroken and retires to bed. However, Browning is not so easily put off.

Wimpole Street is not the ideal place to bring up a large family. Mr Barrett will move to the country. Meanwhile, Browning has a plan. Elizabeth and he will move to Italy, where she can pursue her love of poetry and grow well in a healthier, outdoor climate, taking her servant and her dog, Flush, with her. Mr Barrett gets wind of this, and tries to stop the couple at the railway station. Parental love, he avers, is the highest form of all. Elizabeth knows this is not so – woman and man are made for each other. Browning marries Elizabeth and the couple set out for their new, happy life in Italy. There is nothing her father can do to stop her.

Music and Songs

A romantic musical triumph with music and lyrics that summon up the happiness of the Victorian era, plus its more shadowy side as an age of dark, suppressed emotion, and love finally victorious in ballads and character-revealing numbers. These include 'The world outside' (Elizabeth), 'Moon in my pocket' (Robert), 'You only to love me' (Elizabeth), 'I know now' (Elizabeth and Robert), 'Escape me never' (Robert) and 'The girls that boys dream about' (the Barrett children).

Did You Know?

✱ Because of rivalry between the Littler Brothers, *Robert and Elizabeth* remained at the Lyric Theatre in Shaftesbury Avenue, unable to move to a larger theatre. Despite selling out and a long run, the elaborate and costly production did not make a profit.

✱ Due to legal problems with an earlier draft of the show, *Robert and Elizabeth* did not get the chance to repeat its success in America at the time.

The Critics

'The show with just about everything to guarantee success in a London musical . . . Ron Grainer's score sounded as if it had been soaked in minor Novello rhapsodies for several decades' – Sheridan Morley

---

Recommended Recording

Original London cast (CD) EMI Records 0777 7 89059 2 9
By a large margin the preferred recording. The original cast are strong-voiced and accurate, and the effect is still thrilling. It was recorded again when there was a revival at Chichester, and this does contain a little extra material, but it lacks the thrilling June Bronhill and Keith Michell partnership.

The Rocky Horror Show

LYRICS ✴ Richard O'Brien
MUSIC ✴ Richard O'Brien
BOOK ✴ Richard O'Brien

First Performance

London, Theatre Upstairs, 19 June 1973 (2358 performances)
Transferred to Comedy Theatre (600 performances)
New York, Belasco Theater, 10 March 1975 (45 performances)

Principal Characters

Brad ✴ A nerd
Janet ✴ His girl
Riff-Raff ✴ A sinister presence
Magenta, Columbia
✴ His assistants
Frank 'n' Furter ✴ A creator
Rocky ✴ A man-made creation
Dr Scott ✴ A college tutor
Narrator

Original London Cast

Christopher Malcolm, Julie Covington, Richard O'Brien, Patricia Quinn,
Little Nell, Tim Curry, Rayner Burton, Paddy O'Hagan, Jonathan Adams

Original New York Cast

Bill Miller, Abigale Haness, Richard O'Brien, Jamie Donnelly,
Boni Enten, Tim Curry, Kim Milford, Meatloaf, Graham Jarvis

Plot

Inspired by classic Hollywood B movies and springboarded from the Frankenstein story, *The Rocky Horror Show* finds the all-American newlyweds, Brad and Janet, stranded in a storm and seeking refuge in a castle which has all the Gothic spookiness anyone could wish for. There's something very strange going on. There's the sinister servant, Riff-Raff, and his two assistants, the very odd Magenta and Columbia, who's a terrific tap dancer. The owner is Frank 'n' Furter who likes dressing up in fishnets, lipstick, corsets and suspenders. His main achievement is that he's created a perfect man out of spare human parts – this is Rocky. Frank's sexual habits are omnivorous. By the end of the evening he's had his wicked way with both Brad and Janet. They need help.

To the rescue comes Brad and Janet's tutor, Dr Scott, somewhat incapacitated by being confined to a wheelchair. Dr Scott knows something that Brad and Janet don't. The inhabitants of the castle are aliens, and the real controller is Riff-Raff. Frank has overstepped the mark and, with his creation, is eliminated, as the remaining aliens take off for home in a puff of smoke, leaving behind Brad, Janet and Dr Scott – all of whom have developed a taste for wearing drag clothing in the interim!

Music and Songs

An irresistible mix of driving rock 'n' roll, including 'Science fiction, double feature' (Magenta and Columbia), 'Sweet transvestite' (Frank), 'Time warp' (the company) and 'Hot patootie' (Rocky).

Did You Know?

✶ The original production had action all around and, on nets, above. It soon transferred to an old cinema close by on the King's Road and stayed there for over 2000 performances.

✶ While its success on stage in Britain was not reproduced on Broadway, the film of the show has received some of the most intense cult attention. The late-night audiences come dressed as their favourite characters. They throw rice and frozen peas at the screen while following the dialogue and singing the songs with the film cast.

The Critics

'Richard O'Brien's spangled piece of erotic fantasy is so funny, so fast, so sexy and so unexpectedly well realized, that one is in danger of merely applauding it without assessing it . . . It speaks wonders for Jim Sharman's vivid direction which takes the action round, up and over his audience, that for all its highly sensual ambience as a piece, it is far too jokey to ever be accused of practising the corruptions it pretends to preach' – *Daily Mail*

Recommended Recording

Original London cast (CD) Castle DOJOCD 54
This recording, with all the original cast members and Tim Curry's Frank 'n' Furter under some semblance of control, is the one to have (and there are a number to choose from). It glories in its own tackiness and as a pastiche of B movies.

Film

20th Century Fox, 1975. Starring Tim Curry, Susan Sarandon and Barry Bostwick. Directed by Jim Sharman. Retitled *The Rocky Horror Picture Show*.

Rose Marie

LYRICS ✴ Oscar Hammerstein II and Otto Harbach
MUSIC ✴ Rudolf Friml and Herbert Stothart
BOOK ✴ Oscar Hammerstein II and Otto Harbach

First Performance

New York, Imperial Theater, 2 September 1924 (557 performances)
London, Drury Lane Theatre, 20 March 1925 (851 performances)

Principal Characters

Rose Marie la Flamme ✴ A singer
Jim Kenyon ✴ A fur-trapper
Hard-boiled Herman ✴ Kenyon's friend
Lady Jane
Sergeant Malone (of the Mounties)
Emile la Flamme ✴ Rose Marie's brother

Original New York Cast

Mary Ellis, Dennis King, William Kent, Dorothy Mackaye,
Arthur Deagon, Eduardo Ciannelli

Original London Cast

Edith Day, Derek Oldham, Billy Merson, Clarice Hardwicke,
John Dunsmore, Michael Cole

Plot

Lady Jane owns a hotel in Saskatchewan in Canada. To it comes Jim Kenyon. His hard-drinking, hard-living nature has been tamed by the influence of Rose Marie, a young French Canadian. She's also in the hotel and her brother, Emile, wants to remove her from what he sees as Jim's unwelcome influence. Jim is trying to settle a land claim with Blackeagle and becomes prime suspect when the latter is killed. Jim and his friend, Herman, go to their mountain lodge, where he can keep in touch with his sweetheart by using the Indian love call. Rose Marie's brother tries to blackmail his sister into marrying a richer man, at the price of keeping Jim's escape route secret. Gradually Rose Marie begins to believe that Jim did indeed commit the murder. She tells her brother she intends to go to Quebec to marry a rich suitor, but secretly plans to follow Jim wherever he goes. When Sergeant Malone arrives with a warrant for Jim's arrest for murder, Rose Marie uses the Indian love call to warn her lover to escape alone.

Lady Jane moves to Quebec as well, opens a fancy-goods shop and marries Herman. Jim turns up just before Rose Marie is about to marry Hawley, her rich suitor. He is accompanied by Wanda, the actual murderess. The latter threatens Hawley, who had witnessed the original killing. Malone is also in the vicinity, ready to arrest Jim. As Rose Marie advances towards the altar, Wanda confesses everything, including her love for Hawley. Herman, Malone and Lady Jane rush to Jim's lodgings, and Rose Marie and Jim are united through the Indian love call.

Music and Songs

A musical comedy score with all the charm of operetta and all the impact of American musical comedy. This is one of the most popular of all scores, and includes many fondly-remembered songs such as 'Indian love call' (Jim and Rose Marie), 'The Mounties' (Sergeant Malone and the Mounties), 'Lak Jeem' (Rose Marie), 'Why shouldn't we?' (Lady Jane and Herman), 'Totem Tom Tom' (the chorus) and 'Only a kiss' (Lady Jane).

Did You Know?

✶ The box office gross for the Broadway run of *Rose Marie* remained unequalled or surpassed until the arrival of *Oklahoma!*

✶ The 'Indian love call' (first line, When I'm calling you . . .) featured in the 1996 spoof film *Mars Attacks!* A recording of it disturbed the invading Martians so much that their heads exploded and the earth was saved!

✶ Mary Ellis, who starred in the Broadway production, later came to London and remained there for the rest of her career. She is remembered for her connection with the Ivor Novello extravaganzas.

The Critics

'A bon-voyage basket of musical shows . . . there is drama and melodrama, musical comedy, grand opera and opéra-comique . . . a beautiful composite photograph of a three-ring circus . . . the most entrancing music it has long been our privilege to hear' – *New York Herald Tribune*

Recommended Recording

1999 Media Theatre (CD) Rockwell productions Ltd. IND 99222
This adventurous theatre company is intent upon reviving older shows that seldom get produced. The fact that they are recording them brings us the only chance to hear the score on CD. The quality is not totally professional but it's very playable.

Films

MGM, 1936. Starring Jeanette MacDonald, Nelson Eddy and James Stewart. Directed by W.S. van Dyke.
MGM, 1954 . Starring Ann Blyth, Howard Keel and Fernando Lamas. Directed by Mervyn LeRoy.

Sail Away

LYRICS ✳ Noël Coward
MUSIC ✳ Noël Coward
BOOK ✳ Noël Coward

First Performance

New York, Broadhurst Theater, 3 October 1961 (167 performances)
London, Savoy Theatre, 21 June 1962 (252 performances)

Principal Characters

Johnny Van Mier ✳ A young passenger
Mimi Paragon ✳ A cruise organiser
Nancy Foyle ✳ A novelist's niece
Barnaby Slade ✳ A passenger
Joe ✳ The purser
Alvin Lush

Original New York Cast

James Hurst, Elaine Stritch, Patricia Harty, Grover Dale,
Charles Braswell, Paul O'Keefe

Original London Cast

David Holliday, Elaine Stritch, Sheila Forbes, Grover Dale,
John Hewer, Stephen Ashworth

Plot

Passengers hurriedly board their luxury cruise liner, the *Coronia*. They are
followed by the cruise organiser, Mimi Paragon, whose immediate job is to get to
know the passengers. There's Johnny Van Mier who is hoping to forget a girl.
Then there's famous novelist Elinor Spencer-Bollard and her niece, Nancy Foyle.
The latter longs to fall in love and what better than a cruise to help? How about
Barnaby Slade, who suggests the idea of an exotic romance? Meanwhile, Johnny
has Mimi herself in his sights, but she discourages him – the age difference is a
problem. The cruise proceeds to Gibraltar, on its way to Italy, and Mimi learns
some useful phrases in foreign languages.

The liner docks in Tangier and Johnny decides to go slow on romance for the
time being. Mimi is stuck on board looking after the little ones. Johnny's mother
expresses her opposition to Johnny's liking for Mimi, but that only fuels his
desire. Mimi also feels it can't work out, and tells Johnny so, on the last night of
the cruise. Everyone else seems to be happy as they leave. Nancy is with her friend
Barnaby. Mimi seems to be fated to be the only sad one, until Johnny reappears to
sweep her off to happiness.

Music and Songs

A witty score by Noël Coward, even if the title number was rescued from an earlier show. As a vehicle for Elaine Stritch, words are more important than melody, but there are some good tunes as well in this delightful late score by The Master. They include 'Come to me' (Mimi), 'Sail away' (Johnny), 'Beatnik love affair' (Barnaby), 'Go slow Johnny' (Johnny), 'The little ones' ABC' (Mimi) and 'Why do the wrong people travel?' (Mimi).

Did You Know?

✶ This musical show was one of the few Coward wrote which seemed to follow on from his lighter stage comedies, as opposed to his previous musicals which tended towards operetta.

✶ This was the show that made Elaine Stritch's reputation. Her part was increased when a main character was eliminated, and her role as cruise organiser developed. She played it on Broadway and then for almost twice as long in London. Subsequently she took up residence in Britain for some time and appeared extensively on stage and television here, including a series with Donald Sinden entitled *Two's Company*.

✶ The London cast had Coward's old friend Edith Day in a cameo role, singing with Sydney Arnold the number added for the London production – 'Bronxville Darby and Joan'.

The Critics

'Coward's humorous score is too entertaining to have a serious love story get in its way. It does get in the way, too' – *New York Post*
'*Sail Away*, in spite of all the rocking and shaking, doesn't really go anywhere' – *New York Journal American*

Recommended Recording

Original Broadway cast (CD) Broadway Angel ZDM 0777 7 64759 2 9
While Coward recorded the songs from the show (CD – Harbinger HCD 1701) and that is certainly of interest, this has the unique Elaine Stritch attacking the songs. Strong on comedy and delivered with a Broadway relish.

St Louis Woman

LYRICS ✷ Johnny Mercer
MUSIC ✷ Harold Arlen
BOOK ✷ Arna Bontemps and Countee Cullen,
based on Bontemps' novel *God Sends Sunday*

First Performance

New York, Martin Beck Theater, 30 March 1946 (113 performances)

Principal Characters

Little Augie ✷ A jockey
Della Green ✷ His girl
Biglow Brown ✷ A bar owner
Lila ✷ His previous mistress
Butterfly ✷ A friend

Original New York Cast

Harold Nicholas, Ruby Hill, Rex Ingram, June Hawkins, Pearl Bailey,
Fayard Nicholas

Plot

St Louis, 1898. Little Augie is a jockey who has hit a winning streak, and is making a play for Della Green, the belle of St Louis, and girlfriend of the proprietor of the local bar, Biglow Brown. Della's a free spirit – when she has had enough of Brown's manhandling, she'll be off. Brown has a previous mistress, Lila, who is still around. Then there's the barmaid, Butterfly, who is in love with another jockey, Barney, but an old, unlucky one. She wants a wedding ring before Barney and she get intimate.

It's cakewalk time and Augie wins Della with a virtuoso performance. Later they set up house together and plan marriage. But there's a cloud on the horizon; Augie's off at the racetrack when Della receives an unwelcome visit from Brown, who beats her when she resists him. Lila rushes in and begs to be taken back. Augie returns, a shot rings out and Brown thinks he's been wounded by Augie (in fact it is Lila who shot him). Brown curses Augie, before dying.

Augie is suspected of the killing, but at Brown's funeral Lila, overcome, confesses. Meanwhile, the curse appears to be in operation. Augie's horses aren't winning and Della blames herself. She leaves, pretending she needs a grander lifestyle than Augie can presently provide. Her new friend, the new bar owner, nevertheless tells Augie of Della's true, nobler feelings. Augie feels the curse is just so much mumbo-jumbo. He'll win his next race and he and Della can get back together. He does, and they do!

Music and Songs

This is a top-drawer Arlen and Mercer collaboration, full of wit, smoky humour and touching, sensitive, memorable songs which include the classic Arlen/Mercer standards 'Come rain or come shine' (Della and Little Augie) and 'Any place I hang my hat is home' (Della), plus 'Legalise my name' (Butterfly), 'I had myself a true love' (Lila), 'Lullaby' (Della), 'Leavin' time' (the chorus), 'It's a woman's prerogative' (Butterfly) and 'Ridin' on the moon' (Augie).

Did You Know?

✳ This is the show that started off Pearl Bailey – in a minor role as Butterfly – on the road to stardom.

✳ The Nicholas Brothers, the alarmingly talented dancing and singing couple, were showbusiness veterans from early childhood, and had appeared in sensational routines in '30s musical films.

✳ Harold Nicholas recalls that, as the show depicted the participants as less than virtuous, it was boycotted and picketed by the black community. And white theatregoers stayed away for that reason, too.

✳ The show was originally written as a vehicle for Lena Horne but she would not play a lady of easy virtue and refused the part.

The Critics

'I was lucky enough to see a performance of *St Louis Woman*. It was one of the loveliest musicals I have ever seen – costumes, scenery, lyrics and music' – songwriter Alec Wilder

---

Recommended Recording

1998 Concert cast (CD) Mercury 31453–8150
An exciting modern recording which, against high odds, manages to come out top against a fine original cast version and, of course, the great Pearl Bailey. This City Center Encores! version has the complete score and a wonderful cast headed by Vanessa L. Williams and Charles S. Dutton.

Salad Days

LYRICS ✳ Dorothy Reynolds and Julian Slade
MUSIC ✳ Julian Slade
BOOK ✳ Dorothy Reynolds and Julian Slade

First Performance

London, Vaudeville Theatre, 5 August 1954 (2283 performances)
New York, Barbizon Plaza, 10 November 1958 (80 performances)

Principal Characters

Jane ✳ A recent university graduate
Timothy Dawes ✳ Another graduate
Timothy's mother
Tramp
Uncle Clem
Nigel Danvers
Fiona Thompson

Original London Cast

Eleanor Drew, John Warner, Dorothy Reynolds, Newton Blick,
James Cairncross, Michael Meacham, Christine Finn

Original New York Cast

Barbara Franklin, Richard Easton, Mary Savage, Powys Thomas,
Jack Creley, Tom Kneebone, June Sampson

Plot

A group of dons bid farewell to their new graduates, including Jane and Timothy.
Their parents are putting pressure on the pair to order their lives. Jane must find a
husband and Timothy must get a good job. They agree to meet up again in a
London park. It would make sense for them to marry, and for Timothy to take the
first job he's offered. A tramp appears and offers Timothy £7 a week for a month
to look after his mobile piano. Timothy accepts and finds that when it plays
everyone within earshot has an irresistible urge to dance! Timothy goes to his
Uncle Clem to get a job in the Foreign Office (in fact he spends a lot of time
looking for jobs with various uncles), but he's soon back with Jane and 'Minnie',
the piano in the park.

Nigel, an old friend of Jane's, invites her to a nightclub (not knowing she and
Timothy are already married), and on leaving the club they meet up with Timothy
himself. There's nothing like people having fun for someone to try to suppress it –
in this case news of the piano's properties has reached the desk of the Minister of
Pleasure and Pastimes. He wants to suppress it. Timothy and Jane go to hide it,
but the piano has vanished anyway.

When Jane meets the tramp again he does not seem unduly worried. Jane and
Timothy enlist the help of Timothy's scientist uncle, Zed, who whisks them off in

his flying saucer for a bird's-eye view . The piano is found and handed on to the next couple for a month; they turn out to be Nigel and his new-found friend, Fiona. Meanwhile, Tim and Jane look forward to their future together with hope and confidence.

Music and Songs

Indomitably English – as fresh, clean and innocent as spring, and as timeless and delightful a score as ever came out of this country. It has the simple artlessness that conceals great craft, and which is wonderfully appealing to the English – but this appeal does not extend across the Atlantic. The score includes 'The things that are done by a don' (the chorus), 'We said we wouldn't look back' (Tim and Jane), 'I sit in the sun' (Jane), 'Oh look at me' (the company) and 'We're looking for a piano' (Tim, Jane and the cast).

Did You Know?

✸ This was the longest-running British show in the history of the British musical theatre until it was overtaken by *Oliver!*

✸ Regular, successful revivals have shown that charm, style and melody, coupled with a bit of magic, can still find a place in London's West End.

✸ The title *Salad Days* is from Shakespeare and was suggested by the bar attendant at the Bristol Old Vic where the show first appeared.

The Critics

The Times described the piece as 'reacting sharply against the hard-hitting, hard-boiled American musical'.
Ivor Brown concurred: 'While jet planes crashed the sound barrier, a piano tinkled and we suddenly took this to be the music of the spheres.'

Recommended Recording

Original London cast (CD) Sony West End SMK 66176
The original mono recording with the composer at the piano. It has freshness and is unequalled. The show has had many revivals resulting in two other original cast recordings which are quite acceptable, and there is a 40th Anniversary studio recording with every ounce of music in it and a cast which reads like a British theatrical Who's Who.

Film

Salad Days was televised in 1983 with Julian Slade appearing as a bystander in one scene. Ian Richardson and Simon Green were in the cast.

Sally

LYRICS ✶ Clifford Grey and Buddy de Sylva
MUSIC ✶ Jerome Kern, with additional (ballet) music by Victor Herbert
BOOK ✶ Guy Bolton, based on his and P.G. Wodehouse's
unproduced musical *The Little Thing*

First Performance

New York, New Amsterdam Theater, 21 December 1920 (570 performances)
London, Winter Garden Theatre, 10 September 1921 (387 performances)

Principal Characters

Sally Green ✶ A foundling
Otis Hooper ✶ Of the Vaudeville agency
Connie ✶ The exiled duke
Blair Farquar ✶ An only son
Rosalind Rafferty ✶ Otis' girlfriend

Original New York Cast

Marilynn (subsequently Marilyn) Miller, Walter Catlett,
Leon Errol, Irving Fisher, Mary Hay

Original London Cast

Dorothy Dickson, George Grossmith,
Leslie Henson, Gregory Stroud, Heather Thatcher

Plot

Sally Green is chosen from a group of foundlings to be dishwasher at Greenwich Village's Alley Inn by its proprietress, Mrs Ten Broek. Another member of the staff is the exiled Grand Duke Constantine (Connie) of Czechoslovakia. He'll be allowed off from his job as a waiter for one night to attend a ball in his honour, thrown by Richard Farquar. Farquar has a son, Blair, who visits the inn and is attracted to Sally. Connie is impressed, too, by Sally's dancing and arranges for her to perform at the inn. After her successful performance, a theatrical agent decides to pass her off as a celebrated French dancer, who has just turned down an engagement at the Farquar Ball.

Sally is duly introduced as Madame Nockerova, and is a dancing sensation. Blair is puzzled by the ballerina's close resemblance to Sally – and falls in love all over again! Unfortunately, Sally goes too far and convinces Blair that, as Madame Nockerova, she had engineered Connie's downfall. Blair denounces her and it's left to the theatrical agent to sort things out, and bring the young lovers together for a final-curtain happy ending.

Music and Songs

A charming early romantic Jerome Kern score, including 'Look for the silver lining' (Sally), 'Wild rose' (Sally) and 'The lorelei' (Sally).

Did You Know?

★ The show was the fourth longest-running musical of the 1920s.

★ There was a successful London revival in 1942 called *Wild Rose* with Jessie Matthews.

★ The success of this show and *Irene* brought another entitled *Sally, Irene and Mary*.

★ Dorothy Dickson had come to London as a chorus dancer and became a star.

The Critics

'Sally is Marilynn Miller – from her head to her toes. She danced divinely . . . her performance is one of the daintiest things of this unusual season' – *New York Dramatic Mirror*

Yet the London Sally had her adherents too: 'There was a real sensation in London last night. Miss Dorothy Dickson, who had hardly a speaking part before, danced, spoke and sang her way to one of the season's biggest hits. So great was Miss Dickson's hit that when she twice lost her slipper in the ballet scene and was forced to stop dancing, the audience cheered her to the echo' – *New York Herald*

Recommended Recording

While the original London cast 78s made it onto LP (**Monmouth Evergreen MES 7053**) they have not, as yet, reached CD.

Film

Warner Brothers, 1929. Starring Marilyn Miller, Joe E. Brown and Lawrence Gray. Directed by John Francis Dillon.

Seesaw

LYRICS ✶ Dorothy Fields
MUSIC ✶ Cy Coleman
BOOK ✶ Michael Stewart, based on *Two for the Seesaw* by William Gibson,
subsequently revised by, and wholly credited to, Michael Bennett

First Performance

New York, Uris Theater, 18 March 1973 (296 performances)

Principal Characters

Jerry Ryan ✶ A lawyer
Gittel Mosca ✶ A dancer
David ✶ A young dancer
Sophie
Julio Gonzales
Sparkle

Original New York Cast

Ken Howard, Michele Lee, Tommy Tune, Cecelia Norfleet,
Giancarlo Esposito, LaMonte Peterson

Plot

The impact of New York on innocent out-of-towners can indeed be great. Jerry
Ryan, a simple, handsome young lawyer from America's mid-West, comes to New
York where he gets involved in a romance with a screwball young dancer whose
background, ideas and attitudes are completely different from his own. This is
Gittel Mosca – and the two keep in touch by telephone. They meet and part
through that medium. (Indeed, the original play, on which this musical adaptation
was based, just offered these two characters and their telephones.)

Gittel introduces Jerry to all aspects of her life in New York, peopled as it is
with strange and wonderful characters from every part of the globe. Jerry finds
himself outside X-rated cinema marquees in Times Square and propositioned by
Eighth Avenue hookers.

There are compensatory tender moments for Gittel and Jerry at Lincoln Center.
And other bizarre events. How about a performance of *Hamlet* by a mobile street
theatre – in the original Puerto Rican?! Gittel has a close friend, David, an
aspiring choreographer who dreams up the ultimate Broadway production
number.

Sadly the relationship between Jerry and Gittel fails in the end to lead to
anything more permanent. But both have learned things about themselves and
about their emotional hang-ups – and also about New York, that very special and
exciting city.

Music and Songs

A wonderful kaleidoscope of New York, full of punchy melodies by Cy Coleman at his friskiest, and clever, knowing lyrics. In fact this was the last set of lyrics by one of the greatest wordsmiths of all – Dorothy Fields. The score includes 'Nobody does it like me' (Gittel), 'Welcome to holiday inn' (Gittel), 'It's not where you start' (David and the company) and 'I'm way ahead' (Gittel).

Did You Know?

∗ *Seesaw* combined the intimacy of a two-hander with the big, bold production numbers typical of New York and its heartwarming theatre community.

∗ *Seesaw* was the show that made the name and reputation of Texan dancer (and latterly choreographer/director) Tommy Tune, a major force on the Broadway musical stage for almost 30 years.

∗ This was the last show that Dorothy Fields wrote.

∗ John Lindsay, the New York mayor at the time, joined in the finale when he saw the show and earned a great deal of publicity for both it and New York where the show is set.

∗ Tommy Tune won the Tony Award for his performance in *Seesaw*.

The Critics

The critics enjoyed themselves:
'*Seesaw* is a love of a musical' – Walter Kerr, *New York Times*
'*Seesaw* is well crafted, intelligent . . . literate and tuneful. It has pulse and vibration' – Clive Barnes, *New York Times*
'A brassy, sexy musical' – *WNBC* (New York radio station)
'*Seesaw* is an intimate bittersweet comedy and a big brassy musical'– *New York Daily News*
'One of the best musicals I've ever seen' – Rex Reed

Recommended Recording

Original Broadway cast (CD) DRG CDRG 6108
The only recording of the show. Ken Howard and Michele Lee head a spirited cast in a solid gold Broadway-sounding cast album.

1776

Lyrics ✶ Sherman Edwards
Music ✶ Sherman Edwards
Book ✶ Peter Stone, based on a concept by Sherman Edwards

First Performance

New York, 46th Street Theater, 16 March 1969 (1217 performances)
London, New Theatre, 16 June 1970 (168 performances)

Principal Characters

John Adams ✶ Member of the Congress for Massachusetts
Benjamin Franklin ✶ Member for Pennsylvania
John Dickinson ✶ Member for Pennsylvania
Edward Rutledge ✶ Member for South Carolina
Stephen Hopkins ✶ Member for Rhode Island
Richard Henry Lee ✶ Member for Virginia
Thomas Jefferson ✶ Member for Virginia
Abigail Adams ✶ John's wife
Martha Jefferson ✶ Thomas' wife

Original New York Cast

William Daniels, Howard Da Silva, Paul Hecht, Clifford David, Roy Poole,
Ronald Holgate, Ken Howard, Virginia Vestoff, Betty Buckley

Original London Cast

Lewis Fiander, Ronald Radd, Bernard Lloyd, David Kernan, Tony Steedman,
David Morton, John Quentin, Vivienne Ross, Cheryl Kennedy

Plot

Philadelphia in 1776 is the seat of American political power controlling the thirteen states of North America. There is talk of independence. Indeed, George Washington and the army of the American States are currently up in arms against the British. Should the Americans seek complete independence or maintain strong links with the British Empire – the strongest and most powerful of the time? John Adams wants a new sovereign state, and so does Benjamin Franklin. But the motion must be proposed by a seeming neutral – like Richard Henry Lee, the amiable Southern delegate. These politicians are opposed by members from Pennsylvania who want to maintain ties with Britain.

As events unfold, the balance of power shifts this way and that, through illness and incapacity. Adams must produce a unanimous vote, and therefore must individually win over six delegates who are currently wavering in their allegiances.

Gradually events fall his way. But there are compromises to be reckoned with. The Southern states will only come in for independence if they are allowed to retain slavery. Franklin, with heavy heart, suggests the deletion of the slavery clause – one battle should be fought at a time. The resolution of slavery can wait.

Eventually the Declaration of Independence is signed almost unanimously, even if there is one congressman, Dickinson, still loyal to the Crown who cannot bring himself to sign the document that brings into being the United States of America.

Music and Songs

A fine collection of plot-advancing music, spiced with love songs and dramatic numbers. Edwards' only Broadway score suggests a talent that, sadly, has not been heard of again in this medium. It includes 'Piddle, twiddle and resolve' (Adams), 'Till then' (the wives), 'The Lees of Old Virginia' (Lee, Franklin and Adams), 'Cool, cool, considerate men' (Dickinson), 'Momma look sharp' (Congress trio) and 'Molasses to rum' (Rutledge).

Did You Know?

✳ The creator of the show, former history teacher Sherman Edwards, spent seven years writing it.

✳ 1776 was the first musical ever presented in its entirety at the White House, on 22 February 1970 at a command performance for President Nixon and his guests.

✳1776 won the best musical Tony Award.

The Critics

'It makes even an Englishman's heart beat faster' – *New York Times* (written by an American)
'This is a musical with style, humanity, wit and passion' – Clive Barnes (English)
'A brilliant and remarkably moving work of theatrical art . . . a most exhilarating accomplishment' – *New York Post*
'A magnificently staged and stunning original . . . it is warm with life of its own. It is funny. It is moving' – *New York Daily News*

Recommended Recording

Original Broadway cast (CD) Sony Broadway SK 48215
This is a show that mounts to a magnificently exciting climax, captured well on disc. The London cast was recorded but this has not been issued on CD and there has been a new issue for the 1997 revival.

She Loves Me

LYRICS ✶ Sheldon Harnick
MUSIC ✶ Jerry Bock
BOOK ✶ Joe Masteroff, based on the Hungarian play, *Parfumerie*, by Miklos Laszlo

First Performance

New York, Eugene O'Neill Theater, 23 April 1963 (302 performances)
London, Lyric Theatre, 29 April 1964 (189 performances)

Principal Characters

Amalia Balash ✶ A sales assistant
Georg Nowack ✶ A shop manager
Ilona Ritter ✶ A sales assistant
Steven Kodaly ✶ A salesman
Zoltan Maraczek ✶ A shop owner
Ladislav Sipos ✶ A sales assistant
Arpad Laszlo ✶ An ambitious delivery boy

Original New York Cast

Barbara Cook, Daniel Massey, Barbara Baxley, Jack Cassidy, Ludwig Donath, Nathaniel Frey, Ralph Williams

Original London Cast

Anne Rogers, Gary Raymond, Rita Moreno, Gary Miller, Karel Stepanek, Peter Sallis, Gregory Phillips

Plot

The action takes place in and around Maraczek's Parfumerie, in a town in continental Europe in the mid-thirties. The staff are old-hand Ladislav Sipos, a mature shop worker; young delivery boy Arpad; and Ilona Ritter, who has spent the night with salesman Steven Kodaly. They think no one knows of their assignation – but everyone does. It's a small shop after all.

The shop manager is the gentlemanly Georg who has a secret romance with a penpal he's never met – they address each other fondly as 'Dear Friend', in their warm and intimate letters. Mr Maraczek, the boss, takes a a paternal interest in Georg – he should find himself a girl and settle down. Twenty minutes into the day and Amalia Balash arrives looking for a job. With a crafty piece of selling, she gets one, but she and Georg don't hit it off.

The seasons pass and Mr Maraczek has a problem. His wife is having an affair with a staff member. The only one who visits him is Georg – so it must be Georg, mustn't it? What keeps Georg sane at the moment is the stream of letters from his penfriend. Now he is to meet her at last, at the Café Imperiale. That same night, the owner orders his staff to stay behind and put up the Christmas decorations. Georg and Mr Maraczek finally fall out, and Georg leaves his job and the shop. He goes to the café and sees Amalia there with a red rose in a book – she is his penpal. Meanwhile, a detective comes to visit Maraczek at his now-deserted shop, and tells him that his wife's lover is not Georg, but Steve Kodaly. Maraczek is devastated and shoots himself in the shoulder. Luckily Arpad is still in the shop and gets him to hospital. In the meantime, Georg goes to Amalia's table at the restaurant and completely spoils the evening, without revealing his identity as her penpal. So it's misery all round.

In the days approaching Christmas a lot of things happen. Arpad is appointed a junior shop assistant. Georg is reinstated as manager, Steve is sacked, Ilona discovers a new romance in the library, and as for Amalia . . . When she doesn't return to work the following day, Georg visits her, bringing ice cream. Instead of sacking her, as she expected, he's kind and thoughtful and nice, even if he does tell her there was another (fat, old, balding) visitor at the café who, like her, bore a red rose. Finally, the two set up another meeting, and Georg reveals his true identity as her penpal. Amalia is delighted – it's just what she'd hoped for!

Music and Songs

The sound of Middle Europe between the wars, including the songs 'Good morning, good day' (the company), 'No more candy' (Amalia), 'Will he like me?' (Amalia), 'Ilona' (Steven), 'Dear friend' (Amalia), 'Ice cream' (Amalia) and 'She loves me' (Georg).

Did You Know?

∗ The films *The Good Old Summertime* and *The Shop Around the Corner* were based on the same Hungarian play that formed the basis for this musical.

∗ In the original London staging, the illness of Nyree Dawn Porter meant that a substitute had to be found. This was Rita Moreno and a new song was written for her – 'Heads I win'.

∗ For the London production the score was revisited and the lyrics changed to use English words rather than American. However, the show was still set somewhere in Europe.

∗ Jack Cassidy won a Tony Award for his performance in *She Loves Me*.

The Critics

'A musical play with which everyone can fall in love' – *New York World Telegram & Sun*

Recommended Recording

Original Broadway cast (CD) Polydor 831 968-2
Barbara Cook singing 'Ice cream' tips this into the best. In fact all the performances are wonderful. The London cast recording is fine in its own right and both the recent Broadway and London productions have been recorded. But the original is the one to go for.

Show Boat

LYRICS ✱ Oscar Hammerstein II
MUSIC ✱ Jerome Kern
BOOK ✱ Oscar Hammerstein II,
based on Edna Furber's novel *Show Boat*

First Performance

New York, Ziegfeld Theater, 20 December 1927 (572 performances)
London, Drury Lane Theatre, 3 May 1928 (350 performances)

Principal Characters

Magnolia Hawkes Ravenal ✱ A singer
Gaylord Ravenal ✱ A gambler
Captain Andy Hawkes ✱ Magnolia's father
Julie La Verne ✱ A singer
Joe ✱ A stevedore
Parthy Ann Hawkes ✱ Magnolia's mother
Queenie ✱ Joe's girl
Ellie May Chipley ✱ A soubrette
Frank Schultz ✱ A character actor/singer
Steve Baker ✱ Julie's husband

Original New York Cast

Norma Terris, Howard Marsh, Charles Winninger, Helen Morgan, Jules Bledsoe,
Edna May Oliver, Tess Gardella, Eva Puck, Sammy White, Charles Ellis

Original London Cast

Edith Day, Howett Worster, Cedric Hardwicke, Marie Burke, Paul Robeson,
Viola Compton, Alberta Hunter, Dorothy Lena, Leslie Sarony, Colin Clive

Plot

The showboat *Cotton Blossom* has arrived at Natchez, a port on the Mississippi. At the riverside Magnolia, the daughter of Captain Andy and his wife Parthy, meets the handsome gambler, Gaylord Ravenal. When the show's leading couple, Julie and Steve, are forced off the boat because it is discovered she is of mixed blood, Ravenal and Magnolia take over and fall in love. They marry and also leave.

Ravenal continues to gamble and, for a few years, Lady Luck is on his side. Then the young couple's fortunes change for the worse. Together with their child Kim they are living in sleazy lodgings. Two old friends from the boat, Ellie and Frank, discover them on the brink of eviction. Ravenal decides to leave his wife and daughter and, after a visit to see Kim at her convent school, does so. Frank suggests Magnolia tries for a job at the Trocadero Club where they are about to work. The singer there is an older and more shopworn Julie. Julie had been very close to Magnolia when she worked on the boat and still has a great deal of love for her and so, when she sees her in such a desperate need of a job, she resigns and suggests to the management they take Magnolia on.

It's New Year's Eve and Magnolia is on stage, nervous and not a success. Her father appears with a couple of 'ladies' on his arm and, on seeing his daughter, gets the audience to listen to her. Encouraged by this support, Magnolia wins them over and she is on her way to stardom.

We now move on to the time when Magnolia decides to retire from the stage. Kim is now a star in her own right. Captain Andy comes across Ravenal and invites him to the showboat where he is reunited once more with Magnolia. And so it is a happy ending as they listen to their daughter on the radio.

Music and Songs

The show is one of the towering achievements of musical theatre and includes 'Cotton Blossom' (the chorus), 'Make believe' (Magnolia and Gaylord), 'Can't help lovin' dat man' (Julie), 'Till the good luck comes my way' (Gaylord), 'Life upon the wicked stage' (Ellie and Frank), 'Queenie's ballyhoo' (Queenie), 'You are love' (Magnolia and Gaylord), 'Why do I love you?' (Gaylord and Magnolia), 'Bill' (Julie), 'After the ball' (Magnolia and Cap'n Andy) and, of course, 'Ol' man river' (Joe).

Did You Know?

* Paul Robeson was first choice for the role of Joe on Broadway. This proved not to be possible, but he assumed the role triumphantly for London and for the film.

The Critics

Most American first night reviewers opted to see Philip Barry's *Paris Bound*, which opened the same night as *Show Boat*. When Brooks Atkinson of the *New York Times* did see *Show Boat* he wrote: 'Superlative praise of *Show Boat* does not seem excessive. Faithfully adapted from Edna Furber's picturesque novel, set to an enchanting score by Jerome Kern, staged with the sort of artistry we eulogise in Reinhardt, *Show Boat* becomes one of those epochal works about which garrulous old men gabble for twenty-five years after the scenery has rattled off to the storehouse.'

Recommended Recording

Complete version (3 CDs) EMI CDS 7 49108 2
This studio cast recording by John McGlinn is a masterpiece. It includes songs that did not make the original Broadway opening but deserve such a fine interpretation. The cast, including Frederica von Stade and Jerry Hadley, is excellent. A single CD extract issue from this using what was the original Broadway score has been issued (**EMI CDS 7 49847 2**).

Films

Universal, 1936. Starring Irene Dunne, Allan Jones, Charles Winninger, Helen Morgan and Paul Robeson. Directed by James Whale.
MGM, 1951. Starring Kathryn Grayson, Howard Keel, Ava Gardner, Marge and Gower Champion, Joe E. Brown and William Warfield. Directed by George Sidney.

Silk Stockings

LYRICS ✷ Cole Porter
MUSIC ✷ Cole Porter
BOOK ✷ George S. Kaufman, Leueen McGrath and Abe Burrows, based on the
screenplay for *Ninotchka* by Charles Brackett, Billy Wilder and Walter Reisch, and
suggested by *Ninotchka* by Melchior Lengyel

First Performance

New York, Imperial Theater, 24 February 1955 (478 performances)

Principal Characters

Peter Ilyich Boroff ✷ A composer
Steve Canfield ✷ A Hollywood agent
Ninotchka ✷ A Russian commissar
Janice Dayton ✷ A film star
Ivanov, Brankov, Bibinski
✷ Russian officials

Original New York Cast

Philip Sterling, Don Ameche, Hildegarde Neff, Gretchen Wyler, Henry Lascoe,
Leon Belasco, David Opatoshu

Plot

Peter Ilyich Boroff is a leading Soviet composer living in Paris. Hollywood agent,
Steve Canfield, wants to use his 'Ode to a tractor' in a Hollywood film starring
Janice Dayton. This does not please the Soviet hierarchy, which sends a group of
agents, Brankov, Ivanov and Bibinski, to Paris to take Boroff back to Russia. The
wily Canfield takes on Boroff as a client and claims the composer has a French
father – so he can claim to be French rather than Russian.

Meanwhile, the three agents are enjoying their stay in Paris so much, they are
totally ineffectual at persuading the composer to return. So Ninotchka is sent to
sort things out. Comrade Ninotchka Yaschenko is a totally dedicated party worker
who won't be deflected from her task. Or will she, once she's been exposed to the
good life by Steve Canfield at his most charming?

Steve's client, Janice, arrives. She's going to star in a version of *War and
Peace*. This is not obvious casting for a swimming star . . . As the days pass
Ninotchka finds both Paris and Steve Canfield difficult to resist.

The three Russians originally charged with bringing Boroff back now believe
that Ninotchka herself has 'gone native', and plans to marry the American; so it's
time for them to take up their original assignment! Steve proposes to Ninotchka,
who accepts, even though he admits the hoax about Boroff's 'French' father.
Boroff himself is horrified when he hears what the Americans have done to his
music for the film. It's back to the Soviet Union for him and the agents, and
Ninotchka has no choice either – her work is done.

Poor Steve is left behind with his gift for his fiancée: 365 pairs of silk
stockings. Ninotchka has a new job back in Moscow – she superintends a Soviet

artists commune – and Boroff finds he quite likes decadent, popular music after all. Suddenly Steve Canfield turns up with Commissar Markovitch. Steve can help the commissar to sell his story for big money in the West. Steve also finds a way for Ninotchka to escape with him – and even the three former agents have high hopes of becoming Wall Street billionaires!

Music and Songs

Cole Porter back in Paris with a witty collection of point numbers, as well as a couple of good love songs. The old master may be coasting a bit now, but the score offers many pleasant moments, including 'Too bad' (the Russians), 'Paris loves lovers' (Steve and Ninotchka), 'Stereophonic sound' (Steve and Janice), 'It's a chemical reaction' (Ninotchka), 'All of you' (Steve), 'Without love' (Ninotchka) and 'Josephine' (Janice).

Did You Know?

∗ Don Ameche, Hildegarde Neff and Gretchen Wyler all made their Broadway debuts in this show.

∗ While working on this, his last Broadway show, Cole Porter suffered the bereavement of his wife, Linda.

The Critics

'We can all afford to relax now. Everything about *Silk Stockings*, which opened at the Imperial last night, represents the best goods in the American Musical Comedy Emporium. This is one of Gotham's most memorable shows, on a par with *Guys and Dolls*' – *New York Times*

'There could not be any more pleasant company in the theater than Hildegarde Neff. She is a fascinating actress with a slinky, smoky voice and her singing of "Without love" is the high point of the show' – *New York Daily News*

Recommended Recording

Original Broadway cast (CD) RCA Victor 1102-2-RG
Still the fullest version of this score. It's late Porter with choice moments of enjoyment and some excellent songs.

Film

MGM, 1957. Starring Fred Astaire, Cyd Charisse and Janis Paige. Directed by Rouben Mamoulian.

Song of Norway

LYRICS ✶ Robert Wright and George Forrest
MUSIC ✶ Robert Wright and George Forrest,
adapted from melodies by Edvard Grieg
BOOK ✶ Milton Lazarus,
based on a play by Homer Curran

First Performance

New York, Imperial Theater, 21 August 1944 (860 performances)
London, Palace Theatre, 7 March 1946 (526 performances)

Principal Characters

Louisa Giovanni ✶ An opera singer
Edvard Grieg ✶ A composer
Rikaard Nordraak ✶ A poet
Nina Hagerup ✶ Grieg's fiancée
Count Peppi Le Loup ✶ Louisa's husband

Original New York Cast

Irra Petina, Lawrence Brooks, Robert Shafer, Helena Bliss, Sig Arno

Original London Cast

Janet Hamilton-Smith, John Hargreaves, Arthur Servent, Halina Victoria,
Bernard Ansell

Plot

It's 1860 in Troldhaugen in Norway. Poet Rikaard Nordraak is waiting for the
return of a childhood friend, Nina. Three childhood friends – the third is Edvard
Grieg – will then be back together. Although both boys love Nina, the unspoken
understanding is that she favours Grieg. The local Midsummer Eve Festival will
have two important visitors: Count Peppi and his wife, opera singer Louisa
Giovanni. The count, on arrival, flirts unsuccessfully with Nina and is caught out
by his wife, who thinks this gives her the right to do a bit of philandering herself.
She hears Grieg playing his music and immediately offers him a position as her
accompanist on a forthcoming tour. Grieg is engaged to Nina but the wedding
must be postponed – the tour is to begin immediately.

A year later and Grieg is the toast of the capitals of Europe. Nina and Rikaard
catch up with him in Copenhagen. Rikaard has been ill, but has completed a
patriotic poem which Grieg had promised to set to music. This is pushed to the
back of Grieg's mind when Louisa brings in someone else to meet him, Henrik
Ibsen, the celebrated playwright; now Grieg must write the music for *Peer Gynt*.
Rikaard is depressed that his work is to be further postponed. Nina announces
that she and Edvard Grieg are to be married the following week.

A year later, Grieg is still working on *Peer Gynt*, while Louisa is still intriguing
– this time in the Rome Opera House. Grieg has a visitor, Mr Nordraak, Rikaard's
father. The son has died, and the father has brought the poem for Grieg to set to

music. Grieg has been very selfish; it is time to return to his roots, to Troldhaugen with his wife. It's Christmastime and he has music to write in memory of his friend.

Music and Songs

The score is taken from various vocal and instrumental pieces from the works of the classical composer Grieg and includes 'Freddy and his fiddle' (Einart, Sigrid, and children) – Norwegian Dance No. 2, 'Now' (Louisa) – Second Violin Sonata and Waltz, Op. 12, 'Strange music' (Nina and Edvard) – Wedding in Troldhaugen, 'Midsummer's eve' (Rikaard and Louisa) – Scherzo in E, and 'I love you' (Nina) – 'Ich liebe dich' (a famous Grieg song).

Did You Know?

✷ The producer was so sure of the show's potential that he increased ticket prices from $4.40 to $6.00.

✷ It was the first Broadway show to cross the Atlantic Ocean after the end of the Second World War, beating *Oklahoma!* which had opened on Broadway a year before.

The Critics

'A shot straight into the stratosphere' – *New York Times*
'There's enough in *Song of Norway* to please almost any taste much of the time' – *New York Post*
'A new operetta which is destined to become a classic in the field' – *New York World Telegram*

Recommended Recording

Studio cast (CD) TER CDTER2 1173
A complete and definitive modern recording made under the guiding hands of Wright and Forrest. The extended length gives ample opportunity for the Grieg music to be heard.

Film

Cinerama, 1970. Starring Florence Henderson, Toralv Maurstad and Edward G. Robinson. Directed by Andrew Stone.

The Sound of Music

LYRICS ✳ Oscar Hammerstein II
MUSIC ✳ Richard Rodgers
BOOK ✳ Howard Lindsay and Russel Crouse, based on Maria Von Trapp's
book *The Trapp Family Singers* and its German film version

First Performance

New York, Lunt Fontanne Theater, 16 November 1959 (1443 performances)
London, Palace Theatre, 8 May 1961 (2385 performances)

Principal Characters

Maria Rainer Von Trapp
Captain George Von Trapp
Elsa Schraeder ✳ A family friend
Max Detweiler ✳ A promoter
Mother Abbess
Liesl Von Trapp
Rolf Gruber ✳ A youth
Sister Margaretta

Original New York Cast

Mary Martin, Theodore Bikel, Marion Marlowe, Kurt Kaszner, Patricia Neway,
Lauri Peters, Brian Davies, Muriel O. Malley

Original London Cast

Jean Bayliss, Roger Dann, Eunice Gayson, Harold Kasket, Constance Shacklock,
Barbara Brown, Nicholas Bennett, Olive Gilbert

Plot

Maria Rainer, a postulant at Nonnberg Abbey, is sent by the abbess of her Order to become the latest in a long line of governesses for the children of (the largely absent) widowed Captain Von Trapp, a naval captain. Through common sense and her obvious talent for childcare, Maria wins the children over. However, because of the feelings she has developed for the captain, she leaves to rejoin the convent when he returns with two friends, one of whom is Countess Elsa Schraeder whom he intends to marry.

Back in the convent Maria is told she can't use the convent to escape from life, and courageously returns to the captain's home, to resume her duties. The children make it obvious who they'd prefer as stepmother. So Maria becomes the wife of the captain. On the honeymooners' return, they discover that the Nazis have taken over as the power in the land, and make plans to escape during a local music festival at which the whole family perform. This they successfully achieve, and end up climbing the Alps into Switzerland.

Music and Songs

The last Rodgers and Hammmerstein score, and fully up to the level of the rest. Some of the many well-known songs from the score are 'The sound of music' (Maria), 'Maria' (the nuns), 'My favorite things' (Maria and Abbess), 'Do-Re-Mi' (Maria and the children), 'Sixteen going on seventeen' (Rolf and Liesl), 'How can love survive?' (Elsa and Max), 'Climb every mountain' (Mother Abbess), 'An ordinary couple' (Maria and Captain) and 'Edelweiss' (Maria and Captain).

Did You Know?

★ The London run is the greatest for any Rodgers and Hammerstein show anywhere.

★ The film is one of the most commercially successful of any films of Broadway shows.

★ The additional numbers for the film, 'Something good' and 'I have confidence in me', have lyrics by Richard Rodgers (Hammerstein's last completed lyric for the show was 'Edelweiss').

★ The film has become a cult with special showings where the audience join in with the songs.

★ *The Sound of Music* won five Tony Awards, including best musical, an award it shared with *Fiorello!*

The Critics

'Before the play is halfway through its promising chores it becomes not only too sweet for words but almost too sweet for music . . . the people on stage have all melted long before our hearts do' – *New York Herald Tribune*
'The best of *The Sound of Music* is Rodgers and Hammerstein in good form. Mr Rodgers has not written with such freshness of style since *The King and I*. Mr Hammerstein has contributed lyrics that also have the sentiment and dexterity of his best work' – *New York Times*

Recommended Recording

Original Broadway cast (CD) Sony SK 60583
There are many to chose from and the film's popularity makes it one of the most collected soundtracks. However, Mary Martin and the rest of the original cast are wonderful and there is less syrup to swim through.

Film

20th Century Fox, 1965. Starring Julie Andrews, Christopher Plummer and Peggy Wood. Directed by Robert Wise.

South Pacific

LYRICS ✶ Oscar Hammerstein II
MUSIC ✶ Richard Rodgers
BOOK ✶ Oscar Hammerstein and Joshua Logan, based on stories from
James Michener's *Tales of the South Pacific*

First Performance

New York, Majestic Theater, 7 April 1949 (1925 performances)
London, Drury Lane Theatre, 1 November 1951 (802 performances)

Principal Characters

Nellie Forbush ✶ A nurse
Emile de Becque ✶ A planter
Luther Billis ✶ An entrepreneur
Lieutenant Joe Cable ✶ A marine
Bloody Mary ✶ A local entrepreneur
Liat ✶ Her daughter
Captain George Brackett
Commander William Harbison
Seabee Richard West

Original New York Cast

Mary Martin, Ezio Pinza, Myron McCormick, William Tabbert, Juanita Hall,
Betta St John, Martin Woolfson, Harvey Stephens, Dickinson Eastham

Original London Cast

Mary Martin, Wilbur Evans, Ray Walston, Muriel Smith, Peter Grant,
Betta St John, Hartley Power, John McLaren, Ivor Emmanuel

Plot

Nellie Forbush is a nurse from Little Rock stationed on a Pacific island in World
War II. She knows how far she has come from Little Rock when she falls in love
with the older, foreign, de Becque, a local planter. However, when she finds out
that he is a widower, who is father to two half-caste children, she cannot accept
the situation – because of her small-town upbringing.

Likewise, young Lieutenant Cable from a noble Boston family, in love with the
Polynesian, Liat, whose mother is Bloody Mary, the local entrepreneur, is torn
between love and inborn prejudice.

De Becque, deeply disappointed with Nellie's attitude and coldnesss towards
him, joins an American spy mission on a nearby island, and Nellie subsequently
realises her true feelings for him. Luckily for her, de Becque escapes when the
Japanese attack and comes back to find her serving soup to his children – her
rehabilitation is complete. His companion on the dangerous mission, Lieutenant
Cable, is not so lucky. He is killed and Liat is left alone, deprived of the one man
she would marry.

Music and Songs

Apart from 'Bali hai', there is no South Seas flavour to Rodgers and Hammerstein's exuberant, lusty and often touching score. Well-known songs include 'Dites moi' (Emile's children), 'A cockeyed optimist' (Nellie), 'Twin soliloquies' (Nellie and Emile), 'Some enchanted evening' (Emile), 'Bloody Mary' (the sailors and Bloody Mary), 'There's nothing like a dame' (the sailors), 'Bali hai' (Bloody Mary), 'I'm gonna wash that man right out of my hair' (Nellie), 'A wonderful guy' (Nellie), 'Younger than springtime' (Joe), 'You've got to be carefully taught' (Joe), 'Honey Bun' (Nellie), 'Happy talk' (Bloody Mary) and 'This nearly was mine' (Emile).

Did You Know?

✶ *South Pacific* enjoyed the greatest advance sales and the second-longest Broadway run up to that point.

✶ Sean Connery was in the chorus at one stage of the original show's London run.

✶ Ray Walston, London's Luther Billis, was the only member of either the Broadway or the London cast to repeat their portrayal on the screen.

✶ *South Pacific* won eight Tony Awards, including best musical.

✶ The film is said to have recovered its entire film negative cost from the single extended run at the Dominion Theatre, Tottenham Court Road, London.

The Critics

'Magnificent . . . a tenderly beautiful idyll of genuine people . . . as lively, warm, fresh and beautiful as we had all hoped it would be' – *New York Times*
'What sets the show apart is the Rodgers and Hammerstein score: a great composition, unique characters fully brought forth. A compelling story against a colorful background. Or even: the most popular score ever written' – Ethan Mordden

Recommended Recording

Original Broadway cast (CD) Sony SK 60722
The newly re-mastered CD has bonus tracks, but even without them this recording with the delightful Mary Martin and a perfectly cast Ezio Pinza is way ahead of any other.

Film

20th Century Fox, 1958. Starring Mitzi Gaynor, Rossano Brazzi (voice of Giorgio Tozzi), John Kerr (voice of Bill Lee) and Juanita Hall (sung by Muriel Smith). Directed by Joshua Logan.

Starlight Express

LYRICS ✳ Richard Stilgoe
MUSIC ✳ Andrew Lloyd Webber
BOOK ✳ Story by Andrew Lloyd Webber

First Performance

London, Apollo Victoria, 27 March 1984 (still running)
New York, Gershwin Theater, 15 March 1987 (761 performances)

Principal Characters

Greaseball
Rusty
Ashley
Buffy
Dinah
Pearl
CB
Poppa

Original London Cast

Jeff Shankley, Ray Shell, Chrissy Wickham, Nancy Wood, Frances Ruffelle,
Stephanie Lawrence, Michael Staniforth, Lon Satton

Original New York Cast

Robert Torti, Greg Mowry, Andrea McArdle, Jamie Beth Chandler,
Jane Krakowski, Reva Rice, Berry K. Bernal, Steve Fowler

Plot

The original UK plot: When the children are asleep, their toys play, especially the engines and carriages of the train set. They race across the set in a series of contests. There's the macho Pacific Daylight (better known as Greaseball), the fastest diesel, in contrast to Rusty, the little steam engine who merely works in the sidings. From France there's Bobo (Sudest), Italy offers Espresso (Settobello), and then there are the APT and entries from Russia, Japan and, at the last minute, the electrically powered super engine, Electra (AC/DC). They vie for superiority along with the best cars, trucks and cabooses. Rusty pulls the three boxcars, Rocky I, II and III. No chance for Rusty, it seems, with the smoking car, Ashley, Buffy the restaurant car, or the brand-new Pearl. Just to make his job more difficult, there's a two-timing guard's van called CB, who does all he can to sabotage Rusty and leave the way clear for Electra and Greaseball.

One by one the bigger, more powerful, locos come to grief. Rusty's Poppa wins an eliminator, but Rusty, with the help of the Starlight Express (his guiding star in the sky), must take over. He defeats Electra, and finally Pearl realises that Rusty is her engine. Greaseball may have a future – converted to steam and with Dinah in tow! There's a light at the end of the tunnel, and old-fashioned steam has beaten the new technologies (you knew this was a fairy story, didn't you?).

Music and Songs (Original Version)

Lloyd Webber in his rock 'n' roll mode. Combining mostly heavy rock with a touch of blues, spirituals, gospel and country and Western, this is a tribute to American popular music of the 1960s, '70s and '80s. There were alterations, eliminations and additions made for America, but the basic score includes 'Rolling stock' (Greaseball), 'AC/DC' (Electra and company), 'U.N.C.O.U.P.L.E.D' (Dinah, Ashley, Buffy and Belle), 'I am the Starlight' (Rusty and Starlight Express), 'One rock 'n' roll too many' (CB and Greaseball), 'Only me, only you' (Pearl and Rusty), 'Light at the end of the tunnel' (the company), 'Make up my heart' (Pearl) and 'Next time you fall in love' (Pearl and Rusty).

Did You Know?

✶ The American production used a revised and simplified story, eliminating CB and adding new songs. These changes have been adopted (since 23 November 1992) in the second edition of the version running in London – a rewritten script, new songs and various other alterations added up to half a million pounds worth of changes.

✶ After *Cats* this is the longest-running Andrew Lloyd Webber show.

The Critics

'Andrew Lloyd Webber's new show, with pert lyrics by Richard Stilgoe and book by nobody who is named marks the apotheosis of the High Tech masque' – *The Observer*
'The musical, in its best moments, surges out and around the building, like a stage version of *Rollerball* and ironically establishes the value of steam engines at the expense of diesels' – *Financial Times*
'As spectacle, overwhelming, as engineering, phenomenal. You have to see it – and then you won't believe it' – *The Daily Telegraph*

Recommended Recording

Original London cast (CD) Polydor 821 597-2
Even though Andrew Lloyd Webber has written a number of American-based shows, this is his most American in sound. The full original cast version is a great piece of childhood fun and none the worse for that.

Stop the World, I Want to Get Off

LYRICS ✶ Leslie Bricusse and Anthony Newley
MUSIC ✶ Leslie Bricusse and Anthony Newley
BOOK ✶ Leslie Bricusse and Anthony Newley

First Performance

London, Queen's Theatre, 20 July 1961 (485 performances)
New York, Shubert Theater, 3 October 1962 (555 performances)

Principal Characters

Littlechap
Evie Littlechap ✶ His wife
Jane Littlechap ✶ His daughter
Susan Littlechap ✶ His daughter

Original London Cast

Anthony Newley, Anna Quayle, Jennifer Baker, Susan Baker

Original New York Cast

Anthony Newley, Anna Quayle, Jennifer Baker, Susan Baker

Plot

In the nonstop circus of life, Littlechap thinks he's cleverer than the other clowns. He deserves to be ringmaster, doesn't he?

First of all, it's time to acquire some wealth – a thousand a week should be enough for that trip to Cannes, Capri or Ascot. From his bedsit off South Kensington's Brompton Road. But first, how about chatting up Evie – on the top deck of the 8.30 bus?

So to marriage and his boss is Evie's father; Littlechap is on his way up the ladder. He was the teaboy, and now he's manager of the northern office in Sludgepool!

The flesh is weak, however. On a trip to Russia he's seduced by Anya, then there's German Ilse and American Ginnie (funny how they all look like Evie, though). Meanwhile, there are mountains to build and politicians to charm with the acuity of his responses, not to mention the fellow members of Snobb's Club. Yet, despite his involvement in international affairs, he doesn't seem able to father the son he's always dreamed about.

Littlechap is old now and, on reflection, his life was superficial and added up to nothing. Evie, at last recognised as the most important person in his life, has died. And yet all is not completely lost. Before he dies himself, Littlechap witnesses the birth of his grandson, born to his second daughter, Jane, who will inherit Littlechap's mixed legacy of triumphs and failures.

Music and Songs

As richly and melodiously packed a score as any English show has achieved, including 'Once in a lifetime' (Littlechap), 'Gonna build a mountain' (Littlechap) and 'What kind of fool am I?' (Littlechap), plus 'Typically English' (Evie), 'Lumbered' (Littlechap) and 'Meilinki Meilchick' (Littlechap).

Did You Know?

∗ The 1963 Tony awards found Newley nominated as best actor.

∗ The show was produced in thanks to Anthony Newley who had stepped down from starring in a show in Brighton when a bigger star became available.

∗ This was the first of the three allegorical musicals part-written by, and all starring, Anthony Newley (the others were *The Roar of the Greasepaint* and *The Good Old Bad Old Days*). Unique in the history of British musical theatre, they contain some of the most attractive songs written for the stage in the 1960s and '70s.

∗ The show was performed in the setting of a circus ring, with Newley as a white-faced clown. On Broadway one of his successors was Joel Grey, who would also be in white-face for his role in *Cabaret* some years later.

The Critics

'It is so unexpectedly fresh' – *New York World Telegram & Sun*
'Commonplace and repetitious' – *New York Times*
'The kind of show you are likely to love or to loathe. Frankly we can take it or leave it – mostly leave it' – *Daily Mirror* (US)

Recommended Recording

Studio cast (CD) TER CDTER2 1172
This complete recording has the wonderfully resourceful Louise Gold playing the female roles, and Mike Holloway the role of Littlechap. Those who want to relish the unique talents of both Anthony Newley and Anna Quayle can choose between the original London and Broadway cast recordings – the London one **(Deram 820 958-2)** has the edge.

Film

Warner Brothers, 1966. Starring Millicent Martin and Tony Tanner (who took over from Newley in the London production). Directed by Philip Saville.

Strike Up The Band

LYRICS ✳ Ira Gershwin
MUSIC ✳ George Gershwin
BOOK ✳ Morrie Ryskind, based on an original libretto by George S. Kaufman

First Performance

New York, Times Square Theatre, 14 January 1930 (191 performances)

Principal Characters

Col. Holmes ✳ The Unofficial Spokesman
Gideon ✳ His side-kick
Grace Draper ✳ Founder of the City Air Movement
Anne Draper ✳ Her daughter
Jim Townsend ✳ A journalist
Horace J. Fletcher ✳ A chocolate manufacturer
Joan Fletcher ✳ His daughter

Original New York Cast

Bobby Clark, Paul McCullough, Blanche Ring, Doris Carson, Jerry Goff,
Dudley Clements, Margaret Schilling

Plot

The show is a dream, the happenings bear no resemblance to the truth at all and the fact that Colonel Holmes is rather like President Wilson's adviser, Colonel House, is an amazing coincidence. Horace J. Fletcher is an American chocolate manufacturer who wants the United States to go to war with Switzerland so that he can sell more of his chocolates. He has enrolled Colonel Holmes, the President's confidential adviser, to help and has said that he is willing to put up the cash for the war, as long as it is named after him. Grace Draper is after Fletcher's support for her movement, while her daughter is more interested in a young man. Another romance is on its way, for Joan Fletcher has found out who wrote an unflattering article about her; it was the handsome James (Jim) Townsend. The reason he has written it is to get her attention, and he has succeeded.

The war is a failure, as the troops do not fight, which upsets the tourists hoping to see a good battle. The Swiss troops can never be found (because of clever use of the yodel), and the American troops have all their buttons cut off, making any movement difficult. Fletcher becomes a pacifist, a new general is found and the boys retreat back home. Mrs Draper is pursued by Colonel Holmes as he believes her to be a millionaire and the younger set make up their differences and have a happy ending.

Music and Songs

George and Ira Gershwin at their best. The title song (the only song to get to the film bearing the show's name) is a rousing chorus number enticing people to war.

Comedy numbers such as 'Typical self-made man' (Fletcher, Jim and the Yes-Men) and 'Oh this is such a lovely war' (Soldiers and Swiss Girls) sit nicely with the romantic 'Soon' (Jim and Joan) and 'I've got a crush on you' (Timothy and Anne). And there is always 'The man I love', sung by Joan and Jim before it was cut.

Did You Know?

∗ The show was originally seen in 1927 at Long Beach, New Jersey but it was taken off after two weeks and Morrie Ryskind was brought in to re-write the book.

∗ The re-write took out the original plot that Switzerland and the United States go to war over cheese imports and shifted it to chocolate.

∗ The song 'The man I love' was dropped from the show, a fate that followed it in two more shows.

∗ The pit orchestra was the Red Nichols Band and it included Benny Goodman, Gene Krupa, Glen Miller, Jimmy Dorsey and Jack Teagarden.

The Critics

'I don't remember ever before in a musical comedy having noticed or understood what it was all about. Here all is not clear but really startling. Of all things in the world, here is a bitter, rather good satirical attack on war, genuine propaganda at times, sung and danced on Broadway to standing room only' – *The World*

Recommended Recording

Studio cast (CD) Elecktra Nonesuch 79273 – 2
This fine restored version is based on the 1927 production but includes the new songs brought in for the 1930 Broadway version. It has a fine cast including Brent Barrett, Rebecca Luker and Don Chastain.

Film

MGM,1940. Starring Mickey Rooney and Judy Garland.

The Student Prince in Heidelberg

LYRICS ✶ Dorothy Donnelly
MUSIC ✶ Sigmund Romberg
BOOK ✶ Dorothy Donnelly, based on the play *Old Heidelberg* by
Rudolf Bleichman, adapted from the German play *Alt Heidelberg*

First Performance

New York, Al Jolson Theater, 2 December 1924 (608 performances)
London, His Majesty's Theatre, 3 February 1926 (96 performances)

Principal Characters

Karl-Franz ✶ A student prince
Kathie ✶ A serving girl
Dr Engel ✶ A tutor
Lutz
Captain Tarnitz
Detlef ✶ A student

Original New York Cast

Howard Marsh, Ilse Marvenga, Greek Evans, George Hassell,
John Coast, Raymond Marlowe

Original London Cast

Allan Prior, Ilse Marvenga, Herbert Waterous, Oscar Figman,
John Coast, Raymond Marlowe

Plot

Prince Karl-Franz is about to spend a year at Heidelberg University before taking up his state duties. He goes with his tutor, Dr Engel (who is also, unwillingly, to act as a spy for the court, reporting back on the prince to his grandfather, the king), and lives in Dr Engel's old lodgings, an inn called The Three Golden Apples. This hostelry is graced by the presence of waitress Kathie. Karl-Franz is invited to join the Saxon Corps by student leader Detlef, and embraces student life with all its sensual pleasures. He declares his intention of being just a student while in Heidelberg and not a prince.

Soon the prince has a visitor: his future wife, Princess Margaret. This throws him into a panic. The princess represents everything from which student life has freed him. Impulsively he calls Kathie to escape to Paris with him. But it's too late. News arrives from the palace: the king is dying and Karl-Franz must return to be betrothed to Princess Margaret. He tries to escape, but is unsuccessful. Kathie understands.

It's two years later, and King Karl-Franz, still unmarried, receives a visitor, a waiter from The Three Golden Apples who brings him up to date with the news.

Kathie weeps alone in her room, the inn has failed and is being sold, and the prince's fiery fellow students have sunk into conventional lives.

Karl-Franz returns to Heidelberg, but Princess Margaret has preceded him. She asks Kathie to release the former prince from his marriage proposal, and to leave the city herself and get married. When Karl-Franz arrives, Kathie tells him she is to return to her village to marry her former fiancé, while he, the king, must marry Margaret, who truly loves him.

Music and Songs

One of the most gorgeous, sumptuous and romantic scores of its period, this is Romberg at his best. The score includes 'Golden days' (Engel), 'Come boys, let's all be gay boys' (the Saxon Corps), 'Gaudeamus igitur' (the students), 'Deep in my heart' (Kathie and Karl-Franz), 'Drinking song' (Karl-Franz and the students), 'Serenade' (Karl-Franz) and 'Just we two' (Tarnitz and Margaret).

Did You Know?

✷ Presented originally as a play without music, the story flopped twice. The musical failed first time round in London, too.

✷ The American producers, the Shuberts, were sure the show would fail because it had retained the unhappy ending of the original play, at the composer's insistence. They were duly proved wrong.

✷ The 1954 film was the most successful of any using music by Romberg.

The Critics

'The first rank of shows to which you would not be ashamed to take a real musician' – *Life*
'The production is nicely scored and magnificently sung, and merited even the cheers that were sent across the footlights' – *New York Times*
'Spectacular and triumphant in every sense . . . a musical smash, colourful, gorgeous' – *Variety*

Recommended Recording

Studio cast (CD) TER CDTER2 1172
This is a complete recording starring Norman Bailey, Marilyn Hill Smith, Diana Montague and David Bendall. All you could ask in this beautifully produced double set CD.

Films

MGM, 1927. Starring Ramon Navarro and Norma Shearer. Directed by Ernst Lubitsch. The film had no music.
MGM, 1954. Starring Edmund Purdom (with Mario Lanza's singing voice) and Ann Blyth. Directed by Richard Thorpe.

Sunday in the Park with George

LYRICS ✳ Stephen Sondheim
MUSIC ✳ Stephen Sondheim
BOOK ✳ James Lapine

First Performance

New York, Booth Theater, 2 May 1984 (604 performances)
London, Royal National Theatre, 15 March 1990 (in repertoire)

Principal Characters

George ✳ A painter
Dot ✳ His mistress*
Marie ✳ Their child*

*Dot and Marie are played by the same person.

Original New York Cast

Mandy Patinkin, Bernadette Peters

Original London Cast

Philip Quast, Maria Friedman

Plot

The first act takes place in Paris in 1884. George is an obsessive painter, whose aim is to take a clean sheet of paper and imbue it with order through composition, balance, light and harmony. He's in the open air when we first meet him, sketching his mistress, Dot. Painting consumes him. That evening he cancels a promised evening out with Dot, to complete painting a hat in his latest composition. That's enough for Dot; she leaves him and takes up with pastry cook, Louis.

George meanwhile sketches the visitors to the river bank, for inclusion in his masterpiece, *A Summer Evening on the Island of the Grande Jatte*. His finished painting receives a mixed reception from his art-lover friends. Dot, after a final plea to be reunited with George, plans to leave for America with Louis, and with her baby, fathered by George. The first act ends with all the characters placed in a living tableau of the painting by George – he has imposed his order at last.

A hundred years later, and the completed picture hangs in a Chicago art gallery. Now there's another George, a direct descendant of the painter through his daughter Marie, the present George's grandmother. He's been commissioned to prepare a work in celebration of the famous painting. He comes up with a mechanical performance work that he calls a chromolume. It's number seven in a series. Something goes wrong when it's unveiled, but all is rescued thanks to an ex-NASA scientist.

His 98-year-old grandmother slips in and out of rationality at the launch party. She believes that Children and Art are the most two important things you can bequeath to posterity.

George is invited to La Grande Jatte to present his chromolume there. Marie has died in the interim and George makes the trip alone, except for the scientist, and Marie's red notebook, which she (and now George) has inherited from Dot, complete with grammar exercises. Somehow the ghost of Dot appears, to help her great-grandson disperse the mental creative block from which he's currently suffering. George resolves to move on, as the remaining ghosts of the picture appear and re-form into the living tableau of Seurat's work, as at the end of the first act.

Music and Songs

A superb, shimmering collection that, amazingly, reflects the painterly style of Georges Seurat in music. In addition, the show contains some of the most intensely passionate expressions of emotion written for the Broadway stage: 'We do not belong together' (Dot) and 'Move on' (Dot and George) are good instances of this. Other songs are 'Sunday in the park with George' (Dot), 'The day off' (denizens of the park), 'Everybody loves Louis' (Dot), 'Finishing the hat' (George) and 'Putting it together' (art gallery attendees).

Did You Know?

∗ The Seurat painting which contains all the characters of the first act (except the painter) is in the Art Institute of Chicago.

∗ Although not doing well at the Tonys, *Sunday in the Park with George* won the Pulitzer Prize for drama in April 1985.

The Critics

The critical comments were varied:

'A lovely, wildly inventive score that sometimes remakes the French composers whose revolution in music paralleled the post-impressionists in art' – *New York Times*

'To say that this show breaks new ground is not enough; it also breaks new sky, new water, new flesh and new spirit. That harmless sounding title masks more daring and surprise than the American musical stage has seen for some time' – *Newsweek*

Recommended Recording

Original Broadway cast (CD) RCA RD85042
The only recording of the show so far. However, it would be hard to believe another could better this experimental musical piece. Both Bernadette Peters and Mandy Patinkin are at their best.

Sunny

LYRICS ✳ Otto Harbach and Oscar Hammerstein II
MUSIC ✳ Jerome Kern
BOOK ✳ Otto Harbach and Oscar Hammerstein II

First Performance

New York, New Amsterdam Theater, 22 September 1925 (517 performances)
London, Hippodrome Theatre, 7 October 1926 (363 performances)

Principal Characters

Sunny Peters ✳ A circus rider
Jim Deming ✳ A circus owner
Harold Harcourt Wendell-Wendell, Weenie Winters
✳ A dance team
Siegfried Peters ✳ Sunny's father
Tom Warren ✳ An admirer of Sunny

Original New York Cast

Marilyn Miller, Jack Donahue, Clifton Webb, Mary Hay,
Joseph Cawthorn, Paul Frawley

Original London Cast

Binnie Hale, Jack Buchanan, Claude Hulbert, Elsie Randolph,
Nicholas Adams, Jack Hobbs

Plot

Sunny Peters is a bareback rider in a circus currently tented in Southampton in England. World War I has just ended. An American regiment is in town; they're appropriately grateful for the entertainment that Sunny and her troupe have given them during the war, and consequently serenade her with the show's title song.

One of the company is Tom Warren, and he and Sunny soon resume a previous relationship which rapidly turns romantic. (They had briefly known each other as children.) But their path doesn't run smooth.

Sunny wants to get back to America and resume a full stage career. Luck takes a hand when Sunny turns out to have not enough money for the fare. She becomes an inadvertent stowaway on the boat carrying Tom home, when she goes down to the docks to see him off, fails to leave the ship on the last bell and gets swept away. Tom and Sunny are reunited in a fashionable resort in the Southern states at a Hunt Ball.

The complexities of the remainder of the plot, involving a marriage and planned divorce of convenience, are made no easier by the fact that the alterations were made in London, presumably to satisfy the admirers of Jack Buchanan, who played Jim, the circus owner.

Music and Songs

Some early Kern classics which show the rhythmic bounce and melodic drive of a 20th-century master musician, gradually pulling away from European roots to incorporate the vigour and strength of native American music. The score includes such standards as 'Who?' (Tom and Sunny) and 'Sunny' (Tom), plus 'I might grow fond of you' (Weenie and Harold) and 'D'ye love me?' (Sunny).

Did You Know?

✴ This was the first collaboration between Jerome Kern and Oscar Hammerstein II.

✴ Fred Astaire was credited with having choreographed Marilyn Miller's dance numbers in the show.

✴ The show took over $2.4 million during its run – a considerable achievement for the time.

✴ On screen both Judy Garland and June Haver have portrayed Marilyn Miller and sung the hit song 'Who?'

The Critics

Kern's score was described as 'aristocratic' in the New York Herald Tribune. 'The show was better than Sally' exclaimed the New York Daily News.

Recommended Recording

Original London cast (CD) Pearl 27031 9105/AEI AEI-CD 050
Eight of the songs captured in their authentic 1926 sound from the original 78s. Also on this historical issue are songs from Richard Rodgers' Lido Lady and Jerome Kern's Show Boat and all with their original London casts. The AEI disc has the same material plus additional tracks from the Broadway cast and studio recordings.

Films

Warner Brothers, 1939. Starring Marilyn Miller, Joe Donahue and Lawrence Gray. Directed by William A. Seiter.
RKO, 1941. Starring Anna Neagle, Ray Bolger and John Carroll. Directed by Herbert Wilcox.

Sunset Boulevard

LYRICS ✶ Don Black and Christopher Hampton
MUSIC ✶ Andrew Lloyd Webber
BOOK ✶ Don Black and Christopher Hampton,
based on the Billy Wilder film

First Performance

London, Adelphi Theatre, 12 July 1993 (1529 performances)
Los Angeles, Shubert Theater, 9 December 1993 (369 performances)
New York, Minskoff Theater, 17 November 1994 (977 performances)

Principal Characters

Norma Desmond ✶ A star of the silent screen
Joe Gillis ✶ A young screenwriter
Max von Mayerling ✶ Norma's major-domo
Betty Schaefer ✶ A secretary at Paramount

Original London Cast

Patti Lupone, Kevin Anderson, Daniel Benazi, Meredith Braun

Original New York Cast

Glenn Close, Allan Campbell, George Hearn, Judy Kuhn

Plot

Joe Gillis hasn't had much success as a screen writer. His car runs out of gas on Sunset Boulevard, outside the mansion owned by former silent film star, Norma Desmond. Repossession agents are in hot pursuit of him and his car. He hides the car in the garage and asks if he can phone his friends. But Miss Desmond has another, better, idea. She wants to make a screen comeback. He's a writer, perhaps he can lick her self-penned script, *Salome*, into shape for presentation to Cecil B. de Mille. He can live at the mansion too, all expenses paid. That seems fine. But there's a complication. When he goes back to the studio in an attempt to borrow money, he meets young Betty Schaefer, who subsequently cooperates on another script with him – one of his own. And Norma is jealous.

Back at the mansion, Joe realises that Norma has fallen in love with him. She lavishes expensive gifts on him and attempts suicide when he goes out to a party. Joe finishes the script and Norma prepares to sally forth to present it to de Mille. A phone call from the studio invites her to visit, but all they want is the use of her car for a film. Max, her major-domo (and ex-husband), conceals this from her. Norma goes to the studio and de Mille greets her, but is noncommittal on her script. Norma discovers Joe is having a relationship with Betty, and phones her. Joe, snatching the receiver from Norma, invites her over to see how he's living. When Betty arrives, Joe announces he's leaving with her. Norma is beside herself with rage and grief. She shoots Joe dead. Now totally beyond the bounds of reality, she mistakes the arriving police, come to arrest her, for studio executives. She's ready for her close up, Mr de Mille.

Music and Songs

Lloyd Webber has come up with a fine and brooding score that fits the dark and involving subject. He has written no finer score to date than this. For the heroine there are memorable, throbbing ballads, and for the youngsters, songs that sound as if they came straight out of B movies. 'Just one look' (Norma), 'As if we never said goodbye' (Norma) and 'The perfect year' (Norma) are a nice contrast to the joyous 'Too much in love to care' (Joe and Betty) and 'Girl meets boy' (Joe, Betty and Arnie).

Did You Know?

✶ The show is virtually in two sections: the world of Norma Desmond, complete with her mansion and a brief visit to Paramount Studios; and Joe's outside world, with his friends Arnie and Betty, and the action that takes place in streets, restaurants and public areas of Hollywood itself.

✶ It was originally intended that Miss Lupone would head the casts of both the London and Broadway productions. However, the management decided to offer the part of Norma to Glenn Close, who headed the Los Angeles version.

✶ Daniel Benzali, Max in London, made a name for himself in the TV series, *Murder One*.

✶ The principal role of Norma has attracted many great stage performers over the years, including Elaine Paige, Betty Buckley, Rita Moreno and Petula Clark.

The Critics

'Andrew Lloyd Webber's masterpiece' – *Wall Street Journal*
'In terrific voice, Patti Lupone has most of the star quality required and is magnificently harrowing' – *The Independent*
'*Sunset Boulevard* is a rip-roaring hit' – *The Sunday Times*

Recommended Recording

Original Broadway cast (CD) Polydor 31452 33507-2
The cast that started off in Los Angeles with Glenn Close starring. This version incorporates some revisions to the original London cast version with Patti Lupone. The Broadway cast recording is better simply because of the lead's performance, Glenn Close gets closer to the part and is vocally more sure. An exciting performance captured to perfection on disc.

Film

Paramount, 1950. Starring Gloria Swanson and William Holden. Directed by Billy Wilder. This is the film on which Lloyd Webber based his musical.

Sweeney Todd

LYRICS ∗ Stephen Sondheim
MUSIC ∗ Stephen Sondheim
BOOK ∗ Hugh Wheeler, based on a play by Christopher Bond,
in turn based on *A String of Pearls* (1847) by George Dibdin

First Performance

New York, Uris Theater, 1 March 1979 (557 performances)
London, Theatre Royal, Drury Lane, 2 July 1980 (157 performances)

Principal Characters

Sweeny Todd ∗ A barber
Mrs Lovett ∗ A pie-maker
Judge Turpin
Anthony ∗ A young seaman
Tobias ∗ Mrs Lovett's handyman
Johanna ∗ A young ward

Original New York Cast

Len Cariou, Angela Lansbury, Edmund Lyndeck, Victor Garber,
Ken Jennings, Sarah Rice

Original London Cast

Denis Quilley, Sheila Hancock, Austin Kent, Andrew C. Wadsworth,
Michael Staniforth, Mandy More

Plot

It's fifteen years since Sweeney Todd was last in London; he bids farewell to a fellow seafarer, young Anthony, and makes for Fleet Street. Once Todd had a wife and a child, but the sexual machinations of a wily judge robbed him of both, and landed him with a prison sentence in exile. Now he's back. Todd resumes his profession as a barber in premises above a pie shop, where he plans to kill the judge. In the interim he's recognised by a rival barber, Pirelli. The latter is soon the first victim of Todd's cruel blade.

Anthony plans to run off with Todd's daughter, Johanna, now the judge's ward (and future wife), and thus inadvertently thwarts Todd's plan of revenge. Todd starts on a murder spree, using a special barber's chair. The bodies are recycled by Mrs Lovett, the pie-maker, into the best pies in London.

Anthony rescues Johanna from an asylum where the judge has placed her. The judge falls victim to Todd's blade. So does a beggar woman, who turns out to be Todd's wife. (Mrs Lovett had assured him that his wife was dead, in order to further her own romantic designs on Todd.) He throws Mrs Lovett into the pie oven and is then himself slain by her loyal helper, Tobias. That leaves only Anthony and Johanna as survivors of the carnage. So ends the tale of Sweeney Todd.

Music and Songs

Sondheim at his most melodically glorious and verbally acute, drawing on the styles of English ballads and folk music, and on operatic and common broadsheet melodies. The score is constantly captivating and consistently inventive, and just about every song is a highlight. They include 'The ballad of Sweeney Todd' (the company), 'No place like London' (Todd), 'The worst pies in London' (Mrs Lovett), 'Poor thing' (Mrs Lovett and Todd), 'My friends' (Todd and Mrs Lovett), 'Green finch and linnet bird' (Johanna), 'Johanna' (Anthony), 'Pretty women' (Judge and Todd), 'A little priest' (Todd and Mrs Lovett) and 'Not while I'm around' (Tobias and Mrs Lovett).

Did You Know?

✶ Apart from creating thoroughly authentic and beautiful Victorian ditties and ballads, the composer amused himself by using a William Walton-like musical cadence whenever the word London was set.

✶ The splendid, intimate Royal National Theatre revival cast at the Cottesloe featured Alun Armstrong as Todd (replaced by Denis Quilley on transfer to a larger theatre), Julia McKenzie as Mrs Lovett, and Adrian Lester as Anthony. The original Johanna was in the show's ensemble.

✶ *Sweeney Todd* won eight Tony Awards, including those for both its stars, score and libretto.

The Critics

'Sondheim's score, the most distinguished to grace Broadway in years, owes more to Mahler, Alban Berg and Benjamin Britten than Weill' – *New York Times*
'A staggering theater spectacle and more fun than a graveyard on the night of the annual skeleton's ball' – *New York Daily News*
'In sheer ambition and size there's never been a bigger musical on Broadway . . . Sweeney Todd is brilliant, even sensationally so' – *Newsweek*
'*Sweeney Todd* is one giant step for vegetarianism' – *Time*

Recommended Recording

Original Broadway cast (CD) RCA Victor 3379-2-RC
A definitive recording of a powerful show with both Angela Lansbury and Len Cariou so perfect for their roles. This remains the only English language recording of the show, even though other great performances have been seen in other productions. This, however, could hardly be bettered for its chilling representation of the madness of the characters portrayed.

Film

Sweeney Todd was filmed for television in 1982 with George Hearn and Angela Lansbury.

Sweet Adeline

LYRICS ✶ Oscar Hammerstein II
MUSIC ✶ Jerome Kern
BOOK ✶ Oscar Hammerstein II

First Performance

New York, Hammerstein's Theatre, 3 September 1929 (234 performances)

Principal Characters

Adeline ✶ A singer
James Day ✶ A socialite
Tom ✶ A seaman
Lulu Ward ✶ A musical comedy star
Sid Barnett ✶ A composer
Rupert Day ✶ A devotee of drama

Original New York Cast

Helen Morgan, Robert Chisholm, Max Hoffman Jnr, Irene Franklin,
John D. Seymour, Charles Butterworth

Plot

A musical romance of the Gay Nineties, *Sweet Adeline* tells the story of a talented young singer and waitress who works in a Hoboken beer garden owned by her father. She falls in love with Tom Martin, the first mate on the steamship the SS *Paul*. Tom goes off to fight in the Spanish-American War.

When he returns, Adeline loses Tom to her younger sister Nellie. Adeline subsequently resolves to find success through a theatrical career, and becomes a musical comedy actress under the name Adeline Beaumont. In her rise to the top she is helped by Rupert Day, a lover of the theatre; Lulu Ward, a comic diva; and by a wealthy socialite, James Day, with whom she falls in love. But James' family strongly disapprove of his relationship with an actress, and the couple part. Adeline then turns finally to the composer Sid Barnett for consolation.

Music and Songs

A harmonious and skilful set of songs which bowed graciously to the world of the Gay Nineties. The songs had a plaintive quality and an organic rhythm that was inherently pleasing. For Helen Morgan, playing Adeline, there were also torch songs (passionate songs of unrequited love). Favourite numbers from the score include 'Here am I' (Adeline and Dot), 'Why was I born?' (Adeline), 'Some girl is on your mind' (James, Tom, Sid, Thornton and the male ensemble) and 'Don't ever leave me' (Adeline and James).

Did You Know?

✳ As well as the musical being presented by Oscar Hammerstein II's Uncle Arthur at the Hammerstein Theatre, his Uncle Reginald staged the show – truly a family affair!

✳ The show was written for Helen Morgan after her success in *Show Boat*. She had an omnipresent, archetypal stage mother, so the collaborators named the character of Lulu after her.

✳ The overture to the show did not consist of tunes by Kern, but his arrangements of melodies of the time in which the show was set.

The Critics

'Different and as tuneful and colorful as it is unusual, well acted and full of substance; it is like reviewing history by taking sugar-coated pellets' – *Evening Union*
'A gentle opera with appropriate music . . . one of the politest frolics of the new year' – *New York Herald Tribune*

Recommended Recording

This rather pleasant score has not been served well on disc and there is no recording to recommend.

Film

Warner Brothers, 1935. Starring Irene Dunne and Donald Woods.

Sweet Charity

LYRICS ✳ Dorothy Fields
MUSIC ✳ Cy Coleman
BOOK ✳ Neil Simon, based on the film *Nights of Cabiria*,
directed by Federico Fellini, Tullio Pinelli and Ennio Flaiano

First Performance

New York, Palace Theater, 29 January 1966 (608 performances)
London, Prince of Wales Theatre, 11 October 1967 (476 performances)

Principal Characters

Charity Hope Valentine ✳ A dance-hall hostess
Oscar Lindquist ✳ A punter
Nickie ✳ A hostess
Helene ✳ A hostess
Vittorio Vidal ✳ A film star
Johann Sebastian Brubeck ✳ A Rhythm of Life churchman
Good Fairy

Original New York Cast

Gwen Verdon, John McMartin, Helen Gallagher, Thelma Oliver, James Luisi,
Arnold Soboloff, Ruth Buzzi

Original London Cast

Juliet Prowse, Rod McLennan, Josephine Blake, Paula Kelly, John Keston,
Fred Evans, Joyanne Delancy

Plot

We are in New York's Central Park as Charity is joined by her latest boyfriend
Charley, who, like the others, is only in love with her money and, catching hold of
her purse, he pushes her into the lake and walks off. Later that evening at the Fan-
Dango Ballroom Charity tells her version – but her fellow hostesses know Charity
is lying and she comes to terms with what has happened. Later, outside the
Pompeii Club, the film star Vittorio Vidal is attempting to coax Ursala, his very
angry and jealous girl-friend, back into the club. Accidentally he pushes Charity,
who gets invited into the club and ends up in his apartment where she collects a
few souvenirs. But Ursala returns and Charity spends the night in the closet.

Charity decides to improve herself by joining a cultural group and here she
meets Oscar – only their elevator comes to an unscheduled stop and he is
claustrophobic. When it eventually starts they escape and visit the Rhythm of Life
Church in a converted garage. The police raid the premises and once again they
escape. Safely back on the street, they arrange to meet again and Charity decides
to tell Oscar the truth about herself – only she can't get around to it. Eventually
she has to and she sends him a telegram asking him to meet her. Charity confesses
– only to find he has already discovered what she does for a living and he still
wants to marry her. At the ballroom the girls and Herman, the owner, are

preparing a surprise party. But all is not well when the couple arrive, for Oscar now has doubts and leaves. Once again Charity is alone – but now she is alone with a new ability to shrug off life's problems.

Music and Songs

Cy Coleman, a major Broadway composer, at his brassy best. This is the irresistible sound of Broadway at its most mindblowingly confident. Well-known numbers from the show include 'I'm a brass band' (Charity and friends), 'If my friends could see me now' (Charity), 'The Rhythm of Life' (church members), 'Too many tomorrows' (Vidal), 'There's gotta be something better than this' (Charity and friends) and 'Where am I going?' (Charity).

Did You Know?

✱ This is Cy Coleman's most successful and most often revived show.

✱ Another film by Federico Fellini also provided the plot for a successful Broadway show: $8^{1/2}$ became *Nine*.

✱ The electrifying choreography by Bob Fosse makes *Sweet Charity* one of Broadway's greatest-ever dance musicals, and it earned him the Tony Award.

✱ The original concept had a comic strip concept with comments on the action on the stage appearing in comic strip voice bubbles.

The Critics

'Irresistible' – *Daily Express*
'A triumph' – *The Sun*
'Everybody, but everybody, had a whale of a time . . . a sweet sexy fairy tale – nice and dirty, witty and pretty, with enough energy to pop the corks of every bottle of non-fizz in the West End. And funny, very funny, too' – *Daily Sketch*

Recommended Recording

Original Broadway cast (CD) Columbia CK 2900
A classic Broadway score with Gwen Verdon bringing out every nuance of joy from Dorothy Fields' lyrics. Cy Coleman's dance music is stunning and, while well represented here, can be heard to perfection in the complete studio cast recording on **JAY CDJAY2 1284**. The original London cast version with Juliet Prowse is also good.

Film

Universal Pictures, 1969. Starring Shirley MacLaine, John McMartin, Riccardo Montalban, Chita Rivera and Sammy Davis Junior. Directed by Bob Fosse.

Take Me Along

LYRICS ✳ Bob Merrill
MUSIC ✳ Bob Merrill
BOOK ✳ Joseph Stein and Robert Russell,
based on Eugene O'Neill's play *Ah Wilderness*

First Performance

New York, Shubert Theater, 22 October 1959 (448 performances)

Principal Characters

Richard Miller ✳ Our hero
Muriel Macomber ✳ His sweetheart
Sid ✳ Nat's brother-in-law
Aunt Lily
Nat Miller ✳ Richard's father
Essie Miller ✳ Richard's mother

Original New York Cast

Robert Morse, Susan Luckey, Jackie Gleason, Eileen Herlie,
Walter Pidgeon, Una Merkel

Plot

It's small-town America in 1906. Nat Miller runs the local newspaper, the *Centerville Globe*. His son, Richard, is suffering all the pangs of young love with his girlfriend, Muriel Macomber, and reads her romantic literature. Unfortunately her father overhears and locks up Muriel for a month, banning Richard from seeing her. He also cancels an ad in Nat Miller's paper.

Nat's brother-in-law, Sid, is in town. Can he and Aunt Lily, an elderly spinster, plight their troth? Muriel Macomber's father storms into the house and demands that Richard be punished; Nat, the proud father, refuses to comply.

Meanwhile, Sid, sober for once, proposes to Lily; well, he must stay sober, especially for the Fourth of July picnic. Richard is despondent, for he receives a note in which Muriel calls off their engagement. So he's in the right mood to visit a local saloon with his friend, Wint. At dinner time, Sid is drunk again. Poor Lily.

At the Pleasant Beach House, Richard gets drunk and falls asleep. Back home, his father tries to sober him up, and teaches him a few facts of life into the bargain. Richard learns that Muriel was forced by her father to break off the engagement. They'll find some way of making up. All is now well, and Richard looks forward to going to university. Meanwhile, Lily and Sid will try to make a go of it – but the flesh is weak. He's got to take up again his newspaper job in Waterbury, and Lily is packed and ready to accompany him.

Music and Songs

A really charming old-fashioned set of songs, full of good humour, that captures the magic of O'Neill's play, with its turn-of-the-century snapshot of small-town folks. Numbers include 'I would die' (Richard and Muriel), 'Sid ol' kid' (Sid and the townspeople), 'Staying young' (Nat), 'I get embarrassed' (Lily), 'We're home' (Lily), 'Take me along' (Sid and Nat), 'Promise me a rose' (Lily) and 'But yours' (Lily and Sid).

Did You Know?

∗ The show was originally called *Connecticut Summer*.

∗ The same story but with different songs had been used for an MGM musical, *Summer Holiday*, in 1948, starring Mickey Rooney, Walter Huston and Marilyn Maxwell (this has no connection with the 1962 Cliff Richard film or the stage show that recently appeared based on that film).

∗ Jackie Gleason won a Tony Award for his performance.

∗ Jackie Gleason insisted on being the highest-paid player on Broadway. His salary was the same as Alfred Drake's in *Kismet*, plus $50 a week (a weekly total of $5050). As it turned out though, he wasn't. Ethel Merman in *Gypsy* got a percentage of the profits that put her first.

The Critics

'Substitution enough for gaiety. Everyone is in motion, but nothing moves inside the libretto' – *New York Times*
'This latest winner in the Merrill stable burst into the Shubert Theater last night like a berserk brewery truck' – *New York Journal American*

Recommended Recording

Original Broadway cast (CD) RCA Victor 07863–51050-2
A perfectly-formed Bob Merrill score served so well with a bravura performance by Jackie Gleason, the highest-paid Broadway star of the time, Walter Pidgeon, Eileen Herlie and Una Merkel – a cast the likes of which it is doubtful could ever be brought together again.

They're Playing Our Song

LYRICS ✴ Carol Bayer Sager
MUSIC ✴ Marvin Hamlisch
BOOK ✴ Neil Simon

First Performance

New York, Imperial Theater, 11 February 1979 (1082 performances)
London, Shaftesbury Theatre, 1 October 1980 (667 performances)

Principal Characters

Vernon Gersch ✴ A composer
Sonia Walsk ✴ A lyricist

Original New York Cast

Robert Klein, Lucie Arnez

Original London Cast

Tom Conti, Gemma Craven

Plot

Vernon Gersch is thirty-four years old and at the top of his profession as a song writer; why he's even got a couple of Grammy awards and an Oscar. But he's in need of a new lyricist – perhaps it will be Sonia Walsk. He could do with another girlfriend too. They have a lot in common. Both are neurotic Jewish New Yorkers, and they even visit psychiatrists in the same building.

Sonia turns out to be late for just about everything, including her various work appointments with Vernon. But then, she's breaking up with her boyfriend, Leon. In the end Vernon and Sonia agree to work on five songs, but first, how about a trip to a friend's beach house? They eventually get there, but not before Sonia has broken into the wrong house.

Afterwards, and back in New York, Vernon is disturbed – he can't sleep. This is just as well, because Sonia arrives with her suitcases. She can't throw Leon out of her apartment, so she has come to stay with Vernon. Now she won't be late any more, will she? But what about Leon? He's an unseen but tangible presence. Sonia and Vernon write one last song together and then she leaves – for Leon. The song is a success but Vernon is in hospital – he's been involved in a car crash. Sonia visits him, at the same time as Leon has an appointment there for a white blood cell test. By chance, later on Vernon meets Leon, and likes him. Leon's got a new girlfriend, and Sonia's off to London to work with Elton John – or is she? Vernon asks her if she will work in New York with the new, improved Vernon Gersch. Of course she can – and will.

Music and Songs

A catchy, soft rock score with insistent rhythms and cheeky, catchy melodies that include 'Fallin'' (Vernon), 'If he really knew me' (Vernon and Sonia), 'They're playing my song' (Vernon and Sonia), 'Right' (Sonia), 'When you're in my arms' (Vernon) and 'I still believe in love' (Vernon and Sonia).

Did You Know?

✷ Only two characters appear in the show (although there is a chorus to reveal Vernon and Sonia's inner thoughts, which virtually becomes an important character in its own right).

✷ Lucie Arnez of the Broadway cast is the daughter of Lucille Ball and Desi Arnez.

✷ The show has a quality that makes it suitable for both large and small theatres. As a result, it has become a popular choice in English and Scottish regional theatres.

The Critics

The critics enjoyed this slick, well-packaged show:
'Fun and funny, full of blithe good humour, hilarious jokes and witty and pointed characterizations that are endurable and lovable' – *New York Times*
'In terms of originality this is probably the nearest that the Broadway Musical has ever got to an autobiographical home movie' – *Punch*

Recommended Recording

Original Broadway cast (CD) Casablanca 826 240-2M-1
A hard choice as the London cast recording with Tom Conti and Gemma Craven is almost equally as good. However, Robert Klein and Lucie Arnez somehow have that extra Broadway bounce that the show is about, and this just gives it the lead.

Tip-Toes

LYRICS ✴ Ira Gershwin
MUSIC ✴ George Gershwin
BOOK ✴ Guy Bolton and Fred Thompson

First Performance

New York, Liberty Theater, 28 December 1925 (194 performances)
London, Winter Garden Theatre, 31 August 1926 (182 performances)

Principal Characters

Tip-Toes Kaye ✴ A young dancer
Steve Burton ✴ A rich man
Al Kaye ✴ Tip-Toes' uncle
Hen Kaye ✴ Tip-Toes' other uncle
Sylvia Metcalf
Rollo Metcalf ✴ Steve's relatives
Peggy
Binnie

Original New York Cast

Queenie Smith, Allen Kearns, Andrew Tombes, Harry Watson Jnr,
Jeanette MacDonald, Robert Halliday, Amy Revere, Gertrude MacDonald

Original London Cast

Dorothy Dickson, Allen Kearns, Laddie Cliff, John Kirby,
Vera Bryer, Evan Thomas, Eileen Stack, Peggy Beatty

Plot

Tip-Toes is a young dancer stranded at the railway station at Palm Beach, Florida, with her two rascally uncles, Al and Hen Kaye (together they form a vaudeville trio). When they meet Rollo Metcalf and his wife, Sylvia, at the depot they have an idea. The Metcalfs have come to meet Sylvia's brother, Steve. Rollo makes the mistake of flirting with Tip-Toes. As a result, her uncles tap him for some money to enable Tip-Toes to gatecrash the exclusive Surf Club in style to find a suitable backer. To that end they clothe her lavishly and introduce her to society.

Here she meets Rollo's brother-in-law, a millionaire, who has made his money from glue. This is Steve Burton. Steve is no fool (he's worth $7 million for starters). In order to test her, he claims to have lost all his money, to the discomfiture of the uncles. Imagine his delight when Tip-Toes renounces all desire for wealth, it's Steve she wants for herself. Naturally virtue is its own reward and Tip-Toes, by the end of the evening, has both the man – and his money!

Music and Songs

A brash, early, immediately attractive set of songs, high on appeal and sentiment, low on subtlety, but with an irresistible lip-smacking Gershwin style. Songs include 'Looking for a boy' (Tip-toes), 'When do we dance?' (Binnie and company), 'These charming people' (Tip-toes, Al and Hen) and 'That certain feeling' (Tip-toes and Steve).

Did You Know?

✶ Lorenz Hart wrote Ira Gershwin a fan letter for his lyrics: 'Such delicacies prove that songs can be both popular and intelligent.'

✶ Ira Gershwin always felt that this show was the one where he proved himself to be a good lyricist.

✶ Note the inclusion of Jeanette MacDonald. Her film fame was to eclipse the success of everyone else in the cast.

The Critics

'Bright and gay and good looking, the new musical comedy is made altogether captivating by the pretty, rebellious and infectious music of George Gershwin and, all told, the best score he has written in his days in the theatre. All told, I think the best score anyone has written for our town this season' – *The World*

Recommended Recording

This score has yet to reach CD although selections from the 1926 London production were released on (LP) **Monmouth Evergreen MES/7052.**

Film

British National Pictures, 1928. Starring Dorothy Gish, Will Rogers and Nelson Keys. Directed by Herbert Wilcox.

Trelawny

LYRICS ✳ Julian Slade
MUSIC ✳ Julian Slade
BOOK ✳ Aubrey Woods, adapted from the play *Trelawny of the Wells*
by Arthur Wing Pinero

First Performance

London, Sadler's Wells/Prince of Wales Theatre, 27 June 1972 (177 performances)

Principal Characters

Rose Trelawny ✳ An actress
Arthur Gower ✳ Her friend
Sir William Gower ✳ His uncle
Tom Wrench ✳ An actor/playwright
Avonia Bunn ✳ A star of pantomime

Original London Cast

Gemma Craven, John Watts, Max Adrian, Ian Richardson, Elizabeth Power

Plot

Rose Trelawny is the star of the Wells Theatre, but she is about to leave the company – she's giving it all up to marry Arthur Gower, a toff. At the surprise party her friends bid her farewell. There's Tom Wrench (secretly in love with her), her best pal Avonia, who comes into her own with the Christmas pantomime, and the Telfers, old stagers who run the company as actor/managers.

Rose finds it difficult to settle in Cavendish Square, where Arthur is completely under the control of his formidable relatives – especially the terrifying Sir William Gower. In fact, Arthur is boarded out elsewhere and manages but few intimate moments with his beloved Rose. Things come to a head when some of Rose's theatrical friends arrive to visit her. The resulting fracas causes Rose to leave Cavendish Square with them and return to the theatre.

But Rose has changed. She can no longer play in the stagey, artificial way required by the Telfers. She is sacked from her role in the panto and lives out her days in a poky room in theatrical digs. Sir William comes to visit her there. Arthur has disappeared. Does Rose know where he is? Rose does not. Eventually Sir William is told of Rose's true situation and agrees to put up the money for a new, more naturalistic play in which she will be the star, written by Tom Wrench.

At the first rehearsals, Sir William is concealed in a box, as the cast await the arrival of a new, young actor who is to star opposite Rose. Unbeknown to all except Tom, he turns out to be Arthur Gower, now a 'splendid gypsy' like Rose. Sir William is reconciled. Arthur and Rose can look forward to a future together.

Music and Songs

A wonderful score, possibly Julian Slade's finest, full of tender Victorian ballads, witty music-hall numbers and subtle plot-advancing songs. It features 'The one who isn't there' (Rose), 'Two fools' (Arthur and Rose), 'Ever of thee I'm fondly dreaming' (the company), 'The turn of Avonia Bunn' (Avonia) and 'Life' (Tom Wrench).

Did You Know?

∗ Aubrey Woods' book is remarkably faithful to Pinero's original. The characters of Imogen Parrot and Avonia Bunn have been successfully combined, but otherwise the story is the same.

∗ Gemma Craven, the show's Rose, was to take further important roles in the West End in a *South Pacific* revival, *They're Playing Our Song*, and many others.

∗ Cameron Macintosh produced this show.

The Critics

'The best British musical since *Oliver!*' – *Sunday Express*
'Authentic Pinero transformed with sympathy, tact and taste into a rousing, touching, colourful show . . . the dialogue is always powerful and revealing . . . an agreeable assortment of songs constantly hits off the mood of the show' – *The Stage*
'The score flits from Sullivan via vaudeville to Ivor Novello' – *The Times*

Recommended Recording

Original London cast (LP) Decca SKL 5144
A fine score that should have been reissued on CD but this, as yet, has failed to materialise.

The Unsinkable Molly Brown

LYRICS ✴ Meredith Willson
MUSIC ✴ Meredith Willson
BOOK ✴ Richard Morris

First Performance

New York, Winter Garden Theater, 3 November 1960 (532 performances)

Principal Characters

Molly Tobin ✴ The Unsinkable
Johnny Brown ✴ A prospector
Prince de Long ✴ A European friend

Original New York Cast

Tammy Grimes, Harve Presnell, Mitchell Gregg

Plot

Molly Tobin and her brothers often wrestle together at their shack in Hannibal, Missouri. You can't keep a girl like her down; she's going to be rich and famous.

First she's a saloon singer in the mining town of Leadville, Colorado, where she meets prospector, Johnny Brown. They fall in love and he shows her his newly-built cabin. Now all they need is a brass bedstead. On their wedding night he leaves, and returns a week later with $300,000. Through a mishap it all gets burned up, but Johnny soon has another fortune and he and his feisty wife move to a big house in Denver, where they are shunned by smart society. So Molly sets off for a grand tour of Europe.

She returns from Paris a great social success, with her aristocratic friends in train. She'll show Denver society! Unfortunately her party is ruined by the arrival of her rough, miner friends from Leadville and, despite Johnny's forebodings, Molly decamps back to Europe with Prince de Long.

In Monte Carlo the prince asks Molly to divorce Johnny and marry him. Molly, however, longs for home, and sets sail for the United States on the *Titanic*. Escaping in a lifeboat, she eventually arrives home in Denver, reunited with her true love, Johnny.

Music and Songs

A riotous red-blooded score. It was a good follow-up to *The Music Man* for Willson, although it is certainly less gentle and more raucous. Numbers include 'I ain't down yet' (Molly), 'Belly up to the bar boys' (Christmas and Molly), 'I'll never say no' (Johnny and Molly), 'My own brass bed' (Molly), 'If I knew' (Johnny), 'Chick-a-pen' (Johnny and Molly), 'Dolce far niente' (Prince de Long) and 'I may never fall in love with you' (Molly).

Did You Know?

✷ Molly Brown was a real-life character, and a legend throughout Colorado.

✷ Harve Presnell, making his film debut, was the only original cast member to repeat his performance on screen.

✷ Tammy Grimes won the Tony Award for her performance.

✷ In the film *Titanic* Molly Brown has a significant part and befriends the hero.

The Critics

'A smash hit' – *New York Journal American*
'Far and away the best musical since *My Fair Lady*' – CBS TV
'*The Unsinkable Molly Brown* is delectable' – *New York World Telegram & Sun*
'Meredith Willson's score is one of the brightest features of *Molly Brown*' – *New York Post*

Recommended Recording

Original Broadway cast (CD) Broadway Angel ZDM 0 777 7 64761 2 4
Tammy Grimes in her element. A powerhouse performance backed up by the true sound of Harve Presnell's fine voice. The film version has Debbie Reynolds, and Harve Presnell repeating his stage role, but it is not so complete, and for all her charm, Miss Reynolds's interpretation is not quite as robust as that of Tammy Grimes.

Film

MGM, 1964. Starring Debbie Reynolds and Harve Presnell. Directed by Charles Walters.

Up in Central Park

LYRICS ✳ Dorothy Fields
MUSIC ✳ Sigmund Romberg
BOOK ✳ Herbert and Dorothy Fields

First Performance

New York, New Century Theater, 27 January 1945 (504 performances)

Principal Characters

John Matthews
Rosie Moore

Original New York Cast

Wilbur Evans, Maureen Cannon

Plot

This charming period musical deals with the setting-up and opening of Central Park in the heart of New York's Manhattan Island in the 1870s. There's a young, investigative journalist, John Matthews, who works for the *New York Times*. He is in love with Rosie Moore, the daughter of one of the political henchmen of William Marcey (Boss) Tweed, the power behind Tammany Hall (the corrupt Union HQ).

Rosie wants to become a stage star. She is often in the park, usually near the carousel, where she meets John for the first time. But John is investigating corruption in the building of Central Park, and Rosie's father and his associates are implicated. When Boss Tweed learns of this, he goes to the *New York Times* offices. He's bought himself out of trouble before on many occasions – surely he can do the same again?

But the paper, and its reporter John, cannot be bribed. Tweed's power is broken and Rosie's father crashes with the rest of them. Rosie blames John for the downturn in her family's fortunes. She turns in her despair to Richard Connelly, the comptroller of the city. He promises to help her further her theatrical career, and they get married. Unfortunately it turns out that Richard is already married, and he runs away, only to be killed. Rosie subsequently leaves the city to take up serious vocal studies. A year later she returns to Central Park, to the bandstand on the Mall – and there's John, ready to kiss and make up as the pair reaffirm their love for each other.

Music and Songs

Romberg finished his Broadway career with a success, a lovely collection of turn-of-the-century-style ballads that showed the old master at his most endearing. None have become standards, but all are charming, and include 'April snow' (Rosie), 'Close as pages in a book' (Rosie and John), 'When you walk in the room' (John) and 'Every day is Ladies' Day with me' (John).

Did You Know?

✴ The complicated physical production by Mike Todd highlighted the showman at his best, and included an elaborate skating scene.

✴ This was the last musical that Romberg lived to see produced – and it proved to be one of his most successful.

✴ The settings resembled the etchings sold by Currier and Ives, the firm that was the subject of a song in the show.

✴ The villain of the piece, corrupt Boss Tweed, actually existed. The crusading reporter John was an amalgam of various fearless fact-finders.

✴ Herbert Fields was Dorothy Fields's brother. Their father was Lew Fields, a theatrical producer, and half of the Webber and Fields vaudeville team.

The Critics

'As big as its namesake and it is just as pretty to look at . . . it is long, and to be frank, pretty dull' – *The Times*
'A commendable departure from formula musicals' – *PM Magazine*

Recommended Recording

An Evening with Dorothy Fields (CD) DRG 5167
There was an LP issue (**Decca DL 8016**) but this has not, as yet, been transferred to CD. Miss Fields, the lyricist, reminisced about her career at the 'Y' in New York, and this recording of that evening is a most enjoyable one. It includes 'The big back yard' and 'Close as pages in a book' from this show.

Film

U-I, 1948. Starring Deanna Durbin, Dick Haymes and Vincent Price. Directed by William A. Seiter.

The Vagabond King

LYRICS ✶ Brian Hooker
MUSIC ✶ Rudolf Friml
BOOK ✶ Brian Hooker, Russell Janney and W.H. Post,
based on the play *If I were King* by Justin McCarthy

First Performance

New York, Casino Theater, 21 September 1925 (511 performances)
London, Winter Garden Theatre, 19 April 1927 (480 performances)

Principal Characters

François Villon ✶ A poet
Katherine de Vaucelles ✶ A courtier
Louis XI ✶ The king
Huguette de Hamel ✶ A peasant girl

Original New York Cast

Dennis King, Carolyn Thomson, Max Figman, Jane Carroll

Original London Cast

Derek Oldham, Winnie Melville, H.A. Sainsbury, Norah Blaney

Plot

François Villon, a 15th-century poet, is also a vagabond. His king, Louis XI, has a
lady of the court who needs taking down a peg or two. She is the lovely Katherine
de Vaucelles. So the king dubs Villon king for a day. During that twenty-four
hours he must woo and win Katherine, or his head will be forfeited. This is a
challenge Villon accepts with alacrity, although he already has a love of his own,
the winsome peasant girl, Huguette. Naturally, Katherine and Villon fall in love
with each other.

Meanwhile, there are political problems afoot. The Duke of Burgundy sees his
chance to send troops to Paris and overcome the king's forces – which he does.
Villon has a real battle on his hands now. He rallies his own vagabond friends to
fight for the real king. In the ensuing mêlée Huguette is killed, but the vagabonds
defeat the Burgundians. As a reward, Villon, no longer king, is allowed to marry
Katherine by King Louis.

Music and Songs

A rich, full-blooded score from the composer of *Rose Marie*. Stirring marches and tender love songs make up this hardy perennial, and include 'Song of the vagabonds' (Villon and the vagabonds), 'Some day' (Villon), 'Love for sale' (Huguette), 'Only a rose' (Villon) and 'Love me tonight' (Villon and Katherine).

Did You Know?

✶ Villon actually existed, and his poetry survives, but this story is complete fantasy.

✶ Rodgers and Hart wrote a musical version of the original story in 1922, but the producer they approached, Russell Janney, opted for more famous names to create a Broadway musical on the subject.

✶ There had already been an opera by Edmond de Membrée with Villon as its hero, mounted at the Paris Opera in 1857.

The Critics

'There is no harm in pointing out the essential foolishness of the idea that a man may be so changed in appearance by taking a bath and putting on a costume that his friends can't recognize him ... *The Vagabond King* proves that it survives such monstrosities' – *Journal American*

Recommended Recording

Studio cast (CD) Castle MAC CD 334
Other than the film soundtrack this is all that is available. John Hanson recreates the role he played many times and couples it with another of his favourites, *The Student Prince*.

Films

Paramount, 1930. Starring Dennis King, Jeanette MacDonald and Lillian Roth. Directed by Ludwig Berger.
Paramount, 1956. Starring Oreste and Kathryn Grayson. Directed by Michael Curtiz.

Valmouth

LYRICS ✶ Sandy Wilson
MUSIC ✶ Sandy Wilson
BOOK ✶ Sandy Wilson,
adapted from the works of Ronald Firbank

First Performance

London, Lyric Theatre, 2 October 1958 (84 performances)
Transferred to Saville Theatre, 29 January 1959 (102 performances)
New York, York Play House, 6 October 1960 (14 performances)

Principal Characters

Mrs Hurstpierpoint ✶ A religious fanatic
Lady Parvula de Panzoust ✶ Elderly but amorous
Granny Tooke ✶ The oldest resident
Mrs Thoroughfare ✶ Denizens of Valmouth
Captain Dick Thoroughfare
Lieutenant Whorwood ✶ A visitor
Niri-Esther ✶ The niece of . . .
Mrs Yajnavalkya ✶ A masseuse
Sister Ecclesia ✶ A nun
Cardinal Pirelli ✶ A debauched cleric

Original London Cast

Barbara Couper, Fenella Fielding, Doris Hare, Betty Hardy,
Alan Edwards, Aubrey Woods, Maxine Daniels, Bertice Reading,
Marcia Ashton, Geoffrey Dunn

Original New York Cast

Anne Francine, Constance Carpenter, Beatrice Pons, Philippa Bevans,
Alfred Toigo, Gene Rupert, Gail Jones, Bertice Reading,
Elly Stone, Ralston Hill

Plot

Valmouth is an imaginary Edwardian spa where ancient Roman Catholic ladies
continue to pander to the desires of their long-gone youth. There's the amorous
Lady Parvula, in hot pursuit of a local shepherd; and there's the exotic Mrs
Hurstpierpoint, now a religious fanatic, but once the mistress of a king – she
wears holly inside her clothes as the equivalent of a hair shirt. Mrs Yajnavalkya
comes from the East. She's a masseuse and chiropodist, and something of a
matchmaker in her spare time. Then there's the 120-year-old Granny Tooke . . .

Mrs Yajnavalkya has a lovely niece, Niri-Esther, who has secretly married
Captain Dick, Mrs Thoroughfare's son, and she is pregnant by him. When he
returns to Valmouth with his 'close' friend by his side he admits the relationship,
and his mother arranges another wedding to be solemnized by the visiting

Cardinal Pirelli who, we discover, has been excommunicated for having once christened a dog. The baby is a girl and Mrs Hurstpierpoint decides that Niri-Esther is an infidel and needs converting but strange things are happening and Valmouth is destroyed. The only survivors are Mrs Yajnavalkya, Niri-Esher and her baby, and they are back home on their tropical island. Even so, Mrs Yajnavalkya reflects that there is no place to compare with Valmouth.

Music and Songs

Sandy Wilson at his most baroque. More daring than Cole Porter, and as sophisticated and decadent as Firbank, these sublimely witty and perfumed songs are brilliantly characterised. Of these the best known are 'My big best shoes' (Mrs Yajnavalkya and Granny Tooke), 'Little girl baby' (Mrs Yajnavalkya), 'Magic fingers' (Mrs Yajnavalkya) and 'Only a passing phase' (Lady Parvula).

Did You Know?

∗ One of the best of all cult musicals. Some consider it the forgotten masterpiece of British musical theatre.

∗ In the Chichester revival Mesdames Reading, Fielding, Ashton and Hare repeated their original roles. Sir Robert Helpmann was Cardinal Pirelli.

∗ Cleo Laine took over from Bertice Reading when the show transferred to the West End and is on the recording. However, Bertice Reading recorded her two big numbers and they were released on a 45.

The Critics

Some critics were confused, describing the show on its original outing as 'tasteless' and 'depraved' and asking, 'Has the censor quit?'
'It creates a world of perfumed immorality, but does so with a sort of contemptuous confidence which is the sign of the highest possible style' – *Daily Express*

Recommended Recording

1982 Chichester Revival cast (CD) TER CDTER 1019
Many of the original cast were brought together for this fine revival and it allowed Bertice Reading to play again the part that was written for her, and to be part of the cast recording. On the original CD, Cleo Laine's songs had arrangements by her husband John Dankworth; the theatre arrangements were not used. The rest remains as close to perfection as possible.

Very Good, Eddie

LYRICS ✱ Schuyler Greene
MUSIC ✱ Jerome Kern
BOOK ✱ Guy Bolton,
based on the play *Over Night* by Philip Bartholomae

First Performance

New York, Princess Theater, 23 December 1915 (341 performances)
London, Palace Theatre, 18 May 1918 (46 performances)

Principal Characters

Eddie Kettle ✱ A young bridegroom
Dick Rivers
Georgina Kettle ✱ A young bride
Elsie Darling ✱ A young bride
Madame Matroppo ✱ A teacher of singing
Percy Darling ✱ Another bridegroom

Original New York Cast

Ernest Truex, Oscar Shaw, Helen Raymond, Alice Dovey,
Ada Lewis, John Willard

Original London Cast

Nelson Keys, Walter Williams, Helen Temple, Nellie Briarcliffe,
Veronica Brady, Stanley Turnbull

Plot

Two honeymoon couples have chosen the same trip on *The Catskill*, a Hudson River Dayline ship. They are diminutive Eddie and tall Georgina Kettle, and tall Percy and diminutive Elsie Darling, the prize singing pupil of Madame Matroppo. It turns out the men know each other, and are delighted to introduce each other to their respective wives at the pier head. Through confusion, the couples are separated and Eddie takes off for the trip without his wife. But Percy's wife, Elsie, is on board, while Percy finds himself on dry land with Eddie's wife, Georgina. Now Eddie and Elsie must pretend, for the sake of propriety, to be married to each other. Unfortunately there's a complication – Eddie and Elsie find each other rather attractive.

But this is a musical comedy from the early years of the century, so all will end happily with the right couples restored to peace and harmony together, when they all meet up at the Rip Van Winkle Inn – but not before Eddie and Elsie have endured a number of embarrassing incidents and near misses, and Eddie has discovered a personal self-confidence that had, until that time, eluded him.

In the successful revival, the plot was changed at the end to allow for the joining together of the two couples of similar height; apparently the clergyman who carried out the original weddings wasn't fully qualified!

Music and Songs

This is appealing, very charming early Kern, from the Princess Theater World War I period which some believe was the true dawn of musical comedy. Songs still sung today include 'Some sort of somebody' (Dick and Elsie), 'Isn't it great to be married?' (Eddie, Elsie, Percy and Georgina), 'Thirteen collar' (Eddie), 'Babes in the wood' (Eddie and Elsie), and 'Nodding roses' (Elsie and Dick).

Did You Know?

✱ This was one of the intimate and charming small-scale shows for the Princess Theater on which Kern, Guy Bolton and their collaborators cut their musical teeth.

✱ The Princess Shows, of which this was one, marked the turning point of the American musical show.

✱ At the first night Jerome Kern introduced his old friend P.G. Wodehouse to Guy Bolton, and so began a new and important collaboration.

The Critics

'Will *Very Good, Eddie* ever be as entertaining as *Over Night*? Jerome Kern has furnished the score, which is reminiscent of about every tune he ever wrote for any other piece. The music adds nothing to the enjoyment of the piece' – *The Enquirer* (The answer to the question was, of course, 'Yes'.)

Recommended Recording

Original Revival cast (CD) DRG CDRG 6100
This off-Broadway revival cast is the only recording of this score currently available. Nevertheless, it has charm, is well sung, and remains fairly true to the original.

Very Warm for May

LYRICS ✳ Oscar Hammerstein II
MUSIC ✳ Jerome Kern
BOOK ✳ Oscar Hammerstein II

First Performance

New York, Alvin Theater, 17 November 1939 (59 performances)

Principal Characters

William Graham ✳ Father of May
Jackson ✳ A dancer
May Graham ✳ William's daughter
Johnny Graham ✳ William's son
Kenny
Raymond Sibley
Sonny Spofford ✳ Winnie's son
Liz Spofford ✳ Winnie's daughter
Lowell Pennyfeather
Ogdon Quiler ✳ An artistic director
Jethro Hancock
Winnie Spofford ✳ A patron
Deamish
Schlesinger

Original New York Cast

Donald Brian, Avon Long, Grace MacDonald, Jack Whiting, Ray Mayer,
Richard Quine, Frances Mercer, Max Showalter, Hiram Sherman, William Torpey,
Eve Arden, Len Mence, Seldon Bennett, Bruce Evans

Plot

In the original plot, William Graham has fallen into debt. Unfortunately the creditors are gangsters. And unless William does something illegal for them, his daughter, May, will be harmed. His son, Johnny, is a dabbler on Broadway, so he can help May to hide herself in an out-of-town stock company. This, run by flamboyant Ogdon Quiler, is located on Winnie Spofford's property in Connecticut. Winnie has two stage-struck kids – Liz and Sonny.

Eventually the gangsters discover where Johnny and May are working, and go down to settle up. Luckily the police get involved, and after a bit of shooting and a bit of kidnapping, there's a series of happy endings. Liz ends up with Johnny, and May with Sonny. And guess what? William Graham recognises Winnie as an old flame from his youth.

While this is the plot with which the show went out of town, revisions eliminated the gangster plot, leaving a conventional story in which a young girl rebelled against not being allowed to follow the same career her father had followed when young. This really helped to sink the show, as songs which originally had dramatic credibility seemed marooned by themselves.

Music and Songs

Mature Kern, bursting with romance and memorability, including at least one of his greatest songs, 'All the things you are' (Ogdon, Liz, Carroll and Charles), plus 'Heaven in my arms' (Johnny), 'That lucky fellow' (Raymond), 'In the heart of the dark' (Carroll and Liz) and 'All in fun' (Liz and Johnny).

Did You Know?

✳ This was the last new score Kern was to write. Although it only lasted 59 performances, it has proved a classic.

✳ The cast included future director Richard Quine, talented comedienne Eve Arden, film stars June Allyson, Vera-Ellen (Rohe) and Billie Worth in the chorus (London's *Call Me Madam* star), and dance-director Don Loper.

✳ 'Alvin's Orchestra', the pit orchestra, was in reality jazz great Matty Malneck's band.

✳ The song 'All the things you are' was one that Richard Rodgers said he wished he had written, and Arthur Schwartz stated that it was 'the greatest song ever written'.

The Critics

The critics were confused:
'Inconsequential plot . . . forever slowing things down' – *Cue*
'Dandy . . . but never well developed . . . a confused jumble' – *Variety*
'The book is a singularly haphazard invention that throws the show out of focus and makes an appreciation of Mr Kern's music almost a challenge' – *New York Times*

Recommended Recording

Studio cast (CD) AEI AEI-CD 008
Based on the radio broadcast, this recording includes members of the original Broadway cast. In addition there is a rare recording of Kern at the piano accompanying Tony Martin singing 'All the things you are'.

The Water Gypsies

LYRICS ✷ A.P. Herbert
MUSIC ✷ Vivian Ellis
BOOK ✷ A.P. Herbert,
based on his novel *The Water Gypsies*

First Performance

London, Winter Garden Theatre, 31 August 1955 (239 performances)

Principal Characters

Jane ✷ Albert's second daughter
Lily ✷ Albert's elder daughter
Albert Bell ✷ A musician
Mrs Higgins ✷ A publican
Bunny ✷ Lily's friend
George Bryan ✷ Jane's friend
Fred ✷ A water gypsy

Original London Cast

Pamela Charles, Dora Bryan, Jerry Verno, Doris Hare,
Roy Godfrey, Peter Graves, Laurie Payne

Plot

Meet the daughters of Albert Bell, an out-of-work music hall pit orchestra player.
He's a trumpeter who is romantically involved with Mrs Higgins, the licensee of
the local pub. The first daughter is Lily (who loathes her name), a good-natured,
good-time girl with a hearty cynicism about the opposite sex, especially her wide-
boy boyfriend, Bunny.

However, let's focus on Albert's second daughter, Jane. She has three
boyfriends: first, Mrs Higgins' son Ernest, a pompous young radical; secondly, the
artist George Bryan; and thirdly, a young bargee, Fred, who is illiterate but has
the soul of a poet. He can rhapsodise about life on the canal, its traditionally-
ornamented boats, and the joys of being a bargee on the long boats towed by an
old grey mare.

Jane turns out to be an unsophisticated dreamer and it takes the evening's
events for her to realise what and who she wants out of life. It's not the self-
important, truculent and possessive Ernest. Although infatuated by the lifestyle of
the charming and attractive artist, Bryan, it's not him either. In fact, it is Bryan
who realises Jane's essential innocence, refuses to take advantage of her and
sends her back to the simple life, on the canal with her trusting and loyal bargee,
Fred.

Music and Songs

Characteristic of the quiet, unobtrusive craftsmanship of the most successful partnership of the thirties and forties in British musical comedy – Vivian Ellis and A.P. Herbert. The score includes 'Why did you call me Lily?' (Lily), 'Clip clop' (Fred), 'I should worry' (Bunny and Lily), 'When I'm washing up' (Jane), 'He doesn't care' (Jane), 'Castles and hearts and roses' (Fred), 'Little boat' (Jane), 'Why should spring have all the flowers?' (Albert and Mrs Higgins) and 'This is our secret' (Bryan and Jane).

Did You Know?

✶ This is the show that made a star of Dora Bryan, as Lily, the worldly-wise elder daughter, with her song 'Why did you call me Lily?'

✶ The show was withdrawn when Miss Bryan became pregnant and had to leave the cast.

The Critics

'Their [Herbert and Ellis] enterprise was to write a Cockney pastoral which derived from Dickens and reached, in the *Punch* cartoons of the 1880s, a state of flawless unreality in which Sir Alan has striven to preserve it. And how nearly he has succeeded in making us believe in Hammersmith as a rural hamlet peopled with quaint bargees whose joys are homely and whose destiny is perforce obscure . . . [The music] chimes like cowbells over the meadow' – Kenneth Tynan
'The musical play of Sir Alan Herbert's floats along for the most part with all the square-bottomed and solid assurance of the barge that takes so large a part of it' – *The Times*
'Miss Bryan has a remarkably infectious manner. She lets off at a firmly consistent pressure the steam that prevents the main brew from boiling over into really unbearable sentimentality. Mercifully, Miss Bryan has much to do' – *The Times*

Recommended Recording

Original London cast (LP) His Master's Voice DLP 1097
This original 10 inch LP excluded the hit song 'Why did you call me Lily?' but it was reinstated on a reissue (**World Record Club SH 228**), when the songs from *Bless The Bride* were added.

West Side Story

LYRICS ✶ Stephen Sondheim
MUSIC ✶ Leonard Bernstein
BOOK ✶ Arthur Laurents, based on an idea by Jerome Robbins
and Shakespeare's *Romeo and Juliet*

First Performance

New York, Winter Garden Theater, 26 September 1957 (734 performances)
London, Her Majesty's Theatre, 12 December 1958 (1039 performances)

Principal Characters

Maria ✶ A young Puerto Rican
Tony ✶ Her sweetheart
Anita ✶ Bernardo's girl
Riff ✶ Leader of the Jets
Bernardo ✶ Leader of the Sharks
Doc ✶ A grown-up

Original New York Cast

Carol Lawrence, Larry Kert, Chita Rivera, Mickey Calin, Ken LeRoy, Art Smith

Original London Cast

Marlys Watters, Don McKay, Chita Rivera, George Chakiris, Ken LeRoy,
David Bauer

Plot

Tony, a past member of the American gang called the Jets, is maturing from that youthful phase and is settling into a job at a drugstore. However, Riff, the Jets' leader, persuades him to join one more fight against the Puerto Rican Sharks, led by Bernardo. At the local dance, Tony meets Bernardo's sister Maria, and they fall in love – a fact discovered by Anita, Bernardo's girlfriend. It is a love destined not to succeed, as Tony tries desperately to keep the planned fight to fists, and not weapons. At the fight, Bernardo, furious at the romance between Tony and Maria, goes for Tony. The fight descends into all-out war, with weapons appearing. Bernardo and Riff fight, leaving Riff dead, only to be avenged by Tony killing Bernardo.

Maria knows nothing of these events. Tony finds his way to her bedroom and when he leaves Anita accuses Maria of helping him, the enemy. Meanwhile, the Jets have re-formed and found that the Puerto Ricans are after Tony's blood. Chino, their new leader, has a gun. Anita, in spite of her hate, wants to help Tony for Maria's sake and tries to warn him. However, at the drugstore the Jets molest her and in anger and fright she lies to them that Chino has killed Maria. Tony hears the news, only to find Maria as he walks the streets. As they caress, Chino appears and shoots Tony.

Following the three senseless killings, the rival factions show solidarity and together take Tony's body away. The show ends with an all-round recognition that the gang war must cease and that everyone must learn to live peacefully together.

Music and Songs

One of the greatest musical scores of all – jazzy, sparky, lyrical, aggressive, beautiful, memorable. Songs include 'Jet song' (Riff and the Jets), 'Something's coming' (Tony), 'The dance at the gym' (the company), 'Maria' (Tony), 'Tonight' (Tony and Maria), 'America' (Anita, Rosalia and Shark girls), 'One hand, one heart' (Tony and Maria), 'I feel pretty' (Maria), 'Somewhere' (Consuelo) and 'Gee Officer Krupke!' (Action, Snowboy and the Jets).

Did You Know?

✶ *West Side Story* won the Tony for best choreography but no others.

✶ Originally the lyrics were attributed to Leonard Bernstein and Stephen Sondheim. After its first showing the former took his name off the credits but still retained the royalty.

✶ The original London run exceeded the Broadway original.

The Critics

'The radioactive fallout from *West Side Story* must still be descending on Broadway this morning. The show rides with a catastrophic roar' – *New York Herald Tribune*
'Extraordinarily exciting . . . a provocative and artful blend of music, dance and plot' – *New York News*
'*West Side Story* is a superlative musical. A chiller, a thriller, as up-to-the-minute as tomorrow's headlines' – *New York Mirror*

Recommended Recording

Original Broadway cast (CD) Columbia CK 32603
One of the most exciting of all Broadway cast recordings that no revival cast or studio cast have come up to, which is surprising as Bernstein attempted to better it himself. No collection should be without this.

Film

United Artists, 1961. Starring Natalie Wood, Richard Beymer and Rita Moreno. Directed by Robert Wise and Jerome Robbins.

Where's Charley?

LYRICS * Frank Loesser
MUSIC * Frank Loesser
BOOK * George Abbott,
based on the play *Charley's Aunt* by Brandon Thomas

First Performance

New York, St James' Theatre, 11 October 1948 (792 performances)
London, Palace Theatre, 20 February 1958 (404 performances)

Principal Characters

Charles Wykeham * A student
Amy Spettigue * His friend, a student
Jack Chesney * Another student
Kitty Verdun * A student
Sir Francis Chesney * Charley's uncle
Mr Spettigue * Amy's father

Original New York Cast

Ray Bolger, Allyn McLerie, Byron Palmer, Doretta Morrow,
Paul England, Horace Cooper

Original London Cast

Norman Wisdom, Pip Hinton, Terence Cooper, Pamela Gale,
Jerry Desmonde, Felix Felton

Plot

In Oxford, especially in 1892, it was almost impossible for young male undergraduates to entertain their girlfriends in their rooms. In the case of our heroes, Jack and Charley, they intend to ask Amy and Kitty to marry them on their visit, but the guardian of one of them refuses permission for a trip to Oxford unless a chaperone is present. Sadly, Aunt Donna Lucia, their chaperone, was not on the train that Charley went to meet. But Amy and Kitty will be all right, because Charley will impersonate her. Jack is told by his father that the family is now so poor that it seems he must leave university. Perhaps father could marry Donna Anna, who is an extremely wealthy Brazilian.

Meanwhile, Charley is led a merry dance, doing his own wooing when he's not dressed up as his aunt, and in the meantime fending off advances from two of the fathers. As if that wasn't enough, the real Donna Anna turns up. But she sums up the situation at a glance and herself assumes a false identity, as Mrs Beverly-Smythe. In the end, she and Charley arrange for the two fathers to allow their daughters to marry Jack and Charley. Donna Anna finds a husband for herself – Jack's own father – a former beau, thus solving that family's debt problems. Spettigue, Amy's father, who has been pursuing the false Donna, leaves in high dudgeon when the latter is revealed as Charley, wearing trousers under his dress.

Music and Songs

The versatile Frank Loesser celebrated his move from Hollywood to Broadway with an enduring and viable score, that had an appropriate English touch, typical of the talent of this chameleon-like creator, and featuring the hits 'Once in love with Amy' (Charley), 'My darling, my darling' (Jack and Kitty), plus 'Make a miracle' (Kitty and Charley) and 'Lovelier than ever' (Donna Lucia and Sir Francis). Not that one should forget one of the most stirring marches composed for the Broadway stage: 'The new Ashmoleon marching society and student conservatory band' (Jack, Amy, Kitty, undergraduates and young ladies).

Did You Know?

✷ At the time of its closing, the show had the tenth-longest run of any Broadway musical comedy.

✷ In converting this well-known farce into a musical, the character of Lord Fancourt Babberley, the original friend who dressed up in a frock, was eliminated, and Charley took on the role of his own aunt.

✷ There was no original Broadway cast album even though the show was a success. However, the song 'Once in love with Amy' was recorded by many artists and became a hit.

✷ One of the people to record 'Once in love with Amy' was Norman Wisdom, who a decade later played the part of Charley.

✷ Ray Bolger won a Tony for his performance.

The Critics

'In *Where's Charley?* Mr Loesser was working within the prescribed limits of formula musical comedy. But even within such limits he was exhibiting the wit, perception and lyricism that later were to be so highly praised' – *New York Times*
'There is still agreeably elementary fun to be found in the vintage farce, but it is these songs with their continued fresh tunefulness and charm that give the evening its atmosphere of winning festivity' – *New York Post*

Recommended Recording

Original London cast (CD) EMI West End Angel 0777 7 89058 2 0
Norman Wisdom in great form with an excellent supporting cast. A brisk, fun album that has been released in stereo for the first time.

Film

Warner Brothers, 1952. Starring Ray Bolger, Mary Germaine and Allyn Ann McLerie. Directed by David Butler.

Whistle Down the Wind

LYRICS ✶ Jim Steinman
MUSIC ✶ Andrew Lloyd Webber
BOOK ✶ Patricia Knop, Gale Edwards and Andrew Lloyd Webber
From the original novel by Mary Hayley Bell and the screenplay by
Keith Waterhouse and Willis Hall

First Performance

Washington, The National Theatre, 12 December 1996 (limited season)
London, Aldwych Theatre, 1 July 1998 (1044 performances)

Principal Characters

The Man ✶ An escaped prisoner or Jesus
Boone ✶ A widower with three children
Swallow ✶ Boone's elder daughter
Brat (Bluejay) ✶ Boone's son
Poor Baby (Robin) ✶ Boone's other son
Amos ✶ A boy who wants to get away
Candy ✶ A girl who wants to get away

Original Washington Cast

Davis Gaines, Timothy Nolen, Irene Molloy, Abbi Hutcherson, Cameron Bowen,
Steve Scott Springer, Lacey Hornkohl

Original London Cast

Marcus Lovett, James Graeme, Lottie Mayor, Ashley Andrews, Dean Clish,
Dean Collinson, Veronica Hart

Plot

Boone is a widower with three young children – life is difficult for him it looks as though there will not be many presents this coming Christmas. On their way home Swallow, the oldest child, and her two brothers have met a family friend carrying a sack of kittens he intends to drown. The children rescue the kitttens and hide them in the barn. After a meagre supper they go back to see the kittens and find there 'the man', exhausted and with blood on his hands and body. As he wakes Swallow asks him who he is. The man, startled to find them all looking at him, replies 'Jesus – Christ' which they take as an answer to the question. 'The man' asks them to keep his presence there a secret, but the boys can't keep it quiet and soon a number of other children come to see 'Jesus'.

Elsewhere, the sheriff is warning people to look out for a man who has escaped from prison because his clothes have been found in the vicinity. And there is someone else who wants to escape, young Amos who sees no future at home – a feeling shared by the not-too-moral Candy who agrees to leave with him.

'The man' has had time to rest and collect his strength. The children, however, expect him to be like the Jesus they have read about and want stories – they get stories, but not quite the way they had heard them before. Amos arrives at the barn to say goodbye to Swallow and we see that he is in love with her, and that 'the man' is also smitten. Swallow gets Amos to take her to the train tunnel on his motorbike to pick up a parcel for 'the man', and when there he makes her tell her secret, that her Jesus is in the barn. The sheriff finds the two of them and takes Swallow, with the parcel, back to her father. Amos goes off knowing Swallow is in danger, and knowing too that he has let Candy down. In town the snake preacher has set up a tent and is holding a meeting where the townsfolk test their faith. Here, Amos lets the secret out and the sheriff and townsfolk go on the hunt. Swallow, who seems to have matured overnight, perhaps knows exactly who 'the man' is but, whoever he is, she will not let him down. The mob have no compassion, however, and try to burn 'the man' out of the barn where, when it has burned down, they find no trace of him. Was he Jesus after all?

Music and Songs

Andrew Lloyd Webber in American mode. The sounds of the mid west and religious fervour heighten this score and have encouraged many pop stars to record the numbers. The big hit is 'No matter what' (the children and adults) with 'Tire tracks and broken hearts (Amos and Candy) and the title song (Boone and Swallow). And there is the stiring children's anthem 'When children rule the world'.

Did You Know?

✳ The first musical version of *Whistle Down the Wind* was written for the National Youth Music Theatre by Russell Labey and Richard Taylor.

✳ Andrew Lloyd Webber's *Whistle Down the Wind* transfers the setting from England to the United States and makes the character of Swallow slightly older.

✳ *Whistle Down the Wind* was originally to have had a Broadway opening prior to London but it opened and closed in Washington. The London production is a reworked version staged by a different director.

The Critics

'When I caught Andrew Lloyd Webber's *Whistle Down the Wind* in Washington in 1996, I thought it attractive, touching, altogether more engrossing than those of my American counterparts who punished the uppity British tunesmith with reviews tepid enough to forestall a planned Broadway transfer' – *The Times*
'In *Whistle Down the Wind* religion is the text and the context. The show arrives at the Aldwych much transformed from the Mary Hayley bell novel and Bryan Forbes movie on which it is based. Lloyd Webber rightly argues that Bible-belt Louisiana is a more convincing setting than rural Britain' – *The Sunday Times*

Recommended Recording

Original London cast (CD) Really Useful Records 547 262-2
A two record set containing all the score and all its passion (passion has replaced much of the charm of the original movie). While there is another album with the songs sung by pop stars (**Polydor 559 441-2**), this original cast set is the one to have. Both Marcus Lovett and Lottie Mayor are exceptional.

Wish You Were Here

LYRICS ✶ Harold Rome
MUSIC ✶ Harold Rome
BOOK ✶ Joshua Logan and Arthur Kober,
based on Kober's play *Having a Wonderful Time*

First Performance

New York, Imperial Theater, 25 June 1952 (598 performances)
London, Casino Theatre, 10 October 1953 (282 performances)

Principal Characters

Teddy Stern ✶ A guest
Herman ✶ Her friend
Chick ✶ A waiter
Pinky Harris ✶ The resident Lothario
Fay Fromkin ✶ Another camper
Itchy (Dickie in London) ✶ The social director

Original New York Cast

Patricia Marand, Harry Clarke, Jack Cassidy, Paul Valentine,
Sheila Bond, Sidney Armus

Original London Cast

Elizabeth Larner, Glen Burns, Bruce Trent, Christopher Hewett,
Shani Wallis, Dickie Henderson

Plot

Just as Britain has its holiday camps and recreation centres, America offers a variety of camps to which hard-working young men and women go for holidays in the height of summer. A typical example is Camp Karefree, in the Berkshire Hills. Pretty secretary, Teddy Stern, is a guest for two weeks. She's from the Bronx and is soon in love with one of the waiters at the camp, Chick Miller. He's a law student using his vacation to pay for his next year's tuition. As a result, Teddy dispenses with her current friend, Herman Fabricant, already a well-established businessman.

Meanwhile, there's a taxing programme of social events, led by the social director, the charmingly named Itchy. The camp's resident Romeo is Pinky Harris. He spends all his time in relentless pursuit of the camp's current crop of eligible (and not so eligible) women. He's the cause of a temporary misunderstanding between Teddy and Chick, when it seems as if Teddy has passed the night with Pinky, but all ends happily for the two young lovers.

Music and Songs

A jolly, spirited score that offers fun and romance in equal portions. 'Wish you were here' (Chick) was the main hit. 'Where did the night go?' (Teddy and Chick) also made an impact. Other fine songs were 'Nothing nicer than people' (Fay, Teddy and the girls), 'Certain individuals' (Fay), 'Summer afternoon' (Pinky) and 'Everybody loves somebody' (Fay).

Did You Know?

✶ This was Harold Rome's first musical comedy, all his early work being for revues.

✶ It was advertised as 'The Musical with a Swimming Pool', which indeed was its main set.

✶ This is a rare example of a successful musical rewrite after a New York critical panning; the result was a long-running success.

✶ The English censor was concerned about the lack of clothing on stage as much of the time the cast were in swimming costumes. He was especially concerned when members of the opposite sex got close to each other.

✶ The property man for this complex show won a Tony Award as 'outstanding stage technician'.

The Critics

The New York critics didn't like the show:
'The show lacks dazzle and never really explodes' – *New York Journal American*
'Things are not that bad. They aren't good . . . but going to Camp Karefree in *Wish You Were Here* is not any more fun than going to it would be in real life' – *New York Post*
The London critics were kinder:
'A small masterpiece' – Kenneth Tynan
'It is tremendously alive . . . so I prophesy for it a great success' – *New York Times* London correspondent

---

Recommended Recording

Original Broadway cast (CD) RCA Victor 09026-68326-2
A fun Harold Rome score that is well served by this expertly sung and energetic recording. There was never a full recording of the London cast.

The Wiz

LYRICS ✳ Charlie Smalls
MUSIC ✳ Charlie Smalls
BOOK ✳ William F. Brown, adapted from
The Wonderful Wizard of Oz by L. Frank Baum

First Performance

New York, Majestic Theater, 5 January 1975 (1672 performances)

Principal Characters

Dorothy ✳ A little girl
The Wiz ✳ A magician
Scarecrow
Tin Man
Cowardly Lion
Glinda ✳ A good witch
Evillene ✳ An evil witch

Original New York Cast

Stephanie Mills, André de Shields, Hinton Battle, Tiger Haynes,
Ted Ross, Dee Dee Bridgewater, Mabel King

Plot

There are tornadoes on the way in Kansas, and it's time to batten down the hatches. Aunt Em feels Dorothy isn't doing enough to help – all she does is dream and care about her little dog, Toto. Sure enough, the storm breaks and Dorothy and Toto are whisked away to the land of Oz. The wreck of the farm has squashed Evvamine, the Wicked Witch of the East, and Dorothy has her silver slippers.

The Good Witch of the North tells Dorothy she must go to the Emerald City if she wants to get back to Kansas. So it's off along the yellow brick road with some new friends to accompany her: a worldly-wise Scarecrow, a rusty Tin Man and a Cowardly Lion. They escape the fearsome Kalidahs, thanks to the bravery of two of their number (not, alas, the Lion). Another obstacle, a deadly field of poppies, is overcome, and at last the travellers reach the Emerald City. The Wiz listens to their requests: Dorothy wants to go home; the Scarecrow wants brains; the Tin Man needs a heart; and the Lion requires courage. Simple: the Wicked Witch of the West must die.

But Evillene, the Wicked Witch of the West, knows what's going on, through reports from her slaves, the Winkies. She sends her winged monkeys to capture Dorothy and her friends. By the following week the Tin Man and Scarecrow have been dismembered and Dorothy is a servant girl – even the Lion is a mere water boy. All that the witch needs now are Dorothy's slippers. In defence of the lion, Dorothy inadvertently splashes the witch with water, and the latter melts into a puddle. The Winkies are released and Dorothy's friends restored to their original selves.

Now the Wiz tries to wriggle out of his commitments. He's just a conman from

Omaha, blown by the wind to Oz in his hot-air balloon. He agrees finally to balloon Dorothy back to Kansas, but leaves without her. Luckily, the Good Witch of the North, Addaperle, can summon up Glinda, the Good Witch of the South, who reveals that the secret lies in a click of Dorothy's slippers. So Dorothy says goodbye to her friends, and in three clicks of her heels is back in Kansas.

Music and Songs

A contemporary twist on an old story, with soul, gospel and contemporary pop songs to match. The hits are 'Ease on down the road' (Dorothy, Scarecrow, Tin Man and Lion) and 'If you believe' (Glinda), plus 'Y'all got it!' (The Wiz and company) and 'Soon as I get home' (Dorothy).

Did You Know?

✶ In this version of the story, Dorothy's slippers are silver-, not ruby-coloured.

✶ This is the fifth stage or screen version of L. Frank Baum's perennial story.

✶ *The Wiz* has been seen in many British regional theatres but never in the West End.

✶ *The Wiz* won the best musical and best score Tony Awards and five others.

The Critics

'The show, with all new music and lyrics, is saucy with black urban humor. Its talk is jumping jivernacular, its walk is a big city strut, its dances have a blowtorch frenzy, and its songs range from a warm gospel glow to the rock beat of a riveter mining asphalt' – *Time*

Recommended Recording

Original Broadway cast (CD) Atlantic 18137-2
The original Broadway cast exudes a pounding excitement and electricity that the film lacks. Stephanie Mills is cute and appealing as Dorothy. As nearly always with this story, it is the Scarecrow, the Tin Man and the Cowardly Lion that steal the show.

Film

Motown, 1978. Starring Diana Ross and Michael Jackson. Directed by Sidney Lumet.

Wonderful Town

LYRICS ✳ Betty Comden and Adolph Green
MUSIC ✳ Leonard Bernstein
BOOK ✳ Joseph Fields and Jerome Chodorov,
based on their play *My Sister Eileen*
and stories by Ruth McKenney

First Performance

New York, Winter Garden Theater, 25 February 1952 (559 performances)
London, Princes Theatre, 23 February 1953 (207 performances)

Principal Characters

Ruth
Eileen ✳ Her sister
Bob ✳ Their friend

Original New York Cast

Rosalind Russell, Edith Adams, George Gaynes

Original London Cast

Pat Kirkwood, Shani Wallis, Dennis Bowen

Plot

Greenwich Village is an exciting place in 1930s New York, being home to the city's artistic community. Ruth and her sister, Eileen, take lodgings there. Ruth is a writer and her sister wants a stage career. Their lodgings aren't ideal – there's building work going on all around and a constant stream of bizarre visitors. Eileen is the sort of girl everyone wants to help – and does – with food and free gifts. Ruth is pursuing her newspaper career but Bob Baker, associate editor of the *Manhatter*, is not impressed with her overwritten efforts. He tells her to write from her own experience.

Some young Brazilians have arrived in port and Ruth is to interview them; the visitors only know three words of English – American, Dance and Conga. Naturally, they lead Ruth a merry dance through the streets to Greenwich and are promptly arrested.

Bob actually likes what Ruth has written about the Brazilians, and resigns when his editor turns it down. Will it be back to Columbus, Ohio for the two sisters? Eileen likes Bob, but she's got plenty of suitors already; on the other hand, Ruth is really attracted to him. Then fate takes a hand. The newspapers are full of the blonde bombshell who hijacked the Brazilian Navy. It's Eileen. She's offered a cabaret spot in a nightclub. It's a success and all ends well. Ruth gets her Bob (and a press card). And as for Eileen – there's no need to worry about her!

Music and Songs

Perhaps the warmest-sounding of all the Bernstein musicals, *Wonderful Town* is his second celebration of New York, bringing out the best in Comden and Green, the lyricists, as well. A superb, witty collection of New York numbers and ballads includes 'Wrong note rag' (Ruth), 'A quiet girl' (Bob), 'Ohio' (Ruth and Eileen), 'One hundred easy ways to lose a man', (Ruth), 'A little bit in love' (Eileen), 'Conga!' (Ruth and the company) and 'It's love' (Bob).

Did You Know?

✶ All of Leonard Bernstein's New York–based musicals have been hits, but none based elsewhere – even as near as Washington.

✶ The score was completed in a mere five weeks.

✶ The show won Tony, Donaldson, Drama Critic Circle and Outer Critics Circle awards as Best Musical of the Season.

✶ The London revival with Maureen Lipman outpaced the original London run.

✶ Because of movie rights deals, no film could be made, but the owner of the original film property, Columbia, made its own version with a new (Jule Styne) score, called *My Sister Eileen*.

The Critics

'If *Wonderful Town* belongs to the conventional rather than the adventurous school of musical comedy, its collaborators seem engagingly unaware of the fact; it's all new to them, and they make it all new to you' – *New York Herald Tribune* The *New York Times* called the score 'wonderful' and added that Miss Russell 'makes the whole of the city wonderful; and she will make the whole of the country wonderful when she is elected President in 1956'.

Recommended Recording

Original Broadway cast (CD) MCA Gold MCAD 10050
While there is a complete studio cast, an alternative with Miss Russell from the television production and a good revival English cast with Maureen Lipman, none can top the original Broadway version. Rosalind Russell takes over and hardly ever leaves centre stage with a self-assured and perfect delivery.

Film

A TV production in 1958 featured Rosalind Russell, with Sydney Chaplin and Jacquelyn McKeever.

Zorba

LYRICS ✶ Fred Ebb
MUSIC ✶ John Kander
BOOK ✶ Joseph Stein, based on the novel by Nicos Kazantzakis

First Performance

New York, Imperial Theater, 17 November 1968 (305 performances)
Greenwich, UK, Greenwich Theatre, 27 November 1973 (23 performances)

Principal Characters

Zorba ✶ The Greek
Nikos ✶ A young student
Hortense ✶ An elderly cocotte
The Widow
Pavli ✶ A young man

Original New York Cast

Herschel Bernardi, John Cunningham, Maria Karnilova,
Carmen Alvarez, Richard Dmitri

Original UK Cast

Alfred Marks, Jim Smilie, Miriam Karlin,
Angela Richards, Peter Daly

Plot

Crete, 1924. A young student, Nikos, has just inherited a mine that he plans to restore to life. With his new friend, Zorba, he travels over from Pireus, and finds lodgings with a French woman, Hortense. She and Zorba soon find a romantic interest. Zorba tries to interest Nikos in a young Widow who brings them lunch – but Nikos is cautious. Zorba is a law unto himself. Nikos gives him money to buy mine supplies, but Zorba spends it all on a belly dancer. Hortense meanwhile dreams of marriage with Zorba and a wedding ring. Nikos plucks up courage and visits the Widow. An unstable young man, Pavli, witnesses them and throws himself into the sea.

Next morning, village celebrations are stilled when Pavli's body is washed up. And Zorba is back with no supplies, no money and no wedding ring for Hortense. Nikos tells the Widow how much she means to him – and the feelings are returned. But it's too late. A member of Pavli's family stabs her to death, blaming her for the latter's tragic suicide. More bad news. The mine cannot be reopened – it's too far gone. And Nikos can't understand Zorba's philosophical attitude to those who killed the Widow. You must accept Death as you accept Life, his friend explains; all you can do is dance.

Meanwhile, Hortense is very ill, and in her delirium believes she's a young girl again. Zorba rushes to her side. Nikos and Zorba, in their grief, begin to dance. Nikos decides to return to Athens – and Zorba to go where life takes him.

Music and Songs

Kander and Ebb came up with a raw, ethnic, Mediterranean feel for this score. There's an intense feeling of the pitiless sun and the harshness of living. The effective score includes some touching and effective numbers, such as 'Why can't I speak?' (Widow), 'Only love' (Hortense), 'The first time' (Zorba) and 'I am free' (Zorba).

Did You Know?

✶ Anthony Quinn, the star of film the musical was based on, starred in the Broadway revival.

✶ The Anthony Quinn revival, though it did not play as long on Broadway, recouped its costs, unlike the original.

✶ Boris Aronson won one of his many Tony Awards for his set designs for *Zorba*.

The Critics

'The ethnic Greek element to the music and the cheerfully philosophical note struck by the lyrics – often Mr Ebb is both witty and true, endowing the production with fire and spirit' – *New York Times*

Recommended Recording

Original Broadway cast (CD) Broadway Angel ZDM 7 64665 2 1
A wonderfully atmospheric Kander and Ebb score brought to life by a wonderful cast. The revival cast – even with Anthony Quinn – does not come close to it.

Film

UA, 1964. Starring Anthony Quinn. Directed by Michael Cacoyannis. The film was called *Zorba the Greek*. It preceded the show and had different music.

Composer & Lyricist Biographies

Note: Composer and lyricist names set in **bold** are cross-references to entries elsewhere in this section. Musical names set in **bold** mean that more information is available on that particular musical in the main section of the book which covers major musicals alphabetically.

Lee ADAMS See Strouse

Lynn AHRENS (born 1948, USA)
Stephen FLAHERTY (born 1960, USA)
Lynn Ahrens and Stephen Flaherty's first musical, *Lucky Stiff* (1988), won the 1988 Richard Rodgers Production Award. The next, **Once on this Island** (1990), had eight Tony nominations, and Broadway and London productions. In 1993 their musical version of *My Favorite Year* was produced at the Lincoln Center, New York. In 1996 their latest show, *Ragtime*, opened in Toronto on an extensive pre-Broadway tour, and when it opened on Broadway it won the Tony for best score.

Benny ANDERSSON (born 1945, Sweden)
Bjorn ULVAEUS (born 1946, Sweden)
Benny Andersson and Bjorn Ulvaeus were songwriters for, and male members of, the internationally famous pop group ABBA. Before forming that group, they had been members of other groups, Andersson in the top Swedish pop band The Hep Stars, and Ulvaeus in the folk group The Hootenanay Singers. They came together in 1969. ABBA's international fame came in 1974 when they won the Eurovision Song Contest with 'Waterloo'. They enjoyed a stream of hits until the group split in 1982. A year later one of their concept albums, *ABBACADABRA*, was mounted as a show at the Lyric, Hammersmith (original lyrics by Daniel and Alain **Boublil**, English lyrics by Don Black). In 1986 came the staging of another concept album, written with lyricist Tim **Rice**. This was the musical **Chess** that ran for two years in London, but which did not succeed on Broadway. In 1999 a show written around their ABBA hits opened in London and became the hottest ticket in town. It is called **Mamma Mia!** after one of their greatest hits.

Harold ARLEN (1905–86, USA)
Hyman Arluck (later Arlen) hailed from Buffalo, New York. His father was a cantor in a synagogue where Arlen sang in the choir. He began a theatrical career as a rehearsal pianist for revues and musicals, supplemented by engagements as a jazz singer and pianist in 1920s New York. He appeared on stage, briefly, in **Youmans'** show *Great Day* but found his true metier as a songwriter. His first success with lyricist Ted Koehler was 'Get happy' for Ruth Etting to sing in the *9:15 Revue* (1930). Between 1930 and 1934, Arlen and Koehler worked on the Harlem-based *Cotton Club Revues*; the resulting songs included 'I've got the world on a string', 'Between the devil and the deep blue sea' and

'Stormy weather', introduced by such famous singers as Cab Calloway and Ethel Waters. Arlen wrote the revue *Life Begins at 8:40* (1934) with Ira **Gershwin** and E.Y. **Harburg**, and with Harburg the musical *Hooray for What?* (1937), but his move to Hollywood found Arlen working on twenty films and bringing greater successes, including 'It's only a paper moon' (*Take a Chance*, 1933), 'That old black magic' (*Star Spangled Rhythm*, 1942) and 'Ac-cent-tchu-ate the positive' (*Here Come the Waves*, 1944). With lyricist Johnny **Mercer**, Arlen wrote songs for *Blues in the Night* (1941) and, later on, the all-black Broadway musical **St Louis Woman** (1946). His major triumph in Hollywood was *The Wizard of Oz* (1939), with Harburg as lyricist. He wrote further songs for Judy Garland in *A Star is Born* (1954) and *I Could Go on Singing* (1963). His other Broadway shows were **Bloomer Girl** (1941), which starred Celeste Holm and included 'The eagle and me' and 'Right as the rain', **House of Flowers** (1954) for Pearl Bailey, **Jamaica** with Lena Horne (1957) and *Saratoga* (1959) for Carol Lawrence and Howard Keel. While *Jamaica* could probably have run for as long as the star wished, neither *House of Flowers* nor *Saratoga* was successful.

Howard ASHMAN See Menken

Lionel BART (1930–1999, England)
Lionel Begleiter (later Bart) was born in the East End of London. His first successes came when he wrote rock and skiffle hits for Tommy Steele, including 'Rock with the cavemen' and 'Little white bull' for the film *Tommy the Toreador* (1959), and 'Living doll' for Cliff Richard. After an adaptation of Ben Jonson's *Volpone* for Unity Theatre called *Wally Pone*, he teamed up with Monty Norman for *Fings Aint Wot They Used t' Be*, originally mounted at Stratford East and subsequently in the West End, followed by a collaboration with Laurie Johnson for the Mermaid Theatre of *Lock Up Your Daughters* (1959). The following year he was responsible for both the words and music of **Oliver!** The show became a huge international success, running for 2618 performances. There followed **Blitz!** (1962), *Maggie May* (1964) and *Twang!* (1965), a resounding failure. Since then *La Strada* failed to set America alight in 1969. A semi-musical based on *Sparrers Can't Sing*, called *The Londoners*, ran in 1972 at Stratford East. We still await the long-anticipated musical version of *The Hunchback of Notre Dame*.

Irving BERLIN (1888–1989, Russia)
Irving Berlin was born Israel Baline in Tyumen, Siberia. The Baline family reached the USA in 1893. Three years later the father was dead. Young Berlin busked and became a singing waiter. In 1907 came his first published work, the lyric to 'Marie from sunny Italy' (music by café pianist Nick Nicholson), but he was named Berlin on the cover. The revue *Up and Down Broadway* (1910) contained some of his earliest songs but he really established his reputation with 'Alexander's ragtime band' (1911). His first complete Broadway show was *Watch Your Step* (1914), which was presented on both sides of the Atlantic. All the while he contributed to Broadway productions, especially the *Ziegfeld Follies*. He formed his own music publishing company and also estab-

lished the Music Box Theater for revues. During the '30s much of his best work was in Hollywood, creating standards for Bing Crosby, Ethel Merman, Alice Faye, Ginger Rogers and Fred Astaire. The films included *Top Hat* (1935), *Follow the Fleet* (1936), *On the Avenue* (1937) and *Holiday Inn* (1942). In 1940 Broadway saw the highly successful *Louisiana Purchase*. In 1946 he was asked to take over an assignment intended for Jerome **Kern**. This turned out to be his most popular Broadway show, **Annie Get Your Gun**, written for Ethel Merman. For her, too, he wrote **Call Me Madam** in 1950. Following this, Berlin was to write but one more show, the flagwaving *Mr President* in 1962. Although he could only play the piano in the key of F sharp, he was so successful that Richard **Rodgers** was able to describe him as 'the folk-song composer of our country'. He died at the age of 101.

Leonard BERNSTEIN (1918–90, USA)

Leonard Bernstein was born in Lawrence, Massachusetts. He studied at Harvard and the Curtis Institute. His first musical, **On the Town** (1944), based on Jerome Robbins' idea, had lyrics by Betty **Comden** and Adolph **Green**. The team collaborated again on **Wonderful Town** (1953). After the comic opera **Candide** (1956), Bernstein worked again with Jerome Robbins on a modern-day version of *Romeo and Juliet*, **West Side Story** (1957), with lyrics by Stephen **Sondheim**. Bernstein's last musical was the bicentennial tribute *1600 Pennsylvania Avenue* (1976), which was a failure.

Jerry BOCK (born 1928, USA)
Sheldon HARNICK (born 1924, USA)

Jerry Bock was born Jerrold Lewis in New Haven, Connecticut. He gained experience in student productions at the University of Wisconsin before moving to New York and writing for television and revues. His first hit show, with lyricist Larry Holofcener, was **Mr Wonderful** in 1956; his principal collaborator from then on was lyricist Sheldon Harnick. *The Body Beautiful* (1958) was followed by **Fiorello!** (1959). Harnick was responsible for both music and lyrics for songs in *New Faces* (1952) and *Shangri-La* (1956). After the failures of *Tenderloin* (1960), and the critically-acclaimed **She Loves Me** (1963), the couple wrote **Fiddler on the Roof** in 1964. It ran for over 3000 performances in New York and 2000 in London. Bock and Harnick's *The Apple Tree* (1966) and *The Rothschilds* (1970) were not big hits. The pair then parted company. Harnick also wrote *Smiling the Boy Fell Dead* (1961) with David Baker, *Captain Jinks of the Horse Marines* (1975) with Jack Beeson, and *Rex* (1976) with Richard **Rodgers**. *She Loves Me* has recently been revived on both sides of the Atlantic.

Alain BOUBLIL See Schönberg

Leslie BRICUSSE (born 1931, England)
Anthony NEWLEY (1931–1999, England)

Leslie Bricusse's Cambridge University revue *Out of the Blue* was staged in the West End. He then wrote both music and lyrics for *Lady at the Wheel* (1958), before collaborating with Anthony Newley. The partnership had successes with

Stop the World, I Want to Get Off (1960) and **The Roar of the Greasepaint, The Smell of the Crowd** (1965). Their only other stage show together was *The Good Old Bad Old Days* (1972). The collaboration also contributed songs for films such as *Willy Wonka and the Chocolate Factory* (1971), the title song for *Goldfinger* (1964), with music by John Barry, and *Doctor Doolittle* (1967). Bricusse won an Academy Award for 'Talk to the animals'. Bricusse was responsible for the music and lyrics for the films *Goodbye Mr Chips* (1969) and *Scrooge* (1970), both of which have also been seen on stage. He also wrote the stage show *Sherlock Holmes* (1989) and *Victor/Victoria* (1996), based on the earlier film. Bricusse wrote the lyrics for Frank Wildhorn's version of *Jekyll and Hyde* (1990).

Cy COLEMAN (born 1929, USA)

Seymour Kaufman (later Coleman) was born in New York. After studying at the New York College of Music, he played piano in a jazz trio, and began writing songs with lyricist Joseph McCarthy and then with Carolyn Leigh. Coleman wrote several hit songs: 'Witchcraft' (lyrics by Leigh), for example, was a hit in 1957. His first show was *Wildcat* (1960) for Lucille Ball and this was followed by **Little Me** (1962), based on Patrick Dennis' book. Coleman's new lyricist was veteran Dorothy **Fields**. First came his biggest Broadway success, **Sweet Charity** (1966); then came **Seesaw** (1973). Coleman worked with Betty **Comden** and Adolph **Green** for the revue *Straws in the Wind* (1975) and then **On the Twentieth Century** (1978). **Barnum** in 1980 (lyrics by Michael Stewart) was a big Broadway hit. After a flop, *Welcome to the Club* (1989), Coleman worked again with Comden and Green on *The Will Rogers Follies* (1990). **City of Angels** (1989), with lyrics by David Zippel, was a critical but not a commercial success. In 1997 came *This Life* about street-walkers.

Betty COMDEN (born 1915, USA)
Adolph GREEN (born 1915, USA)

Lyricists Comden and Green met at university, forming a cabaret act at the Village Vanguard with actress Judy Holliday. Here they met Leonard **Bernstein** and together wrote their first show, **On the Town** (1944). *Billion Dollar Baby* (1945), with music by Morton Gould, followed, before the duo moved to Hollywood to write screenplays for a time. Later, their Broadway success continued. With Jule **Styne** they wrote *Two on the Aisle* (1951), **Peter Pan** (1954), **Bells Are Ringing** (1956), *Say Darling* (1958), **Do Re Mi** (1960), *Subways are for Sleeping* (1961), *Fade Out, Fade In* (1964) and *Hallelujah Baby* (1967); with Bernstein again they wrote lyrics for **Wonderful Town** (1953); and with Cy **Coleman On the Twentieth Century** (1978) and *The Will Rogers Follies* (1991).

Sir Noël COWARD (1899–1973, England)

Coward was a self-taught composer, writer, actor and director. His eventual success was to rival that of his American equivalents. His first successful song, 'Forbidden fruit', came in 1916. Subsequently came the revues *On with the Dance* (1925) and *This Year of Grace* (1928), and the book/musical **Bitter Sweet** in 1929. Then came *Conversation Piece* (1934) and *Operette* (1938), as well as *Pacific 1860* (1946), *Ace of Clubs* (1950) and *The Girl Who Came to Supper* (1963). Coward is most famous for his witty songs like 'Mad dogs and Englishmen' from *Words and Music* (1932) and 'The stately homes of England' from *Set to Music* (1939).

Gene Vincent DE PAUL (1919–88, USA)

De Paul was a performing and recording pianist who wrote some memorable songs, including 'I'll remember April' (1941) and 'Star eyes' (1943), before moving to Hollywood. He won an Academy Award for the MGM film musical *Seven Brides for Seven Brothers* (lyricist Johnny **Mercer**). It was put on stage in New York in 1982 and in London in 1985. For Broadway, De Paul and Mercer wrote the show **L'il Abner** (1956) which ran for 693 performances. A film version was released in 1959.

Al DUBIN (1891–1945, Switzerland)
Harry WARREN (1893–1981, USA)

Dubin and Warren joined forces in the thirties in Hollywood and wrote scores for film musicals such as *Roman Scandals, 42nd Street, Gold Diggers of 1933, Footlight Parade* (all 1933), *Wonder Bar, Moulin Rouge, Twenty Million Sweethearts, Dames* (1934), *Go Into Your Dance* and *Gold Diggers of 1935*. The stage production of **42nd Street** utilised their vast catalogue. Harry Warren had a career on Broadway writing for *Sweet and Low* (1930), *The Laugh Parade* (1931) and *Billy Rose's Crazy Quilt*.

Fred EBB See Kander

Vivian ELLIS (1904–96, England)

Vivian Ellis was born in London. He began writing songs as a teenager and contributed songs to shows and revues before providing half the songs for his first hit **Mr Cinders** (1929). For Sophie Tucker he wrote the bulk of *Follow a Star* (1930). *Jill Darling* (1934) was a further success, as was the revue *Streamline*. Then came *Running Riot* (1938) and *Under Your Hat* (1938). After World War II came *Big Ben* (1946) and a huge success, **Bless the Bride** (1947). *Tough at the Top* (1949) and *And so to Bed* (1951) followed, then came **The Water Gypsies** (1955). Ellis lived to see a resurgence of interest in his music with a revival of *Bless the Bride*, and in 1992 a musical revue of his output, entitled *Spread a Little Happiness*, served to remind of the strength and diversity of his musical output. 1996 saw a revival of his charming children's show *Listen to the Wind*.

Dorothy FIELDS (1904–74, USA)

Lyricist/librettist Dorothy Fields, from Allenhurst, New Jersey, initially wrote with with composer Jimmy **McHugh**, including 'I can't give you anything but love', which featured in both *Delmar's Revels* (1927) and *Blackbirds of 1928*, and 'On the sunny side of the street' from *The International Revue* (1930). In Hollywood Fields worked with Jerome **Kern** on the Fred Astaire/Ginger Rogers films *Roberta* (1935), writing 'Lovely to look at' and 'I won't dance', and *Swing Time* (1936), including 'The way you look tonight'. Back on Broadway, she wrote the librettos of Cole **Porter**'s *Let's Face It* (1941) and *Mexican Hayride* (1944), and Irving **Berlin**'s biggest success, **Annie Get Your Gun** (1946). In 1966 she joined Cy **Coleman** on **Sweet Charity**, which included 'Big spender', and also wrote lyrics for his show **Seesaw** (1973).

William FINN (born 1952, USA)
William Finn was born in Boston, Massachusetts, and has had three successful musicals to date. The first was *In Trousers* (1979), the second *March of the Falsettos* (1981) and the third *Falsettoland* (1990). The last two (all three featured the same characters) were combined in one show – *Falsettos* (1992). He subsequently tried a treatment of the book *Muscle*, but that came to nothing, and provided a scenario for the dance musical *Dangerous Games* (1989). The same year there was a Shakespeare Festival mounting of his *Romance in Hard Times*.

Stephen FLAHERTY See Ahrens

George FORREST (born 1915, USA)
Robert WRIGHT (1914–1999, USA)
Brooklyn-born George Forrest and Florida's Robert Wright have worked exclusively together as lyricist and composer team, whose greatest successes have involved adaptations of classical music for Broadway shows. Their first film hit was 'The donkey serenade', an adaptation of Friml's 'Chansonette' in *The Firefly* (1937). On Broadway **Song of Norway** (1944) was an adaptation of Grieg's music; *Gypsy Lady* (1946) used Victor Herbert's music, and *Magdalena* (1948) had a score by Villa-Lobos. Their biggest success was **Kismet** (1953), which freely adapted themes from Borodin. *Kismet* was filmed in 1955 with Howard Keel and Dolores Gray. *Anya* (1965), about the Grand Duchess Anastasia, used the music of Rachmaninov, and *The Great Waltz* (1970) that of Johann Strauss. Their shows with their own music were *Kean* (1961) and *Grand Hotel* (1989), a new collaboration with Maury Yeston based on their earlier failure, *At the Grand* (1956).

Harold FRASER-SIMSON (1878–1944, England)
Harold Fraser-Simson was a successful ship-owner who wrote several songs during the early 1900s, but his crowning glory was his score for **The Maid of the Mountains** (1916), a show that ran for over 1000 performances in London. This was followed by *Bonita* (1911), *A Southern Maid* (1917), *Our Peg* (1919), *Head Over Heels* (1923), *Our Nell* (1924), *Betty in Mayfair* (1925) and *Toad of Toad Hall* (1929). His A.A. Milne settings were used in *Winnie the Pooh* (1970).

Rudolf FRIML (1879–1972, Czechoslovakia/USA)
After a stint as piano accompanist to violin virtuoso Jan Kubelik, Czech-born Rudolf Friml settled in the United States in 1906, devoting himself to composition (his piano concerto premiered in 1906). In 1912 he was chosen to compose the score for *The Firefly* and its tempestuous prima donna star Emma Trentini. His scores were graceful, charming, highly melodic – easy to sing and easy to remember. His enduring scores include *Katinka* (1915), *Ziegfeld Follies*

of 1921 and 1923, **Rose Marie** (1924), **The Vagabond King** (1925) and *The Three Musketeers* (1928). These were essentially old-fashioned romantic operettas whose vogue eventually passed. From 1930 onwards Friml's time as a successful stage composer was over as far as new work was concerned. *Luana* (1930) flopped on both sides of the Atlantic. Friml moved to Hollywood but failed to produce any significant new scores. He did however make recordings and appear on television in later years. He died in Hollywood.

Noël GAY (1898–1954, England)

Reginald Moxon Armitage was appointed deputy organist of Wakefield Cathedral when he was only twelve years of age. At fifteen he won a scholarship to the Royal College of Music, and at eighteen was musical director at St Anne's, Soho. After studies at Christ's College, Cambridge, he began writing popular songs under the pseudonym Noël Gay. In 1925 his songs were included in the revue *Stop Press. The Charlot Revue of 1926* and *Clowns in Clover* (1927) also included songs by him, the first of many memorable songs in musicals, films and revues. 'The sun has got his hat on' (1932), 'Leaning on a lamp-post' (1937), sung by George Formby in the film *Feather Your Nest*, and 'Love makes the world go round' (1938), from *These Foolish Things*, were all subsequently incorporated into the successful revival of **Me and My Girl**. This was originally staged at the Victoria Palace, London in 1937. It ran for 1646 performances. Its hit song, 'The Lambeth walk', inspired a dance craze. The show was filmed in 1939 as *The Lambeth Walk*, and was successfully revived in London in 1984 and the following year on Broadway. Other shows by Noël Gay were *Wild Oats* (1938), *Present Arms* (1940), *Susie* (1942), *La-di-da-di-da* (1943), *The Love Racket* (1943), *Meet Me Victoria* (1944), *Sweetheart Mine* (1946) and *Bob's Your Uncle* (1948).

George GERSHWIN (1898–1937, USA)
Ira GERSHWIN (1896–1983, USA)

One of the greatest tragedies in the history of musical comedy was the premature death of one of the art form's greatest exponents. George and Ira Gershovitz were the sons of Russian-Jewish immigrants. In 1914 George took his first job working as a song-plugger for a music publisher, where he began to write songs. He was rehearsal pianist on Jerome **Kern**'s *Miss 1917*. He was soon engaged by music publisher T.B. Harms. Ira continued his education and submitted verse to newspapers and other periodicals. George encouraged him to write song lyrics; their first collaboration, 'The real American folk song', was sung by Nora Bayes in *Ladies First* (1918), with Ira's name hidden under the pseudonym Arthur Francis. In 1919 George wrote his first Broadway show, *La La Lucille*, and had a hit with 'Swanee'. He contributed to *George White's Scandals* from 1920 until 1924. In 1924, George and Ira wrote **Lady, Be Good!** together. Ira's incisive, smart lyrics were ideally coupled to George's wonderful music. 1924 saw *Rhapsody in Blue* premièred at the Aeolian Hall. The Gershwins continued their Broadway progress during the 1920s and '30s with the political spoofs **Strike Up the Band** (1928/30) and **Of Thee I Sing** (1931) which picked up a Pulitzer Prize, and succeeded in Hollywood with *Shall We Dance?* (1937), *A Damsel in Distress* (1937) and *The Goldwyn Follies* (1938). In

1935 the glorious opera, *Porgy and Bess*, was not universally admired. While working on the *Goldwyn Follies*, George fell ill and died, unexpectedly, on 11 July at the age of 38. Ira continued his career as a lyricist with others after his brother died. His collaborators included Kurt **Weill** (**Lady in the Dark**, 1941), Jerome **Kern** (*Cover Girl*, 1944), Harry Warren (*The Barkleys of Broadway*, 1949) and Harold **Arlen** (*A Star is Born*, 1954).

Sir W(illam) S(chwenk) GILBERT (1836–1911, England)
Sir Arthur SULLIVAN (1842–1900, England)
Gilbert wrote comic verse, plays, comic operas and burlesques before joining forces with Sullivan in 1871 to write short pieces for the Gaiety Theatre. Richard D'Oyly Carte commissioned them to write *The Sorcerer* (1877) for him and there followed *HMS Pinafore* (1878), **The Pirates of Penzance** (1880), *Patience* (1881), *Iolanthe* (1882), *Princess Ida* (1884), **The Mikado** (1885), *Ruddigore* (1887), *The Yeomen of the Guard* (1888), *The Gondoliers* (1889), *Utopia (Limited)* (1893) and *The Grand Duke* (1896). Their partnership was full of tension and Sullivan, especially, felt trapped by it as he felt it cheapened his talent. They both worked extensively with other partners. Their career has led to books, plays and films – the latest being the award winning *Topsy Turvey* (1999).

Adolph GREEN See **Comden**

Marvin HAMLISCH (born 1944, USA)
Hamlisch's parents arrived in the United States in 1937. At the age of seven, Hamlisch became the youngest student to be admitted to the Juilliard School, America's most prestigious music academy. A schoolfriend, Liza Minnelli, recorded his song 'Travellin' man'. In 1965 he wrote his first hit 'Sunshine, lollipops and rainbows'. He worked on Broadway as a rehearsal pianist and arranger on *Fade Out, Fade In*, creating special material for Ann-Margret and Liza Minnelli along the way. He wrote music for films between 1968 and 1973, including *The Swimmer* (1968), *Take the Money and Run* (1969) and *The Sting* (1973), the latter winning an Academy Award for best adapted score. In the same year he also picked up another two Academy Awards for the Barbra Streisand film, *The Way We Were* (best original score and song). On Broadway he had a success with **A Chorus Line** in 1975, which received nine Tony awards and a Pulitzer Prize, and was filmed in 1985. **They're Playing Our Song** followed in 1979. Later shows, *Jean* (1983) at the Royal National Theatre, *Smile* (1986) and *The Goodbye Girl* (1993) were not successful on Broadway, although the latter was given a London run in 1997.

Oscar HAMMERSTEIN II (1895–1960, USA) *Also see Rodgers.*
Oscar Hammerstein II was born into a theatrical family. After dutifully study-ing law at Columbia University, he became stage manager to his Uncle Arthur Hammerstein, writing the libretto and lyrics for his first musical, *Always You*, in 1920 (music by Herbert Stothart). Hammerstein, often with Otto **Harbach**, was responsible for **Friml's Rose Marie** (1924) and **Romberg's The Desert Song** (1926). His libretto for Jerome **Kern's Show Boat** (1927) was a ground-breaker. Kern provided the music for **Sweet Adeline** (1929), **Music in the Air** (1932)

and **Very Warm for May** (1939). In 1943 he began his most successful partnership with composer Richard **Rodgers**, on **Oklahoma!** which, like *Show Boat*, took place in an American setting. The partnership continued with **Carousel** (1945), **South Pacific** (1949), **The King and I** (1951) and **The Sound of Music** (1959), as well as some less successful shows. **Carmen Jones**, Hammerstein's adaptation of Bizet's *Carmen*, was staged with a black cast in 1943.

Otto HARBACH (1873–1963, USA)

Otto Harbach, from Utah, was an English teacher, journalist and copywriter. His *Three Twins* (1908) was a hit, written with Karl Hoschna. Harbach wrote *The Firefly* (1912) with composer Rudolf **Friml**, and often collaborated with Oscar **Hammerstein** II, as on Friml's **Rose Marie** (1924). Harbach later contributed lyrics for **Kern's Roberta** (1932), which included 'Smoke gets in your eyes'.

E.Y. HARBURG (1898–1981, USA)

Born Isidore Hochberg in New York, Edgar 'Yip' Harburg attended the same City College as lyricist Ira **Gershwin**. Harburg wrote his first lyrics for Earl Carroll's *Sketch Book* (1929), which had music by Jay Gorney. 'Brother can you spare a dime?' (also with Gorney) graced the revue *Americana* (1932). Harburg also worked with Vernon Duke on *Walk a Little Faster* (1932) and Burton **Lane** on *Hold on to Your Hats* (1940) and **Finian's Rainbow** (1947), but his most successful collaborator was Harold **Arlen**. For Broadway they wrote *Hooray for What!* (1937), **Bloomer Girl** (1944) and **Jamaica** (1957). In Hollywood the pair wrote songs for *Gold Diggers of 1937* and *The Wizard of Oz* (1939). Harburg's last Broadway show was *Darling of the Day* (1968), with music by Jule **Styne**, which starred Patricia Routledge and Vincent Price.

Sheldon HARNICK See Bock

Lorenz HART See Rodgers

David HENEKER (born 1906, England)

Heneker served in the army until 1948. He scored successes in 1958 with *Expresso Bongo*, and the English adaptation of Marguerite Monnot's **Irma-la-Douce** with Monty Norman (later composer of the 'James Bond theme'). *Bongo* was filmed in 1959 with Cliff Richard. Among others, Heneker has also written for **Half a Sixpence** (1963) for Tommy Steele, **Charlie Girl** (1965) for Joe Brown and Anna Neagle, and *Phil the Fluter* (1969) for Evelyn Laye and Mark Wynter. 1966 saw the fox-hunting musical *Jorrocks*. Other Heneker shows include *The Biograph Girl* (1980) and *Peg* (1982).

Jerry HERMAN (born 1933, USA)

Self-taught New Yorker, Jerry Herman, studied drama at Miami University before returning to New York, where he worked briefly in nightclubs and began writing for television. *I Feel Wonderful*, his first revue, was staged off-Broadway in 1954; then came *Nightcap* (1958) and *Parade* (1960). *Milk and Honey* (1961), his first Broadway show, won a Tony Award for the composer/lyricist. *Madam Aphrodite* (1961) failed but he then scored with **Hello, Dolly!** in 1964, a huge success for Carol Channing. It was Broadway's longest-running show at that time, with 2844 performances when it closed. **Mame** in 1966, starring Angela Lansbury, ran for 1508 performances (with a further 443 in London) but subsequent shows *Dear World* (1969), also with Lansbury, **Mack and Mabel** (1974) and *The Grand Tour* (1979) were all relatively unsuccessful. Herman had to wait until 1983 before another Broadway, but not London, hit with **La Cage aux Folles**, the first Broadway musical show with homosexuality as its subject. Recently, Herman composed the television musical *Mrs Santa Claus* (1996) for Miss Lansbury.

Arnold B. Horwitt (1918–1977, USA)
Albert Hague (born Germany 1920)
Arnold Horwitt was a writer and lyricist who wrote extensively for American revue. His sketches and lyrics are included in *Make Mine Manhattan* (1948), *The Girls Against the Boys* (1959), *Two's Company* (1952) and *Call Me Mister* (1946). Albert Hague's career was as a composer and an actor. As an actor he is fondly remembered for his role in the television series *Fame* in the eighties and as a composer for Broadway shows such as Redhead (1959) *Café Crown* (1964) *The Fig Leaves Are Falling* (1969), *Miss Moffat* (1974). Their one collaboration was **Plain and Fancy** (1955).

Sir Elton JOHN See Rice

John KANDER (born 1927, USA)
Fred EBB (born 1932, USA)
Kansas City's John Kander started out as a rehearsal pianist, then as a conductor and arranger. His first, unsuccessful, show was *The Family Affair* (1962), but after joining forces with lyricist Fred Ebb he wrote *Flora, the Red Menace* (1965), which gave Liza Minnelli her first starring role. Like Kander, Ebb had studied at Columbia University and contributed to Broadway revues such as *From A to Z* (1960), writing the book for *Morning Sun* (1963) and working on the US version of the TV series *That Was the Week That Was*. Kander and Ebb followed *Flora* with **Cabaret** in 1966. *Cabaret* was filmed in 1972 with Minnelli as its star. Kander and Ebb's other shows include *The Happy Time* (1968), *70 Girls 70* (1971) and the hard-bitten **Chicago** (1972), plus *Woman of the Year* (1981). In 1990 they had another hit with **Kiss of the Spider Woman**, based on Manuel Puig's novel, which opened in Toronto and London before finally moving to Broadway. *Steel Pier* in 1997 flopped, unlike the same year's revival of *Chicago*.

Jerome KERN (1885–1945, USA)
The father of American musical theatre, Jerome Kern studied at the New York College of Music and in Heidelberg, where his first composition, a piano piece called 'At the casino', was published in 1902. Back in New York he added songs to imported European shows, including 'How'd you like to spoon with me?' from *The Earl and the Girl* (1905). An Anglophile, he married Eva Leale, the daughter of a pub landlord. Kern's first Broadway show was *The Red*

Petticoat (1912). He continued to have more success with his interpolated songs, before joining librettist Guy Bolton for a series of shows originally based at the Princess Theater, including *Nobody Home* (1915) and **Very Good, Eddie** (1915). P.G. Wodehouse became lyric-writer in 1917, and the group scored a string of quick hits: *Have a Heart, Oh Boy* and **Leave it to Jane** (all 1917), *Oh, Lady! Lady!* (1918) and *Sitting Pretty* (1924). **Sally** (1920) was Kern's first transatlantic success. **Show Boat** (1927), with lyrics by Oscar **Hammerstein II**, changed the face of the Broadway musical: set in a realistic America, it was light years away from the never-never land of operetta, and it came with songs integral to the plot, not merely interpolations. In the 1930s Kern found himself writing for Hollywood's finest performers, including Irene Dunne and Deanna Durbin, Fred Astaire and Ginger Rogers, with films like *Roberta* (1935), the film version of the 1933 show, and *Swing Time* (1936), plus *High Wide and Handsome* (1937), *Can't Help Singing* (1944) and the posthumously released *Centennial Summer* (1946). 'The last time I saw Paris' was included in the film of Gershwin's **Lady, Be Good!** (1941) and won an Academy Award. In 1945 Kern returned to New York to begin work on a musical featuring Ethel Merman, based on the life of Annie Oakley, but died suddenly of a heart attack on 11 November. **Annie Get Your Gun** was written by Irving **Berlin**.

Henry KRIEGER (born New York, 1945)

Krieger leapt into the big time with the lively score for **Dreamgirls** (1981), which was followed two years later by another for *The Tap Dance Kid* (1983). Next came a further collaboration with his partner in *Dreamgirls*, Tom Eyen, on *Dangerous Music* (1988) and a children's musical for Leicester in England called *Fat Pig* (1988).

Burton LANE (1912–96, USA)

Burton Levy (later Lane) from New York worked initially for music publishers, Remick, as a pianist and staff writer when only fifteen. Encouraged by George **Gershwin**, he wrote songs for Broadway revues, including *Three's a Crowd* (1930), *Earl Carroll's Vanities* (1931) and *Americana* (1932). Moving to California in 1933, he wrote songs for the films *Folies Bergère* (1935), *Swing High, Swing Low* (1937) and *Babes on Broadway* (1941). He stayed out West until 1954, returning to Broadway for *Hold on to Your Hats* (1940), *Laffing Room Only* (1944) and **Finian's Rainbow** (1947). The latter was a collaboration with E.Y. **Harburg** and included the songs 'How are things in Glocca Morra?' and 'That old devil moon'. It was filmed in 1968 with Fred Astaire, Tommy Steele and Petula Clark. In Lane's only two subsequent shows, **On a Clear Day You Can See Forever** (1965) and *Carmelina* (1979), Alan Jay **Lerner** was the lyricist.

Mitch LEIGH (born 1928, USA)

Brooklyn's Irwin Mitchnick studied at Yale University with Hindemith. After working as a jazz musician he wrote radio and television commercials, forming his own company. The musical play, **Man of La Mancha**, came in 1965. An adaptation of Cervantes' *Don Quixote*, it was originally intended for television.

Lyrics were by Joe Darion. It remains Leigh's biggest Broadway hit and was filmed, starring Peter O'Toole, in 1972. The subsequent shows *Chu Chem* (1966), *Cry for Us All* (1970), *Odyssey* (1974), *Home Sweet Homer* (1976) and *Sarava* (1978) were not as popular.

Alan Jay LERNER   See Loewe

Lord Andrew LLOYD-WEBBER (born 1948, England)

Andrew Lloyd-Webber, son of composer Dr William Lloyd-Webber (1914–82), went to Westminster School. He wrote his first composition at the age of six, and had a piano suite published when he was nine. He studied at the Guildhall School of Music and the Royal College of Music. In 1965 he worked with lyricist Tim **Rice** on their first show, *The Likes of Us*, which was never produced. In 1968 **Joseph and the Amazing Technicolor Dreamcoat** was written for Colet Court, the junior wing of St Paul's School, London. It was originally published for school use, but was expanded somewhat for subsequent recording, and further expanded for the Edinburgh Festival in 1972, and performances in London and New York. Then came **Jesus Christ Superstar** on Broadway in 1971 and London in 1972 (at the Palace Theatre, later bought by Lloyd Webber), where it ran for 3358 performances. With Alan Ayckbourn, Lloyd Webber wrote the unsuccessful show *Jeeves* (1975, but revised and successfully revived in 1996), before resuming work with Rice on **Evita** (1976), an LP; after scoring a No. 1 hit with 'Don't cry for me, Argentina', the show opened in 1978. *Evita* was his final collaboration with Rice, and has recently been filmed with Madonna. Then came **Cats** (1981), using T.S. Eliot's poems. Subsequently he worked with Don Black for *Song and Dance* (1982), and Richard Stilgoe for both **Starlight Express** (1984) and **The Phantom of the Opera** (1986). He worked with Don Black again on **Aspects of Love** (1989) and **Sunset Boulevard** (1993). Jim Steinman is his lyricist for **Whistle Down the Wind** (1997) and Ben Elton for **The Beautiful Game.**

Frank LOESSER (1910–69, USA)

Loesser was born into a classical musical family, but he was more interested in pop. He was a journalist and member of a variety act while writing pop lyrics. 'In love with a memory of you', his first published song (1931), was written with composer William Schuman. Lyrics for *The Illustrator's Show* (1936) resulted in a contract from Universal Pictures in Hollywood, where he wrote for over twenty film musicals, and contributed to some forty others. He then wrote his own music for army shows, including *Skirts* and *About Face* (both 1944), and *OK, USA* (1945). In 1948 he wrote the music and lyrics for his first Broadway show, **Where's Charley?**, adapted from Brandon Thomas' farce *Charley's Aunt.* Then came his masterpiece, **Guys and Dolls** (1950), and **The Most Happy Fella** (1956), almost operatic in feeling, followed. *Greenwillow* (1960) was unsuccessful. **How to Succeed in Business Without Really Trying** (1961) ran longer than any of his other shows (1417 performances, plus 520 in London) and became only the fourth musical to win a Pulitzer Prize. His last show, *Pleasures and Palaces* (1965), based on the story of Lieutenant Potemkin, didn't reach Broadway. *Hans Christian Anderson* (1952) is his best-known Hollywood score, and was adapted for the London stage in 1974.

Frederick LOEWE (1901–88, Germany)
Alan Jay LERNER (1918–86, USA)

Busoni and d'Albert were Berlin-born Frederick Loewe's piano teachers, and he studied composition with Reznicek. He emigrated to the USA in 1924. His first show, *Great Lady*, appeared in 1938, but *Salute to Spring* (1937) contained some of his songs, which were subsequently recycled in *Life of the Party* (1942), with a book by Alan Jay Lerner. New York-born Lerner had studied at the Institute of Musical Art and at Harvard before working as a scriptwriter on radio. Loewe was to be his composer partner from then on, beginning with *What's Up?* (1943). Their first success was **Brigadoon** (1947), set in Scotland, followed by their only show set in America – *Paint Your Wagon* (1951). **My Fair Lady** (1956) was the team's biggest success, and then came the film *Gigi* (1958). Richard Burton starred in **Camelot** (1960). After *Camelot* (filmed in 1967), Lerner and Loewe worked together one more time, on the film *The Little Prince* (1974). Lerner also collaborated with composers Kurt **Weill** on *Love Life* (1948), Burton **Lane** on **On a Clear Day You Can See Forever** (1965) and *Carmelina* (1979), André Previn on *Coco* (1969), Leonard **Bernstein** on *1600 Pennsylvania Avenue* (1976) and Charles **Strouse** on *Dance a Little Closer* (1983).

Galt MacDERMOT (born 1928, Canada)

Galt MacDermot's first show was his 'tribal love-rock musical' **Hair** (1967). The book and lyrics were by Gerome Ragni and James Rado. It was filmed in 1979. MacDermot's later shows were *Isabel's a Jezebel* (1970) and *Two Gentlemen of Verona* (1971), a successful Shakespeare adaptation, followed by two failures, *Dude* and *Via Galactica* (both 1972).

Richard MALTBY JNR (born 1937, USA)
David SHIRE (born 1937, USA)

Richard Maltby from Wisconsin and Buffalo's David Shire have collaborated on many songs and a number of musicals which never reached Broadway. The songs formed the basis of two successful musical revues, *Starting Here, Starting Now* and *Closer than Ever*. Happily, both *Baby* (1983) and *Big* (1996) proved to be fine both melodically and lyrically, even if neither proved to be commercially successful. Both partners have also pursued separate and successful careers. Maltby has gained renown as director and conceiver of *Ain't Misbehavin'*, and also directed the Broadway production of *Song and Dance*. He wrote the splendid lyrics for **Miss Saigon** (1993). Shire is also a highly successful composer of film scores, including *Saturday Night Fever, Return to Oz, The Taking of Pelham 1-2-3, All the President's Men, Farewell My Lovely* and *The Hindenberg*.

Henry MANCINI (1924–94, USA)

The film composer responsible for *Peter Gunn* (1958) and *The Pink Panther* won Academy awards for both 'Moon river' from *Breakfast at Tiffany's* (1961) and the theme song from *Days of Wine and Roses* (1964), both with lyrics by Johnny **Mercer**. His only musical film was *Victor/Victoria* (1982), earning the composer another Academy Award. It became a Broadway show in 1996, after the composer's death.

Hugh MARTIN (born 1914, USA)
Ralph BLANE (born 1914, USA)
Alabama's Hugh Martin sang in Harold **Arlen**'s *Hooray for What?* (1937), where he met Ralph Blane, also in the cast. Oklahoma-born Blane was born Ralph Uriah Hunsecker and had previously appeared on Broadway in *New Faces of 1936*. Martin and Blane began a songwriting partnership, forming a vocal group, The Four Martins. Their first show together, *Best Foot Forward*, came in in 1941. In 1943 Hollywood beckoned and they supervised the show's screen adaptation, before writing songs for *Thousands Cheer* (1943), *Meet Me in St Louis* (1944), *The Girl Rush* (1955) and *The Girl Most Likely* (1957). On Broadway, Martin wrote his own lyrics for *Look Ma, I'm Dancin'* (1948). Other Blane and Martin shows were *Make a Wish* (1951) and *Three Wishes for Jamie* (1952).

Jimmy McHUGH (1894–1969, USA)
Jimmy McHugh was rehearsal pianist for the Boston Opera before becoming song-plugger for Irving **Berlin**'s music company. In the 1920s he wrote songs for the *Cotton Club Revues*, and in 1928 wrote for the first time with lyricist Dorothy **Fields**: their early successes included 'On the sunny side of the street' from *The International Revue* (1930). In Hollywood they wrote songs like 'Cuban love song' (used as the title song for the 1931 film), as well as songs for *Flying High* (1931) and *Hooray for Love* (1935). McHugh, with Harold Adamson, wrote such songs as 'That foolish feeling' from *Top of the Town* (1937), the title song from *That Certain Age* (1938) and 'I couldn't sleep a wink last night' from *Higher and Higher* (1943). Back on Broadway he wrote the scores for *The Streets of Paris* (1939), *Keep Off the Grass* (1940), with Al Dubin's lyrics, and *As the Girls Go* (1948) with Adamson.

Alan MENKEN (born 1951, USA)
Howard ASHMAN (1951–91, USA)
New Yorker Alan Menken enjoyed a classical musical training before deciding to pursue a career on Broadway. He swiftly met up with Baltimore-born lyricist, Howard Ashman, who began his career off-off Broadway. They collaborated on the *Real Life Funnies* (1981), and scored a hit with the rock musical **Little Shop of Horrors** (1982), based on the 1961 Roger Corman film. The show was filmed in 1986. The same year came their unsuccessful show *Smile*. Menken also had other Broadway shows, including *God Bless You, Mr Rosewater* (1979) and *A Christmas Carol* (1995). Menken's Hollywood work, especially for Disney, has established him. This began with *The Little Mermaid* (1989), and continued with **Beauty and the Beast** (1991), *Aladdin* (1992), including the Oscar-winning 'A whole new world' (lyrics by Tim **Rice**), *Pocahontas* (1995) and *The Hunchback of Notre Dame* (1996), the latter two involving lyricist Stephen **Schwartz**.

Johnny MERCER (1909–76, USA)

The Southern gentleman, John Herndon Mercer, reached New York in 1927. He was a sometime vocalist with Paul Whiteman. His song 'Out of breath and scared to death of you' (music by Everett Miller) appeared in the *Garrick Gaities of 1930*. He soon became a successful and prolific lyricist. Mercer's collaborators included: Harold **Arlen** on *Blues in the Night* (1941) and **St Louis Woman** (1946); Hoagy Carmichael on *Walk with Music* (1940) and *Here Comes the Groom* (1951); Robert Emmett Dolan Texas on *L'il Darlin'* (1949) and *Foxy* (1964); Jerome **Kern** on *You Were Never Lovelier* (1942); Henry **Mancini** on *Breakfast at Tiffany's* (1961), *Days of Wine and Roses* (1962) and *Charade* (1963); Gene **De Paul** on **L'il Abner** (1956); and Harry Warren on *The Harvey Girls* (1946). The show *Top Banana* (1951) had both music and lyrics by him. He co-founded Capitol Records in 1942.

Bob MERRILL (1921–1998, USA)

Henry Robert Merrill, New York actor and wartime show producer, also worked in television as a writer and director, and after producing a pop hit with 'If I knew you were coming I'd have baked a cake' (1950, written with Al Hoffman), he turned to full-time songwriting. *New Girl in Town* (1957) and **Take Me Along** (1959) were Merrill's first Broadway scores; **Carnival** (1961) was a hit. In 1964 came the lyrics for Jule **Styne's** **Funny Girl**. He was to work with Styne again on *Sugar* (1972). *Henry, Sweet Henry* (1967) was not a hit.

Anthony NEWLEY See Bricusse

Ivor NOVELLO (1893–1951, Wales)

Cardiff's David Ivor Davies had a singing teacher mother, and his father was an amateur musician. His first song was published when he was 17. In 1914 came 'Keep the home fires burning', one of the most popular songs of World War I. It was originally called 'Till the boys come home'. In 1919 he acted for the first time in the film *The Call of the Blood*, and throughout the 1920s and '30s was a stage and screen matinée idol. He concentrated on writing plays, but very few songs, until 1935, when he returned to music, composing **Glamorous Night**. He normally took the nonsinging lead role in his own musical plays, including *Careless Rapture* (1936), *Crest of the Wave* (1937) and **The Dancing Years** (1939). The latter, his most successful show, was filmed in 1947 and revived in 1968. **King's Rhapsody** (1949) and *Gay's the Word* (1951) were his last works. The principal role in the latter was played by Cicely Courtneidge.

Richard O'BRIEN (born 1942, New Zealand)

Richard O'Brien was the deviser and composer of music and lyrics for the movie spoof, **The Rocky Horror Show** (1972). He also played a principal role in it. Neither a further show, *T Zee* (1976), nor *Shock Treatment* (1982), a film sequel to *Rocky Horror*, proved anything like as successful.

Cole PORTER (1891–1964, USA)

Cole Porter was born into a wealthy family in Peru, Indiana. His mother encouraged his musical ambitions, and had his piano piece 'The bobolink waltz' published in 1902. He wrote football songs, and contributed to amateur shows at Yale University; then, after brief law studies at Harvard, he took courses in harmony and counterpoint. Before moving to Paris he staged his first show, *See America First*, in 1916. He joined the French Foreign Legion for a three-year stint. *Hitchy-Koo* of 1919, a revue with an all-Porter score, made him independently wealthy. He also married wealth, his socialite wife being Linda Thomas. They held fashionable parties at which he performed his own sophisticated songs. Other shows and revues with Porter songs were staged in London and New York during the 1920s. *Paris* (1928) and *Fifty Million Frenchmen* (1929) were followed by *Gay Divorce* (1932), **Anything Goes** (1934) and *Red, Hot and Blue* (1936). Porter was permanently and painfully injured by a riding accident in 1937. He lost his left, and then his right, legs and spent his later years in constant pain. After a series of musical flops during the 1940s, he returned with **Kiss Me Kate** (1948) and **Can-Can** (1953), and the film *High Society* (1956), all of which were very popular. His legacy of standards includes 'Night and day', 'Let's do it', 'Begin the beguine', 'Miss Otis regrets' and 'Anything goes'.

Sir Tim RICE (born 1944, England)
London's Timothy Miles Bindon Rice worked for EMI records, became a pop singer and then met up with Andrew **Lloyd Webber** in 1965 to write *The Likes of Us*, an unproduced musical about Dr Barnardo. The first success came in 1968 with **Joseph and the Amazing Technicolor Dreamcoat**, followed by **Jesus Christ, Superstar** (1971) and **Evita** (1976). Rice later worked with classical opera composer, Stephen Oliver, on the musical *Blondel* (1983) about the Crusades, and former ABBA members and songwriters Benny **Andersson** and Bjorn **Ulvaeus** for **Chess** (1988). Academy awards followed for the songs 'A whole new world' from Disney's *Aladdin* (1992, music by Alan **Menken**), 'Circle of life' from **The Lion King** (1994, co-written with Elton John) and 'You must love me', an extra song added to the 1996 film of *Evita* starring Madonna. The latest collaboration with Elton John is *Aida*; after problems out of town the show opened in 2000 to become a popular hit.

Richard RODGERS (1902–79, USA)
Lorenz HART (1895–1943, USA)
Richard Rodgers from New York had his first song published in *My Auto Show Girl* in 1914. Four years later at Columbia University he met Lorenz Hart, a play translator. Their first published song together was 'Any old place with you' from *A Lonely Romeo* (1919). After Columbia's varsity production, *Fly with Me* (1919), they contributed seven songs to *Poor Little Ritz Girl* (1920). *The Garrick Gaities* of 1925 was their first big hit. *Dearest Enemy* (1925) was an integrated musical as opposed to the slapdash formats of the time. After an unsuccessful stay in Hollywood (1930–4), Rodgers and Hart returned to Broadway with *Jumbo* (1935), **On Your Toes** (1936) and **Babes in Arms** (1937). **Pal Joey** (1940) was an astonishing show, with its rough, heartless, ruthless characters. The pair separated when Hart turned down the offer to adapt the play *Green Grow the Lilacs*. He died shortly after the show based on the novel,

Oklahoma!, opened to great acclaim. At the time of his death he had once more been working with his former partner, contributing new songs for a revival of A Connecticut Yankee.

Richard RODGERS (1902–79, USA)
Oscar HAMMERSTEIN II (1895–1960, USA) *Also see separate entry.*
Rodgers' new collaborator on **Oklahoma!** was Oscar Hammerstein II. Together they formed the most important, inventive and commercial partnership of the era. The newly integrated song/dance/drama style produced **Carousel** (1945), **South Pacific** (1949), **The King and I** (1951) and **The Sound of Music** (1959), all of which have proved to be perennially popular. On Hammerstein's death, Rodgers continued working with various collaborators. He wrote the lyrics of *No Strings* (1962) and teamed up with Stephen **Sondheim** for *Do I Hear a Waltz?* (1965), Martin Charnin for *Two by Two* (1970) and Sheldon **Harnick** for *Rex* (1976).

Sigmund ROMBERG (1887–1951, Hungary)
An engineering student, Romberg also studied the violin and eventually adopted the theatre as the basis for his career, which ranged between London and New York, as a pianist then as the leader of a hotel orchestra. He started writing musicals for the Shubert Brothers in New York. *Maytime* (1917) started a successful series including *Blossom Time* (1921), which used music by Schubert. **The Student Prince in Heidelberg** (1924) and **The Desert Song** (1926) were massively popular. Of the next series, only **The New Moon** (1927) lived up to expectations. The last shows before his death were the successful **Up in Central Park** (1945) and *My Romance* (1948), a failure. Afterwards came *The Girl in Pink Tights* (1954), a posthumous show; it was not a success either.

Harold ROME (born 1908, USA)
Connecticut-born Harold Rome worked in summer camps and as a draughtsman before writing an amateur review, to be performed by members of the New York Garment Union, called *Pins and Needles*. *Sing out the News* and *Call Me Mister* were revues that added to the composer's reputation. Then came the 1952 musical **Wish You Were Here** (1952), a hit on both sides of the Atlantic. An adaptation of the Marcel Pagnol story called **Fanny** (1954) was followed by the Western musical **Destry Rides Again** (1959) and *I Can Get it for you Wholesale* (1962). Versions of the *Gone with the Wind* story – *Scarlett* (1970) and *Gone with the Wind* (1972) – proved to be the last shows Rome was to have produced on Broadway or in the West End.

Harvey SCHMIDT (born 1929, USA)
The longest-running musical of all time was created by two Texans, Tom Jones and Harvey Schmidt, who created **The Fantasticks** in 1960. It is now heading for forty years off-Broadway. They had been pals at university and contributed to various small-scale revues, including *Demi Dozen*, *Pieces of Eight* and *Shoestring 57*. After their record breaker, the pair produced more conventional large-scale Broadway musicals, including *110 in the Shade* (1963), which was a version of *The Rainmaker*, I Do! I Do! (1966), *Celebration* (1969), *Colette*

(1970, revised 1982 and 1983), *Philemon* (1973) and *Grovers Corners* (1987), a version of Thornton Wilder's *Our Town*. The collaborators have established the Portfolio Theatre for trying out experimental musicals.

Claude-Michel SCHÖNBERG (born 1944, France)
Alain BOUBLIL (born 1941, France)

Record company music producer Claude-Michel Schönberg's first show was *La Revolution Française* in 1973, originally a pageant after being a concept LP. The show **Les Miserables** (1980) was seen in Paris by London producer Cameron Mackintosh, who interested the Royal Shakespeare Company in mounting it in Britain in 1985. It transferred from the Barbican to the West End, where it has remained ever since. Next, in 1989 Boublil and Schönberg came up with a modern-day version of Puccini's great opera *Madama Butterfly*. It was called **Miss Saigon** (1989) and has become the longest-running show ever mounted at the Theatre Royal Drury Lane. Finally, in 1996 came a third show for the West End – **Martin Guerre**.

Arthur SCHWARTZ (1900–84, USA)

Arthur Schwartz is better remembered for his wonderful songs than the shows from which they came. His main lyricists were Howard Dietz and Dorothy **Fields**, and he worked extensively on both sides of the Atlantic. *The Bandwagon* (including 'Dancing in the dark') (1931) for the Astaires was a huge hit, and the songs were recycled for a film twenty years later. *Revenge with Music* (1934) was a fine version of Manuel de Falla's *The Three-Cornered Hat*. *Between the Devil* (featuring 'By myself') (1937) and *Virginia* (1937) were not successful. *Stars in Your Eyes* (1939) had lyrics by Dorothy Fields, and Ira **Gershwin** contributed the lyrics for *Park Avenue* (1946). *A Tree Grows in Brooklyn* (featuring 'I'll buy you a star') (1951) was a wonderful show, but it was followed by a failed attempt to repeat its success for star Shirley Booth, with *By the Beautiful Sea* (1954). *The Gay Life* (1961) also failed and even a show for Mary Martin called *Jennie* (1963) suffered the same fate. He acted as film producer for *Night and Day* and *Cover Girl*. The films *Thank Your Lucky Stars* (featuring 'They're either too young or too old') (1943) and *The Time, the Place and the Girl* (featuring 'Gal in calico') (1946) had wonderful film scores.

Stephen SCHWARTZ (born 1948, USA)

New York-born composer/lyricist Stephen Schwartz studied piano and composition at the Juilliard School, America's top music school. His first Broadway success came with the rock musical **Godspell** (1971); the show's album, produced by Schwartz, won two Grammy awards. He followed *Godspell* with **Pippin** (1972), *The Magic Show* (1974) and *The Baker's Wife* (1978). As a lyricist he collaborated on Leonard **Bernstein**'s Mass (1971), a biblical show for London. *Children of Eden* (1991) was not successful. Recently he has worked with Alan **Menken** on Disney's *Pocahontas* (1994) and *The Hunchback of Notre Dame* (1996).

David SHIRE See Maltby

Julian SLADE (born 1930, England)
Julian Slade wrote his first shows and incidental music for the Bristol Old Vic
from 1951 onwards, including much incidental music for Shakespeare plays
and *The Duenna.* A production of *The Comedy of Errors* was transmitted by
BBC TV in 1954, but it was **Salad Days,** a bewitchingly simple, artless musical
comedy that proved to be the longest-running show of the 1950s. There followed **Free as Air** (1957), *Hooray for Daisy* (1959) and *Follow That Girl* (1960).
Wildest Dreams (1960), *Vanity Fair* (1962) and *Nutmeg and Ginger* (1963) were
followed after a long gap by Slade's masterpiece, **Trelawny** (1972). A version
of J.M. Barrie's *Dear Brutus* is waiting in the wings.

Stephen SONDHEIM (born 1930, USA)
The fact that he attended the same school as one of Oscar **Hammerstein II**'s
sons turned out to be a godsend for the young Sondheim. His parents had separated and the youngster's talent was nurtured by Hammerstein. He wrote four
musicals before he was twenty-one, and took composition lessons from Milton
Babbitt. His work during the 1950s included television scripts, and he also
wrote an unproduced musical, *Saturday Night.* In addition, he contributed incidental music to Broadway plays. Leonard **Bernstein** chose him as lyricist for
West Side Story (1957), and he followed this with Jule **Styne's Gypsy** (1959).
A Funny Thing Happened on the Way to the Forum (1962) was Sondheim's
first successful work as lyricist and composer, although his subsequent show,
Anyone Can Whistle (1964), flopped. 1970 saw the beginning of an eleven-
year partnership with director Hal Prince. Their innovative shows included
Company (1970), which used songs to comment on the drama; **Follies** (1971),
which used pastiche to illustrate the inner thoughts of unhappily married
couples; and **A Little Night Music** (1972), which included the hit 'Send in the
clowns'. **Pacific Overtures** (1976), the operatic **Sweeney Todd** (1979) and the
chronologically reversed **Merrily We Roll Along** (1981) were the other
Sondheim/Prince productions. Sondheim won a Pulitzer Prize in 1984 for
Sunday in the Park with George. His innovative approach has continued with
the recent productions **Into the Woods** (1991), *Assassins* (1992) and **Passion**
(1994). His latest is *Wise Guys* that was given a showcase in New York in 2000
and is due for a commercial production in 2001.

Charles STROUSE (born 1928, USA)
Lee ADAMS (born 1924, USA)
Strouse was a songwriter from the age of twelve, and after studies at the
Eastman School of Music and the Berkshire Music Center, he worked as a
Broadway rehearsal pianist. Once there, Strouse began collaborating with lyri-
cist Lee Adams, a native of Mansfield, Ohio. They contributed songs for off-
Broadway revues, including *Catch a Star* (1955) and *Ben Bagley's Shoestring
Revue* (1956); and for London, *Fresh Airs* (1956). Their first full-length score
was **Bye Bye Birdie** (1960), which was filmed in 1963 starring Dick Van Dyke
and Ann-Margret. An unsuccessful sequel, *Bring Back Birdie*, followed in
1981. Further shows included *All American* (1962), **Golden Boy** (1964),
Applause (1970) and *Six* (1971). Subsequently, Strouse collaborated with other
lyricists, including Martin Charnin on **Annie** (1977). He also wrote music for

several films, such as *Bonnie and Clyde* (1967) and *The Night They Raided Minsky's* (1968).

Leslie STUART (1864–1928, England)

Thomas Augustine Barrett was born in Southport, Lancashire. He wrote minstrel-style songs under the pseudonyms Lester Barrett, and later Leslie Stuart, while organist at Salford Cathedral. In 1895 he went to London and wrote songs for *An Artist's Model* and *The Shop Girl*. Stuart's minstrel songs were performed by leading blackface performer Eugene Stratton, an American singer and dancer who had settled in London. Their hits together included 'Lily of Laguna' (1898), and their partnership continued until Stratton's retirement in 1915. Meanwhile, Stuart wrote a full-length score, **Florodora** (1899), a big success on both sides of the Atlantic. Later Stuart musical comedies were not as successful, and the composer spent much of his time pursuing his passion for horse racing.

Jule STYNE (1905–94, England)

Styne's family settled in Chicago in 1914 (he was born in London), and he made his début as a pianist with the Chicago Symphony Orchestra. He subsequently performed in, and arranged music for, dance bands, producing a hit song with 'Sunday' in 1926. In 1940 in Hollywood he worked with lyricists Sammy Cahn, Frank **Loesser** and E.Y. **Harburg**. With Cahn, Styne wrote his first Broadway show, *High Button Shoes*, in 1947. Leo Robin provided the lyrics for **Gentlemen Prefer Blondes** (1949), filmed in 1953 with Marilyn Monroe and Jane Russell. Other important shows include **Bells are Ringing** (1956), with a book by Betty **Comden** and Adolph **Green**, **Gypsy** (1959) for Ethel Merman, with lyrics by Stephen **Sondheim**, and **Funny Girl** (1964) with Bob **Merrill**. Unhappily, his last show, *The Red Shoes* (1993), was no more successful than *Look to the Lilies* (1970) or *One-Night Stand* (1980) had been.

Arthur SULLIVAN See Gilbert

Harry TIERNEY (1890–1965, USA)

Tierney worked in music publishing as a staff pianist and composer, writing songs for revues, including four *Ziegfeld Follies*, as well as **Irene** (1919), which became Broadway's longest-running show of the time with 670 performances. *Irene* made a star of Edith Day, for whom Tierney had conceived the songs. Other shows included *Kid Boots* (1923) for Eddie Cantor. His 1927 show **Rio Rita** was one of the first Broadway musicals to be filmed as a talking picture in 1929. Encouraged by its success, Tierney moved to Hollywood where he wrote songs for films, but was unsuccessful there, as he was on a return to the theatre. None of his subsequent shows reached Broadway.

Pete TOWNSHEND (born 1945, England)

Peter Dennis Blandford Townshend was born in London. He played banjo with trumpet player John Entwhistle, in trad-jazz groups while at school. Together with Roger Daltrey and Keith Moon, they formed The Who. Townshend wrote the band's early hits 'My generation' (1965), 'Substitute' (1966) and 'Pictures of Lily' (1967). Their 1967 album, *The Who Sell Out*, contained a 'mini-opera' prelude to a much more ambitious undertaking, the full-length rock-opera *Tommy* (1969). After performances by the band on tour it was first a stage show in 1973. Ken Russell's film version, starring Daltrey, Tina Turner and Elton John, appeared in 1975, and the show was revived on Broadway in 1994, for which Townshend contributed a new song, 'I believe my own eyes'. Townshend planned another rock opera, *Lifehouse*, which was abandoned, and its songs found their way into the album *Quadrophenia* (1973), which was filmed in 1979.

Bjorn ULVAEUS See Andersson

Harry WARREN See Dubin

Kurt WEILL (1900–50, Germany)
Kurt Weill's career divided neatly into two: his operas in Germany; and his Broadway shows and films. The composer of *Die Dreigroschenoper* (1928) and *Happy End* (1929) in Germany also wrote *My Kingdom for a Cow* (1935), which was produced in London. He then moved to America, where a new Broadway career began. *Johnny Johnson* (1936) was followed by *Knickerbocker Holiday* (1938) for Walter Huston and a show for Gertrude Lawrence, **Lady in the Dark** (1941). Mary Martin was the star of **One Touch of Venus** (1943). 1945 produced an elaborate failure, *The Firebrand of Florence*, the story of Benvenuto Cellini. *Street Scene,* adopted by the world's opera houses, came in 1947; *Love Life* (1948) and a version of *Cry the Beloved Country*, **Lost in the Stars** (1949), ended his Broadway career.

Meredith WILLSON (1902–84, USA)
Meredith Willson was Sousa's principal flautist before joining the New York Philharmonic Orchestra in 1922. He subsequently conducted on radio, continued to study and wrote two symphonies, songs and other works; he also arranged Charlie Chaplin's music for the film *The Great Dictator* (1940). His song 'May the good Lord bless and keep you' was for Tallulah Bankhead's radio programme, *The Big Show*. For Broadway he wrote **The Music Man** (1957), filmed in 1962, followed by **The Unsinkable Molly Brown** (1960), filmed in 1964, and *Here's Love* (1963), all of which were successes.

Sandy WILSON (born 1924, England)
Wilson was born in Cheshire. At Oxford he wrote for and appeared in revues. In London he contributed to the revues *Slings and Arrows, Oranges and Lemons* (both 1948), *See You Later* (1951) and *See You Again* (1952). In 1953 he wrote **The Boy Friend** which, after performances at the Players' and Embassy theatres, ran for a record-breaking 2084 performances at Wyndham's Theatre. The New York show, which ran for 485 performances, starred newcomer, Julie Andrews. It was filmed in 1972 with Twiggy in the leading role. Wilson followed with *The Buccaneer* (1955) and cult musical **Valmouth** (1958). He contributed songs to later shows, including *Pieces of Eight* (1959), *As Dorothy Parker Once Said* (1969) and *Aladdin* (1979). *Divorce Me Darling*

(1964) was an unsuccessful 1964 sequel to *The Boy Friend*. Unfortunately, there was no more success for two fascinating later shows, *His Monkey Wife* (1971) and *The Clapham Wonder* (1978).

Robert WRIGHT See Forrest

Vincent YOUMANS (1898–1946, USA)

Youmans began composing while doing navy service during World War I. 'Hallelujah' was turned into a popular march by Sousa. His first published song was 'The country cousin' in 1920, and his first show, with Paul Lannin, was *Two Little Girls in Blue* in 1921. Both this and *Wildflower* (1923) succeeded and led on to his biggest hit, **No, No, Nanette** (1925), featuring 'Tea for two', written with Irving Caesar. The show was filmed in 1930 with most of Youmans' music replaced. **Hit the Deck** (1927), which featured his old navy tune 'Hallelujah' with added lyrics, was his last successful show, although many of his individual songs became standards. He moved to Hollywood in 1933 to write the music for *Flying Down to Rio*, including the song 'Orchids in the moonlight'. In 1934 he succumbed to tuberculosis, which forced him into premature retirement.

A Short Glossary

Book	The story and spoken words of the stage musical.
Choreographer	The man or woman who creates the dancing for a show.
Conductor	The man or woman who controls the pit orchestra, and conducts the on-stage singers.
Dance captain	The person who rehearses the dancers in the absence of the choreographer.
Director	The person who tells the actors and singers what to do on stage. Together with the creative team, he or she also selects the performers.
Eleven o'clock number	A last-minute show-stopper for the star to send the audience home in a happy mood (e.g. 'I'm going back where I can be me' from *Bells are Ringing*).
Extravaganza	A big, gaudy spectacle of a show – part pageant, part revue, part musical.
Lyrics	The words of the songs of a stage musical.
Matinée	An afternoon performance.
Musical comedy	The two most glorious words in the English language!
Opera	The weightiest form of music drama. If part of it is spoken rather than entirely sung it is often classified as comic opera – even if the plot is far from funny.
Opéra comique	A form of sung light musical entertainment popular in France, related to German and Austrian operetta.
Operetta	Lighter than opera but rather weightier than musical comedy. A musical play popular in Austria and Germany.
Point number	A song designed to show off the versatility and brilliance of the performer rather than to advance the plot (e.g. 'Tschaikovsky' in *Lady in the Dark*).
Producer	He or she buys the property (book, music, lyrics), raises the money, gets the theatre organised, engages the director and performers, arranges the publicity and closes the show.
Revue	An unconnected series of songs, sketches, dances and possibly tableaux.
Show-stopper	A song that halts the show for extended applause.
Swing	A versatile dancer who has to learn everyone else's dancing role and is prepared to substitute when called on to do so.

Musical Title Index

Song Title Index

437